INTIFADA

INTIFADA

Palestine at the Crossroads

Edited by
JAMAL R. NASSAR
and
ROGER HEACOCK

PRAEGER

New York
Westport, Connecticut
London

Library of Congress Cataloging-in-Publication Data

Intifada : Palestine at the crossroads / edited by Jamal R. Nassar and
  Roger Heacock.
    p. cm.
   Includes bibliographical references.
   ISBN 0–275–93411–X (alk. paper)
    1.West Bank—History—Palestinian Uprising, 1987–   2. Gaza Strip—
History—Palestinian Uprising, 1987–   I. Nassar, Jamal R. (Jamal
Raji) II. Heacock, Roger.
DS110.W47I56   1990
956.9405′4—dc20   89–22879

Library of Congress Catalog Card Number: 89–22879
ISBN: 0–275–93411–X

First published in 1990

Praeger Publishers, One Madison Avenue, New York, NY 10010
A division of Greenwood Press, Inc.

Printed in the United States of America

The paper used in this book complies with the
Permanent Paper Standard issued by the National
Information Standards Organization (Z39.48–1984).

10 9 8 7 6 5 4 3 2 1

To Those Who Dare to Struggle for
the Dignity of All

Contents

PART II.   THE PARTICIPANTS

PART III.   REGIONAL AND INTERNATIONAL REACTIONS

PART IV. IMPACT ON THE MAIN PROTAGONISTS

PART V. CONCLUSION

Preface

The Palestinian *intifada* (uprising) is not a transitory phenomenon that sprang up from nowhere and may be expected to pass as mysteriously as it arose. To be sure, as the chapters that follow demonstrate, the uprising represents the acceleration of an ongoing process of resistance. The *intifada* also exhibits the volatility of the Middle East, a region that is vital to world security and economic stability. It is clear today that serious analysts cannot study the politics of the Arab-Israeli conflict, and in particular its Palestinian dimension, without coming to grips with the Palestinian uprising.

This volume is a modest attempt at tracing and assessing the *intifada*. The principal emphasis throughout is upon the dynamics of its rise and the patterns of its development and consequences. Our aim is to be comprehensive. As always comprehensiveness is subverted by time and necessity. Therefore some important chapters will be left to the future. The book is also designed to provide the reader with expert summary and analysis. The majority of the contributors are, in fact, experts on the subject. Most are Palestinian professionals on the West Bank, many have not only witnessed the *intifada* but actually participate in it. Many have paid the price for their political activism and involvement in Israeli jails. Other contributors are experts of long standing on the issues on which they write. Combined, their contributions provide the reader with detailed discussion that is not otherwise possible.

While this volume grows out of the Palestinian *intifada*, it stands in stark relief to the suffering and pain of those who reside in the land we call holy. It is the product of the combined experiences of editors and contributors, many of whom stand witness to "the revolution of the stone." When this volume was planned in the West Bank, the editors agreed that editorial control would reside with the authors of the individual chapters. Each contributor was left to reach his/her own conclusions. The collection may, however, surprise many. The conclusions are similar and harmonious as if by design. This may be a reflection of Palestinian national unity among the masses and at the grass-roots level. The contributors simply mirror their society. Most are Palestinian. After all, the *intifada* is a Palestinian phenomenon, and Palestinian intellectuals should naturally be the ones to present it to the world. Being Palestinians under occupation, they are part of the *intifada*. Being intellectuals, they are natural critics of their society. Thus, each is an observer as well as a participant in the *intifada*. In the process, they have provided the necessary link between theory and practice.

Many, besides the editors and contributors, have extended their aid to the project. Bir Zeit University and Illinois State University have both provided resources and support services. The Fulbright Foundation made it possible for Professor Nassar to be on the West Bank and live through the *intifada*'s first year. We also wish to acknowledge the invaluable assistance rendered by numerous persons, many of whom were occupied and preoccupied more than full time by the theories and praxis here described.

Those who must be singled out for their invaluable technical assistance in producing the manuscript (translation, editing, typing, and reading) are Leena Masad, Leena Ghattas, Donn Hutchison, Muhammad Masad, and Paula Masad. All of these giving individuals reside in the Occupied Territories and are linked to one or another educational institution. Across the ocean from them, three Illinois State University graduate students also extended necessary services. They are Theresa Miller, Mark Mullenbach, and especially Hamdi Shaqqura, who went the extra mile to help in this project. To all of them, we are eternally grateful.

Bir Zeit University as an institution must be singled out as well. Its moral and material support enabled this project to get off the ground at a time when the university itself was dealing with the crisis of military-ordered closure, multiple restrictions on personnel, funds, and equipment, and a constant threat to its very existence. We also acknowledge with thanks the generous grant by the Friedrich Ebert Foundation, Bonn, Federal Republic of Germany, to those among our contributors who researched and wrote their chapters on socioeconomic matters within the Occupied Territories.

Very important also were our wives, Hanan Nassar and Laura Wick, who courageously and patiently supported this undertaking. We are indebted to them and to our children for their understanding and support through many months of work on this volume. Finally and most of all, we wish to thank the dozens of persons—whose identities must remain anonymous—who gave their time and expertise to insure that our data and their interpretation are based on a true rendering of events. These people represent the hundreds of thousands of unheralded activists whose struggle has left its mark on contemporary world history. Our sincere thanks to them because they are the people of the *intifada*.

INTIFADA

1

Introduction

ON ACHIEVING INDEPENDENCE

Ibrahim Abu-Lughod

Without question, the *intifada* (uprising) is a watershed in the Palestinian historical quest for independence. It marks a decisive break with the articulation of past objectives and opts for a significantly different mode of achieving independence. The new mode contrasts very sharply with previous Palestinian practice and, equally important, with those modes pursued by Third World independence movements. The *intifada* reflects, then, both continuity and innovation in the Palestinian struggle for independence. Thus far the analysis, writings, and portrayal of the *intifada* have tended to emphasize its unique qualities; and more frequently such analysis tends to relate these unique techniques or processes to the specific context of the West Bank and Gaza wherein independence is being achieved in reality.

Such a portrayal is of course both valid and of considerable historical and social value. But unless the *intifada* is placed in comparative Palestinian perspective and set against the backdrop of the historical quest for Palestinian statehood, its theoretical and practical significance will be difficult to assess and appreciate. Our task in this discussion is to raise some of these historical and comparative issues, suggest instances of continuity as well as change in the quest for statehood, and relate both to the altered social and political environment in which the Palestinian struggle as a whole, in and outside Palestine, has been waged.

Whether the *intifada* was initiated on December 7, 8, or 9, 1987, may not be that significant; what is significant, at substantive and symbolic levels, is that

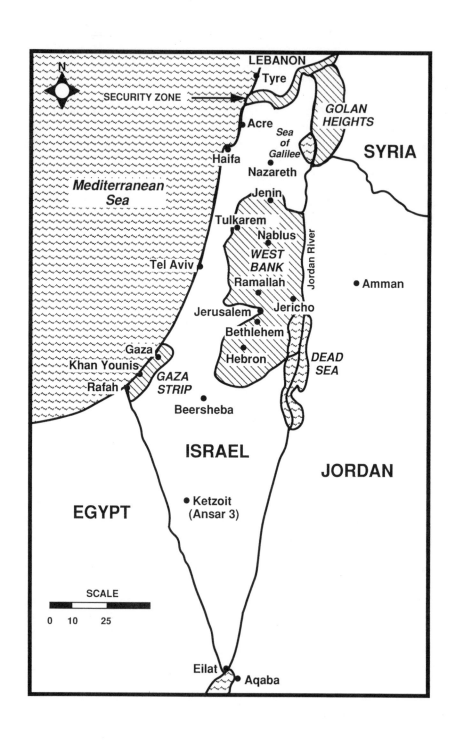

the outbreak occurred exactly seventy years after Palestine was militarily occupied by the British forces then commanded by General Edmund Allenby. Those forces, theoretically allied with the Arab revolt of 1915, entered Jerusalem between December 7 and 9, 1917.

The *intifada* began in Gaza; shortly thereafter it spread to the rest of the Palestinian territory—the so-called West Bank. In an entirely different form and manner Palestinians in other geopolitical regions joined the *intifada*. Without question Palestinian communities elsewhere—in Israel, Jordan, the Gulf region, as well as throughout the rest of the world—have been active participants in the struggle, rendering political, financial, moral, and informational support to the *intifada*. Admittedly the support varied from one area to another, but the positive interaction with the *intifada* on Palestinian soil made the overall Palestinian endeavor a national one aimed at a solution to the question of Palestine.

Instant reactions to and commentaries on the *intifada* reflected the predilections of the commentators; some were emphatic in their assessment of the *intifada* as a spontaneous event; others suggested that it was manipulated if not induced by "external" elements, specifically agents of the Palestine Liberation Organization (PLO). Those who accepted the validity of the "spontaneity" hypothesis were politically motivated in that they refused to accept the centrality of the Palestine Liberation Organization to the national struggle of the Palestinian people. On the other hand, many such commentators expected and/or wished the *intifada*'s early dissipation and eradication. Those who accepted the "external" hypothesis believed that severe internal coercive measures coupled with imposition of serious constraints on the alleged external supporter—the Palestine Liberation Organization—would rapidly bring the *intifada* to an end. Both groups believed in the fragility of the *intifada* and the efficacy of the countermeasures to be carried out by the Israeli army of occupation.

The *intifada* is now in its third year; its strength and viability are no longer in question. A vitally interested "observer," the chief of staff of the Israeli army, stated publicly that "there is no such thing as eradicating the *intifada*."[1] The Palestinians in the occupied Palestinian territory strongly believe that the *intifada* has become a way of life for all Palestinians. It is clear, then, that the early prognosis turned out to be based on false premises or wishful thinking. Palestinians and Israelis who have dealt more objectively with the *intifada* have taken into account different variables, which have led to diametrically opposed conclusions.

It is clear now that the *intifada* is primarily a political act of resistance seeking the achievement of a political objective. It derives its major values, aspirations, and premises from the collective existential experiences of the Palestinian people, especially those who have encountered British and Israeli colonialism over the past seven decades; and in carrying its purpose forward the *intifada* has benefited from the previous militant experience of the Palestinians as they struggled for national independence.

While the *intifada* seeks to bring Israel's military occupation to an end, the fact that it occurs seventy years after Palestine's occupation and control by British colonialism conveys graphically an important dimension of the Palestinian struggle. It is a struggle of a people who have been denied their historic right to national independence first by Britain and later by Israel. Thus the *intifada* reaffirms the historic Palestinian assertion that the fundamental cause of the conflict between Israel and the Palestinians is the persistent colonial denial of the right of the Palestinian people to self-determination. The denial was initially voiced publicly by Lord Balfour when he stated in 1919 that "in the case of Palestine we deliberately and rightly decline to accept the principle of self-determination" and added equally arrogantly, "In Palestine we do not even propose to go through the form of consulting the wishes of the inhabitants of the country."[2] Denying the Palestinian right to self-determination was necessary so that Britain would be able to carry out the commitments that it made to Zionism in the November 2, 1917, Balfour Declaration. Israel's denial has been forcibly practiced by its military occupation of the West Bank and Gaza since June 1967.

The *intifada* is essentially about the right of the Palestinians in the West Bank and Gaza to determine their destiny. The exercise of that right would entail the termination of Israel's occupation of the West Bank and Gaza. In view of Israel's evident intention of continuing its military control, effecting and benefiting from its policy of exploitation of the human and material resources of the people and the territories, the encounter between Israel and the Palestinians has been viewed as one between a colonial power and a colonized population. As such Israel established an unequal relationship between Israelis and Palestinians. Such encounters and relationships are usually conflictual: the colonizer tries, ultimately unsuccessfully, to perpetuate the colonial condition. Social, political, and economic conditions in the West Bank and Gaza are of necessity oppressive and exploitative; hence the enduring Palestinian struggle to alter the colonial condition and bring the military occupation to an end.

A cursory examination of Palestinian history throughout the past seven decades clearly reveals that Palestinians struggled against both Britain and Israel as colonizing powers. Whereas Britain wanted its control of Palestine for specific imperialist reasons—reasons of empire, protection of lines of communication, strategy, and so on—it had the additional objective of discharging Balfour's commitment of facilitating "the establishment in Palestine of a national home for the Jewish people." Israel's occupation of the West Bank and Gaza in June 1967 might have been premised on some Zionist territorial imperative; its reality *in situ* has, however, conformed to the general practices of imperialism in the Third World. Israel has used the West Bank and Gaza as a captive market for its goods and services, has transformed the population into a source of cheap labor, and has diverted water resources. Thus Palestinian resistance to both powers has been consistent with the struggle of the colonized in general; yet each phase of the struggle acquired a specific character that stemmed from the particular context in which it has been waged.

Though the *intifada* is generally noted for many of its unprecedented qualities and attributes, its closest parallel in the annals of the Palestinian struggle is clearly the 1936–39 revolt. First, the revolt was recognized by Palestinians and the British against whom it was waged as a major revolution. The Palestinians referred to it as *al-Thawra al-Arabiyya al-Kubra*—the Great Arab Revolt.[3] The Peel Commission, dispatched by the British government in the wake of the general strike that lasted for six months, from April to October 1936 (also unprecedented in its duration and comprehensiveness), referred to it as a revolt. The commission wished to correct the generally dismissive terms that the Mandate administration used in its portrayal of the "events" to minimize the gravity of the manifestations and political implications of the encounter with the Palestinians. Then, as in the early phases of the *intifada*, both British and Israeli officers referred to the violent encounters between Palestinian nationalists and armies of occupation as "riots," "disturbances," "terrorist acts," and so on. In neither case was there a willingness on the part of the colonizer to admit the political and nationally cohesive nature of the resistance and the political solution that it sought. The Peel Commission clearly understood the political bases of the general strike and the underlying sources of conflict that led to the armed revolt. It was forthright in stating that the Palestinians aimed at independence. The commission understood clearly that Palestinian political independence would enable them to halt the establishment of the Jewish national home. The commission accepted the legitimacy of the Palestinian assertion but restricted the scope—in its projected solution—of its geopolitical implementation.[4]

Today Israel treats and interacts with the *intifada* as a major act of resistance and revolution; but in a deliberate policy of denying its comprehensiveness and legitimacy, it referred to it initially as riots, terrorism, violence, and disturbances. Israel now refers to Palestinian resistance simply as the *intifada*. While increasing sectors of Israel's public recognize the political dimensions of the *intifada*, the government's policy remains firmly anchored in its stubborn denial of the legitimacy of Palestinian independence.

Both revolts shared the common aspiration of independence; in the first instance it was the independence of Palestine as a whole; in the second the *intifada* stressed the goal of ending Israel's occupation of the West Bank and Gaza, which led the national leadership, the Palestine Liberation Organization, to proclaim the state of Palestine and to imply its location in the occupied Palestinian territory. The achievement of the goal of the 1936–39 revolt would have negated the establishment of Israel, while the achievement of Palestinian independence in the West Bank and Gaza does not conflict with Israel's existence. The differing territorial as well as social, cultural, and political implications of Palestinian independence have enabled other states and people to endorse the political agenda of the *intifada* as it has been expressed externally by the Palestine Liberation Organization.

Although the territorial scope of the newly projected independent Palestinian state is more restricted, Britain's and Israel's reaction to both revolts has been quite similar. Both powers resorted to major acts of coercion to bring the uprisings to an end. The fatalities of 1936–39 revolt exceed those of the *intifada* between December 1987 and April 1989. It is estimated that more than 5,000 Palestinians were killed by British troops and Jewish militias between 1936 and 1939. Between December 7/8, 1987, and April 1989 Israeli troops killed more than 500 Palestinians. It will be recalled that the notorious Defense Regulations, which Israel uses liberally to detain, interrogate, and imprison Palestinians, were in fact initially enacted by Britain in 1936–37 (later amended in 1946 to deal with rising Jewish terrorism) precisely to suppress the 1936 revolt. Britain constructed and expanded prisons to accommodate the more than 10,000 Palestinians detained for varied periods between 1936 and 1939. It is useful to point out that some of the same prisons, such as Sarafand, have been used by both colonial powers to imprison political activists. Both powers have resorted to home demolitions, collective punishments, banishment of alleged "leaders" to achieve the political decapitation of the population, curfews, and beatings to intimidate the population and "restore law and order."[5]

The success of British colonialism in suppressing the Palestinian revolt of 1936–39 can be attributed to the adoption and vigorous enforcement of a very brutal policy of suppression as well as structural weaknesses in the Palestinian resistance itself. Palestinian studies of the revolt point out that the leadership was both confused and indecisive in the pursuit of the objectives of the national movement; they document important divisions within both the community and leadership which weakened the national cohesion and purpose. The leadership's reliance on the "dependent" Arab states made it more difficult to successfully mobilize the population toward certain goals.

While Israel, like all other colonial powers that have confronted national revolts, is relying on a policy of brute force to suppress the *intifada*, the Palestinian leadership *in situ* (the Unified National Leadership and the popular committees) as well as the national leadership—the Palestine Liberation Organization—have absorbed the lessons of the earlier (and subsequent) struggles and charted a path of resistance to Israel that is politically more feasible and more likely to succeed. The leadership understood the significance of the overwhelming disparity between the contending forces in terms of available lethal power. After all, not only is Israel an atomic power, but it has extensive access to America's arsenal for any kinds of weapons that may be necessary to contain the *intifada*. The leadership understood fully Israel's more than evident eagerness to use weapons of repression to enforce its policy of denying the Palestinian right to self-determination. Israel's devastating 1982 invasion of Lebanon with its incredible toll in Palestinian and Lebanese lives served as a constant reminder of the enormous cost entailed in an uprising that might depend on the use of weapons. And such weapons are in any case difficult if not impossible to obtain in the hermetically sealed West Bank and Gaza. For these and for equally important subjective reasons as well the *intifada* expressed itself in extremely militant but not violent means. To refer to stones thrown by kids as "violent" acts is a ludicrous charge to justify Israel's continuing resort to systematic violence.

The *intifada* and its leadership understood the fundamental law applicable to the achievement of independence in colonial situations: a colonial system can be defended and maintained successfully as long as the benefits a colonial power derives from the colonized exceed the costs. After all, the underlying rationale of all colonial systems is the successful exploitation of the colonized. The challenge to the colonized becomes one of increasing the costs to the colonizer to such an extent that it no longer pays to maintain the colonial condition.

The history of national independence movements in Africa and Asia is essentially one of increasing the costs of maintaining the colonial system. In response to the nationalists' sustained pressure—strikes, demonstrations, economic boycotts, civil disobedience, nonpayment of taxes, and occasional violent acts—the colonial powers invariably resort to brutal and violent measures to repress the nationalists. Eventually the colonizer concludes that the costs incurred in acts of repression are in fact prohibitive, economically, politically, and morally. There comes a point in the struggle when the two antagonists reach the inevitable conclusion that a negotiated agreement that leads to independence and the exit of the colonial power is preferable to continued strife.

What this suggests is that national independence is rarely achieved by military means; few former British or French colonies would have achieved independence by militarily defeating the colonial power. One can even go further: liberation movements that engaged the colonizer in what became known as wars of national liberation, for example, in Algeria, Mozambique, and Angola, also achieved their victory over the colonizer by resorting to means other than sustained wars. Some degree of selective violence contributes, often psychologically and informationally, to the successful consummation of the struggle. Cases of successful decolonization that were brought about by inflicting a decisive military defeat on the colonial power are exceptional. It is usually the case that exerting a combination of economic, social, and political pressures—domestic, regional, and international—on the colonial power alters the balance in favor of the nationalists and assures their victory. In short, one can state that the history of Third World independence is a testimony to the triumph of the colonized by means that relied minimally upon actual violence; the systematic use of violence has been more characteristic of colonial powers.

It should be made clear that rarely do the colonized recognize the validity of the law of independence stated above. Generally speaking, the colonized resort to some kind of violence initially—for psychological, informational, or other reasons. Only with extensive experience, with more pervasive politicization of the population, and greater clarity of the objectives and dynamics of the struggle do the colonized recognize the utility and validity of quasi-nonviolent but militant techniques of national resistance.[6] This certainly has been true of the Palestinian experience in the course of the *intifada,* which for all practical purposes can be considered as the latest—though the most original—phase in the Palestinian struggle for independence. It drew many of its lessons not only from the first phase—the Mandate period—but also from the second, articulated and led by the Palestine Liberation Organization essentially from outside the occupied Palestinian territory. That phase came to an end with the exodus of the Palestine Liberation Organization and its cadres from Beirut in the summer of 1982. In both phases some degree of violent means—exaggerated by self-serving antagonists—was part of the strategy of achieving independence. Additionally, and especially in the Beirut phase of the movement's struggle, there was much greater emphasis on the role and recruitment of Palestinians of the diaspora and on consolidating and strengthening diasporic national institutions as these were sustained by the Palestine Liberation Organization.

The exodus from Lebanon helped considerably in refocusing the struggle on the occupied areas; the Palestine Liberation Organization and its constituent groups implemented more effective policies of sustaining, supporting, and fostering national institutions in the West Bank and Gaza while carrying out the international political and diplomatic struggle for the legitimacy of Palestinian independence.

These efforts and concerns appeared at a time when fundamental transformations had already occurred in the West Bank and Gaza. Not only had Israel's occupation policies become more repressive and more openly annexationist (by then more than 60 percent of the Palestinian domain of the West Bank and Gaza had been confiscated, and the areas had been much more effectively "integrated" into Israel), but the Palestinians themselves reached a much higher level of political consciousness and organizational effectiveness. A new generation of Palestinians had matured in the occupied areas; it was much more clear in its views of the future and more realistic in assessing its adversary's intentions, policies, practices, and powers. The generation that was either pacified during the Jordanian interregnum or whose activist components were neutralized by Israel on the basis of information in police files left by the departed Jordanian authorities was by then effectively displaced by a newer generation more able to cope with and confront the occupation intellectually, politically, and militantly. The newer generation of Palestinians understood more sharply that colonial facts were and are reversible; they have looked into Palestinian history and discovered that despite the many adversities that confronted the Palestinians during the Mandate and under varied forms of occupation and exile, they have in fact succeeded not only in maintaining and consolidating their national and political identities—admittedly at terrible cost to themselves—but in acquiring skills— organizational and otherwise—that would help them reach their goal of self-determination. They understood and acted upon the understanding, which Israel never did, that the Palestinian people, irrespective of place and condition, constitute a national community and thus must seek a "national" solution to their existential problems of occupation and exile. And to do so the occupied areas must remain the focus of the struggle for self-determination. By the mid–1980s that generation, highly organized, somewhat experienced, with extensive networks inside and outside the occupied Palestinian territory, and sufficiently creative in integrating external support from Palestinian and Arab sources, seized the initiative in confronting the Israeli army of occupation. Not only had demonstrations, stone throwing (the Palestinian artist Isma'il Shammout depicted the stone-throwing events in several paintings titled *Atfal al-Hijara* in 1985), and other forms of confrontation become more common by the mid–1980s, but the political objectives of such confrontations were more clearly stated.

The various political initiatives of the Palestine Liberation Organization, pursued after the Algiers National Councils (1987 and 1988), drew considerable support and sustenance from the Palestinians under occupation. The travail of the Palestinians in Lebanon added to the urgency of reaching a political settlement of the national problem of independent Palestinian existence.

Israel's failure to eradicate the *intifada* is not hard to discern. For it is clear from our narrative that the *intifada* is neither an event nor a happening, but the culmination of a historical process of liberation and state building. Precisely because there is a broad Palestinian consensus inside and outside the occupied Palestinian territory on the political goals of the *intifada*, the leadership—again inside and outside—mapped a strategy of national action calculated to translate the political goals into reality. Observers of the *intifada* are unanimous in evaluating the viability and strength of that strategy. Based upon broad sectoral, functional, and political consultations and organization, it simultaneously avoided the pitfalls of the 1936 revolt and responded to and anchored itself in an altered national, regional, and international environment. The sustained mobilization of the people, their incredible discipline, especially when confronted with the severe provocations of a unique army of occupation, and their militancy in breaking the chains that the occupier forced on them contributed enormously to the emergence of an entirely new Palestinian political and social order. The new order acquired legitimacy and thus de facto rendered the occupation and all its institutions totally illegitimate. The norms and values that now govern the population emanate from the new political order. In less than a year after the outbreak of the *intifada* an alternative society was in place; the governance of that society is effectively Palestinian.

The actual practice of Palestinian independence on the ground is manifested differentially: Palestinians now exercise more effective control over their work, institutions, and behavior. Rules and regulations issued by the national leadership generally have greater legitimacy and thus are implemented where possible. To give but one recent illustration of the effectiveness of the alternate legitimate order: in April 1989 the Unified National Leadership of the *intifada* decreed that daylight saving time would be in effect by mid-April; Israel's normal daylight saving time was to begin on May 1. For two weeks the two areas ran on different times. Despite Israel's harsh punishment of Palestinians who observed Palestinian daylight saving time—which included breaking the wrists and the watches of such individuals—it was all too evident that the two areas are indeed separate and distinct from each other. Clearly the two societies cannot be held together by an army of occupation; hence the reality and inevitability of independent statehood.

Israel of course continues to resist the inevitable outcome; but its economic, political, and moral losses are considerable. While estimates of the economic costs of the *intifada* to Israel vary—from increased costs of maintaining a larger army of occupation, loss in tourism income, and losses from the increasing efforts of Palestinians at self-sufficiency—they are thought to be over a billion dollars annually.[7] The moral and political costs worldwide have already produced considerable criticism within Israel itself. Equally important, the *intifada* rendered Jordanian hopes for the retrieval of its hegemony in the West Bank illusory. Thus King Hussein's announcement severing Jordan's links with the West Bank reflected the de facto transformation of the juridical status of the West Bank. But, most important, the *intifada* enabled the Palestine National Council (PNC), the highest acknowledged Palestinian legislative organ, to proclaim the state of Palestine and seek its full independence. Chairman Yasser Arafat, subsequently elected by the PNC's Central Council to the post of president of the state of Palestine, in his major address to the United Nations General Assembly and his subsequent press statements in Geneva on December 13 and 14, 1988, clarified and elaborated on the territorial meaning of the state of Palestine, the potential relationship between that state and Israel, and the Palestinian commitment to reaching a political solution to the Palestine-Israel conflict. It was in the wake of those pronouncements that the United States resumed its substantive dialogue with the Palestine Liberation Organization and that more than ninety countries extended varied forms of recognition to the state of Palestine.

The *intifada* has demonstrated the futility of a military solution to the conflict between Palestinian Arabs and Israeli Jews; it has similarly rendered the military occupation of the West Bank and Gaza obsolete. The *intifada* has done so by the clarity of the political program it has projected by the creative, militant, but nonviolent techniques of organization and pressure it has used, and by the concrete daily practices of the people as they struggle to translate independence into reality. The *intifada* has additionally shown the way out of the Palestinian-Israeli impasse; it called for and accepted the reality that in Palestine there are two national communities, with two separate and distinct national identities who have distinct values and norms and are governed by two sets of social, cultural, and political institutions. One political structure may not meet satisfactorily the national needs of the two people; each must seek its expression equally independently in a structure of its own making on the same soil. The *intifada* and its national leadership openly call for direct negotiation among the parties—including Israel and the Palestine Liberation Organization—in the context of an international peace conference. It is their expectation that successful negotiation within that framework will lead to the comprehensive and just settlement of all issues of contention: land, people, and sovereignty. Such a settlement, premised on full respect for each people's right to self-determination, including national independence and sovereignty, will be respected and honored by both people.

NOTES

1. Quoted by Anthony Lewis, *New York Times,* April 16, 1989, p. A25. See also Rabin's statement, *New York Times,* December 5, 1989, p. A3.

2. Statements are reproduced in Doreen Ingrams, *Palestine Papers, 1917–1922* (New York: Braziller, 1973), pp. 61, 73.

3. See, *inter alia,* A. W. Kayyali, *Palestine: A Modern History* (London: Croom Helm, n.d.), especially pp. 187–227; Bayan A. al-Hout, *al-Oiyadat wa al-Mu'assasat al-Siyasiyya fi Filastin, 1917–1948* (Beirut: Institute of Palestine Studies; 1981), pp. 331–409; and the chapters by David Waines and Barbara Kalkas in *The Transformation of Palestine,* ed. I. Abu-Lughod (Evanston, Ill.: Northwestern University Press, 1987).

4. Great Britain, Royal Commission on Palestine, *Report,* presented by the Secretary of State for the Colonies to Parliament, July 1937 (London: His Majesty's Stationery Office), 1937.

5. See M. C. Bassiouni and L. Cainkar, eds., *The Palestinian Intifada—December 9, 1987-December 8, 1988* (Chicago: Data Base Project on Palestinian Human Rights, 1989); Raja Shehadeh, *Occupier's Law: Israel and the West Bank* (Washington, D.C.: Institute of Palestine Studies; 1988); and al-Haq: Law in the Service of Man, *Punishing a Nation: Human Rights Violations During the Palestinian Uprising, December 1987-December 1988* (Ramallah: al-Haq, 1988).

6. Gene Sharp's *The Politics of Non-violent Action* (Boston: Porter Sargent, 1973), is very suggestive.

7. UNCTAD's secretariat report title of "Recent Economic Development in the Occupied Palestinian Territories . . . " (Geneva; August 8, 1988), though dated, is very helpful in estimating the "costs" of the *intifada* to Israel and to the Palestinians.

I

THE PRECONDITIONS

2

The Sociology of an Uprising
THE ROOTS OF THE *INTIFADA*

*Samih K. Farsoun and
Jean M. Landis*

Contrary to the expectations of experts, the Palestinian uprising against Israeli occupation, the *intifada,* persists, its momentum stabilizing despite intensified hardships suffered by the Palestinian people. It occurs nearly forty years after the partitioning of Palestine and the creation of the Israeli state, and twenty years after the Six Day War and the Israeli occupation of the West Bank and Gaza. While during this time the Palestinians have always resisted Israeli rule, the *intifada* represents their first sustained, mass-based popular revolt. The duration, scope, innovative tactics, and accomplishments of the *intifada* make it a historic movement organizing Palestinian political unity around a clear and simple objective: ending the occupation and paving the way for self-determination.

Recognition of the categorical nature of the *intifada* is essential. Most important, the uprising of the Palestinian people against Israeli rule does not derive from civil rights issues or issues related to general "social conditions." The individual deprivations and denial of human rights suffered by the Palestinian population must be examined in the context of the deprivation of national existence; therefore the *intifada* cannot be analyzed as merely a social protest movement seeking change within an existing nation/state structure. Neither does it constitute a revolution in the classic sense, attempting to overthrow an indigenous ruling class and state, or *ancien regime*, as did the French or Bolshevik revolutions. Finally, it cannot be considered an independence movement of the American type, as the Palestinians and the Israelis do not originate from the same nation. Alternatively, it is more accurately conceptualized as a rebellion against colonial occupation, and as such is closely akin to national liberation struggles throughout the colonized Third World. However, while the *intifada* shares many similarities with such struggles and has much the same aim, that is, self-determination, it is situated in its own historic matrix of forces. Its character results from the historical development of an oppression/resistance dialectic structured by the political, economic, and social realities within which the Palestinian people have struggled to gain control over their daily lives in the face of Israel's attempts to Judaize the Occupied Territories and entrench its control over them.[1]

The *intifada* is a historical product of all previous efforts to resist dispossession and suppression of Palestinian national identity. It constitutes the fourth major movement in defense of a Palestinian homeland. The first was the 1936–39 revolt against authorities of the British Mandate, the second was the 1947–48 resistance to the partitioning of Palestine, and the third was the founding of the Palestine Liberation Organization in 1964–65. Unlike these previous movements, the *intifada* has been successful in joining together the young and the old, men and women, city dwellers and villagers, Muslims and Christians, the poor and the rich, and all political currents to form a genuine people's movement. The *intifada* represents the latest climactic expression of the collective Palestinian will, one asserting national consciousness, resisting dispossession, and reclaiming Palestinian political rights.

The primary purpose of this chapter is to examine the social roots of the *intifada*: Why and how did the uprising emerge?[2]

THEORETICAL PERSPECTIVES

In attempting to identify the roots or causes of the *intifada,* or for that matter, any other movement of collective action/violence, one must be guided by a theory. "The facts" cannot speak for themselves. Rather, they must be constructed and interpretively assembled by social scientists who are guided by certain theoretical assumptions. The consumer of one's "facts" is most advantaged when these guiding assumptions are stated explicitly. And there are many theories of collective violence from which to choose.[3] These theories can be categorized into at least three major models, among which it is important to distinguish, as all of them have been applied to the *intifada* in current political discourse as well as in the popular press.[4]

The "outside-agitator model" often is espoused by incumbent power-holders faced with rebellious insurgency. This perspective "imagines revolutions and lesser public disturbances to be the work of subversives who, with a sinister genius for cajolery and coercion, provoke otherwise disinterested masses to violence."[5] Needless to say, this model has been invoked frequently (and erroneously, we might add) to describe the relationship of the Palestine Liberation Organization (PLO) to the uprising of Palestinians within the Occupied Territories.[6]

The "volcanic model" has been a favorite among Western sociologists and political scientists.[7] While there are several different variants of this model, in general it attributes episodes of collective violence to "periodic eruption of social-psychological tensions that boil up in human groups like lava under the earth's crust."[8] Thus, collective violence is theorized as resulting from the existence of a critical mass of individuals possessing a "revolutionary state of mind."[9] From this perspective, a collective uprising such as the *intifada* is viewed as a spontaneous outburst of mass anger and hostilities resulting from the sum of individual deprivations and frustrations. Given the duration and the level of deprivations, human rights violations, and humiliations suffered by the Palestinians under Israeli rule, it is tempting to invoke this model, as have some sympathetic commentators. However, as Rod Aya correctly notes, this model treats episodes of collective violence as if they were natural disasters—exploding or erupting—and in doing so precludes meaningful analysis of the complex interplay of social and political forces that condition forms of reaction to, or expression of, collective grievances.[10]

The third model, the "political process model," is the most useful theoretical starting point for analyzing the origin and continuing dynamics of the *intifada*.[11] This model takes as its point of departure the notion that collective violence is one form of collective action, and as such constitutes only "politics by other means" rather than "abnormal" behavior.[12] Moreover, popular collective action is conceived of as deliberate and undertaken for discernable practical reasons, that is, "principled complaints over recognized bones of contention."[13] It results from the failure to give contending groups legal redress of grievances and failure to legitimize and accommodate their complaints within the legal political structure. When political struggles can be resolved legally, they are not dangerous; they spill into the streets when people recognize that legal solutions are impossible.[14]

Rejecting the volcanic model in favor of the political process model as the most appropriate for analyzing the roots of the *intifada* has been poignantly advocated by Salim Tamari:

Frustration is what you feel when your beloved has not returned your amorous overtures. What we have here is repression. It is not a psychological state of mind, but a political response to a physical state of affairs. The word frustration obfuscates the relationship between Israel and the occupied territories. One, because it obscures the hierarchical form of control. Two, because it misconstrues the nature of the response, which is not a mindless eruption but a politically motivated act, spontaneous, but with clear political objectives.[15]

Theoretically, political exclusion can be viewed as a necessary condition for the outbreak of collective violence; however, it should not be considered a sufficient one. The "physical state of affairs" that inspires, indeed requires, the political response is the true root of any collective action. Thus, a sociologically grounded analysis cannot focus solely on the political dimensions of conflict, but also must examine the historical interplay among political, economic, social, and ideological factors that impact upon the development of both the nature of the political question and the capacity of groups to act collectively upon it.[16] Key to this examination is the recognition that the calculus of political struggle changes in relation to changes in the overall structure of societies, as the composition of aggrieved groups, their social basis of solidarity, the strategies and tactics available to them, as well as the very substance and understanding of their grievances derive from the social structure within which they are embedded.[17]

Note, however, that this relationship between social structure and political action is never a one-way, passive pattern of causation; rather, it is dialectical or "reflexive." To borrow from Marx, while not under conditions of their own choosing, men and women, through their active resistance to structurally generated oppression, do indeed make their own history.[18] As groups struggle to resolve the conflicts that arise from developing contradictions within a given structure, they, in fact, continually restructure the conditions under which they are oppressed, transforming at the same time the balance of political, economic, social, and ideological forces brought to bear on the struggle, the objectives of struggle, as well as the strategies appropriate to it.

THE COLONIAL ROOTS OF THE *INTIFADA*

Guiding our analysis is the definition of the Occupied Territories as an internal colony of Israel. It is this militarily imposed status that has generated the political, economic, social, and ideological conditions of oppression and the forms of resistance to them that have developed in dialectical unity to shape both the character of the uprising and the Israeli reaction to it. The colonial drive for expropriation and dispossession of the natives, resisted by indigenous determination to persevere and overcome, generated a strategy of struggle best characterized, in Gramscian terms, as a "war of position."[19] By creating a web of "popular sovereignties"—institutions, social relations, and ideology in response to Israeli colonial oppression—the Palestinian natives wove an opposing "fabric of hegemony" through which collective action could be mobilized and sustained and Palestinian society could be reconstructed and preserved in the face of Israeli colonialism. But having won the war of position in a long and difficult struggle, the Palestinians were prepared to initiate a new strategy—the "war of maneuver"—an uprising that needed only a precipitous trigger. Exposition of how the Palestinians, despite terrible odds, did indeed wage a successful war of position will be the focus of this chapter.

Israel began life as a Zionist settler colony within historic Palestine, and after the withdrawal of the British, consolidated to maintain colonial relationships thus established.[20] With the creation of the state of Israel in 1948, over 770,000 Palestinians were forcefully displaced and effectively dispossessed of their ancestral heritage.[21] Upon the indigenous Palestinians who remained to become citizens of the newly created state, Israel imposed a complex regime of internal colonization, subjugating them socially, politically, and economically.[22] In the course of the June 1967 war, Israel conquered the remaining parts of historic Palestine, the Old City of Jerusalem, the West Bank, and Gaza, displacing an estimated additional 350,000 Palestinians.[23] These territories and their remaining population became captive under Israeli military authority and in effect were cut off from the rest of the Arab world. Soon after their conquest, Israel proceeded to impose upon them a colonial regimen not unlike that previously practiced upon the Palestinians in Israel, albeit one employing more drastic measures and more intensified processes.[24]

Four major processes of hegemonic subjugation articulate in the creation and maintenance of this internal colony: political suppression, economic exploitation, institutional "destructuring," and ideological and cultural repression. Israeli policy intends these processes to prevent, or at least to impede, the development of a societal infrastructure (a civil society) conducive to sustaining, either politically or economically, an independent Palestinian entity or state, while at the same time strengthening and expanding the state of Israel. In succeeding, Israel would perhaps dispossess those Palestinians remaining on their homeland (the West Bank and Gaza) and eliminate the question of Palestine. These processes of subjugation have generated both formal (aboveground) and informal (underground) organizational structures of resistance supported economically by outside sources, primarily from the exiled Palestinian nationalist movement (namely, the PLO, including its separate constituent parts). Thus, in effect, the process of internal colonization has sown the seeds of its own destruction—it has generated discontent, blocked legitimate means for redressing grievances, and created new "facts" of resistance—a hegemonic, nationalist ideology, the organizational structure and indigenous leadership that has been capable of mobilizing and articulating the expression of grievances into systematic, innovative community-wide acts of resistance. In other words, it has created the need for and conditioned the nature of "politics by other means."

POLITICAL SUPPRESSION

The first necessary aspect of establishing a regime of colonialism is political control. For Israel, political suppression of the Palestinians in the Occupied Territories is the obvious and most publicized method of subjugating the West Bank and Gaza. Since 1967 both the West Bank and Gaza have been under military rule, which grants Israel complete control over all aspects of Palestinian life: legal, civil, and political rights, land and water rights, licensing, taxation, trade, services, security, education, health, and social welfare. Military orders making or suspending laws require no public review, nor are they subject to review by governmental or public bodies within Israel.[25]

Municipal elections in the Occupied Territories were last held in 1976, and in those elections nationalist, pro-PLO mayoral candidates emerged as the people's choice. In 1982, after successfully organizing a National Guidance Committee (NGC) that worked on behalf of uncompromised Palestinian self-determination, the mayors were dismissed, municipal councils were disbanded, and the NGC was banned. Simply put, Israel prohibited any meaningful political activity on the part of Palestinians in the Occupied Territories. Palestinian political parties or organizations were outlawed, as were political demonstrations or mere collective gatherings of more than ten people.[26]

While Palestinians under occupation and in exile have long recognized the PLO as their legitimate representative, since 1980 they have been subject to criminal prosecution for unauthorized contact with PLO representatives or for expressing support for the organization. This stance toward PLO support was part of a larger Israeli policy initiative begun by the newly elected Likud government in 1977.[27] Termed by the Israelis themselves the "Iron Fist," it was designed to forcefully put down growing Palestinian resistance to Israeli colonization and Palestinian nationalism under the leadership of the PLO among Palestinians outside of historic Palestine.[28]

This increasing strength and visibility of Palestinian nationalist sentiment coincided with and possibly contributed to the victory of the conservative Israeli nationalist Likud coalition in 1977 and a quantum escalation of the colonization process, against which nationalist, PLO-aligned resistance was targeted. Israel responded with the Iron Fist leveled against Palestinian resistance and self-assertion in general, and the PLO in particular. The foreign policy aspect of the Iron Fist was manifest in the 1982 Israeli invasion of Lebanon, the subsequent defeat of the PLO there, and the massacres of Sabra and Shatila that killed over 1,000 Palestinian refugees. However, rather than beating the Palestinians into submission, the Israeli Iron Fist fueled the embers of rebellion even further, serving, in part, as the long-term catalyst for the *intifada*.[29]

The escalation of the Iron Fist policy provoked greater Palestinian anger and active resistance. Meron Benvenisti reported that between 1977 and 1982, the average annual number of "acts of violence" in the Occupied Territories was approximately 500, but he noted a cycle of escalated violence beginning in 1981.[30] From 1981 to 1982, 4,400 incidents of civil violence were documented, and between 1982 and 1987 the number of these incidents averaged approximately 3,000. The yearly count six months prior to the outbreak of the *intifada*, from April 1986 to May 1987, stood at 3,150.[31]

The sustained levels of "acts of violence" in the Occupied Territories between 1981 and 1987 testify to the inability of Israel's Iron Fist to control the mounting political self-assertion of the Palestinian people. In the two years prior to the *intifada*, sanctions against Palestinian political expression became even more arbitrary and harsh. On August 4, 1985, Israel's National Unity government initiated Iron Fist II to deal with increasing Palestinian defiance of the occupation.[32]

In accordance with the Iron Fist policies, Israel arrests political activists and holds them indefinitely in administrative detention without charging them. From the declaration of Iron Fist II to the outbreak of the *intifada* (1985–87), at least 316 administrative detention orders were issued, and at least forty persons were deported.[33]

In response to this suppression of aboveground political organization, underground grass-roots Palestinian activism proliferated. This too Israel attempted to stifle. To suppress grass-roots Palestinian political activity, in addition to deporting and administratively detaining community leaders, trade unionists, journalists, lawyers, and student activists, Israel has meted out a variety of collective punishments and arbitrary harassments. Mass arrests have been common: it has been estimated that over 200,000 out of a population of 1.7 million Palestinians had been arrested during the occupation prior to the *intifada*.[34] Extended curfews have been routinely imposed upon villages, towns, and refugee camps. From 1985 to 1987 a minimum of 125 Palestinian homes were demolished or sealed.[35]

In addition to the escalation, beginning in 1985, of administrative detentions, deportations, curfews, and home demolitions, Israel's Iron Fist policies included less quantifiable forms of collective repression manifest in "a campaign of harassment." As Jan Abu-Shakrah testifies:

The campaign [begun in 1985] was marked by the use of humiliating and degrading practices, such as forcing men to stand for long periods on one leg with their hands in the air, ordering them to dance, to bray like a donkey, to walk on all fours, and so on. Residents were ordered to remove their clothes and to perform humiliating acts, and were beaten if they refused. Soldiers entered houses, destroying furniture, shooting at water tanks, and beating residents, including women, if they complained.[36]

Less well publicized has been the continuing torture and inhumane treatment of those politically active Palestinians officially under Israeli care. In 1987 approximately 4,700 political prisoners could be found in Israeli detention centers. Long-standing Israeli practices of prisoner abuse and torture as a means of coercing confessions and denying legal rights have been well documented, as have the generally inhumane and overcrowded conditions of detention facilities.[37]

Obviously, Israeli Iron Fist attempts to control Palestinians in the Occupied Territories did not have the intended consequence of making the Palestinians atomized and passive Israeli subjects subdued in their political aspirations, but rather propagated the seeds of resistance that had been rooted historically in the overall conditions of colonial occupation; this in turn contributed to collective resistance and hence the blossoming of the *intifada*.

As suggested earlier, the nature of the historic and ongoing political repression experienced by the Palestinians under Israeli occupation alone is insufficient to explain the mass-based support for the *intifada*, its mobilization, and its sustained momentum in the face of increasingly violent Israeli attempts to control it. Rather, this political suppression must be viewed in relation to the other three processes of internal colonial subjugation that have produced the social bases of this support, namely, economic exploitation, institutional destructuring, and cultural and ideological repression, all of which articulate with one another at the political level.

ECONOMIC EXPLOITATION

In the second major process of internal colonization, Israel strives to harness the economic resources and labor power of the indigenous Palestinians in the service of the Israeli economy. Although officially considered independent economic units, the Gaza Strip and the West Bank have been forced, through post–1967 war Israeli policies, into dependency on the physical integration into Israel's economic system. As aptly put by Mohammed K. Shadid, "The occupation has helped transform Israel into a state with an imperial economy, relying for its well-being on the captive human and material resources of the occupied territories."[38] More specifically, over the course of the occupation, Israel has taken control of the service infrastructure of the West Bank and Gaza, confiscated Palestinian land and water resources, exploited and degraded Palestinian labor, held the Occupied Territories as a captive market, and restricted their external trade.[39]

The physical infrastructure and the transportation and communication systems in the West Bank and Gaza have been recast into Israel's.[40] Similarly, the Occupied Territories' electric generation units have been linked to and controlled by the Israeli grid.[41]

More important, Israel pursues a policy of "creeping" or de facto annexation through the confiscation of land and the establishment of Israeli colonial settlements throughout the Occupied Territories (see Chapter 3).[42] In addition to its unabashed annexation of the Old City and East Jerusalem in 1967, Israel has confiscated, or brought under Israeli military control, over 52 percent of the land in the West Bank and between 30 and 40 percent of Gaza's land.[43] As of April 1987, confiscated Palestinian land supported 18 Jewish settlements in Gaza, with over 2,700 settlers, and 118 settlements in the West Bank, with over 65,000 settlers.[44]

Land confiscation and construction of Israeli settlements in the West Bank and Gaza followed general patterns corresponding to the respective parties that controlled the Israeli government.[45] While the labor alliance governing Israel between 1967 and 1977 initiated the policy of land confiscation and colonial settlements, it tended to avoid erecting such bases/settlements in the midst of Palestinian population concentrations. Rather, it surrounded and contained such centers. However, soon after the Likud victory (1977–83), a more overtly political strategy was implemented.[46] The Likud government, with its Iron Fist policy, escalated the processes of land confiscation and colonization and planted settlements right in the midst of Palestinian urban concentrations. The provocative character of these developments triggered sharp conflict between Israeli authorities and local Palestinians. Such conflict became more spectacular as settler vigilantes took matters into their own hands.[47] Despite this open and escalating conflict, the first National Unity government (Likud and Labor from 1983 to 1988) renewed the Likud strategy and backed it up with Iron Fist II.

To support Israeli settlements, and to preserve the deteriorating water supply within the borders of Israel proper, water indigenous to the Occupied Territories is confiscated (see Chapter 3).[48] As with land confiscation, this process escalated under the Likud government, which in 1982 transferred management of the water systems from the military government to Israel's national water company, Mekorot.[49] Consequently, the quality and quantity of water available for domestic and agricultural consumption by the Palestinian population within the Occupied Territories have been made increasingly dependent on the consumption "requirements" of both Jewish settlers and Jewish Israelis, requirements defined by Israel. Constraints on water usage imposed by Israel on Palestinian farmers have kept the area of irrigated land unchanged since 1967.[50]

The Occupied Territories have become captive markets for Israeli exports (see Chapter 3). The Occupied Territories constitute Israel's second most important commodity export market (the United States is the first). The export of Israeli goods into the Occupied Territories was, and remains, unrestricted, while Israeli-imposed tariffs and other barriers have circumscribed trade with the outside world. In 1986 the West Bank and Gaza imported $780.3 million worth of Israeli goods, constituting 89.4 percent of their total imports.[51]

In contrast to the unrestricted export of Israeli-produced goods into the Occupied Territories, quotas are imposed on the type and amount of goods that can be exported from them into Israel, and the export of some regional commodities to Israel or its overseas markets is completely prohibited.[52] Moreover, Israel protects its markets at the source through outright restrictions on production, which in recent years have become more severe.[53] Thus, forced dependency on Israel for trade is exacerbated by protection of the Israeli market from competition, effectively distorting the productive sectors of the West Bank and Gaza in a manner that maximizes the profitability of this arrangement for Israel.

Through Israeli control over the Occupied Territories' infrastructure, its confiscation of prime agricultural land and restriction of water usage for irrigation, as well as its control over trade throughout the postwar period, the structure of production in the Occupied Territories has been reoriented and regulated by the needs of the Israeli economy rather than by the development requirements of the territories themselves (see Chapter three).[54] This situation of dependency has resulted in the overall stagnation of industry and agriculture over the duration of the occupation. The significant exception to this stagnation has been the growth of the construction sector in both the West Bank and Gaza.[55] This growth is attributable largely to a rise in the demand for residential housing, rather than to the construction of production-related facilities.

Overall economic stagnation and concomitant low levels of productive investment have forced Palestinians, both skilled and unskilled, to seek employment outside the West Bank and Gaza, primarily in Israel and the oil-producing Arab peninsula (see Chapter three). Most significantly, as the occupation progressed, increasing agricultural stagnation resulted in a rapid depeasantization and partial proletarianization of large segments of the West Bank and Gaza peasantry and small farmers. For a time, employment in Israel and labor migration to the Gulf states counteracted the lack of employment opportunities for unskilled and semiskilled workers in the territories, increasing the purchasing power of the population.

By official accounts, in 1986 over 94,000 Palestinian workers were crossing into Israel for work every business day; this number would increase by 25–30 percent if unofficially employed workers were included.[56] However, as other ethnic groups (Sephardic Jews and "Israeli-Arabs") experienced upward mobility as a result of a structural upgrading of occupations, West Bank and Gaza Palestinians remained substantially overrepresented in the declining low-status ones, primarily as manual labor in construction and agriculture; they had in fact remained Israel's "hewers of wood and drawers of water."[57]

While employment in Israel was becoming less appealing to a new generation of Palestinian youth, opportunities to work in the Gulf states were drying up. Emigration out of the Occupied Territories averaged 17 per 1,000 population during the oil boom era between 1973 and 1982. By 1985 the Bank of Israel reported that the rate of emigration had dropped to 3 per 1,000.[58] Accordingly, cash remittances from Palestinians laboring in the Gulf have steadily declined since 1982. Juan Tamayo reports that remittances into Jordan, much of which were destined for the Occupied Territories, dropped from $1.5 billion in 1982 to $887 million in 1988.[59] This sharp drop had a profound impact on the general well-being of the people in the Occupied Territories, which, when combined with the near closure of channels of opportunity, undoubtedly increased perceptions of structural oppression, especially among youths seeking first employment. In the context of a very youthful population, this situation was bound to create volatile conditions, and it constituted a pivotal catalytic factor contributing to the timing of the uprising.

The colonial economic regime that Israel imposed on the Occupied Territories and the Palestinians escalated progressively from the start of the occupation. Each escalation of the Iron Fist policy had its economic component. For example, as part of Iron Fist II, Israel's new minister of defense, Yitzhak Rabin, initiated another turn of the economic screw over the Occupied Territories when he declared upon his appointment in 1984, "There will be no development initiated by the Israeli government, and no permits will be given for expanding industry and agriculture which may compete with the state of Israel."[60] Needless to say, this policy intensified the economic squeeze on the Palestinians and degraded their economic well-being—a factor crucial in preparing the context of the uprising. Palestinian economic survival, or, as the Palestinians labeled it, steadfast economic perseverance (*sumud*) in the face of labor degradation and resource dispossession, has been the most critical aspect in winning one strategic battle in the "war of position" against Israel.

INSTITUTIONAL DESTRUCTURING

Israel's colonial regime over the West Bank and Gaza extended to Palestinian social and economic institutions. As with the political organizations, the occupation authorities, through direct and indirect means, attempted to inhibit, if not altogether destroy, organized, autonomous Palestinian economic institutions. For example, when the two Palestinian territories were occupied in 1967, one of the first acts of the occupation authorities "was to demolish the existing Arab financial and monetary institutions. . . . the earliest military orders closed the 31 branches of Amman-based and other banks, imposed the authority of the Bank of Israel over all banking matters, made the Israeli [currency] legal tender (jointly with the Jordanian dinar) and imposed Israeli foreign exchange controls."[61] These measures have had a profound impact on subsequent monetary conditions such as the practice of real savings and investment. Thus, Palestinians under occupation were forced to revert to premodern and traditional institutions: money changers, merchants, and landowners who provide varied forms of service, currency exchange, money transfers, credit, borrowing, and lending. "Although Israeli banks were encouraged to operate in the occupied territories, the policy was not wholly designed to integrate Arab financial life with Israel as a subordinate but profitable annex; it was principally designed with a political aim to weaken and undermine independent Arab economic development."[62]

The Israeli military occupation authorities had the power to issue or withhold licenses and permissions for varied social and economic activities. They used this power liberally in a clear effort to obstruct the development of an autonomous Palestinian civil society. For example, trade union activity is severely controlled and circumscribed. In Gaza

trade union activity . . . is restricted to six unions. . . . Founded in 1964 under Egyptian rule and banned by the Israeli government from 1967 to 1980, these unions have a total membership of about three hundred and are not allowed to recruit individuals who were not members before 1967. Furthermore, unions cannot hold elections, accept funds from abroad, register any workers without prior permission, hold educational and cultural lectures or hold any meeting without an Israeli officer in attendance.[63]

In the West Bank, Israel allowed trade union organizations according to the 1960 Jordanian labor laws. But by the late 1970s, Israeli occupation authorities withheld licenses from new trade unions and circumscribed the activities of existing ones, often by simply closing offices or altogether banning them. Union leaders were held under administrative detention, town or house arrest, and were subjected even to deportation. Harassment and intimidation of activists, leaders and members alike, were other forms of repression routinely practiced by Israel in an effort to disrupt or deter the work of union men and women. In response to these measures, Palestinian union activity and the labor movement in general organized on a more informal, quasi-underground, semilegal basis with diffuse and quickly replaceable leadership. In the course of this restructuring, the labor unions became more politicized, emphasizing the nationalist struggle (against Israel) over the class struggle and socialist ideology.[64] During the 1970s, in spite of severe repression by military authorities and internal divisiveness and socio-political competition, trade unionism and the labor movement grew in numbers and strength with the rapid process of depeasantization and partial proletarian-ization of the Palestinian labor force. Even informal and indirect union support was extended to migrant Palestinian workers inside Israel.

Israeli occupation authorities succeeded not only in delegitimizing Palestinian economic institutions but also in circumscribing educational and other social service activity. For example, the entire educational and manpower development infrastructure has seriously deteriorated, as evidenced by declines in educational standards and in the square footage of school rooms, stagnation of vocational and technical training, and total elimination of agricultural manpower training.[65] There has, in fact, been an extensive deskilling of Palestinian manpower under occupation.[66] Further, the lack of public investment in health facilities led to a decline in the number of hospital beds from 26 per 10,000 population in 1974 to 18 in 1985.[67]

Israeli efforts at destructuring Palestinian institutions, intended to truncate or destroy *organized* Palestinian activity, were responded to with significantly more political and nationalist activism. Thus, grass-roots organizations sprang forth in all areas of communal life: medical relief, agricultural relief, local councils, professional associations, trade unions and even union federations, women's committees, and all manner of self-help educational, cultural, welfare, and char-itable societies. Even productive cooperatives evolved, as did agricultural and industrial credit service and manpower training centers. These committees filled the gap of needed communal services and operated in spite of the obstructionist military occupation. "In the process, they laid the groundwork for organized, institutional resistance to the occupation."[68] Like the trade unions, these com-mittees were infused with Palestinian nationalism, and they prepared the ground for the brilliantly successful popular committees of the *intifada*.

The Palestinian civil society that emerged in dialectical opposition to hege-monic Israeli control—grass-roots based, decentralized, voluntary, self-reliant, and politically conscious—developed and strengthened itself in spite of heavy-handed Israeli depredations. Joost Hiltermann notes that these local, mass-based organizations originated in the early 1970s "when local activists, in many cases school children, began organizing to address the basic social and infrastructural problems in Palestinian society."[69] George Abed estimates that currently "there are more than 400 local organizations, institutions, associations, and committees operating in virtually all Palestinian towns and villages and refugee camps."[70] Many of these local organizations have taken on new tasks and provided the organizational, experiential, and ideological (collectivist and nationalist) foundation for the popular committees that have sprung up so quickly to mobilize and deploy the Palestinian people in the *intifada*.

Ironically, then, the efforts of the colonizing power to atomize, degrade, control, and dispossess a native population triggered a dialectical oppositional response that produced an authentic organizational structure, knitting the people together in a web of reciprocal relations, mutual cooperation, and solid, politically conscious bonds, creating a "woven fabric" of hegemony that could unite many threads of Palestinian society which traditionally were separated by conflicting objective interests. As the struggle intensified, Palestinian unity strengthened in this war of position: all internal divisions dissolved, and a remarkably popular and determined movement of the oppressed against a colonial oppressor developed.

CULTURAL AND IDEOLOGICAL REPRESSION

The fourth and final aspect of Israel's colonial regime over the West Bank and Gaza is a structure of cultural and ideological repression. This was practiced not merely in the Israeli effort to block the mobilizing ideology for organized Palestinian activity but also to suppress the sense of collective identity, and ultimately, collective will.

Israeli repression of Palestinian culture and ideology has reached such extremes as to prohibit artists from painting or exhibiting works in which the four colors of the Palestinian flag are used simultaneously. There is also a great deal of interference in the content of the educational curriculum, especially regarding the history and culture of Palestine and the Palestinian people. As Muhammad Hallaj testifies:

The word "Palestine" has been expunged from all textbooks used in the schools and methodically replaced by "Israel." Many books, most of them classics of Arabic literature, have been black-listed and libraries are forbidden to possess them.

Palestinian Arab historic sites have been bulldozed or pillaged. Even Palestinian folk items, traditional costumes, and foods are being robbed and marketed abroad as Israeli creations. The Arabic names of towns, hills, and streets are being erased and changed to Hebrew names. UNESCO was correct in concluding that "the Israeli authorities [are] adopting policies in Gaza and the West Bank designed to paralyze Palestinian culture."[71]

Under the 1945 Defense Emergency Regulations Israel requires licensing of all publications and grants the minister of the interior unreviewable discretion to refuse, suspend, or revoke such licenses.[72] In addition, all publications, Israeli and Palestinian alike, are subject to continual censorship: "Items are subject to censorship even if they are verbatim translations of materials already published in the Hebrew or foreign press, or disseminated by major news agencies."[73] Specific military orders further restrict freedom of the press. These orders (1) prohibit the importation or distribution of publications without a permit from local military authorities (1967); (2) forbid the publication of anything having "political significance" (1967, 1971, and 1981); (3) allow the confiscation of any publication, even those having a permit and those having passed the Israeli censor (1970); and (4) require the publication of all military announcements in newspapers.[74]

The Israeli efforts to control and suppress the free flow of information, education, and other cultural activity extended to prohibition of festivals, exhibits, and public lectures.[75] However, illegal though it is according to the occupier's law, such activity never ceased. Further, an underground system of oral and popular communication helped resist fragmentation, allowed coordination, and reinforced cultural and national identity. Art, poetry, prose, and even graffiti at times took on a cryptic and symbolic style in order to circumvent the censor. Increasingly over the last decade, such innovative Palestinian cultural activity raised as well as deepened and spread national consciousness. It has been instrumental in developing the ideological terrain upon which Palestinians have come to oppose and mobilize against colonial Israeli occupation, becoming, indeed, the "culture of the *Intifada*."[76]

One important ideological theme that emerged among the Palestinians through the dialectic of oppression/resistance was *sumud,* or steadfast perseverance. *Sumud* emerged in the second half of the 1970s as "a collective and third way between submission and exile, between passivity and . . . violence to end the occupation."[77] This ideology expressed a strategy of perseverance under Israeli hegemony, the pressures of which were causing the deterioration and threatening the integrity of Palestinian society, and thus the continued presence of the Palestinians on their national soil. Monies pumped in through the Steadfastness Aid Fund of the Jordanian-Palestinian Joint Committee, established by the Arab Summit Conference in Baghdad in 1978, were largely what Ibrahim Dakkak calls "static *sumud*": maintenance of Palestinians on their land.[78] This soon was transformed into a more dynamic *sumud muqawim* (resistance *sumud*), an ideology and practice that helped energize and spread self-help local service committees. Among the most successful of these in the early 1980s were the medical relief committees: doctors from Jerusalem hospitals on their days off would go out to establish and man clinics in villages. "By 1983 every section of the West Bank and Gaza was covered by one of eight such organizations. Together they formed the Union of Palestinian Medical Relief Committees," which became the exemplar for many other types of committees.[79] An incredible new politically conscious and mobilizing dynamism developed, characterized by enthusiasm coupled with a new spirit of service and sacrifice. From a static *sumud*, characterized by an attitude of resignation (perhaps even self-pity), albeit coupled with the determination to stay put on the land, the *sumud muqawim* emerged as activist and effective in seeking ways to build alternative institutions, and thus to resist and undermine the occupation.

CONCLUSION: POPULAR SOVEREIGNTIES AND THE CONJUNCTURAL MOMENT

The *intifada*, a popular national liberation movement of the Palestinian people under internal Israeli colonization, is an example par excellence of "politics by other means." Indeed, under conditions not of their own choosing, the Palestinian people, men, women, and children, made dramatic history by developing the ideological, organizational, and mobilizational means to resist oppression. Through their active participation in the dialectic of oppression/resistance, they have transformed qualitatively the balance of political, economic, social, and ideological forces in the area; they have won the war of position.

This feat is all the more remarkable when one considers the power, resources, and arrogance of the colonizer. The means that the Palestinian people developed to resist centralized, overpowering, and hegemonic Israeli oppression were "popular sovereignties," local and self-reliant committees that provided popular empowerment. As Israel was successful in preventing and suppressing the establishment of a central, coherent, national Palestinian leadership in the Occupied Territories—witness the fate of the National Guidance Committee, the Palestine National Front, and even the nationalist elected mayors—the Palestinian people created the "popular sovereignties" of first the local and then the popular committees, a most effective mechanism of active resistance. These popular sovereignties emerged as a blend of traditional and modern structures of social organization, communication, and mobilization. Their disseminative and empowering capacities have been crucial reasons for the reproduction, and therefore the momentum, intensity, and scope of the *intifada*.

The final question to be addressed concerns the timing of the *intifada*. Why then?

The root cause of the Palestinian *intifada* is clearly the cumulative effects of two decades of Israeli colonialism in the Occupied Territories of the West Bank and Gaza. This colonialism, deliberately and systematically perpetrated, drastically transformed the structure of Palestinian society: demographically, economically, politically, institutionally, and ideologically. Perhaps as important, the colonial policies and actions of Israel were coupled with a rhetoric and ideology, emanating from both the government and the political movements, which laid claim to the Palestinian land and its resources and which did not hide the wordless wish of ridding these lands of the indigenous Palestinians. This threat of dispossession, dispersion, and loss of identity was not lost on a people who had experienced these tragedies a generation earlier in 1948. Despite a frightful war in 1967, most Palestinians in the West Bank and Gaza stayed put and did not flee out of harm's way.

During and immediately upon conclusion of the war, a slogan became popular among the Palestinians, *al-Ard qabl al-'Ard*, or "land before honor"; it reversed the sentiment that in 1948 led to massive flights of Palestinians into exile. For the Palestinians this slogan expressed the recognition that the loss of land would mean the final destruction of their society, their dispossession, loss of identity, and dispersed exile. It was as if the motto expressed a collective will, a determination to stay put, grit one's teeth, and persevere. This collective determination, infused by the collective memory of 1948, undoubtedly undergirded the spirit of resistance so pivotal to fighting the war of position against dispossessive Israeli colonialism. This spirit expressed itself as Palestinian nationalism under the leadership of the PLO.

The Palestinian nationalist movement, however, transformed its ideology and goals in two broad phases. As Tamari observes, in the first phase of Palestinian resistance,

until the mid–1970's, the Palestinian nationalist movement in both rhetoric and program, had as its goal the establishment of a secular state in all of Palestine; . . . [after] the October War [of 1973] . . . a significant shift occurred in the ideological formulations of Palestinian nationalist objectives. That strategy called for Israeli withdrawal from the Occupied Territories and the establishment of a Palestinian state in those areas . . . co-existing with the state of Israel.[80]

The ideological change from "liberation" to "independence" signaled a new strategy for the PLO inside the Occupied Territories: building embryonic institutions of power. "By the late 1970s, [this strategy] had established the complete political hegemony of Palestinian nationalism and the PLO as the single articulator of Palestinian aspirations."[81]

In the late 1970s, Palestinian nationalism clashed head on with a more aggressive Israeli colonialism initiated by the triumphant right-wing Likud government. This clash intensified greatly after the Camp David Accords and the bilateral peace treaty between Israel and Egypt. The coincidence of the neutralization of Egypt from the Arab-Israeli conflict and the success of Palestinian nationalism may have encouraged Israel to unleash its Iron Fist policy toward all three targets: the Palestinians under occupation, the Palestinians inside Israel proper, and those in exile, particularly the PLO in Lebanon.

Within this political context, four catalyzing events propelled the Palestinians in the Occupied Territories to move from a war of position to a war of maneuver in their struggle against Israeli colonialism. The first was Israel's forced retreat from its invasion of Lebanon. The 1982 invasion not only showed Israel's brutal aggression clearly to international public opinion, but, more important, was defeated by a determined Lebanese resistance. The myth of Israeli invincibility was broken. Taking matters into one's own hands and acting accordingly became a popular concept. Thus, a strong ideology of self-reliance finally replaced that of dependence on external powers.

Second, the downturn in the Arab oil economy undermined the economic well-being of Palestinians under occupation. This precipitous decline closed off work opportunities, and Palestinian emigration rates dropped commensurately. Thus, an effective escape valve for energetic young men who otherwise had few domestic resources available to provide for their families was clogged. The resultant emiseration and degradation of labor manifested itself politically in increased civil disobedience; witness the rapid increase in "acts of violence" noted above. This obvious ferment among Palestinians brought on in 1985 Israel's Iron Fist II.

However, despite the increased repression, discontent, and ferment, Palestinian activism in the Occupied Territories in the mid–1980s remained sporadic, factionalized, and uncoordinated. In other words, the climate was politically charged, but the political forces active in the war of position remained fragmented. The third catalyzing event brought them together; this was the reunification of the principal constituent parts of the PLO in a meeting of the Palestine National Council (PNC) in Algiers in 1987. After nearly five years of divisiveness and paralysis, the Palestinian national movement found the means to regroup, reunite, and expand its formal ranks. Noteworthy is the legitimation and formal acceptance of the Palestinian Communist party (active and effective in the underground in the Occupied Territories) by the other PNC participants, uniting, perhaps for the first time, the respective Palestinian political factions in the Occupied Territories. Suddenly, self-reliant, experienced, determined activists found their impetus for cooperation and coordination: an underground, united, organic leadership was born, and a strategic battle in the war of position was won.

The fourth and final catalyzing event occurred in November 1987. Arab leaders, meeting in a summit conference in Amman, Jordan, 40 miles away from the Occupied Territories, declared that the Arab enemy was Iran, 1,000 miles to the east, while the Israeli occupation soldiers were beating up Palestinian school girls in the West Bank. In the communiqué of the summit, the Palestine question was relegated to the end, almost as an afterthought, outraging Palestinians under occupation and in exile.

The conjunctural moment had arrived. The political climate was charged, the social and economic discontent high, and the conflicts generated by the practice of oppression/resistance intense. In this context, the emergence of a united organic leadership and the bonding of the vast majority of people in a web of popular sovereignties, cemented together by a collectivist and nationalist ideology, were sufficient to mobilize the Palestinians for action, transforming a war of position into a war of maneuver. All that was needed for a general uprising, the Palestinian war of maneuver, was a precipitous event, any event, to launch it. That tragical incident occurred on December 9, 1987.

NOTES

1. See Naseer Aruri, "Dialectics of Dispossession," in Naseer Aruri, ed., *Occupation: Israel over Palestine* (Belmont, Mass.: Association for Arab American University Graduates, 1983).

2. Other projects with this same purpose can be found in Samih K. Farsoun, "The Roots of the Intifadah," *The Return* 1, no. 2 (September 1988): 4; Ann Mosley Lesch, "The Palestinian Uprising—Causes and Consequences," *Field Staff Reports*, 1988–89/ no. 1, Africa/Middle East (Indianapolis: Universities Field Staff International, 1988–89); Bernard Sabella, "Why the Intifadah?" *The Return* 1, no. 5 (December 1988): 13.

3. See James B. Rule, *Theories of Civil Violence* (Berkeley: University of California Press, 1988).

4. These "models" are taken from Rod Aya, "Theories of Revolution Reconsidered: Contrasting Models of Collective Violence," *Theory and Society* 8 (1979): 39–99.

5. Ibid., p. 49.

6. For example, see *Jerusalem Post*, October 14, 1987.

7. Aya, "Theories of Revolution," p. 49.

8. Ibid., p. 42.

9. For example, see James C. Davies, "Toward a Theory of Revolution," *American Sociological Review* 27 (1962); Ted R. Gurr, *Why Men Rebel* (Princeton, N.J.: Princeton University Press, 1968); Samuel P. Huntington, *Political Order in Changing Societies* (New Haven, Conn.: Yale University Press, 1968); Chalmers Johnson, *Revolutionary Change* (Boston: Little, Brown, 1966); Neil J. Smelser, *Theory of Collective Behavior* (New York: Free Press, 1963).

10. Also see Charles Tilley, *From Mobilization to Revolution* (Reading, Mass.: Addison-Wesley, 1978), and Rule, *Theories of Civil Violence*, for thorough critiques of this approach.

11. This model was developed and advanced by Tilley, *From Mobilization to Revolution*.

12. Aya, "Theories of Revolution," p. 49.

13. Ibid., p. 72.

14. Quintin Hoare and Geoffrey N. Smith, eds. and trans., *Selections from the Prison Notebooks of Antonio Gramsci* (New York: International Publishers, 1987).

15. Salim Tamari, "What the Uprising Means," *Middle East Report*, no. 152 (May-June 1988): 28.

16. Aya, "Theories of Revolution," pp. 76–78; see also Tilley, *From Mobilization to Revolution*.

17. Tilley, *From Mobilization to Revolution*.

18. Karl Marx, *The Eighteenth Brumaire of Louis Bonaparte* (New York: International Publishers, 1987), p. 15.

19. Hoare and Smith, *Antonio Gramsci*.

20. See Maxime Rodinson, *Israel: A Colonial Settler State?* (New York: Monad Press, 1973); Samih K. Farsoun, "Settler Colonialism and Herrenvolk-democracy," in Richard P. Stevens and Abdelwahab M. Elmessiri, eds., *Israel and South Africa: The Progression of a Relationship* (New York: New World Press, 1976).

21. Aruri, *Occupation*; Janet Abu-Lughod, "The Demographic Transformation of Palestine," in Ibrahim Abu-Lughod, ed., *The Transformation of Palestine* (Evanston, Ill.: Northwestern University Press, 1987).

22. Rodinson, *Israel*; Farsoun, "Settler Colonialism." See also Elia Zureik, *The Palestinians in Israel: A Study in Internal Colonialism* (London: Routledge and Kegan Paul, 1979).

23. J. Abu-Lughod, "The Demographic Transformation."

24. See generally Aruri, *Occupation*; I. Abu-Lughod, George T. Abed, ed., *The Palestinian Economy* (London: Routledge Champan & Hall, 1988).

25. Sara Roy, *The Gaza Strip Survey* (Boulder, Colo.: Westview Press, 1986), p. 123.

26. Lea Tsemel, "Personal Status and Rights," in Aruri, *Occupation*, p. 64.

27. See Aruri, "Dialectics of Dispossession," pp. 16–19.

28. For example, see John Quigley, "Human Rights and Palestine," in Ibrahim Abu-Lughod, ed. *Palestinian Rights* (Wilmette, Ill.: Medina Press, 1982).

29. Lesch, "Palestinian Uprising."

30. Meron Benvenisti, *1987 Report: Demographic, Economic, Legal, Social and Political Developments in the West Bank* (Boulder, Colo.: Westview Press, 1987), p. 40.

31. Ibid.

32. Note that neither Iron Fist I nor II were innovative responses to unique circumstances. They simply endorsed the reinstatement or escalation of certain repressive practices and intensification of the violence that had been part of the (unpublicized) Israeli repertoire since the outset of the occupation. See Muhammad Hallaj, "Israel's Palestinian Policy," in I. Abu-Lughod, ed. *Palestinian Rights*, pp. 95–106; see also Aruri, "Dialectics of Dispossession."

33. Benvenisti, *1987 Report*, citing al-Haq.

34. M. Cherif Bassiouni and Louise Cainkar, eds., *The Palestinian Intifada—December 9, 1987—December 8, 1988: A Record of Israeli Repression* (Chicago: Data Base Project on Palestinian Human Rights, 1989).

35. Benvenisti, *1987 Report*, p. 40, citing al-Haq. See also Bassiouni and Cainkar, *Palestinian Intifada*, and U.S. State Department, *Country Reports on Human Rights 1988*, Washington, D.C.: U.S. Department of State, 1989, p. 1381.

36. Jan Abu-Shakrah, "The Iron Fist, October 1985 to January 1986," *Journal of Palestine Studies* 15, no. 4 (Summer 1986): 121.

37. See Ghassan Bishara, "The Human Rights Case Against Israel: The Policy of Torture," *Journal of Palestine Studies* 8 (Summer 1979): 3–30. See also Bassiouni and Cainkar, *Palestinian Intifada*.

38. Mohammed K. Shadid, "Israeli Policy Towards Economic Development in the West Bank and Gaza," in Abed, *Palestinian Economy*, p. 121.

39. See especially Abed, *Palestinian Economy*; Simcha Bahiri, *Industrialization in the West Bank and Gaza* (Boulder, Colo.: Westview Press, 1987); David Kahan, *Agriculture and Water Resources in the West Bank and Gaza (1967–1987)* (Boulder, Colo.: Westview Press, 1987); Yusif A. Sayigh, "The Palestinian Economy Under Occupation: Dependency and Pauperization," *Journal of Palestine Studies* 15, no. 4 (Summer 1986): 41–67; Roy, *Gaza Strip Survey*; Fawzi A. Gharaibeh, *The Economies of the West Bank and Gaza Strip* (Boulder, Colo.: Westview Press, 1985); Sara Graham-Brown, "The Economic Consequences of the Occupation," in Aruri, *Occupation*, pp. 167–222.

40. Benvenisti, *1987 Report*; Tamari, "What the Uprising Means."

41. Gharaibeh, *Economies*, p. 99.

42. See Ibrahim Matar, "Israeli Settlements and Palestinian Rights," and Peter Demant, "Israeli Settlement Policy Today," in Aruri, *Occupation*, pp. 117–64.

43. Meron Benvenisti with Ziad Abu-Zayed and Danny Rubenstein, *The West Bank Handbook: A Political Lexicon* (Boulder, Colo.: Westview Press, 1986); Roy, *Gaza Strip Survey*.

44. Benvenisti, *1987 Report*.

45. Graham-Brown, "Economic Consequences"; Geoffrey Aronson, *Creating Facts:*

Israel, Palestinians and the West Bank (Washington, D.C.: Institute for Palestine Studies, 1987).

46. Graham-Brown, "Economic Consequences."

47. See Jan Abu-Shakrah, *Israeli Settler Violence in the Occupied Territories, 1980–1984* (Chicago: Palestine Human Rights Campaign, 1985).

48. See Meron Benvenisti, *1987 Report*; Benvenisti et al., *West Bank Handbook*; Roy, *Gaza Strip Survey*; Gharaibeh, *Economies*; Kahan, *Agriculture and Water Resources*.

49. Benvenisti, *West Bank Handbook*, p. 225.

50. Gharaibeh, *Economies*.

51. Benvenisti, *1987 Report*.

52. Benvenisti, *1987 Report*; Roy, *Gaza Strip Survey*; Gharaibeh, *Economies*.

53. Roger Owen, "The West Bank Now: Economic Development," in Peter F. Krogh and Mary C. McDavid, eds., *Palestinians Under Occupation: Prospects for the Future* (Washington, D.C.: Center for Contemporary Arab Studies, Georgetown University, 1989), p. 49.

54. Benvenisti, *1987 Report*; Roy, *Gaza Strip Survey*; Gharaibeh, *Economies*.

55. Antoine Mansour, "The West Bank Economy: 1948–1984," in Abed, *Palestinian Economy*; Roy, *Gaza Strip Survey*.

56. Benvenisti, *1987 Report*; Gharaibeh, *Economies*, p. 50. See also Roy, *Gaza Strip Survey*; Moshe Semyonov and Noah Lewin-Epstein, *Hewers of Wood and Drawers of Water: Noncitizen Arabs in the Israeli Labor Market* (Ithaca, N.Y.: International Labor Relations Press, 1987).

57. Semyonov and Lewin-Epstein, *Hewers of Wood*.

58. Danny Rubenstein, "Economic Woes in the Territories," *Davar*, November 18, 1984; Zio Rabi, "Demographic Update," *Ha'aretz*, November 28, 1984.

59. Juan O. Tamayo, " 'Gucci Kingdom' Jordan Falls from Riches to Rags," *Miami Herald*, March 19, 1989. According to an estimate cited by Owen, "West Bank Now," p. 50, "Over a third of the income of the West Bank and Gaza was then [early 1980s] coming directly in aid and remittances from outside."

60. Cited in Owen, "West Bank Now," p. 49.

61. Laurence Harris, "Money and Finance with Undeveloped Banking in the Occupied Territories," in Abed, *Palestinian Economy*, p. 191.

62. Ibid., p. 220.

63. Roy, *Gaza Strip Survey*, p. 60.

64. Joost Hiltermann, "The Dynamics of Mass Mobilization and the Uprising: The Case of the Labor Movement," paper presented at "The Palestinians: New Directions," Fourteenth Annual Symposium, Center for Contemporary Arab Studies, Georgetown University, May 4–5, 1989.

65. George Abed, ed., *The Palestinian Economy: Studies in Development under Prolonged Occupation* (London: Routledge Champan & Hall, 1989), p. 16. One exception should be cited. This is the successful establishment and expansion of institutions of higher learning in the Occupied Territories. As George Abed notes, "The private educational system expanded quantitatively, even if lack of resources limited the extent of qualitative improvements" ibid., p. 18.

66. See Raja Khalidi, "The Economy of the Palestinian Arabs in Israel," and Atif A. Kubursi, "Jobs, Education and Development: The Case of the West Bank," in Abed, *Palestinian Economy*; see also Abed, in ibid.

67. Abed, *Palestinian Economy*, p. 6.

68. Hiltermann, "Dynamics," p. 5.

69. Ibid., p. 2.

70. Abed, *Palestinian Economy*, p. 19.

71. Hallaj, "Israel's Palestinian Policy," p. 99.

72. Committee to Protect Journalists and Article 19, *Journalism Under Occupation: Israel's Regulation of the Palestinian Press* (Jerusalem: Committee to Protect Journalists and Article 19, October 1988), p. 53.

73. Ibid., p. 52.

74. Ibid., pp. 60–61.

75. Roy, *Gaza Strip Survey*, p. 68.

76. Hanan Mikhail-Ashrawi in a lecture at "The Palestinians: Future Directions," Fourteenth Annual Symposium, Center for Contemporary Arab Studies, Georgetown University, May 4–5, 1989.

77. Committee to Protect Journalists and Article 19, 1988, p. 11.

78. Ibrahim Dakkak, "Development from Within: A Strategy for Survival" in Abed, *Palestinian Economy*, p. 289.

79. Owen, "West Bank Now," p. 50.

80. Tamari, "What the Uprising Means," p. 26.

81. Ibid.

3

The Effects of Israeli Occupation on the Economy of the West Bank and Gaza Strip

Samir Abdallah Saleh

The Israeli occupation of the West Bank and Gaza Strip in June 1967 led to deep changes in their economy. Most important among economic factors introduced by the occupation were (1) measures regulating Palestinian economic activities; (2) the opening of the Palestinian market to Israeli goods and entrepreneurs; and (3) the so-called open bridges policy, which linked the Occupied Territories to the Arab world via Jordan.

The Israeli occupation is colonial-settler and neocolonial in nature, seeking to destructure the Palestinians' socioeconomic as well as cultural existence in order to force large numbers among them out of their homeland, while those who remain are harnessed to Israeli needs.[1] The nature of the occupation contradicts Palestinian aspirations in all fields, including the economic field.

The economic facet of Israeli policy consists in separating the Palestinian people from the sources of their sustenance and development, while expanding Israeli socioeconomic formation at their expense. This can be seen in Israeli measures with respect to land, water, energy, investment, human resources, and infrastructure in the Occupied Territories.

All Palestinian social classes were thus harmed by the occupation and found little room to prosper and expand. And all sectors of the population have therefore resisted the occupation. In the process of defending their economic structures, they even attempted to strengthen and expand them with the goal of creating the prerequisites for an independent state.

Israeli businessmen seek maximum profits in the Occupied Territories and attempt to use them as a bridge for expansion in the Arab world. As will be seen, however, the goal of profit maximization is not always achieved, certainly not without creating unexpected by-products, because the market has its own laws whose outcome cannot always be predicted.

The tying of the occupied economy to that of Israel has had tangible effects on the course of Palestinian economic and social development. For example, the influx of tens of thousands of Palestinian workers into the Israeli labor market led to the accumulation of experience and technical know-how in some areas. It also made it possible for Palestinian businessmen to buy certain types of technology, particularly in the fields of agriculture and construction. In human terms, the process was painful, with the separation of tens of thousands of individuals from their own means of production in agriculture and handicrafts, and their transformation into a migrant proletariat making a living by selling its labor power.

On the level of political consciousness, however, these previously dispersed and somewhat isolated producers residing in villages and towns developed a certain unity and solidarity in capitalist workplaces and companies as well as a larger degree of exposure to economic, social, and political issues. This process helped to create a social base for the national struggle.

The following pages examine the effects of direct policies, economic integration, and "open bridges" on Palestinian economic development from 1967 to 1987 and analyze the role of economic factors in the *intifada*.

ADMINISTRATIVE AND LEGISLATIVE PRACTICES OF THE AUTHORITIES

The occupation authorities have directly or indirectly affected economic activities in five areas: (1) reducing the sources of growth in the Palestinian economy; (2) controlling the course of Palestinian investment; (3) controlling external trade; (4) neglecting the Palestinian economic infrastructure; and (5) levying excessive taxes.

Reducing Sources of Growth in the Palestinian Economy

The authorities reduced growth in the Palestinian economy and prevented Palestinians from freely utilizing their material and human resources. This was done by restricting the use of land and water, impeding capital accumulation, and reinforcing distortions in professional training.

Restrictions on Land Use

The Israeli authorities seized more than 52 percent of the West Bank and Gaza Strip from the Palestinian people.[2] This they accomplished through the appropriation of government land, land confiscation, closing off the land, and forged sale deals. They also designed and carried out land use plans in accordance with Israeli geostrategic and economic interests without any consideration for Palestinian interests. The latter thus lost a significant portion of their fertile agricultural land, and the cultivated area dropped 22 percent from 1967 to 1984, from 2,267 to 1,768 thousand dunums (1 dunum = 1000 square meters).[3]

Control Over Water

The authorities imposed a monopoly on water distribution and tightly monitored existing Arab wells. This enabled them to remove more than 450 million cubic meters of the West Bank water supply,[4] or 78 percent of renewable waters, and some 30–60 million cubic meters of Gaza Strip water annually,[5] or close to one-third of its renewable water supply. The amount left for various uses by the Palestinians does not exceed 120 million cubic meters in the West Bank and 100 million cubic meters in the Gaza Strip.

One of the main results of Israeli control over and removal of the waters of the Occupied Territories was a reduction in irrigated agricultural areas. It also became difficult for Palestinian farmers to intensify production. Many villages were left with no drinking water system, and cities faced water shortages.

Denying the Means for Capital Accumulation

One of the first steps taken by the authorities was to close down Arab banks operated in the West Bank and Gaza and to prevent the creation of any Palestinian financial institutions with banking functions. This step had severe economic consequences, as it denied the Occupied Territories the instruments and means of capital accumulation, indispensable to the development of contemporary economies. Individual savings remained scattered in the society rather than being pumped back into the economy in the form of investment. With no national banking system, it becomes difficult for individual savings to make their way into productive local investment. Aside from this, the unavailability of the means for amassing savings and preserving their value against inflation usually pushes their owners to spend them quickly by smuggling them abroad or by purchasing consumer products and precious jewelry. These uses of savings have negative effects on the national economy.

The opening of branches of Israeli banks in the Occupied Territories was meant to make it easier for Israeli businessmen to control their market and for the Israeli authorities to collect taxes and pay the salaries of the Palestinian employees of the government.

In 1981 the Bank of Palestine, Gaza, was allowed to reopen after fourteen years. The restrictions placed on its functioning, however, notably the prohibition of all foreign exchange transactions and the obligation to do all of its business in Israeli shekels, have marginalized it. It has a single branch in Gaza City, and must objectively be seen, despite any efforts on the part of its managers, as nothing more than a weak appendage of the Israeli financial system.

In 1986, after almost twenty years, the Jordan-based Cairo-Amman Bank was allowed to function in the West Bank. But it reopened under conditions that in practice limited it to the functions of receiving local savings, easing the transfer of these savings to and from Jordan, and paying the salaries of Jordanian government employees in the West Bank, while collecting the loans owed that government.

Due to the absence in the Occupied Territories of the instruments of capital accumulation, there was weakness and misuse in local savings, capital fled the area, and Palestinian businessmen were deprived of the credit necessary for economic expansion.

Reinforcing Distortions in Professional Training

The policy of the occupation in the area of training Palestinian human resources may be summarized as the willful reinforcement of distortions inherited from the Jordanian administration of the West Bank and the Egyptian administration of the Gaza Strip. The existing educational systems suited Israeli policy perfectly. The authorities mainly intervened in curricula when the latter contradicted Israeli and Zionist political and historical myths.

Not only Jordanian and Egyptian educational policies in the Palestinian lands, but United Nations Relief and Works Agency (UNRWA) policies as well, were directed toward the production of large numbers of students who could then be exported as clerks, employees, and teachers in Arab administrations, or university graduates who would also be likely to emigrate. What the West Bank and Gaza Strip lacked were vocational training programs in agriculture and industry. Vocational training was seen in a negative light by the prevailing educational philosophy. This led to the creation of successive waves of graduates qualified for one thing only: leaving their homeland. This is, of course, why the occupation authorities tolerated the expansion of university education. The unanticipated rise of organized Palestinian nationalism which was a political by-product of this expansion, however, meant that this toleration was short-lived.

Serious attempts were made locally to change this situation but all concessions were refused by the occupation. An-Najah National University in Nablus, for example, was refused permission to develop a school of agriculture. When overwhelming Israeli economic interests required, the authorities consented to open vocational centers attached to labor exchange bureaus, so as to provide crash training for the Palestinian labor force in Israeli factories.

Distortions in the Palestinian labor force became even more apparent with the dramatic rise in unemployment among Palestinian university graduates in all fields, including doctors, engineers, and scientists. This unemployment is on the face of it structural, with supply far outstripping demand. But when measured against objective need, it can be seen to be an artificial phenomenon, linked to the deterioration of economic and social conditions. It can clearly be seen that health, industry, construction, and education are all fields marked by stagnation or decline. This, rather than any "overqualification" of the population, is therefore the real explanation for unemployment in these fields.

Controlling the Course of Investment

The occupation authorities imposed direct control over the course of investment in the Occupied Territories by maintaining the right to accept or reject every investment project in every economic field. The establishment of any company in industry, agriculture, tourism or commerce requires prior approval by permit. Permit applications are usually granted or refused based on the economic and political interests of the occupation. Projects deemed "threatening" to (i.e., competing with) Israeli economic interests, or ones which more generally would strengthen the Palestinian productive base, are routinely rejected. Most agricultural projects and all projects for electricity production and water storage have been rejected. Many cooperative housing projects have been rejected, and thousands of construction permits are refused annually. The authorities have not objected to projects deemed not to contradict Israeli economic and political interests. In some areas, they have even facilitated their implementation; examples include quarrying, stone-cutting, and the production of other construction materials. This has likewise been the case for industries moved by Israeli businessmen to the Occupied Territories, often because of lower labor costs: clothing, textiles, shoe-making.

Controlling External Trade

The authorities imposed tight controls over the external trade of the Occupied Territories. For more than twenty years, almost all exports to any place in the world except Jordan were banned. Especially harmful was the unavailability of Western European markets. One of the achievements of the *intifada* has been to force the lifting of that ban where Western Europe is concerned, although bureaucratic obstacles and probably even sabotage have limited the impact of this new avenue of trade. Gaza citrus was allowed to be exported to Eastern Europe, with difficulty. Export across the bridges to Jordan, on the other hand, was permitted, but with high levies placed on exporting trucks and drivers.

Neglecting the Palestinian Economic Infrastructure

Through their monopoly on land, energy, water, and transportation planning, the Israeli authorities subjected the development of the Palestinian economic infrastructure to their will. The result was purposeful neglect, in violation of their duties as the de facto authority.

Irrigation projects have been blocked, municipal planning strictly limited, and the creation of industrial zones stymied. Annual government spending on investment for the period 1977–83, for example, did not exceed $35 million on average ($22 million in the West Bank and $13 million in the Gaza Strip), a figure representing only 12 percent of total fixed capital in the Occupied Territories.[6]

In contrast, the Israeli settlements in the Occupied Territories were equipped with a complete infrastructure of roads, electricity, water, and telephones. In the process, no consideration was given to the interests of the Palestinian population. Sometimes the settlements' infrastructures were planned in a way that was harmful to Palestinian economic interests. For example, highways and electricity lines were built on agricultural land so as to surround towns and villages, halting their expansion.

Levying Excessive Taxes

While military government spending on basic services and infrastructure was strictly limited, its budget was swollen by repeated amendments to the income tax laws, the imposition of the value-added tax, and continuous increases in prices of various permits and procedures, including travel. In 1984, for example, the military government's revenue from only two sources, income tax and net indirect taxes on local production, equalled 12 percent of the Occupied Territories' GNP. Those two sources alone covered all of its budget expenses.[7] As a result, budget revenues from other sources were transferred to the Israeli government treasury, a net gain of $150 million for 1984.[8]

Economically, such tax policies further limited Palestinian incomes, demand, and investment.

THE FORCED INTEGRATION OF THE PALESTINIAN MARKET INTO THE ISRAELI MARKET

Market processes constitute the second principal way in which the occupation affected economic processes in the West Bank and Gaza Strip. The Palestinian market was rapidly integrated into that of Israel after the occupation began. This integration was accomplished through a combination of market forces and coercive measures of an administrative and legal nature. The latter guaranteed the protection of Israeli businessmen and companies faced with vulnerable Palestinian producers, who were forced into an unequal confrontation.

The Activities of Israeli Entrepreneurs

Due to the enormous discrepancy between Israeli and Palestinian economic development, market integration took place under conditions of exchange even worse than those that existed between metropolises and colonies during the colonial era. At that time, great geographical separation and transportation costs constituted a factor yielding advantages to the colonies in some instances. The on-the-spot integration of the Israeli and Palestinian economies and the non-existent differences between internal and external trade have eliminated any cost advantage to the occupied economy. The occupier's economic apparatus likewise benefited from the geographic split between Gaza and the West Bank, while connecting both to the Israeli industrial and commercial centers through the road-grid serving the settlements. At the same time the existing Palestinian road system was left to stagnate, effectively hampering intra-Palestinian economic exchanges.

In addition to the unfair terms of exchange imposed on the Palestinians, Israeli businessmen benefited from their more advanced technological level, governmental protective measures, credit facilities, and virtual monopoly position. They thus penetrated all facets of economic activity in the Occupied Territories, as suppliers of the inputs of agricultural and industrial production and internal trade, and the main purchasers of materials and merchandise unavailable on the Israeli market. This disrupted the natural relationship between production and consumption, with Palestinian production becoming heavily dependent on Israeli demand, while Palestinian consumption became heavily dependent on Israeli supply. This type of double dependency is a classic feature of the relationship between colonies and metropolises. But the West Bank and the Gaza Strip display certain unique characteristics.

Due to the scant availability of natural resources in the Occupied Territories, to the possibility for Israeli businessmen directly to exploit available resources, and to minimal transportation costs, the relative advantages of Palestinian producers are narrow, limited to a few industrial processes requiring intensive labor and to those industries lacking a large and profitable market. Even in the latter, however, Israeli entrepreneurs are free to enter at any time.

Relative advantages to Palestinian producers are likewise minimized by direct Israeli measures. Land and water confiscation in the Jordan Valley, for example, has made it possible for Israeli settlers to produce early crops and compete with long-established Palestinian producers.

The Vicissitudes of the Israeli Economy

The ups and downs of Israeli economic life are automatically shifted to the Occupied Territories as a result of market integration, the introduction of the Israeli currency as legal tender, and the daily migration of 40 percent of the Palestinian work force to Israel. Without playing any role in the creation of Israel's economic cycles, and being deprived of the means to deflect any of their effects (which only governmental measures can ensure), the economy of the Occupied Territories has been subjected to their full force.

THE OPEN BRIDGES POLICY

The authorities' open bridges policy with respect to West Bank–East Bank trade had two primary objectives: furthering Palestinian emigration and facilitating Israeli economic expansion into the markets of the Arab world. Some of the by-products of the policy were the following:

• creating dependence on the part of the West Bank's economy, and, increasingly, that of the Gaza Strip, on those of the Arab world;

- preserving the link to the Jordanian dinar (along with the Israeli shekel) as official currency and as a recourse for Palestinian savings and long-term payments in the Occupied Territories; through this link, Palestinians became dependent on Jordanian economic and financial processes;

- dealing with the economic results of Israeli policies in the Occupied Territories by allowing an ebb and flow of Palestinian workers over the bridges, particularly workers rendered jobless by the flooding of the Occupied Territories' markets by Israeli agricultural and consumer items;

- allowing the entry and exit of funds: money transfers from workers in the Arab world meant greater consumption (largely of Israeli goods), and the departure of Palestinian businessmen's uninvestable surpluses meant indirectly encouraging migration, especially to Jordan, which, despite difficult economic conditions, enjoyed a better investment climate than the Occupied Territories. Increased consumption, combined with stagnant production and employment, decidedly favored Israeli businesses and increased integration into and dependence on the Israeli market;

- receiving assistance from the Arab states: such assistance resulted in an increase in economic activity, but benefits depended on the uses of the aid. Israeli screening and channeling of assistance meant that it went almost entirely to the service sector, thus benefiting Israeli businesses, rather than being invested in local production. One by-product was, of course, the building of important Palestinian institutions, which helped large numbers of people, reducing their dependence on institutions run by the occupation authorities. But the latter also benefited from this reduction in demands placed on them to provide basic services (which, as the occupying power, they are obligated to do under international law).

CONTRADICTORY EFFECTS OF OCCUPATION POLICIES

The various direct and indirect policies of the occupation were for twenty years complementary, limiting as they did the development of the Palestinian people while blocking independent socioeconomic formation. Nonetheless, the two types of processes, direct and indirect, were different in their outcomes and by-products.

Direct policies were purely negative in their economic results, stifling economic development and, because they were the doing of an absolute political authority, ruling out secondary results contradictory to occupation goals.

But the market operates according to laws whose outcomes, notably in a capitalist economy, are unpredictable. In this respect, the interests of Israeli entrepreneurs selling merchandise to the Occupied Territories and purchasing Palestinian labor power contradicted those of the occupation authorities: whereas the latter sought to promote the departure of the Palestinians by reducing their capacity to develop in their homeland, the former had a stake in increasing spendable income in the Occupied Territories. It can therefore be said that there was a contradiction between the short-term (economic) and the long-term (strategic) interests of the occupation. The neocolonial nature of the occupation, seeking maximum gain, clashed with its Zionist settler-colonial nature. This contradiction between market processes and the aims of the direct policies of the occupation is fundamental to an understanding of the nature and outcomes of economic relations and political processes in the West Bank and Gaza Strip through twenty years of occupation.

The effects of occupation policies on four aspects of the Palestinian economy are examined: economic growth, migration, structural distortion, and dependency on the Israeli economy.

Economic Growth, 1967–1987

The period 1967–87 was characterized by three successive stages. Relatively fast growth took place through the mid 1970s, with statistics showing considerable rises in all indicators: GNP, production, consumption, and investment. This process was accompanied by the rapid destruction of the natural economy, which, being independent of the market, is not included in the statistics. Tens of thousands of poor peasants, for example, who had made a living from subsistence agriculture before the occupation, and whose activities were not included in GNP figures, began after the occupation to work in Israeli factories and companies, where their wages were included in the GNP.

Both seasonal and masked unemployment were minimal during this stage because the voracity of Israeli businessmen in exploiting the cheap Palestinian labor force created opportunities for tens of thousands of laborers, likewise contributing to the rise in growth indicators.

The boom experienced by the Israeli economy in the wake of the 1967 war indirectly contributed to accelerating economic growth in the Occupied Territories. Demand for labor and some of the Occupied Territories' products increased. And the process of strangling the Palestinian economy had not begun in earnest. Exports enjoyed support from the occupation authorities, and taxes were not yet being collected on a wide scale.

Economic growth slowed considerably from the mid-seventies to the early eighties. This period witnessed the beginning of large-scale measures by Israel designed to curtail or seize Palestinian resources, particularly after the rise to power in 1977 of the Likud. The rise in oil prices and the accompanying economic boom in the Arabian Gulf states, with resulting money transfers by Palestinians working in the Gulf, as well as increased Arab aid to the Palestinians under occupation, notably in the form of "steadfastness funds" after 1978, offset some of the Israeli policies and helped preserve economic activity and positive growth rates in most sectors.

Stagnation and recession began in 1982–83 and have continued to the present. All economic indicators turned downward, influenced by the intensification of direct Israeli policies of a restrictive nature; the severe economic crisis that shook Israel and directly affected the Occupied Territories, which were so dependent on and integrated into the Israeli economy, 40 percent of the work force being employed in Israel, and Israel being their main import and export market; and a downturn in the economies of the Arab world due to the decline in oil prices and the Iran-Iraq war.

Taking into account the interplay of factors, it is not surprising to find that growth rates for the Gaza Strip and West Bank over the two decades 1967–87 were inferior to those of Jordan, particularly after the mid-seventies. Thus, for example, real GNP increased by 119.5 percent in the West Bank and by 86.4 percent in the Gaza Strip, whereas the Jordanian economy grew by 155 percent during the same period.[9] Moreover, real GNP in the West Bank and Gaza Strip in 1985 was less than it had been in 1979 and equal to 1980–81.[10] Similar trends are to be observed with respect to per capita income and per capita GNP, whose real value in the mid-eighties dropped from the level reached during the late seventies.

Large-Scale Migration

In the aftermath of the Israeli occupation, the Occupied Territories witnessed a large-scale migration of the population and work force. After the forced migration due to the June 1967 aggression, the main reason was economic, and bound to Israeli occupation policies as well as control of the market by Israeli businessmen. The economic expansion of the Arab oil-producing states in the late seventies also provided a magnet that further promoted emigration. Dislocations in the economy of the Occupied Territories created a labor surplus, compelling workers to seek employment elsewhere. A significant number had to seek it in the Israeli job market. The rest of the surplus labor force sought employment outside. Available figures show that during the period 1970–86 the West Bank economy created 16,000 jobs, while the Gaza Strip's market shrank during the same period. Those employed in the West Bank rose from 99,800 in 1970 to 115,700 in 1976; the numbers for Gaza fell from 52,900 to 50,700 during the same years. At the same time, the Israeli economy absorbed 95,000 laborers from the West Bank and the Gaza Strip.[11]

Based on the census taken in late 1967 in the West Bank and Gaza and on a net estimated population increase of between 3 and 3.5 percent, one obtains a figure of between 347,000 and 514,000 Palestinian emigrants between 1967 and 1986.

Using either estimate (in the author's view, 3.5 percent is more accurate), it is seen that one out of every four Palestinian citizens was forced to migrate. If we add the results of actions taken by the invading Israeli army in 1967 against Jordan Valley refugee camps (bombarded and emptied of their inhabitants), Qalqilya town (partly razed), Yalu, Imwas, and Beit Nuba villages (razed to the ground), etc., the number of Palestinians forced to migrate ranges between 600,000 and 750,000. Other estimates have put the number even higher, at 761,000 for the period 1967 to 1984, 152,000 of them from the active population.[12]

Distortion of the Structure of the Palestinian Economy

The economic structure of the West Bank and Gaza Strip was seriously distorted during two decades of occupation from 1967 to 1987. There were prominent aspects of this distortion.

First, productive sectors declined in importance in the makeup of GNP, particularly the agricultural sector, whose contribution fell from 34 percent in 1970–73 to 23 percent in 1984–86. The industrial sector had been and remained the weakest in terms of its contribution, not exceeding 8 percent during the period.[13]

Second, transportation, trade, and private services, the distribution or tertiary sector, expanded at the expense of productive sectors, as mediators between the Israeli economy and Palestinian consumers. This sector became the most important, especially in the West Bank.[14]

Third, in the industrial sector, some branches grew massively, while others withered or disappeared. Because of Israeli demand, quarries, stone-cutting factories, and units for the production of other building materials increased. Textiles, sewing, and shoemaking, largely subcontractors to Israeli companies, likewise increased. On the other hand, no modern industries (chemicals, engineering, etc.) appeared while the traditional industries functioned at about half their productive capacity.[15]

The Dependency of the Palestinian Economy on the Israeli Economy

The weakening of economic growth and the distortion of development reduced production diversity and the capacity to satisfy local needs. Palestinian producers likewise oriented themselves toward the Israeli market, either directly (construction) or indirectly, through Israeli companies (textiles, shoemaking, sewing). The following figures give an idea of the depth of dependency:

1. The percentage of GNP originating outside the Occupied Territories increased from 16.7 percent in 1970–73 to 25.2 percent in 1982–85 in the West Bank, and from 20.9 percent to 42.3 percent in the Gaza Strip. More than half this income came from those working in Israel.[16]

2. The percentage of private consumption compared with gross domestic product (GDP) in the Occupied Territories increased from 107.3 percent in 1970–73 to 113 percent in 1982–85, due mainly to the situation in the Gaza Strip (from 104.3 percent to 130.3 percent), despite a slight improvement for the West Bank, where it declined from 109 percent to 107 percent.[17]

3. The percentage of imports increased from 67 percent of GDP in 1970–73 to 77 percent in 1982–85 in the West Bank, and from 82 percent to 148 percent in the Gaza Strip during the same period. For the two combined the increase is from 72 percent to 92.5 percent. Taking into account that some 90 percent of imports in the Occupied Territories come from Israel, the level of dependency on Israel as a supplier is graphically expressed.[18]

4. As for exports, their percentage rate remained roughly stable from 1970–73 to 1982–85, ranging from 28 percent to 31 percent of GDP for the West Bank, and climbing from 43 percent to 54 percent for the Gaza Strip (peaking in 1978–81 at 60 percent). The Israeli market absorbed more than one-half of West Bank exports in the 1970s, and 65 percent in 1986. The Gaza Strip, for its part, sells more than 80 percent of its exports in the Israeli market (85 percent in 1986).[19]

THE ECONOMIC SITUATION AND THE *INTIFADA*

Weak economic growth, a distorted economic structure, multiple dependency on the Israeli economy: such, then, were the disastrous economic results of twenty years of occupation. All three of these phenomena testify to the success of the occupation in exploiting the economy of the West Bank and Gaza Strip and steering it in such a way as to avoid conflict with its strategic interests. Some people, based on these successes of the occupation, drew hasty conclusions and began speaking of the irreversibility of the situation and the impossibility of realizing the dream of Palestinian independence. Various slogans were used by such analysts, such as "salvaging the salvageable," "taking advantage of the last chance" because "time is working against the Palestinians." Some Palestinians proposed to run in the Jerusalem municipal elections or even invited Israel to annex the Occupied Territories so that Palestinians could participate in Knesset elections.

The uprising put an end to such reasoning, slogans, and proposals by demonstrating their falseness. They had, indeed, been based on an exaggeration of the significance of the occupation's economic successes. For these very economic successes actually intensified the conflict between the Palestinian people, unwilling to resign themselves, and their occupiers.

This is not to say that the causes of the *intifada* were economic, a result of the undeniable decline of economic indicators prior to its outbreak. Some have indeed seen the December 1987 explosion as the result of the accumulated resentment of all Palestinian social classes of their difficult plight. This "economic" reading of the uprising is certainly quite different from the more or less "defeatist" conclusions reached by some Palestinian intellectuals prior to December 1987, described above. But both arguments have in common that they exaggerate the significance of statistical aspects of the conflict, notably in the economic sphere. The essence of the conflict between the Palestinians and the occupation is, however, not economic but political: that between imposed foreign political control and the Palestinian people who resist it, striving for its removal and the right to self-determination and an independent state under the leadership of their sole political leadership, the Palestine Liberation Organization.

It is therefore impossible to make a direct causal connection between economic trends and the rise or decline of the national struggle. No general, stable, and independent relationship can be established between the economic situation and this (or any other) national liberation struggle.

One may and must, however, question, in each specific instance, the role of economic factors in the progression of events. And as we have seen, their role was not negligible. First of all, in the twenty-year period leading up to the *intifada*, the proletarianization of a significant portion of the West Bank and Gaza Strip's population helped promote collective political consciousness; second, the deteriorating economic situation had a great deal to do with the uprising's inclusiveness and the dynamics of its development. Each and every social class was harmed economically by the twenty-year occupation. Camp, village, and city, worker, peasant, employee, and entrepreneur—all geographical and social sectors had by 1987 been left with the feeling that the occupation harmed and threatened them. This increased the general commitment to liberation and the willingness on the part of all sectors to participate actively in the struggle for it. In other words, occupation excesses resulted in a weakening of the conflicts between the short-term interests of some relatively privileged social groups and the national interest of the Palestinian people as a whole. This was reflected in a popular consensus unprecedented in the Occupied Territories.

The effect of the economic situation on the dynamics of the *intifada* was found in the gradual and concatenated nature of its progress. Because of economic changes that had occurred over the previous two decades, certain struggle practices, such as the boycott of Israeli goods and of work in Israel, had to be carried out with a good deal of flexibility. On the other hand, the *intifada* itself tangibly influenced the economic situation. It provided growing protection for Palestinian products and succeeded in a widespread boycott of Israeli goods for which local alternatives were available. Furthermore, with growing mass consciousness and austerity among Palestinian consumers, Israeli luxury products were increasingly boycotted. Large numbers of people refused to pay taxes to occupation authorities or delayed their payment as long as possible (i.e., until seizure of goods or cash by troops and tax collectors had been carried out). There was likewise an unprecedented increase in home economy (gardening, livestock rearing, bottling, etc.), with an eye to achieving self-reliance and improving the use of family resources. This trend in turn heightened the people's capacity to resist measures to crush the *intifada* by siege, curfew, fines, taxations, closure of shops, and other measures.

Palestinian workers increasingly resorted to general strikes as a weapon in their national struggle. On general strike days called by the United National Leadership of the Uprising, up to 100,000 workers stayed away from jobs in Israel. Production in Israel was thus disrupted in thousands of workshops, factories, hotels, fields, and building sites, with the construction and textile sectors being hardest hit.

The Occupied Territories, because of *intifada* practices, became tangibly less profitable to occupation authorities and Israeli entrepreneurs. Benefits to those living off of Palestinian day labor also shrank in many cases. And the cost of maintaining Israeli troops and police in the Occupied Territories increased under the impact of the *intifada*. Israel also lost hundreds of millions of dollars in tourism revenues.[20] The Israeli finance minister at one stage calculated *direct* losses to Israel due to the *intifada* at some 3 million shekels ($1.9 million) daily.[21]

CONCLUSION

The following conclusions may be drawn:

1. Economic processes in the West Bank and Gaza Strip are determined by destructive factors, connected with the colonial-settler and neocolonial nature of the occupation, and constructive factors, connected with the economic activity of the Palestinian people. Without the latter's unswerving devotion to its political objectives and the struggle to achieve these goals in all domains, including the economic field, the effects of the occupation on the economy could have been even worse.

2. Direct administrative factors affecting the economy and market processes furthered by the occupation constitute an integrated whole, and their effects on the economy of the West Bank and Gaza Strip have been, generally speaking, negative.

3. There were, nonetheless, significant contradictions between the strategic interests of the occupation—marginalizing the material and spiritual existence of the Palestinians, and exercising pressures to drive them from their homeland—and its immediate interests: maximizing profits to the Israeli economy through the control and exploitation of the Occupied Territories and their inhabitants. These contradictions left a margin, albeit a limited and decreasing one, for some economic development.

4. The reasons for the overall success of the occupation in controlling economic processes in the Occupied Territories are threefold: the administrative and legal monopoly, the economic weakness and underdevelopment of the Occupied Territories, and the superiority of the Israeli economy.

5. The outcome of twenty years of occupation was disastrous for West Bank and Gaza Strip economic development, leading to the weakening, then the end, of economic growth, the distortion of the economic structure, and the deepening of dependency on external economies, particularly Israel's. These results of the occupation, however, in fact intensified the Palestinian people's struggle against it.

6. The uprising was not caused by the deterioration of the economic situation: the *intifada,* as a stage in the ongoing Palestinian struggle, is an inevitable product of the occupation as the embodiment of the forceful imposition of foreign domination. This stage would have been reached no matter what the purely economic picture may have been.

7. The uprising is, however, influenced by the deteriorating economic situation, which has made it more comprehensive socially and geographically, and has affected the dynamics of its progress.

8. The *intifada* showed that the state of dependency imposed upon the Occupied Territories' economy could be used to cause heavy losses to the Israeli economy through the boycott of Israeli goods and of work in Israel. It has also confirmed the fact that the Palestinian people can transfer the Occupied Territories from a limitless source of profit for the occupation authorities and Israeli companies into liabilities both to the army of occupation and to the Israeli economy itself.

NOTES

1. United Nations Committee on Trade and Development (UNCTAD), "Living Conditions of the Palestinian People in the Occupied Territories" (A/40/373-Geneva, 1985), p. 3; and UNCTAD, "The Palestinian Financial Sector Under Israeli Occupation" (UNCTAD/ST/SEU/3-Geneva, 1987), p. 1. See also Meron Benvenisti, *West Bank Handbook* (Jerusalem: Jerusalem Post Publications, 1986), p. 121.

2. UNCTAD, "Living Conditions."

3. Benvenisti, *West Bank Handbook*, p. 224.

4. Ziad Abu Amer, "Iktisad Qita' Ghaza ila ain?" (Whereto the Gaza Strip's Economy?), *al-Katib* (Jerusalem), no. 86 (June 1987): 82.

5. Samir A. Saleh, *Trends and Problems of the Construction Sector's Development in the West Bank and Gaza Strip*, Nablus: An-Najah National University, 1986, p. 3 (in Arabic).

6. UNCTAD, "The Palestinian Financial Sector," p. 101.

7. Ibid., p. 102.

8. Ibid., p. 101.

9. Samir Abdallah, "At-Taghaiurat-ar-raisia fi masader addakhel al-kawmi fi ad-Daffa al-gharbia wa Qita' Ghaza" (Principal Transformations in the Sources of GNP in the West Bank and Gaza Strip), *al-Katib*, no. 98 (June 1988): 5.

10. Calculated from Central Bureau of Statistics (CBS-SAI), *Statistical Abstract of Israel*, 38 (Jerusalem, 1987).

11. Ibid., p. 723.

12. UNCTAD, "The Palestinian Financial Sector," p. 5.

13. C. Kosseifi, "The Forced Migration of Palestinians from the West Bank and Gaza 1967–1983," ESCWA *Population Bulletin* (UNCTAD/ST/SEU/31, December 1985), p. 1.

14. Abdallah, "Principal Transformations," p. 39.

15. Samir Abdallah, *Mashakil wa Itijahat Tatawir al-Qita' as-Sina'i fi al-dafa al-Gharbia wa Kita' Ghaza* (Problems and Directions in the Development of the Industrial Sector in the West Bank and Gaza Strip) (Nablus: An-Najah National University, 1986), pp. 38–39.

16. Abdallah, "Principal Transformations," p. 46.

17. Calculated from several issues of CBS-SAI.

18. Ibid.

19. Ibid.

20. *At-Tali'a* (weekly) August 4, 1988.

21. Ibid.

4

The Development of Political Consciousness Among Palestinians in the Occupied Territories, 1967–1987

Lisa Taraki

The unprecedented mass uprising in the occupied West Bank and Gaza Strip has generated considerable interest in the ways in which the daily struggle is organized, and in the political and community structures that sprang up to direct and further the insurrection. No commensurate attention has been accorded, however, to examining the historical process that gave birth to this revolt against the occupation.

This chapter examines one aspect of this historical process, namely, the crystallization of political consciousness among Palestinians in the West Bank and Gaza Strip in the two decades preceding the uprising. This political consciousness was the product of the convergence of the many factors and events that have fashioned the collective experience of the Palestinians, the most salient of which are the ambivalent position of Arab regimes regarding the Palestinian cause; the rise of the Palestinian resistance in the 1960s; the founding and growing authority of the Palestine Liberation Organization; and the special circumstances of life under Israeli rule in the Occupied Territories.

"Political consciousness" as used here refers to a distinctive *Palestinian* (as opposed to Arab or Jordanian) identity and an outlook whose central tenet is the idea that the establishment of a Palestinian national authority can alone fulfill Palestinian national aspirations. Another, less pronounced, component of Palestinian political consciousness is a socially progressive outlook. While this essentially leftist ideology has been overshadowed by the predominant nationalist outlook, it has constituted an important component of political consciousness and cannot be ignored.

Political consciousness among the Palestinians of the Occupied Territories evolved and took shape primarily within the context of the Palestinian national movement. And since the movement in the Occupied Territories expressed itself in concrete organizations, institutions, and activities, it will be important for this chapter to ground itself as well in these concrete realities. The most important frameworks through which political consciousness was mediated were political parties and fronts; mass organizations; artistic and literary groupings and associations; the press; national institutions, particularly universities and community colleges; a number of charitable societies; and a host of other ephemeral or more permanent efforts and groups.

This chapter will examine the development of political consciousness through the most important of the groupings and organizations outlined above. Most of these frameworks were affiliated with the national movement, either directly, as in the case of political and mass organizations, or indirectly, in the sense that their members identified with the movement. It should be obvious, then, that this study of the development of political consciousness is also a study of the crystallization of a substantial, organized, and articulate social base for the national movement and, by extension, the PLO.

The following periodization of the two decades after 1967 will help us locate some of the critical turning points in the dual and interrelated processes of the consolidation of a social base for the national movement and the crystallization of a unique political consciousness in the Occupied Territories. What will interest us in particular is the emergence of two political and social trends that provided the background against which political consciousness and the national movement were consolidated: the evolution of open frameworks for political action and the increase in mass participation in political activity; and the gradual incorporation of new social forces, especially peasants, refugees, and the urban poor, into national institutions and organizations and, by extension, into the national movement.

HISTORICAL ANTECEDENTS: 1957–1967

The first stirrings of Palestinian political consciousness date to the early years of this century, when Palestinians began to confront the increasing tide of Jewish immigration to Palestine. Until the late 1950s, the Palestinian cause and national identity were not articulated in distinctively Palestinian forums or organizations. It was not until the founding of the Palestinian National Liberation Movement (Fateh) in 1957–58 that a new stage in the Palestinian struggle and national identity was inaugurated. The further elaboration during the early 1960s of a distinctive Palestinian political identity and of Palestinian political institutions has been generally attributed to two developments on the Arab level: the disbanding of the United Arab Republic in 1961, dashing expectations of a unified

Arab effort to liberate Palestine; and the success of the Algerian revolution in 1962, which showed how a people with little outside assistance can fight and win a war of liberation.[1]

The founding of the Palestine Liberation Organization in 1964 was one further step in the process of the crystallization of an independent Palestinian identity. It was also the beginning of the consolidation of an independent Palestinian institutional infrastructure that came to encompass political and military organizations; mass organizations such as unions and women's and students' associations; and other institutions. The introduction of armed struggle by Fateh in 1964–65 was another important development on the symbolic and political levels. In addition to denoting Palestinians' determination to form their own fighting forces, it also ushered in a new stage in the relations between the Palestine national movement and the Arab regimes. The uneasiness among Arab regimes, particularly Jordan, at the presence of armed Palestinians in their territories has been one of the constant themes in Palestinian-Arab relations since that time.[2]

The inauguration of what Palestinians call "the Revolution" came on January 1, 1965, when Fateh's military arm, Sa'iqa, began guerrilla operations against Israel from Syria, Jordan, and Lebanon. Israeli reprisals, particularly raids carried out in the West Bank towns of Jenin and Qalqilya in 1965, and in villages in the Hebron area in 1966, brought Palestinians there into the struggle, albeit in an indirect way, as victims of these actions. But a more important impact of these raids was the growing identification of the Palestinian population in the West Bank with the PLO and their increasing resentment at the Jordanian regime's position regarding armed Palestinian action and the PLO.

The Israeli attack on the village of Samu' and two other neighboring villages in the Hebron area in November 1966, which precipitated wide-scale demonstrations and bloody clashes with Jordanian security forces in Hebron, Nablus, Tulkarm, Jenin, and Jerusalem, is a case in point. While the slogans raised and statements issued during what has been called "the Uprising of 1966" did not reflect a clear and distinct Palestinian political consciousness, they did reflect the growing conflict of interest between the nascent Palestinian institutions and the Jordanian regime, and presaged the disengagement of the Jordanian and Palestinian elements from the Jordanian national movement.[3]

ARMED RESISTANCE AND THE BEGINNINGS OF POLITICAL MOBILIZATION: 1967–1971

The real flowering of the Palestinian resistance, which played a crucial role in the consolidation of Palestinian political consciousness, came after 1967. The political, military, and psychological defeat of 1967 was indeed a turning point in the history of the yet fledgling Palestine national movement. Barely three months after the occupation, Fateh inaugurated its campaign of guerrilla operations, launched mainly from Jordanian territory. The battle in the Jordanian village of Karameh, in which Palestinian guerrillas and Jordanian forces inflicted heavy casualties on the assaulting Israeli army in March 1968, did a great deal to bolster Palestinian morale and belief in the efficacy of armed action against Israel. After the battle of Karameh and the swelling of the ranks of the resistance, the two main guerrilla organizations, Fateh and the Popular Front for the Liberation of Palestine (PFLP), began to create a network of popular militias in the refugee settlements in Jordan, Syria, and Lebanon, and to provide training and political education to political cadres.[4]

The aim of the resistance was the creation of a popular revolutionary movement that would encompass and unite Palestinians both inside and outside the Occupied Territories. Protracted struggle, composed of a long series of small battles, was a stage that all resistance leaders in the late 1960s were convinced was necessary. In their view, the expansion of destruction resulting from the ever-widening circle of Israeli targets would only serve to expand the community of those suffering from the destruction. As sizeable portions of the population became drawn both into the resistance and the support of the Palestinians, they believed, the level of political consciousness would rise, and sooner or later the realization would become universal that either the people will succeed in resisting Zionism or be crushed by it.[5]

The resistance succeeded in mobilizing significant sectors of the Palestinian refugee population in Jordan and Lebanon, and in politicizing them through military, social welfare, and mass organizations. In the occupied West Bank, a popular revolutionary movement such as the one envisioned by resistance leaders did not materialize, despite efforts by Fateh immediately after June 1967 to bring in arms and create an underground network there.[6] Therefore, the fact that no significant organizational base for the resistance existed there meant that armed struggle was basically external, that is, consisting of operations carried out by infiltrators who returned to their bases once their missions were accomplished. Many of the few guerrilla cells that did operate in the West Bank during 1967 and 1968 were infiltrated and destroyed by the Israeli intelligence forces; this is thought to have been partly facilitated by the detailed records of the Jordanian intelligence service captured by the Israelis.[7]

In the Gaza Strip the situation was different. Substantial quantities of light weapons from the Egyptian army and the Palestine Liberation Army remained there, and guerrillas blended into the population and sought refuge in the refugee camps and poor areas or hid in the thick orange groves. A civil disobedience campaign of demonstrations, strikes, and the boycott of Israeli products was also launched.[8] The years 1967–71 witnessed dramatic armed actions carried out by the resistance, mainly in the form of grenade attacks on Israeli targets. Israeli retribution reached its peak in 1971; curfews were imposed on refugee camps to facilitate search and interrogation operations, and 12,000 people, relatives of suspected guerrillas, were deported to detention camps in the Sinai Desert. At least 13,000 were forced to vacate their homes as roads were bulldozed through the camps to facilitate the army's movement.[9] The crushing of the resistance by the end of 1971 was also accomplished by the deportation to Jordan of large numbers of guerrillas; between 1967 and 1971 at least 333 Palestinians were deported from the Gaza Strip, virtually all of them guerrillas.[10]

The real importance of the Occupied Territories for the Palestine national movement has not been their ability to sustain the armed struggle, despite the admiration and respect accorded to the resistance there. Rather, the West Bank and Gaza have constituted an important arena for the development of the political struggle waged by the national movement, and a strong social base *inside* Palestine for its constituents. The process through which the Occupied Territories gained importance as a locus for the national struggle, and through which a unique political consciousness was fashioned there, will be the focus of the remainder of this chapter.

No substantial mass-based political initiative emerged in the first years of the occupation, although the process of forming national frameworks to resist the occupation began in this period. The formation of the Higher Islamic Council and the National Guidance Committees (NGCs) immediately following the annexation of East Jerusalem in June 1967 was the first step in this process. The NGCs, the more important of the two frameworks, were semi-clandestine political coordinating committees and included representatives from different political groups and the Higher Islamic Council.[11] Still, it should be pointed out that the protests, petitions, and statements emanating from the political and civic leaders of the West Bank at the start of the occupation called for the restoration of the status quo ante, that is, the return of the West Bank to Jordanian sovereignty.[12]

In the Gaza Strip, the United National Front was formed at about the same time as the West Bank NGCs to coordinate political action. The Front consisted of communists, Ba'thists, members of the Arab Liberation Front, and a number of nationalist figures in the Gaza Strip. Like the political initiative in the West Bank, the Front's program called for a return to the status quo ante, in this case the return of the Egyptian administration.[13]

Israeli measures against the national leadership in the West Bank, which at that time included many persons with administrative, political, and financial ties with Jordan and the Jordanian regime, dealt a severe blow to attempts to mobilize the population against the occupation. These measures included mass arrests, temporary banishment, the demolition of homes, and deportation to Jordan. By 1969 the NGC structure in the West Bank was virtually destroyed. The United National Front in Gaza, which did not have a wide base from the start, was also severely eroded as a result of the successive blows dealt to its members by the Israeli security forces. By 1971 the Front had ceased to exist as a political force in the Gaza Strip.[14]

NATIONAL RENAISSANCE: 1972–1975

Political Developments

The suppression of the Palestinian resistance in Jordan in 1970–71 led to the increasing isolation of the Palestine national movement in the Arab arena. This, coupled with the realization that the occupation of the West Bank and Gaza was progressing rapidly toward the de facto annexation of these areas, forced the movement to reassess both its strategy and its demands. It may seem paradoxical that these grim facts facing the national movement should at the same time have generated a national renaissance among a people rapidly losing control over what remained of its historic homeland. But it is precisely these challenges that provided the impetus to Palestinians to assert their national identity and formulate an independent political agenda.

In the Occupied Territories, the most significant development was the founding of the Palestine National Front (PNF). The endorsement of the PNF by the Palestine National Council in 1973 marked the beginning of a joint political effort between the PLO leadership outside and the political forces in the Occupied Territories. More important, however, it represented the first response by the Palestinian leadership to an initiative originating in the Occupied Territories. The PNF encompassed some of the elements of the NGCs and the United National Front in Gaza, most of the resistance organizations, and representatives of professional, labor, students', and women's organizations.[15]

The PNF was officially launched in August 1973. It announced that it was ''an integral part of the Palestinian national movement as represented by the Palestine Liberation Organization,'' and declared that it would support ''mass organizations, such as trade unions, students' and women's federations, religious and social clubs and associations, in their efforts to defend the interests of the groups they represent, and [to mobilize] their energies for the struggle against the occupation.'' On the cultural level, the PNF committed itself to ''protect [Arab] culture and history from Zionist manipulation and distortion, . . . [and] to revivify [the] popular heritage and the literature of the Resistance as being an embodiment of [the people's] attachment to their land and their heroic struggle to defend it.''[16]

The PNF was successful in organizing a campaign of civil disobedience and public protests on a scale not witnessed before. A number of measures, the most severe of which was the deportation of PNF leaders, were used by the military authorities in order to check the continuous expansion of resistance activities.

This period also witnessed a reassessment by the Palestinian leadership of the strategy and aims of the Palestinian struggle as a whole. The PLO began to accord more importance to political mobilization inside the Occupied Territories and to strengthening mass and other organizations there.[17] A further development came at the twelfth session of the Palestine National Council held in June 1974, when the council resolved that ''the PLO will struggle by every means . . . to liberate Palestinian land and establish the people's national, independent and fighting sovereignty on every part of Palestinian land to be liberated.''[18] This decision was widely interpreted to mean that the PLO accepted a state in part of Palestine. More important, it meant that the quality and scope of the struggle of the people in the Occupied Territories, the locus of the future state, was of crucial importance.

Cultural-Political Renaissance

The political initiative represented by the PNF in the Occupied Territories was accompanied by other initiatives that contributed both to the amplification of mass participation in the national movement and to the heightening of political consciousness, especially among youth. One outstanding example is the voluntary work movement, which from the beginning became a framework for mobilizing and politicizing Palestinian youth.[19]

The voluntary work movement was founded in 1972 by a number of college and school teachers, youth professionals, and youth living in the Jerusalem-Ramallah area. Under the patronage of the mayor of al-Bireh (later deported for his activism) they plunged into community work, which consisted mostly of manual labor. They also held weekly meetings at the public libraries of the twin towns of Ramallah and al-Bireh, where they would plan their work schedule and discuss literary and political works by Arab and international writers. By the end of 1973, committees began to form in Nablus, Hebron, and Jericho, and more groups were formed in other areas in the next two years. Most of the work consisted of paving roads, reclaiming land for agriculture, and assisting farmers with the harvest.

The voluntary work effort expanded and acquired increased political significance after 1976, when nationalist figures were elected to local councils all over the West Bank. Municipalities hosted voluntary work camps and allowed community youth to work alongside city public works employees in municipal projects. Other forms of voluntary work included assistance to farmers during harvest time, especially during the olive-picking season, and literacy campaigns in villages and refugee camps.

Two aspects of the voluntary work movement are relevant to the shaping of a progressive political consciousness among Palestinian youth in the Occupied Territories. The first has to do with the fact that voluntary work constituted the first substantial community effort that brought young men and women together. The second aspect concerns the nature of the activities carried out by the voluntary work committees. It is not coincidental that manual labor was the dominant form of work; it was a deliberate decision, taken with the aim of breaking down the barrier between intellectual and physical labor, and of spanning the gulf separating the town from the countryside. This outlook is naturally a reflection of the fact that the idea of voluntary work originated in the towns, and in particular among middle-class intellectuals, professionals, and students with little contact with workers or peasants.

With the progressive politicization of voluntary work, work camps became forums for political and cultural expression. Thus began a showdown with the military authorities, who arrested organizers and participants and banned work camps either through directives issued to community elders or by the erection of military checkpoints on roads leading to worksites.

The voluntary work movement played an especially crucial role in the politicization of youth. Many leaders of the student, trade union, and women's movements in the late 1970s and 1980s claim to have received their initiation in national politics in the voluntary work committees of the early 1970s.

The early to mid–1970s also witnessed the beginnings of an artistic and literary renaissance. Several theater groups, many composed of young people active in the voluntary work committees, were formed in the Ramallah-Jerusalem area. Budding artists began to exhibit their works, and a literary movement began to find a home in the emerging Palestinian press, such as the newspapers *al-Fajr* and *al-Sha'b*, founded in 1972. There also began during this period a serious effort to preserve through documentation and collection various aspects of Palestinian cultural heritage. The Society for the Regeneration of the Family (Jam'iyyat In'ash al-Usrah), which had been founded in the West Bank town of al-Bireh in 1965, was the spearhead of this effort. In 1974 the first issue of its journal *Heritage and Society* appeared, dedicated, since then, to the preservation of Palestinian folk traditions and material culture.

The flowering of Palestinian artistic, literary, and political expression came during the next period, with the establishment of broader-based organizations, forums, and institutions that gave it direction and continuity. While these developments and others will be examined in the following section, it is appropriate to point out here that the Occupied Territories were, at the end of 1975, on the threshold of qualitative changes, both on the level of national organization and of political consciousness.

BUILDING THE NATIONAL MOVEMENT: 1976–1981

The strengthening of the national movement and the crystallization of political consciousness in the Occupied Territories during this stage are best studied through the concrete activities and organizations that served as their vehicles. This period witnessed the emergence of open frameworks for political, social, and cultural action; the amplification of mass participation in political activities; and most important, the incorporation of new social forces, particularly the less advantaged sectors of society, into Palestinian institutional life. The emergence of the mass organizations and the expansion of the universities during this period were perhaps the most significant developments.

An atmosphere of heightened political activity prevailed in the Occupied Territories after 1967. The West Bank municipal elections in 1976, the Israeli "autonomy" scheme announced in 1977, and the Camp David Accords signed in 1978 all contributed to this atmosphere. The nationalist municipal councils elected in spring 1976 and the second National Guidance Committee formed in 1978 were the first nonclandestine political frameworks. The NGC, which rapidly assumed national importance, was composed of several mayors and representatives of the professional associations, trade unions, the student movement, charitable societies, women's organizations, and the Islamic establishment. Representatives from the Gaza Strip and individuals in their personal capacities completed the membership of the NGC.[20]

Mobilization against the Israeli, Egyptian, and U.S. political initiatives reached unprecedented levels during this period. Universities, particularly Bir Zeit University, became the focus of nationalist events; mass rallies there and in other institutions became a potent instrument of politicization and mobilization during this period. It is not surprising, therefore, that Israeli attempts at suppressing this mass upsurge of nationalist and anti-occupation sentiment also escalated during this period. In 1982 the NGC was banned, and several nationalist mayors were removed from office by the Israeli authorities.

We now turn to an examination of the major organizations, groupings, and forums that during this period (1976–81) played a crucial role in the consolidation of the national movement and the crystallization of political consciousness in the Occupied Territories. We shall also examine in closer detail the content of this unique political consciousness and discuss some of its features.

THE MASS ORGANIZATIONS

Aside from the clandestine political organizations, the mass organizations have proven to be the most resilient Palestinian institutions. They are open structures with public agendas, and aim to mobilize the largest number of students, workers, women, and youth into organizations serving each of these sectors.[21]

The formation of the mass organizations came at a time when Israeli measures against the national movement and its institutions were taking unprecedented forms. Several factors may be adduced to explain the emergence of the mass organizations at this juncture.

First, the banning of official bodies and institutions such as the NGC and the municipalities presented the national movement with two options: confining itself to underground activities at the risk of losing a growing mass base; or expanding its activities by sponsoring institutions which, because of their informal and seemingly amorphous nature, would be more difficult to target and destroy. The second option was executed with great imagination and creativity: it presented the Israeli military and intelligence forces with a new set of problems and sent them on a fruitless chase after organizations without fixed premises and officers.

Second, there was the growing belief in progressive circles within the national movement that existing organizations were not able to respond adequately to the real problems of Palestinians under occupation. The social distance between these organizations and the people, coupled with the conservative nature of their membership, were viewed as major factors limiting their effectiveness in dealing with issues such as the exploitation of Palestinian workers in Israel, the condition of women, the neglect of agriculture, poor health conditions in the countryside and refugee camps, and other pressing social issues. The founding of mass-based organizations was thus viewed as a social responsibility the national movement had to shoulder.

The major mass organizations in the Occupied Territories are labor unions and union blocs, and voluntary work, student, and women's organizations. While these organizations are active in both the West Bank and the Gaza Strip, their presence is much more pronounced in the former. Gaza mass organizations, with some exceptions, are chapters of parent organizations founded and based in the West Bank.

Most mass organizations are described as "mass democratic frameworks" in their publications. The emphasis on "democratic" is meant to distinguish them from the more formal "establishment" organizations such as charitable and social welfare societies, women's organizations, and professional associations. Decentralization of structure and democratic decision making are often pointed to by these organizations as features that distinguish them from the other frameworks mentioned above. Another distinctive feature of the mass organizations is the class character of both their leadership and constituency: the vast majority are from peasant, refugee, and lower-middle-class urban backgrounds.

While the agendas of the mass organizations differ according to the needs of the sectors served by each, they may all be viewed as agents of political mobilization not only in their constituencies, but also in society at large. The mass organizations see themselves, collectively and individually, as an active component of the national movement, and carry out activities in keeping with that self-definition.

By the beginning of the 1980s, the mass organizations had become an integral part of the infrastructure of national institutions in the Occupied Territories. They had succeeded in mobilizing tens of thousands of youth, workers, women, and students in the service of the national movement, in addition to imparting organizational skills to a significant number of young men and women. They also served as the main channel through which social groups that had traditionally been excluded from Palestinian political and institutional life not only became visible but also assumed leadership positions in the national movement.

CULTURAL FORUMS

Concurrent with the founding of the mass organizations there emerged what may be broadly termed cultural forums through which a new generation of writers and artists began to fashion and express a unique Palestinian consciousness. These forums consisted of newspapers, literary and political journals, theater groups, musical ensembles, and later, groupings and associations of writers, artists, and journalists. Two general tendencies may be identified in the cultural discourse of this period: a nationalist tendency centered around the preservation and elaboration of the Palestinian folk heritage; and a less parochial, more left-leaning tendency. These tendencies were not mutually exclusive; they came together and overlapped frequently in activities, works of art, and other forms of cultural expression.

Literary Forums

The main forum for Palestinian writers in the years preceding 1967 was the relatively short-lived but influential Jerusalem literary journal *al-Ufuq al-Jadid*. The writers whose works appeared in this journal, and who later came to be known as "the generation of *al-Ufuq al-Jadid*," were instrumental in establishing the standards to which Palestinian literature still aspires. The figures of that period, such as Muhammad al-Batrawi, Yahya Yakhlif, Nimr Sirhan, Subhi Shahruri, Khalil al-Sawahri, and Hakam Bal'awi, have become authoritative figures in the history of contemporary Palestinian literature.

In the first years after the occupation, and in the absence of serious literary forums, many Palestinian writers from the West Bank and Gaza turned to literary journals produced by Palestinians inside Israel, especially those published under the aegis of the Israeli Communist party. The journals *al-Jadid* and *al-Ghad* and the newspaper *al-Ittihad* became forums for Palestinian writers under occupation, some of whom published their work under assumed names.[22] This experience opened the way for the reunification of Palestinian literature. The availability of a leftist press also helped strengthen the progressive tendency in poetry and fiction.

Palestinian literature in the Occupied Territories came into its own and began to reach a mass audience in the 1970s, first with the appearance of literary pages in the local newspapers *al-Sha'b*, *al-Fajr*, and *al-Quds* and a few journals in the early 1970s, and then with the founding of the literary journal *al-Bayadir* in Jerusalem in 1976. Other publications such as *al-Muntada al-Adabi* (Gaza, 1975), *al-Katib* (Jerusalem, 1979) and *al-Fajr al-Adabi* (Jerusalem, 1980), and publishing houses such as Salah al-Din also played an important role in providing a forum for both established and young writers of poetry and fiction.

Poetry, especially during the early years of occupation, was the most popular and dominant genre in Palestinian literature. The works of the Palestinian "poets of resistance" in Israel, such as Salem Jubran, Tawfiq Zayyad, Mahmud Darwish, and Samih al-Qasim, served as models for West Bank and Gaza writers, who often imitated their widely read works.[23] The popular form of fiction was the short story, which was indebted to the tradition established by Ghassan Kanafani and Emile Habibi in the previous decade.[24]

The themes found in poetry and fiction were, as might be expected, those dealing with national dispossession, attachment to the land, and the assault upon Palestinian culture and society by the occupier. Issues of class and gender also found their way into this literature, especially at the hands of leftist writers whose works appeared in *al-Bayadir* and *al-Katib*.[25] Palestinian literature during this period also found inspiration in the oral tradition of rural Palestine; many works were written in the colloquial and drew upon folkloric material.[26]

Aside from the publications that provided an opportunity for writers to reach an increasingly wide audience, an important vehicle for the development of a popular literary movement was the founding of writers' circles and associations.

The first group, the Writers of *al-Bayadir*, was formed in May 1977; as the name indicates, the membership was centered around the journal, which by then had established itself as the only serious literary journal in the Occupied Territories. This forum was followed by the short-lived Writers' Group based at Bir Zeit University and the Writers' Circle sponsored by the Arab Thought Forum. One of the most important activities of these groups was the sponsorship of seminars, lectures, and meetings where established and budding writers and critics discussed works written by local poets and short-story writers. The events sponsored by these groups helped writers not only to improve their style and technique, but also to formulate positions regarding the role of the writer and of literature in the national struggle.

Other Cultural Forums

This period also witnessed the initiation or expansion of other frameworks with a broadly cultural mission. The most outstanding is the Society for the Regeneration of the Family. Its journal, *al-Turath wal-Mujtama'*, became one of the primary organs for the preservation of Palestinian oral traditions and regional customs. The society also sponsored the publication of several folkloric studies and initiated work on a dictionary of the colloquial Palestinian dialect. The folklore museum, as well as sponsoring folk festivals and cultural events, aimed at preserving Palestinian traditional heritage.

A number of academics and writers played an important role in furthering this revival of folk traditions, especially songs, folk tales, and proverbs. In addition to contributing to the society's journal, they did much to introduce the public to Palestinian folklore and folk literature through their books, which by now have become standard references in the field.[27]

The "national folklore revival," while performing an important function in affirming Palestinian identity, has at the same time had a regressive influence, in the sense that it has muted the openness to other cultural influences and has retarded the adoption of a more internationalist perspective. The preoccupation with preserving the Palestinian cultural heritage, particularly of peasant culture, has another strange and paradoxical aspect: while it had begun largely at the hands of urban middle-class intellectuals, it was later amplified by people who were still *living* that culture in many of its components. Thus we witness a situation where what is still part of daily life for many people—including many intellectuals—has been relegated to the museum and regarded as something that must be put on display. This "museumization" of Palestinian culture reached unusual proportions in the erection of a life-size styrofoam "Palestinian village" on the grounds of a cultural festival at Bir Zeit University in 1984. The remarks of a well-known Palestinian cultural critic summarize this irony:

The vast majority of our people live in villages and partake in village life. They live from agriculture, and know the most intimate details of village life beginning with the oil press and the plough and ending with the bread oven, *musakhkhan* and thyme bread. Our villages have not become another Indian Pueblo [where people come from all over to ogle at the destroyed Indian life]. Did this truth escape those who thought of erecting the "Palestinian village" as part of the festival?[28]

Other important forums for cultural and political expression were the public events sponsored by student councils at universities and colleges, trade unions, and other institutions. Events such as the annual Palestine Week at Bir Zeit and other universities, and literary festivals and contests were occasions where the public had an opportunity to sample the emerging definition of national culture. The military authorities were well aware of the significance of these occasions; they often placed military roadblocks to prevent people from reaching some of these activities, in addition to banning certain events altogether.

Musical and theatrical groups also served as important vehicles for the articulation of Palestinian political consciousness. Both these mediums witnessed a remarkable expansion in the late 1970s, with the founding of many musical ensembles and theater groups, primarily in the central part of the West Bank.[29] This music and theater were decidedly political in nature and drew freely from Palestinian folk traditions and forms. Theater in particular had a progressive and cosmopolitan outlook, as attested to by the titles and themes of the major plays produced during the 1970s and 1980s. While musical groups had more mobility and could thus reach a larger audience both through concerts and cassettes, theater was primarily restricted to the urban areas and did not make as large an impact as other forms of artistic expression. Another medium worth mentioning in this regard is painting and drawing, which also experienced a revival in this period. As with music and theater, this art was in large part explicitly political, and drew both on folkloric images and international symbols of resistance.[30]

A traditional genre of singing called the *zajal* became very popular and widespread in the 1970s and 1980s. In this type of song, the traditional form is infused with new words with a political message. The medium was perfected by the popular singer Rajeh al-Salfiti, who became a roaming troubadour very much in demand at cultural festivals, weddings, and even political rallies. This type of vocal music was not new; there are songs from the early part of this century recording the Palestinian struggle against Zionist encroachment, as well as songs reflecting the positions of different political parties and movements and used by them in spreading their ideas.[31]

The Palestinian press constitutes another forum through which Palestinian political consciousness was mediated. This press has almost exclusively been based in Jerusalem due to the severe censorship regulations that prevail in the West Bank and Gaza. This has not meant, of course, that the press in Jerusalem has escaped the scissors of the military censor or the edicts of the courts, which have found some publications inciteful and thus deserving of temporary or permanent closure. Despite the censorship and self-censorship imposed upon the Palestinian press, it has nevertheless performed an important role in shaping public opinion. Because of this, it has been subjected to the most severe scrutiny by the Israeli authorities.

The press has reflected the various political tendencies active in the Occupied Territories; even the Village Leagues produced two newspapers during the early 1980s before their defeat by the national movement. In terms of general outlook, most of the periodicals in the Occupied Territories may be called nationalist in that they have adhered, more or less closely, to the national consensus as embodied in positions articulated by the PLO. The nationalist press established itself in the early 1970s, with the publication in 1972 of *al-Fajr* and *al-Sha'b*. Other influential nationalist publications appearing between 1976 and 1981 were *al-Bayadir, al-Tali'a, al-Shira', al-Mithaq, al-Katib, al-Fajr al-Adabi*, and *al-Bayadir al-Siyasi*.[32]

NATIONAL INSTITUTIONS

Palestinians use the term "national institutions" to refer to institutions which, under conditions of national sovereignty, would be subsumed under the state. This nomenclature reflects the reality created after the mid–1970s, when the drive to establish a national infrastructure of organizations and institutions was initiated in the Occupied Territories.

Palestinian universities have played a role far out of proportion to their size in furthering the national movement and serving as a forum for the promotion of political consciousness. The importance of universities, of course, lay in the fact that they provided the ideal—and in some ways the freest—environment within which the student component of the national movement could grow and proliferate.

University and college enrollment increased significantly in the early 1980s. The financial aid policy adopted by institutions of higher education began to change the social character of these institutions, which had previously catered to the children of the urban middle class. Students from peasant, refugee camp, and lower-middle-class urban backgrounds began to form the majority of the student body. Today, a very small percentage of university students are from the towns or the upper class.

The major activity of the student movement was in national politics. During the late 1970s and 1980s, it led anti-occupation activities and organized strikes, demonstrations, and other forms of protest. The universities became a major public forum for political and cultural expression and the site of political rallies attended by hundreds of youths from universities, high schools, and mass organizations. Student newspapers published by student organizations after the early 1980s, and leaflets and other material distributed at public events, also played an important role in initiating youth into the language and practice of politics.

CONSOLIDATION OF THE NATIONAL MOVEMENT: 1982–1987

This period in the life of the Palestinian national movement in the Occupied Territories witnessed a slow but steady consolidation of the national movement and an expansion of its social base, in spite of several developments that could have doomed it were it not for the advances already made: the expulsion of the Palestinian resistance from Lebanon and the Israeli disbanding of the NGC, both of which took place in 1982, and the rise of an Islamic movement generally hostile to the national movement.

The Lebanon War and the breakup of the NGC marked the beginning of a period of internal divisions within the national movement, which at times seriously threatened the national unity forged over the preceding years. Yet at the same time this factionalization of the national movement had a direct impact on the rate of proliferation of the mass organizations, which were one of the main vehicles for political mobilization and politicization. Competition between the different political forces led to the rapid expansion of women's, workers', students', and other organizations. While this situation had many negative results, its positive impact was that it drew more and more sectors of society into the national movement.[33]

The emerging Islamist trend did not threaten in any serious way the national movement's social and political hegemony, despite some significant inroads it made into the student movement. Particularly in the West Bank, the Islamist tendency, whose main component was the Muslim Brethren, in fact was not interested in creating and gaining control of organizations and institutions on a wide scale. Its main ambition appeared to be the formation of Islamic blocs at universities and a few youth associations and charitable societies. The situation in the Gaza Strip was somewhat different. There, the Islamic Center (al-Mujamma' al-Islami) and to some extent the Islamic University became centers for the dissemination of Islamic political thinking. While the Islamist movement and the Muslim Brethren in particular generally worked at cross-purposes with the national movement and did not subscribe to its basic tenets, the Islamic Jihad Organization, which appeared in Gaza in the late 1970s, has been more amenable to cooperation with the national forces. On balance, however, it may be said that the Islamist movement was not able to stem the spread of nationalist sentiment and the consolidation of the national movement. Even the Islamic Jihad, which has significant political legitimacy in the Gaza Strip, has gained this legitimacy because it parted ways with the more conciliatory Muslim Brethren.

The 1980s witnessed the incorporation of increasingly significant sectors of society within a wide variety of organizational frameworks. Most of these frameworks viewed themselves as part of the national movement, and carried out activities and drew up agendas in keeping with national priorities as articulated by the political organizations and the PLO in general. Many organizations that played a key role in politicizing their constituencies were either created or expanded during this period: associations of writers, artists, performers, journalists, academics, professionals, and even university graduates. The main function of these bodies was to give political and professional identity to previously unorganized or partially organized elements, in addition to serving as vehicles for political expression. As mentioned earlier, the mass organizations witnessed a significant expansion during this period, especially with the incorporation of increasing numbers of women, workers, and youth from villages and refugee camps.

Our treatment of the organizational frameworks within which the national movement and political consciousness developed would not be complete without reference to one institution that has played a significant role in the politicization of Palestinians, especially the youth: the Israeli prison system, through which tens of thousands of Palestinians have passed over the two decades of occupation.[34] Israeli jails, a powerful symbol in the political folklore of the Occupied Territories, are often considered by their "graduates" as the ideal place for acquiring a political education. There, isolated from the routine of normal life, prisoners organize seminars and study circles, conduct Hebrew and English lessons, and teach the illiterate among them how to read and write. The impact of this collective experience is no doubt a lasting one.

CONCLUSION

I have attempted in the preceding pages to outline the major contours of the political process that facilitated the birth of the uprising: the consolidation of the Palestinian national movement and the crystallization of Palestinian national consciousness. The considerable media attention accorded to the popular revolt in the Occupied Territories might give the misleading impression that the uprising represents a fundamental departure from and a radical break with the past. Without undermining the important new realities created by the uprising, it is essential to stress that it has relied on and utilized most of the channels of mobilization and politicization developed over the years by the national movement. Moreover, a significant proportion of the activists and leaders of the uprising acquired their organizational skills and political outlooks through their association with the many national organizations, institutions, and forums created during the period preceding the uprising.

The process through which the national movement struck roots in Palestinian society was fraught with difficulties, and was more than once retarded by forces emanating from both inside and outside the Occupied Territories. Yet this movement succeeded in building a substantial infrastructure of organizations and institutions in the West Bank and Gaza and in disseminating a particular form of consciousness among wide segments of the society.

In this chapter, emphasis has been placed on the formal institutions, organizations, and forums that have facilitated the creation of a politicized social base for the national movement. But we cannot ignore the experiences arising out of the very conditions of life under alien rule that have also shaped this process: thousands of Palestinian families have at some point had a member or a relative detained; thousands of families have applied, often without success, to have relatives granted a permit to live in their own land; tens of thousands of Palestinian peasants and refugees have experienced wage labor in Israel under exploitative and often dehumanizing conditions; and all Palestinians have encountered the various forms of control and punishment practiced by the occupying forces.

It remains to be said, however, that the experience of life under alien rule has never constituted in itself the necessary and sufficient means of release from that rule. Without a political movement and doctrine to direct their struggle, the occupied remain an unorganized mass, unable to take hold of their future.

NOTES

1. For discussions of these points and an overview of the period, see Fuad Jabber, "The Palestinian Resistance and Inter-Arab Politics," in William Quandt et al., *The Politics of Palestinian Nationalism* (Berkeley: University of California Press, 1974), pp. 155–216; William Quandt, "Political and Military Dimensions of Contemporary Palestinian Nationalism," in ibid., pp. 43–153; and 'Issa Shu'aibi, *Palestinian Statism: Self-Consciousness and Institutional Development, 1947–1977* (Beirut: PLO Research Center, 1979), pp. 47–97 (in Arabic).

2. Syria, and to some extent Algeria, were the main supporters of Fateh during this period. See Samir Abraham, "The Development and Transformation of the Palestinian National Movement," in Naseer Aruri, ed., *Occupation: Israel over Palestine* (Belmont, Calif.: AAUG Press, 1983), pp. 394–95. For the positions of other Arab governments regarding Fateh's military activities, see Jabber, "Palestinian Resistance," pp. 163–65.

3. For views on the significance of the demonstrations of 1966 and statements issued at the time, see 'Isam Sakhnini, "The Palestinian Entity, 1964–1974," *Shu'un Filastiniyya*, nos. 41–42 (January-February 1975): 61–62 (in Arabic); and Shu'aibi, *Palestinian Statism*, pp. 124–26.

4. Hisham Sharabi, *Palestine Guerrillas: Their Credibility and Effectiveness* (Beirut: Institute for Palestine Studies, 1970), p. 23.

5. Ibid., p. 36. This account is based on official statements by Fateh and the PFLP, and interviews conducted by Sharabi in 1969 with members of these organizations.

6. Jabber, "Palestinian Resistance," p. 189.

7. Al-Haytham al-Ayyubi, "Ten Years from the Life of the Palestinian Armed Struggle," *Shu'un Filastiniyya*, nos. 41–42 (January-February 1975): 245 (in Arabic).

8. Ann Lesch, "Gaza: Forgotten Corner of Palestine," *Journal of Palestine Studies* 15, no. 1 (Autumn 1985): 55.

9. Ibid.

10. The vast majority (290) were sent into exile in 1970 and 1971. See Ann Lesch, "Israeli Deportation of Palestinians from the West Bank and the Gaza Strip, 1967–1978," *Journal of Palestine Studies* 8, no. 2 (Winter 1979): 104, 110 (Part I).

11. Ibrahim Dakkak, "Back to Square One: A Study in the Reemergence of the Palestinian Identity in the West Bank, 1967–1980," in Alexander Scholch, ed., *Palestinians over the Green Line* (London: Ithaca Press, 1983), pp. 70–71.

12. For example, memoranda issued by Muslim personalities, physicians, lawyers,

engineers, pharmacists, unionists, and others immediately after the war affirm the Jordanian identity of the West Bank. See Shu'aibi, *Palestinian Statism*, pp. 137–38, 147–48.

13. "The United National Front in the Gaza Strip," in *The Palestinian Encyclopaedia*, 2nd ed., vol. 2 (Acre: Dar al-Aswar, 1986), p. 28 (in Arabic).

14. Ibid.

15. Shu'aibi, *Palestinian Statism*, p. 192.

16. *International Documents on Palestine 1973* (Beirut: Institute for Palestine Studies, 1976), pp. 459–60.

17. The Palestine National Council, while stressing the preeminence of armed struggle, committed itself at its session in January 1973 to a program of mass mobilization in the Occupied Territories. See *International Documents on Palestine, 1973*, p. 407.

18. *International Documents on Palestine 1974* (Beirut: Institute of Palestine Studies, 1977), p. 449.

19. Information on the voluntary work committees was obtained from interviews conducted with individuals who were instrumental in the founding of the first committees and in the activities of the movement during the 1970s and 1980s. A number of local publications were also consulted.

20. Dakkak, "Square One," pp. 84–85.

21. Information on the mass organizations was obtained from interviews conducted with founding and current members of the major categories of mass organizations, and from the substantial literature produced by these organizations. This literature consists of leaflets, newspapers, magazines, and statements of purpose and internal bylaws.

22. As'ad al-As'ad, "A Look at the Palestinian Cultural Movement," *al-Katib* (Jerusalem), nos. 21–22 (November 1981): 3 (in Arabic).

23. Hanan Mikhail Ashrawi, "The Contemporary Palestinian Poetry of Occupation," *Journal of Palestine Studies*, 7, no. 3 (Spring 1978): 84–85.

24. Hanan Mikhail Ashrawi, *Contemporary Palestinian Literature Under Occupation* (Bir Zeit: Bir Zeit University Publications, 1988), pp. 43–44.

25. Surveys of the themes found in Palestinian literature during this period can be found in *al-Bayadir*, vol. 2, nos. 2 and 8, and vol. 3, no. 7; *al-Katib*, nos. 19–20 (September-October 1981) (all in Arabic); and Ashrawi, *Contemporary Palestinian Literature*.

26. This "folklore revival," in the words of one critic, gave the literature a somewhat defensive and extreme coloring and weighed it heavily with the task of aggressively expressing and affirming Palestinian identity. While it initially gave momentum to the literary movement, it then became a rigid pattern, depriving the literature of much of its originality and vitality. See Ashrawi, "Contemporary Palestinian Poetry," p. 82.

27. Among these writers are 'Abdul-Latif al-Barghuthi, Nabil 'Alqam,'Ali al-Khalili, Walid Rabi', and Musa 'Allush.

28. Muhammad al-Batrawi, "Birzeit Nights . . . Were Not Lit by Moons!" *al-Katib*, no. 53 (September 1984): 120–21 (in Arabic).

29. For information on the theater groups established in the West Bank since 1970, see the series of articles in *al-Katib*, nos. 92–99 (December 1987-July 1988).

30. It should be noted here that a number of Palestinian critics and intellectuals found the theater, literature, and art of this period to be preoccupied with political content at the expense of aesthetic quality. For discussions of these issues, see the early issues of *al-Bayadir*, especially vol. 1, no. 2, and vol. 2, nos. 2 and 3 (in Arabic).

31. 'Abdul-Latif al-Barghuthi, *Arab Popular Songs in Palestine and Jordan* (Bir Zeit: Bir Zeit University Publications, 1979), pp. 50–51 (in Arabic).

32. For details on the history of the Palestinian press under occupation, see Radwan Abu-'Ayyash, *The Press of the Occupied Land* (Jerusalem: Dar al-'Awdah, 1987) (in Arabic); and Muhammad al-Faqih, *Journalistic Institutions in the Occupied Territories* (Jerusalem: Arab Journalists' Association in the Occupied Territories, 1987).

33. It must be stated, however, that some of these organizations existed on paper only, having been created for the purpose of bolstering the influence of the political organizations to which they were affiliated.

34. A poll conducted by the newspaper *al-Fajr*, ABC-TV, and *Newsday* magazine in the West Bank and Gaza in 1986 showed that 47.5 percent of the respondents or members of their families had been arrested for political reasons. See *Palestinian Public Opinion Poll* (Jerusalem: al-Fajr Publications, n.d.), p. 9.

5

The Emergence of an Infrastructure of Resistance

THE CASE OF HEALTH

*Mustafa Barghouthi and
Rita Giacaman*

Any analysis of the extraordinary events of 1988, the first year of the Palestinian uprising, is by necessity linked to an examination of the developments that occurred throughout the previous twenty years of Israeli military rule of the West Bank and Gaza Strip. It is equally important to trace the consequences of such events within the context of an ongoing and intense struggle for Palestinian self-determination. While this struggle has been marked by severe repressions, it has nevertheless given birth to many popular creative initiatives, including those in the field of health, in a prolonged effort to achieve national independence.

In the case of health conditions and services, resistance to military occupation resulted from the concrete conditions that developed in the wake of the events of June 1967. Perhaps it is best to begin by recalling a little-known effort to rescue al-Maqassed Hospital in Jerusalem from Israeli attempts to take it over soon after the West Bank fell under Israeli military rule. At the time, Israeli takeover was the fate of the majority of existing health institutions. In the case of Maqassed, then still under construction, hundreds of people mobilized immediately after the occupation of Jerusalem to transfer equipment, including some private possessions of health professionals, hospital beds, and even patients to the new hospital premises. The authorities were thus prevented from assuming control over al-Maqassed Hospital, which became one of the last remaining independent Palestinian health institutions.

While such early and spontaneous forms of resistance are difficult to compare with the more organized course that this resistance took at a later stage, it is important to emphasize that resistance was generated immediately after occupation by the sheer force of the struggle for survival. The forms of such resistance changed through the course of struggle and were shifted and modified by the influence of a multitude of determinants.

In this chapter, we intend first to delineate the conditions that emerged immediately after Israeli military rule and that led to the development of three distinct yet interrelated trends in resisting military rule through the provision of health services to the Palestinian population of the Occupied Territories. We will then elaborate the content of each trend bringing to light the particular ways in which health services and the national struggle are conceived and the consequences of such conceptions on policy formulation and action. Finally, we will evaluate the outcome of the activities of each trend leading to the period of the uprising and the role of the newly established Palestinian health care system in sustaining the uprising and the health and medical needs of the population of the future Palestinian state.

HEALTH CONDITIONS AND SERVICES: A REVIEW

Although the dearth of information regarding health levels in the West Bank and Gaza Strip in the pre–1967 period makes it impossible to produce comparative time-trend delineations of their course during the twenty years of Israeli rule, available evidence suggests that health conditions, as measured by infant mortality in the region, continued a trend of improvement that was evident in the pre–1967 period.[1] But variations across time and region were substantial, and depended primarily on the effects of colonial policy measures on living conditions and incomes. Overall health conditions remained inadequate throughout the twenty years of Israeli military rule. Infant mortality in the region was persistently high, estimated at 50–100 deaths per 1,000 live births for the West Bank and Gaza Strip for the late 1970s and early 1980s.[2] Morbidity levels were also high for the entire period, further confirming a picture of poor health conditions among the population. Malnutrition affected a substantial proportion of children under the age of five reaching a level as high as 50 percent of all the children in some communities.[3] Parasite infestation remained a major public health hazard, reaching 50 percent infestation levels among school children in Gaza[4] and similar levels among preschool children on the West Bank.[5] Altogether, it would be safe to state that health conditions under Israeli military rule were unacceptably poor.

Moreover, these health conditions in general compared unfavorably with improvements in health conditions scored in the Jordanian state, and very unfavorably with health conditions in Israel. When the infant mortality rate for Israel was 14 deaths per 1,000 live births for 1985, 60 per 1,000 for Syria, and 55 per 1,000 for Jordan for the same year, it was found to reach 70 per 1,000 for the West Bank and Gaza Strip.[6] Clearly, military rule created conditions in which the health status of the population lagged behind those of populations in other

Arab countries; and even after twenty years of occupation, they differed substantially from health conditions in Israel.

On the eve of occupation three systems for health service provision were operating in the area: the governmental, supervised and controlled by the government of Jordan for the West Bank and by that of Egypt for the Gaza Strip; the United Nations Relief and Works Agency (UNRWA), specializing in service provision to refugees; and the private sector, which at the time included health services provided by charitable institutions. It was the governmental health sector, where the majority of people sought and received health care, that was most negatively affected by military rule. Health services budgets were slashed, and hospital and other health facilities were closed down (such as the blood bank and the Beitin Hospital in the Ramallah area) or deprived of critical personnel. For instance, the physician-to-population ratio reached the low level of 8 per 10,000 in the West Bank and Gaza Strip for 1986, compared with 28 per 10,000 for Israel and 22 per 10,000 for Jordan.[7] In addition, by the mid–1980s it was becoming apparent that the governmental health system suffered from serious inequalities in the distribution of health services, neglecting primary health care and health in the rural areas, where the majority of people lived. More important, it also became evident that the authorities' agenda of the first fifteen years of occupation—aiming at the breakdown of the existing basic health infrastructure and reducing it to dependency on Israeli services—had succeeded.[8] Once this became apparent, a new Israeli policy evolved in recent years, focusing further developments in the health services sector toward "creating services especially for the Arabs." From the Palestinian point of view, these new measures served to reinforce previous fears that "as long as dependency of the West Bank and Gaza on Israel presupposes the dependence of the health services sector as well, it is appropriate to develop a second-rate sector for Palestinian Arabs to exclude them from the Israeli first-rate services, which are reserved for Israelis and, at the same time, win the reputation of having developed health conditions in the Occupied Territories."[9]

THE PALESTINIAN RESPONSE

Palestinians were consequently left with the private health sector as the only territory within which to mount a response to the events taking place in the public health sector.[10] Note that the infrastructure breakdown and the consequent dependence on Israeli structures in all aspects of life were the hallmarks characterizing military rule, and in this sense the deterioration in the health services system was not an exception.[11]

The development of resistance at the level of improving health conditions and services therefore fell within the context of a wider and more generalized trend within the Occupied Territories aiming at preserving whatever could be preserved, and building independent Palestinian institutions capable of supporting current needs and at the same time functioning as the infrastructure for the future Palestinian state.[12]

Although the private health sector did not fall completely under the control of the authorities, as happened with governmental health services, it was subjected to serious curtailment and distortion. Even early on, the authorities attempted to contain activities within this sector through various means, including the imposition of heavy taxation on health establishments and institutions, denial of permits to expand premises or build new ones, the harassment of individual health professionals for conducting health activities to serve the needy public, and the closure of professional unions, to name only a few of these measures.[13]

Perhaps the most serious problem faced in the private sector was coordinating health activities. The absence of a national health apparatus made it very difficult to coordinate action both within that sector and between it and governmental and UNRWA institutions. Partially as a result of these conditions, and partially due to problematic conceptions of health and health services among key Palestinian professionals—in the sense of favoring hospital-based medicine to primary and rural health care work—a somewhat disjointed, doctor-heavy health care system arose, characterized by an overemphasis on curative medicine, a neglect of primary health care, and an unequal distribution of health services in favor of towns and urban centers. This system failed to fulfill people's basic health needs.[14]

These developments gave rise to three prototypic Palestinian responses. Emerging in the early years of occupation, the first of these responses simply called for adaptation to Israeli administration and hegemony and advocated acceptance of the new status quo. The substance of the argument was that given the inability of Palestinians to effect change in their condition, there was no alternative but to accept Israeli domination and to make the best of it. Adherents of this view supported attempts to bring about improvements, no matter how small, in the governmental health apparatus controlled by the occupation authorities. The rationale for such an approach is that, in the end, these institutions serve Palestinians, and any services provided must be considered an achievement.

The promoters of this view were primarily physicians who had dominated the old medical establishment and who have had considerable influence in shaping the medical care system in the country. Mostly members of the "old school" and graduates of the 1940s and 1950s, they constituted the medical elite and generally came from well-to-do backgrounds, with ties to the West, viewing the health services networks as another arena within which "development"— equated with Westernization—could be achieved. They understood health, disease, and medical care as simple and pure biological phenomena, divorced from social, economic, and political contexts, and within a strict biomedical framework.[15] Consequently, they equated health development with technical and mechanical development of premises, instruments, and procedures.[16]

Both the content of this position and the affiliation of those espousing it precluded the possibility of spreading and consolidating this view. It was quickly shown to contain serious political flaws. For instance, this approach led to efforts to solicit financial assistance to develop the governmental health apparatus, which was under the total control of the Israeli military and was often seen to be used as an instrument of political control. Moreover, the advocates of this view were resigned to adapting to the military authorities' policies, which were directed toward reducing the governmental health services in the West Bank and Gaza to a low-cost appendage of the Israeli health care system and making it one of the elements in their plans for the so-called autonomy/civil administration policies that had begun to become apparent in Israeli policy after the October 1973 war and following the Camp David Accords.[17] In the end, this trend failed to take root, for it appealed neither to the seasoned nationalists nor to the budding new constituency of the medical establishment, which had radically different priorities—producing a progressive view of health and health services and pro- viding an alternative to urban and hospital-based medicine. This set the stage for the development of alternative Palestinian health sector responses to Israeli military rule.

Emerging in the early 1970s and taking the lead in the middle and late 1970s, the second response promoted the idea of developing medical and health activities independent of the military authorities but nevertheless within the boundaries of the military government's laws and regulations. Consistent with the more general "steadfastness" response to military occupation that was championed by the majority of nationalists during that period,[18] this trend advocated struggling with the authorities to obtain permits for new health initiatives. It was pioneered by elements with cultural and political ties clearly rooted in Arab and Palestinian nationalism, and understood colonialism—or military rule—to be the major cause of ill health and an impediment to the development of health services in the area.[19] Consequently, the thrust of this trend was directed almost exclusively toward disengagement from the military-controlled governmental health appa- ratus and the building of an independent Palestinian health infrastructure.

This response manifested itself primarily in the sometimes intense struggle of charitable societies such as Maqassed Hospital in Jerusalem, the Red Crescent societies of the West Bank and Gaza, and other similar groups with the military government to obtain permits to operate needed health facilities. It was through the concerted efforts of those who supported this viewpoint that the backbone for the curative centralized segment of the health infrastructure was built in the 1970s. The period was characterized by an almost obsessive drive to establish autonomous health institutions and projects whenever possible, although pri- marily in towns and urban centers. The drive of these activists was directed toward improving technical facilities and know-how in specialty medicine. While such a direction for health infrastructural development was warranted in some instances,[20] it was clearly excessive in others and was largely due to a bias toward curative technical medicine at the expense of primary health care. Yet, despite these problems, that period witnessed a relatively successful expression of Palestinian national identity through the establishment of medical institutions serving as the main mode of resistance to occupation in the health sector.

The Israeli authorities were selective in their granting of permits. Palestinian attempts to fulfill people's health needs meant a reduction in the health care costs incurred by the authorities for the occupied population. Simultaneously, these conditions provided them with the opportunity to use health care provision as an instrument of political control. Therefore, although Palestinian groups embarking on the path of project building within the boundaries of the occupier's law achieved considerable gains, they were faced with tremendous and sometimes insurmountable difficulties in their exchanges with the authorities. Some were completely broken by the pressure of Israeli conditions, gradually changing their political positions to obtain permits to operate medical and health activities. Others, such as the Red Crescent and Patient's Friend's Societies, were subjected to substantial delays and deferrals that rarely led to any concrete result.

The consequences of such a stance even proved to be catastrophic in some instances. The control, indeed, the suppression of the activities of such societies reached a point where even a health education session required a special permit from the authorities. Thus, if some succeeded in penetrating the circle of the law and managed to establish nuclei for promising activities, they did so at the expense of facing continual threats of shutdown. The closure of some of these institutions during the uprising, such as the Patient's Friend's Society/Friends of the Sick in Tulkarm on August 23, 1988, for the usual ambiguous "security reasons," testifies to this unfortunate fate. The success of the authorities in forcing hospitals (government and private) periodically to submit lists of names of those injured in the uprising and admitted for medical care, realizing full well the dangerous implications of such disclosures for the wounded, is equally telling of the unfortunate predicament of these institutions and the limitations of this approach to health infrastructure development in the face of military rule. In other words, although considerable gains were achieved utilizing this approach, it nevertheless reached a limit where it could no longer fulfill the fast developing needs of the time.

The third response to military rule emerged from the accumulation of this collective experience in "steadfastness" and in health infrastructure development and the increasing realization that locating the struggle with the military within the field of rules, regulations, and Israeli military law was becoming a counterproductive strategy. Although it was clearly necessary for some institutions to continue espousing this approach, others were increasingly being prompted to find new ways to develop further the Palestinian health infrastructure. The new approach reflected the increasing concern with the need to disengage from destructive Israeli policies by building independent Palestinian alternatives and as an integral part of a strategy of struggle for the establishment of an independent Palestinian state.[21]

It was therefore through practice, trial and error, and the accumulation of experience that the third approach, the alternative health movement, was formulated. Alternative denotes an approach calling for reaching people with basic health services, an emphasis on preventive and health education activities and people's participation in the solution of health problems, in contrast to purely curative, urban-based medicine focusing on the mechanical solution to health problems, otherwise known as the engineering approach to medical care. It does not negate the need for or the importance of curative centralized medical care but rather advocates redressing the balance between the two types of care in compliance with prevailing health conditions in the area and the majority of the population's needs. Alternative also means here an approach calling for the stepping up of defiance against the authority of the Israeli military, and for the opening up, whenever possible, of health services without necessarily waiting for permission from the authorities.

This movement, developing and consolidating itself in struggle with the occupying forces, based its strategy for the development of health services under Israeli military rule on the refusal to recognize the authority of Israeli law and to accept the hegemony of the authorities or their licensing and closure order forms of control. It drew its legitimacy from the needs of the population, from national interest, and from basic human rights principles—including the Hippocratic Oath—to practice medicine and assist people in improving their health conditions.

The new movement emerged in the late 1970s and took root in the early 1980s.[22] It drew on the experience generated by a new generation of activists who in the 1970s developed mass-based social and political action organizations by founding a network of committees rallying the support of volunteers from different sectors of society, such as the voluntary work movement and the women's movement.[23] Thus the new movement developed on the basis of cooperation at the grass-roots level with these mass-based political and social organizations. But it also drew on the experience and the problems of the previous generation of medical and health care providers.

Founded primarily by urban-based health professionals in their twenties and thirties with broadly progressive inclinations and rather strong links to the mass-based organizations increasingly active in the towns, villages, and refugee camps of the West Bank and Gaza, this movement was also posited by its founders as a critical response to purely curative and hospital-based medicine:

"The low standard of living and the lack of appropriate medical services have contributed to the poor health conditions prevailing in the impoverished areas of the occupied Territories. . . . The Union [of Palestinian Medical Relief Committees] is particularly concerned with primary health care and preventive medicine."[24]

It extracted its power primarily from people—men and women volunteer physicians, nurses, and other health professionals and workers—in contrast to the power of money, equipment, and buildings that generally characterized previous endeavors in medical and health care promotion:

"The foundation of its activities rests on the voluntary work of its members, who, during their holidays, practice medical and health related work in rural areas and refugee camps where the population is denied access to health services."[25]

Thus this movement developed as a rebuttal to the approach used by previous health initiatives in that it generated new ways of struggling with the Israeli military and, equally important, new ways of conceiving health and disease and health care provision. In other words, its approach entailed a populist egalitarian dimension previously unknown to Palestinian health care provision. It therefore entailed alternative visions to both the national and health problems in the area.

While those who sponsor this approach have in the past and continue today to face serious harassment at the hands of the Israeli military, especially during the uprising, when emergency health activities were intensified,[26] they succeeded in establishing this form of health service provision as another prototype for resistance not only among health professionals, but among those working in other sectors as well. Moreover, the sponsors of this approach had to face another type of opposition, this time within Palestinian society, most notably from some of the members of the old school, who opposed the social content of the alternative health movement's platform.

Those who opposed the new movement rejected its guiding principle—transferring health services to the rural areas and refugee camps under the slogan "reaching people with services instead of people having to reach the services in urban areas"—and the concept of primary health care provision utilizing health workers other than the ones acknowledged by the old school—that is, physicians, nurses, etc. However, the speed with which this new approach to health care provision under Israeli military rule took root and flourished, its success, and therefore the legitimacy it acquired[27] paved the way for its eventual acceptance by the medical establishment as an important and effective approach to health care provision within the prevailing political context. Because primary health care had considerable appeal to international aid agencies such as UN agencies and church and solidarity groups from Europe and the United States, its superficial elements were even appropriated by the very same people who a decade before were so vehemently opposed to it.[28] Note here that although the terminology used by all trends is now unified and almost identical—calling for primary health care at the rural and refugee camp level as a priority in health care provision—the content of these calls is in fact disparate: while to the new movement primary health care essentially means simple curative techniques supporting preventive measures and consciousness-raising/educational efforts, to others who have appropriated the terminology without its essence primary health care is establishing a clinic in a village and placing X-ray machines and other gadgets in it to be "at the service of people."

The new combined political/social health alternative proved to be a success in more than one way. It overcame some of the problems faced by the centralized curative health sector, which was being constrained by licensing problems imposed by the military: whenever the traditional sector was unable to function, the new groups often succeeded in filling the gap. They also introduced new concepts and methods in health care provision, ones better able to fulfill people's health needs at the grass-roots level. In this way the new movement succeeded in building and developing the indispensable missing segment in the Palestinian health infrastructure, the primary health care network. But, perhaps one of its most important achievements is that, along with those espousing the second approach of building of independent Palestinian institutions within the boundaries of the law—such as Maqassed Hospital, Patient's Friend's and Red Crescent societies—it also embarked on the difficult task of planning for and building an independent health infrastructure for the country that took into consideration the inevitability of the erection of a Palestinian state. Indeed, on the eve of the uprising the stage was already set for the swift and flexible development of an effective medical and health care support system for a population that was to go through perhaps one of the most important historical periods in its struggle for national liberation.

A NATION UNDER SIEGE: MEDICAL AND HEALTH CARE IN THE UPRISING

The spectacular political and social transformations taking place during the uprising manifested themselves at two critical levels: a sharp rise in the collective consciousness and an unforeseen major increase in the participation of various sectors of society in political and social action. The consequences of such transformations for medical and health care were profound.

The widespread participation of the unarmed population in the struggle against the Israeli army and armed Israeli civilians, coupled with a dramatic rise in the use of physical force by the Israeli authorities to quell people's protests, led to exponential increases in the number of dead and injured. In the first year of the uprising alone, conservative estimates listed 389 documented deaths and over 20,000 casualties, all sustained as the direct result of army violence.[29] Such a scale of injuries necessitated a swift and effective response from the country's medical and health care system. With the governmental hospital system overwhelmed by events, having suffered considerable neglect under the administration of the military authorities,[30] and with staff not possessing the freedom necessary for effective action, it was up to the Palestinian medical/health sector and that of UNRWA to mount the needed response.

At first, the events were dislocating: the system was unprepared for this scale of injury; medical care providers lacked experience in wartime trauma medicine; there was no room for the injured in Palestinian health establishments, which also lacked medications and equipment. Moreover, the military authorities took additional measures to limit further the capacity of the governmental health services system for medical care under such conditions. Thus, the already deficient governmental health budget was cut 50 percent, plans were made to reduce health services staff, the fees paid for health care were raised, and patient transfer to Israeli hospitals was terminated.[31] In a letter to Israeli Defense Minister Rabin, Member of the Knesset Dedi Zucker charged that

dozens of residents of the West Bank have died since the start of the uprising, because of the drastic reduction in hospitalization days [in Israel]. . . . Three months after the start of the uprising, virtually all hospitalization of the West Bank residents [in Israel] ceased. . . . a whole category of persons with malignant illnesses—who have paid government insurance in the West Bank—are no longer arriving in Israeli hospitals, because of sanctions by the Civil Administration.

In the same letter, Zucker further clarifies that referrals to Israeli hospitals are made by an administration officer, and can thus be influenced by external pressures, not only by medical considerations.[32] In other words, these measures—intended to punish the population for having successfully mounted one of the most significant resistance responses to military rule—expose further the fact that the Israeli military, whenever needed, uses health services as an instrument of political control. Coupled with the violent army reactions to the uprising, these events also help to reinforce the Palestinian point of view that Israeli military rule is very hazardous to the Palestinian people's health.

Yet, despite what appeared to be insurmountable problems, the system adapted. All three health sectors responded collectively to treat the injured. This wide-ranging participation, although varying among the sectors, reflected the consequences of deep-rooted Israeli policies that resulted in the alienation of all sectors of Palestinian society. Consequently, even the government-controlled sector participated in the relief campaign, rebelling against some of the orders imposed by the authorities and therefore beginning to adopt an attitude of defiance to military rules and regulations similar to that of the alternative health movement.[33]

However, the emergency medical campaign and the needs of the uprising demonstrated the widely differing abilities of each health sector to respond to these needs. For instance, although the governmental health sector succeeded in rebelling against some of the military orders restricting their ability to treat the wounded, and although those working in this sector did contribute to the network of cooperation in emergency medical care provision, it remained incapable of providing minimally acceptable services to the injured. Especially in the Hebron, Gaza, and northern regions of the country, inadequate budgets, equipment, and manpower precluded the possibility of providing basic emergency and medical needs to the population. This factor, coupled with Israeli control over these health institutions, made it impossible for Palestinian health professionals working in this sector to mount a continuous and adequate response to emergency medical needs.

Independent Palestinian curative services reacted by expanding hospital facilities, increasing the number of staff, and improving their emergency rooms
and ambulance services, and the alternative health movement began a systematic
effort to extend urgently needed services to the injured in villages and refugee
camps who could not reach hospitals in the main urban centers.[34] Appeals were
directed to health and humanitarian institutions worldwide, calling for condemnation of Israeli violence, harassment of medical personnel, assaults on hospitals
and clinics, and disruptions of medical care provision to the injured.[35] Meanwhile, donations and voluntary work campaigns continued locally. Supported
by the rising spirit of collectivity and togetherness, these campaigns succeeded
in rallying the support of many institutions and individuals in the Palestinian
health establishment. In other words, with an autonomous medical/health system
in place as a consequence of the efforts of the national and alternative health
movements, defiant of—and at times hampered by—military orders, and supported by increasing sympathies toward the plight of Palestinians worldwide,
Palestinian medical and health care providers succeeded in responding to this
state of emergency and adapting to newly emerging needs.

The reaction of the Palestinian health sector to the conditions and events of
the uprising reflected the general political mood. As in other historically decisive
moments, almost all sectors of society united in one determined response. For
Israeli policies had succeeded in undermining the interests of all sectors and
classes in Palestinian society. The unifying and collective spirit of the moment
predominated in the health sector as well and sharply influenced the way in
which the three health trends responded to the events and to each other as
components of the national struggle. While the relationship among the three
trends might have appeared as chaotic and overwhelmed on occasions by competition, in fact the urgency of the prevailing circumstances produced an acute
realization of the necessity of cooperation and coordination, leading to the rise
of a definitive shape for an independent health services infrastructure.[36] Along
with the efforts exerted in other sectors, it is precisely this infrastructure that
succeeded in sustaining the uprising through the force of a strongly emerging
collective consciousness, through the realization that health sector planning must
take into consideration a balance between national and professional considerations and, in the end, through the strong sense of empowerment that was reinforced with the declaration of the Palestinian state on November 15, 1988.

The empowerment and unity forged in the special conditions of the Palestinian
uprising are nonetheless not necessarily permanent. Many obstacles lie ahead in
the struggle to build an appropriate and equitable health care system for the
emerging state. National liberation, as many nations before have learned, is the
beginning and not the end of the struggle for a developed and equitable society.
Health conditions and health provision are linked to social and economic
inequalities—between classes and sectors of society and between men and
women—and are directly affected by them. This is precisely why addressing
social inequalities must be considered an integral part of any effective strategy

for improvements in health conditions and services. This is why the Palestinian health agenda must reflect the social content of the Palestinian struggle—both to liberate the nation and to build an equitable society where good health and access to health care are a fundamental human right.

NOTES

1. Alan Hill, "The Palestinian Population of the Middle East," *Population and Development Review* 9, no. 2 (June 1983): 302–3.

2. U. O. Schmelz, G. Nathan, and J. Kenvin, *Multiplicity Study of Births and Deaths in Judea, Samaria and Gaza Strip, North Sinai*, Technical Publication Series no. 44 Jerusalem; Israel Central Bureau of Statistics, 1977, p. 2; J. J. Puyet, *Infant Mortality Studies Conducted Among Selected Refugee Communities in the Near East* (Vienna: UNRWA, 1979), p. 3; R. Giacaman, "Inquietantes distorsions: les conditions sanitaire en Cisjoranie," *Revue d'études palestiniennes*, no. 12 Summer 1984; 25–26 (in French); *An Overview of Health Conditions and Services in the Israeli Occupied Territories* (Jerusalem: Union of Palestinian Medical Relief Committees, West Bank and Gaza Strip, August 1987), pp. 8–9

3. Sara Roy, *The Gaza Strip Survey* (Jerusalem: West Bank Data Base, 1986), p. 111; *A Profile of Life and Health in the Village of Biddu* (Bir Zeit: Union of Palestinian Medical Relief Committees and The Community Health Unit of Bir Zeit University, Interim Report, September 1986), p. 23; R. Giacaman, *Life and Health in Three Palestinian Villages* (London: Ithaca Press, 1986), pp. 122–29; *Ain al-Dyuk, Village Health Study* (Bir Zeit: Union of Palestinian Medical Relief Committees and University of Bir Zeit Community Health Unit, August 1988), pp. 31–34.

4. *A Report to the World Health Organization* (Jerusalem: Israel Ministry of Health, 1986), p. 137.

5. *Profile of Life and Health*, p. 23; Giacaman, *Life and Health*, pp. 129–32; *Ain al-Dyuk*, pp. 24–30.

6. *Overview of Health Conditions*, p. 10.

7. Samir Katbeh, *The Status of Health Services in the West Bank* (Jerusalem: Jordan Medical Council, 1977) (in Arabic); *Overview of Health Conditions*, pp. 12–17.

8. Giacaman, "Inquietantes distorsions"; *Overview of Health Conditions*, pp. 34–37.

9. *Overview of Health Conditions*, p. 36.

10. The observations and analysis contained in this section are based on the authors' experience and active participation in a variety of committees for health infrastructure development in the West Bank and Gaza Strip from 1980 until the present time, the proceedings and records of which are unfortunately inaccessible.

11. See Chapter 3 in this volume. Also see N. Aruri, ed., *Occupation: Israel over Palestine* (London: Zed Press, 1984), and M. Benvenisti, *The West Bank and Gaza Data Base Project, Pilot Study Report* (Jerusalem: The Jerusalem Post 1982).

12. This spirit of resistance is probably best expressed in Abdul Sattar Kassim, ed., *Funding Sources for Development in the Occupied Territories* (Jerusalem: Arab Thought Forum, September 1986) (in Arabic).

13. The Palestine Red Crescent Society in Gaza, for instance, attempted for ten consecutive years to obtain a permit to build a much needed pediatric hospital and failed.

Another example is that of the Patient's Friend's Society, which for two years has been trying to obtain a permit to establish a clearly needed rehabilitation center for the physically handicapped for the area and has also failed. Numerous other examples of attempts to stunt the natural development of health services in the area exist, especially during the period of the uprising; they include the closure of the headquarters of the Professional Unions in Jerusalem on August 26, 1988. See al-Haq: Law in the Service of Man, *Punishing a Nation: Human Rights Violations During the Palestinian Uprising, December 1987-December 1988* (Ramallah, al-Haq, 1988), p. 320. Harassment of medical personnel and institutions is described clearly in *The Casualties of Conflict: Medical Care and Human Rights in the West Bank and Gaza Strip. Report of a Medical Fact Finding Mission by Physicians for Human Rights* (Somerville, Mass.: Physicians for Human Rights, March 30, 1988); and in *A Letter of Appeal* (Jerusalem: Union of Palestinian Medical Relief Committees, West Bank and Gaza Strip, January 18, 1988); *News Briefing: Doctors in Detention* (Jerusalem: Union of Palestinian Medical Relief Committees, West Bank and Gaza Strip, July 2, 1988); and *A Letter of Appeal* (Jerusalem: Union of Palestinian Medical Relief Committees, West Bank and Gaza Strip, August 30, 1988).

14. *Overview of Health Conditions*, pp. 18–27.

15. For a useful description and analysis of "biomedical" Western scientific medicine, see L. Doyal, *The Political Economy of Health* (London: Pluto, 1983), pp. 27–36.

16. For a characteristic view of health development needs as expressed by those that espouse this view, see *Health Conditions of the Arab Population in the Occupied Territories, Including Palestine. A Report of the Special Committee of Experts Appointed to Study the Health Conditions of the Inhabitants of the Occupied Territories* (Geneva: World Health Organization Document A36/14, April 28, 1983), p. 6.

17. Examples of advocates of this trend include health professionals holding important administrative posts within the governmental health system and even some international aid agencies, most notably the United Nations Development Program's (UNDP) local office, who have funnelled a considerable amount of funds to health institutions controlled by the Israeli military under the heading "developing and strengthening of health institutions." For a revealing breakdown of UNDP assistance expenditures in the area for the period 1987–88, see *Programme of Assistance to the Palestinian People, Project Catalogue 1987/88* (Jerusalem: UNDP, 1988).

18. This term embodies a policy of resistance to occupation through attempts to remain on the land at all costs. For interesting accounts of the content and limitations of the steadfastness response to military rule, see I. Dakkak, "Back to Square One: A Study of the Reemergence of the Palestinian Identity in the West Bank 1967–1980," in A. Scholch, ed., *Palestinians over the Green Line* (London: Ithaca, 1983), and "Round Table Discussion of National Struggle Issues in the West Bank and Gaza Strip," *Shu'un Filastinia*, No. 103, 1981 (in Arabic).

19. For typical elaborations of this trend, see Katbeh, *Status of Health Services*; A. Baidoun, *The Role of Health in Economic Development in the West Bank* (Jerusalem: Arab Thought Forum, 1981); and the statements made by the Palestine Liberation Organization representative to the Thirty-Fourth World Health Assembly in *Thirty-Fourth World Health Assembly, Summary Records of Committees* (Geneva: World Health Organization Document WHA34/181/Rec/3, May, 4–22 1981), pp. 344–46.

20. Such as in the case of Maqassed Hospital in Jerusalem where, clearly, technical backup and know-how were in fact what was needed for the further development of the establishment.

21. See Dakkak, "Back to Square One"; "Round Table."

22. It was led by the Union of Palestinian Medical Relief Committees.

23. See Chapter 4 in this volume.

24. *Statement of Purpose* (Jerusalem: Union of Palestinian Medical Relief Committees, 1984), p. 1; and *Report of Activities During 1984* (Jerusalem: Union of Palestinian Medical Relief Committees), p. 1.

25. *Annual Report, 1985* (Jerusalem: Union of Palestinian Medical Relief Committees, April 1986).

26. See Union of Palestinian Medical Relief Committees, West Bank and Gaza Strip, *Newsletters No. 1* through *8* (Jerusalem, 1988).

27. This legitimacy was enhanced by the fact that "respectable" international health establishments were not only espousing primary health care as an important form of health care provision in developing countries, but were in fact promoting its principles. For example, the World Health Organization had as its policy slogan "Health for all by the year 2000." See *The Alma Ata Declaration* (Geneva: World Health Organization, 1978).

28. We recall the obstacles, difficulties, and lack of credibility encountered in the early 1980s by those introducing these "new" ideas on primary health care. One of the present authors was accused by the head of the Union of Physicians at the time of being unprofessional for suggesting the initiation of a training course for midwives to deal with poor prenatal care and its problems in the rural areas. The other was accused of "cheapening medicine," with his group described as "barbers" for participating in initiating volunteer group health care that was beginning to reach villagers with simple and needed health care in their domiciles as opposed to health care providers waiting in urban-based offices for the villagers to reach them.

29. See the various estimates listed elsewhere in this volume.

30. Physicians for Human Rights, *Casualties of Conflict*, pp. 28–34.

31. This information was obtained by the authors from Palestinian health professionals working within the governmental health system.

32. Joel Greenberg, "Zucker Charges Palestinian Deaths Related to Hospital Policy," *Jerusalem Post*, December 25, 1988, p. 2.

33. Early on in the uprising, the medical directors of governmental hospitals were served military orders prohibiting them from treating the wounded without charging them for the services provided, and requiring them to provide the military with a list of names of all injured admitted to hospital. While the directors were obliged to submit lists of names of the injured, they did succeed in defying the payment order and have been treating the injured free of charge.

34. Note that the large majority of the injured were reluctant to seek care in hospitals because of the high possibility of a later arrest by the army, with the injury as evidence of guilt. So, if the injury allowed, many opted to stay in their locality, with basic medical and primary health care services reaching them via emergency mobile teams organized by the alternative movement. For example, from January 13 to 17, 1988, the Union of Palestinian Medical Relief Committees succeeded in treating 2,599 patients and in distributing 3,000 first aid kits. Needless to say, not all treated were injured; some were seeking regular medical care through mobile services, having been prevented from receiving ordinary services because of curfews, roadblocks, checkpoints, and states of seige. See Union of Palestinian Medical Relief Committees, *Newsletter No. 1*, January 13–17, 1988.

35. The first such appeal was launched as early as January 7, 1988, and was signed

by thirty-two independent Palestinian medical/health institutions. See *An Open Letter to Health and Humanitarian Institutions* (Jerusalem, January 7, 1988).

36. A good example of cooperation is the program launched by the Union of Palestinian Medical Relief Committees, in cooperation with the hospitals of the country, to screen the blood types of potential blood donors in the various districts of the West Bank. In this way the Union succeeded in drawing up lists of names and addresses for potential donors, with their blood types, to be utilized by hospitals on the West Bank in emergency situations. So far, 20,000 persons have been screened, with lists of their particulars provided to all hospitals, including government ones. This project found considerable success in view of the fact that no appropriate blood banking system exists for the West Bank to date. The program is already known to have contributed to the saving of many lives.

II

THE PARTICIPANTS

6

The Role of the Refugee Camps

Adil Yahya

In 1948 more than three-quarters of a million Palestinians became refugees in the neighboring Arab countries and in the remaining parts of Palestine when 78 percent of the historic land of their country became the state of Israel. As of December 31, 1988, the number of Palestinian refugees registered with United Nations Relief and Works Agency was 2,301,919.[1] The actual number, however, is certainly higher, as UNRWA's records exclude all refugees living out of UNRWA's area of operation in the Near East, as well as refugees living in Israel and the Palestinians who were displaced as a result of the 1967 war. Today there are more than 850,000 refugees in the West Bank and Gaza Strip, representing more than 50 percent of the total population of about a million and a half.[2] Less than 50 percent of these refugees (359,183) are still living in refugee camps: 255,831 in the eight camps of the Gaza Strip (Jabalia, 55,488; Rafah, 51, 847; Beach, 43,086; Khan Yunis, 35,951; Nuseirat, 29,681; Bureij, 17,646; Maghazi, 11,679; Deir el Balah, 10,453), and 103,352 in the twenty camps of the West Bank (Balata, 13,094; Tulkarm, 10,137; Jenin, 9,234; Askar, 8,303; Dheisheh, 7,258; Shufat, 5,890; Kalandia, 5,683; Jalazone, 5,577; Am'ari, 5,306; Arrub, 5,475; Nur Shams, 4,778; Far'a, 4,401; Camp No. 1, 3,943; Fawwar, 3,870; Aqabat Jabr, 2,796; Aida, 2,527; Beit Jibrin, 1,267; Deir Ammar, 1,256; Ein el-Sultan, 696; Nu'eima, which was demolished).[3] It is this category of Palestinian refugees, and in particular their role in the current uprising, that this chapter addresses.

TWENTY YEARS OF OPPRESSION, TWENTY YEARS OF RESISTANCE

Judging from Israeli measures, the authorities consider refugee camps their number one enemy, seeing a potential "terrorist" in every camp resident. Being a camp resident has been deemed a "conviction" in itself, provoking especially brutal treatment at check posts or in prison, and extra suspicion when inside the pre–1967 borders.[4] The so-called carrot and stick policy has never been applied to refugee camps; they were ruled by the stick alone or, as officially named since 1984, the "Iron Fist." In the past twenty years of occupation refugee camps became familiar with all kinds of Israeli measures. As a 15-year-old girl, Salwa Ibrahim from Rafah camp, commented on her painting of a scene from the uprising, "We are left with nothing, our vocabulary is full of words, demolition, beatings, killings, and closures."[5]

While it is difficult to comprehend the burden of occupation on camps, one might look at the number of houses demolished and sealed for political reasons. Between 1985 and 1987, forty-two houses in the West Bank refugee camps were demolished or sealed, while the number of houses affected by this policy in the rest of the West Bank in the same period was ninety-eight.[6] One should keep in mind here that the camp population represents only 10 percent of the total population of the West Bank.

The logic of Israeli measures seems to be that through repression, camps submit to military occupation and stop their resistance, which would mean the end of Palestinian resistance, since the latter is centered in camps. The evidence, as will be shown, points to the opposite conclusion. Israeli measures backfired; instead of creating a deterrent, they fueled anger among the refugees, who lost their fear of the Israeli army and threw themselves into the national struggle in a radical way.

THE SOCIOPOLITICAL ORGANIZATION OF CAMPS

Statistically, the average Palestinian refugee registered with UNRWA is twenty-seven years old and comes from a family of five children; one-third of the total population is under fifteen years of age.[7] The main source of income for Palestinian refugees in the West Bank and Gaza camps is wage labor. A study conducted by the Bir Zeit Research Center showed that more than 77 percent of the work force in the Ramallah camps are wage laborers in Israel and the West Bank.[8] They are employed in factories, construction, municipal, and agricultural work. Other categories of income sources include employment by UNRWA in teaching, health, clerical, and cleaning jobs; employment in government offices; work abroad; and shopkeepers. Refugees who are able to set up private businesses are few in number and tend to leave camps and live in neighboring towns or villages.

The living standards in the West Bank camps, although slightly higher than those in the Gaza camps, are very low. The rate of unemployment in camps is very high, about 20 percent.[9] This can be felt during any visit to a refugee camp, where hundreds of young people sit in coffee shops without work, a phenomenon not seen in towns or villages in the West Bank. Many families in the camps depend wholly or partially on UNRWA's social welfare. About 61,000 persons were listed as special hardship cases by UNRWA in the West Bank and Gaza camps in 1988, qualifying for assistance because they are unable to make a living.[10] If a family has a male member between the ages of eighteen and sixty, it cannot be listed as a special hardship case and thus does not receive any assistance. The 1987 report of the Commissioner General states clearly that "families applying for assistance are subjected to strict verification, and once enrolled in the program, to annual verification."[11]

Looking at the housing conditions as an indicator of life in camps, we find that 96 percent of the refugees in the Ramallah area camps do not own their houses; 97 percent of the houses have no dining room, 89 percent have no sitting room, and 86 percent have no bathrooms. The average refugee family of five has a house with 1.55 bedrooms.[12]

The small and crowded houses that refugees live in today were built in the early 1960s by UNRWA. At the time, they replaced the mudbrick shelters that UNRWA had provided in the 1950s. Before that refugees lived in tents given to them by the International Committee of the Red Cross. Many refugees had managed to add one or more rooms to their houses, but with the coming of occupation many found themselves back in the Red Cross tents of the late 1940s and early 1950s.

Political organization is a distinguishing feature of camp life. Even though it is to a great extent a reflection of Palestinian politics in general, it has its own characteristics: intensity, radicalism, violence, and dedication.

The camps provided an ideal environment for the Palestinian resistance, which flourished and deeply rooted itself among refugees, who most felt the burden of occupation and thus were even more attached to the principle of national independence.

Israeli behavior toward the camps strengthened the will of their residents to resist occupation. The presence of Israeli troops, stationed permanently at camp entrances and at the gates of UNRWA schools, caused tension and resulted in confrontations on an almost daily basis. High concrete walls, concrete-filled barrels, and chain-link fences erected alongside roads crossing or passing by camps served as reminders of the misery of life under occupation. Refugees have neither grown accustomed to living under occupation nor come to terms with it; on the contrary, resistance grew over the years, and camps became centers of dedicated activism, "centers of violence" from the Israeli point of view.

Camp residents can be divided into three main political categories: national political activists, the religious movement, and independents besides a small network of collaborators.

National Political Activists

Most influential and most active in almost all refugee camps, this category is made up mainly of youth, students, laborers, and professionals. Due to the socially conservative nature of refugee camps, the political role of women is marginal. The only role they have is within this category, and even here it is minimal. They function independently from their male counterparts in most cases. The most active Palestinian groups within the West Bank and Gaza camps are Fateh, the Popular Front for the Liberation of Palestine, the Palestine Communist party, and the Democratic Front.

The Religious Movement

Traditionally, but wrongly, refugees are accustomed to labeling all members of religious movements as Muslim Brothers. In fact, the religious movement is no less divided than the national movement. The main religious groups in camps are the Muslim Brotherhood, the largest and most active religious group; al-Jihad al-Islami, more militant, with stronger ties to the national movement; Hezb al-Tahrir; and the Sufis, less political and more religiously oriented. These groups are united around the mosque, promoting religious beliefs and opposition to secularism.

The Independents

Also known as ''nonpolitical'' or ''nonaligned,'' the independents are mainly elders and stand in the middle between the first two groups. It is said that ''their minds are with the religious movement and their hearts with the nationalists.'' Their role is quite significant, as they soothe tension between and within the different groups.

Collaborators

It is not possible to talk of political life without commenting on the most significant problem facing refugee camps, especially the political activists. The Israeli authorities were very successful in setting up a huge network of collaborators in camps, using threats, drugs, bribery, and blackmail. Due to the nature of life in the camps, which is characterized by intensity, poverty, openness, and awkward social organization, the system of secret informers was more effective there than in towns or villages. It is beyond the scope of this chapter to explain this phenomenon in all its aspects. It is important, however, to note that leaflets listing names of persons believed to be collaborators were secretly distributed in past years, often including names of persons from camps. Such lists of names can also be seen once in a while attached to camp walls. It is hard to determine the degree of accuracy of these lists, especially since most of them are signed by vague groups or not signed at all, but names of camp residents make up a large share of such lists. A leaflet distributed in Ramallah in July 1988, for example, included eighty-five names from the area, twenty-eight (32 percent) of them from camps, while refugees in camps are roughly 6 percent of the total population of the region. These elements presented a serious challenge to the national movement, creating suspicion and fear among refugees. The problem was so great that committees to fight collaboration were created in camps. The Jenin camp Committee against Collaborators is an example. It was created in October 1987 to expose the names of collaborators and to mobilize in order to boycott and isolate them.[13]

WHOSE UPRISING?

For many Palestinians in the Occupied Territories, the uprising did not start until December 9 or even later. For refugees in camps, however, it started more than twenty years earlier. Confrontations and clashes with the Israeli army in the form of stone throwing, Molotov cocktails, strikes, as well as raising Palestinian flags, chanting, and decorating walls with nationalist slogans, are daily practices in most refugee camps. The uprising can therefore be described as the spreading of these forms of resistance from refugee camps into towns and villages, and the intensification of resistance in the camps.

The birthplace of the uprising is Jabalia, in the Gaza Strip. It broke out first in this densely populated camp on December 9, 1987, in response to the December 8 incident in which a truck driven by an Israeli swerved into a line of cars carrying Gaza workers, killing four, including refugees from Jabalia.[14] The next day, another refugee from Jabalia camp, Hatem al-Sisi, was shot dead, marking the beginning of a long-lasting uprising. Demonstrations spread throughout the Gaza Strip, centered in refugee camps.

Demonstrations spontaneously spread to the West Bank refugee camps, particularly Balata, where four people, two women and two children, were shot dead on December 11.[15] The other West Bank camps then joined the struggle, especially the ever active camps Jalazone, Am'ari, and Dhesheh. Some people argue that the December phase of the uprising was primarily a war of the camps versus the army.[16] It is more accurate, however, to say that the whole first phase of the uprising, from December 1987 to February 1988, was primarily a refugee camp phase. The uprising did not sweep villages and towns until mid-February 1988.

During this phase, camps were inflamed with resistance, while neighboring towns and villages were less able to organize. Their role was primarily focused on solidarity work in the form of collecting and delivering food donations to besieged and curfewed camps. While even an active center such as Bir Zeit University found its students busily celebrating the founding anniversaries of their groups—the PFLP on December 11 and Fateh on January 1—their comrades in the camps were constantly clashing with the army.

By mid-December, huge demonstrations and popular confrontations became daily practices in the Gaza camps and in some West Bank camps. By the time Peace Day was celebrated by Palestinians on both sides of the Green Line on December 21 (a general strike day), all other West Bank camps had joined the uprising, demonstrations having swept into Jenin, Tulkarem, Far'ah, Arroub, Kalandia, Shufat, and other camps. Clashes with the army continued in spite of the curfews. The practice of challenging curfew orders started in camps well before the United National Leadership of the Uprising (UNLU) called for it on February 27, 1988.[17] In Jenin camp, for example, huge demonstrations took place every day from February 4 to 7 in spite of the curfew, some of them lasting twenty-four hours.[18] Curfews were also broken on numerous occasions in Jalazone, Jabalia, Balata, and Am'ari. Strike forces were set up in camps in the early days of the uprising to carry out stone-throwing missions when huge demonstrations and public confrontations were impossible, using hit-and-run tactics.[19]

Efforts to organize the uprising at the grass-roots level started in camps and spread from there to neighboring towns and villages. In the beginning, youths mobilized themselves to defend their communities against settler attacks and army raids. Guard committees were organized around the middle of December in Am'ari, Kalandia, and Shufat. At the end of December, they spread to all camps and to some towns and villages. Later in the uprising, central committees were formed in each camp to coordinate between the different local committees and to allow for an around-the-clock guarding system. These committees proved to be very useful in keeping camps alert, using a good system of communication by means of lights, loudspeakers, whistles, and human voices. Many wanted persons escaped arrest during army raids, and settlers were prevented from entering camps. On February 4, for example, guard committees in Shufat camp discovered settlers attempting to enter the camp. The people clashed with them until the army came and imposed a curfew on the camp. In Jalazone, settlers also tried unsuccessfully to enter the camp but were discovered by camp guards, whereupon the settlers abducted a boy and ran away.[20] Popular committees in the form of coordination committees between the different political groups existed in camps long before the uprising. Their usual role was to coordinate the activities of these groups. When the uprising started, local committees were formed to meet the new challenges. Food relief committees were formed to obtain and distribute food within the camp in times of siege or curfew. Medical, educational, and even information committees were also created and were later connected with larger national committees. The committees expanded in number and enrollment.

Practices differ from one camp to another. In some camps the committees are unified: in others they are split, each major political group having its own committees. All committees are connected to the leadership of the uprising through the faction that they belong to, receiving communiqués and publications, distributing them, and carrying out the program of the uprising in their camp.

The highest committee in the camp is the coordination committee, whose function as a coordinator between the different political groups and committees continued during the uprising. It is true that the camps followed the program of the UNLU. In many cases, however, they anticipated it, as in the previously mentioned area of breaking curfew orders. In punishing collaborators, camps did not wait for the leadership to call upon them to carry out the mission. This order was issued on March 10, whereas camp residents started attacking collaborators from the very first day of the uprising.[21] Some collaborators were interrogated, beaten, expelled from the camps, or made to renounce their ties with the authorities. Communiqués No. 10, 11, 16, and 26 called for punishing these elements unless they renounced their actions. Camp residents used this opportunity to settle their accounts with collaborators. Several individuals were killed in different refugee camps, such as Aqbat Jabir, Jalazone, Jabalia, and others. Collaborators were then frightened and the flow of information to the Israeli intelligence services was partially blocked, which allowed for the continuation of the uprising. Camps have thus become less vulnerable than before.

THE ISRAELI REACTION

"Our impression is that the unrest has been dealt with in a way that may serve to create more turbulence rather than improve security. . . . there seems to have been a rather heavy-handed reaction in some cases."[22] These were the diplomatic words of Giorgio Giacomelli, Commissioner-General of UNRWA, on the conclusion of his visit to the Occupied Territories on December 16–20, 1987. Giacomelli also expressed concern at the disruption of UNRWA's services.

According to UNRWA figures, 20 Palestinians were killed and 200 were wounded in clashes with the army during the first two weeks of the uprising. Most of these casualties were camp residents, including five martyrs from Jabalia and four from Balata.[23] The army attacked camps with an extraordinary range of measures during the first phase of the uprising. Camp residents were subjected to prolonged curfews and sieges, massive arrest campaigns, restrictions of movement, and beatings. Clearly, the Israeli efforts were aimed at preventing the uprising from reaching the towns and villages of the Occupied Territories.

A study conducted in Far'ah camp on casualties and injuries sustained from December 12, 1987, to March 12, 1988, showed the following results:

	No. of cases	*Incidence*
Injuries from live ammunition	23	5/1,000
Injuries from beatings and tear gas	38	9/1,000
Number of arrests	44	10/1,000(24)

If this pattern had been repeated for all camps over the same period, the total number of casualties would be 1,720 injuries from live ammunition, 3,060 from beating and tear gas, and 3,400 arrests. The real figures are certainly higher, as Far'ah is far from being an active camp by refugee standards. Moreover, the injuries reported in that study and elsewhere represent only a fraction of the actual number. Many injuries were not reported, either because people feared reprisals or because they were unable to report their injuries.

THE MARTYRS OF THE CAMPS

The uprising claimed the lives of no less than 400 people in its first year, while the Israeli authorities recognized only those who were shot dead by the army, 230 people.[25] Of the martyrs 119 were camp residents: 19 from Jabalia, 17 from Shatei', 10 each from Balata, Bureij, and Jenin, 6 each from Nuseirat, Khan Yunis, and Askar, 5 each from Maghazi and Rafah, 4 from Arroub, 3 each from Dhesheh, Deir El-Balah, and Tulkaram, 2 each from Nurshams, Am'ari, Deir Ammar, and Ein Beit El-Ma', and 1 each from Jalazone, Ein Al-Sultan, Far'ah, Kalandia, and Shufat. Seventy martyrs from the camps were shot, 11 were beaten to death, 20 died of tear gas suffocation, and 9 died in suspicious circumstances.[26]

Clearly, the fact that refugee camps spent much of the uprising under curfews and sieges did not save them from Israeli brutality.

INJURIES IN THE CAMPS

It is hard to estimate the number of camp residents who have been wounded in the first year of the uprising for the following reasons: (1) Estimates of total casualties differ widely from one source to another, ranging from 20,000,[27] to 23,000,[28] and even as high as 45,000,[29] while Israeli military sources recognize only 3,640 injuries.[30] (2) UNRWA figures include refugees who are not living in camps. (3) The numbers of injuries in camps differ from one month to another.

Judging from the casualty tolls of January and September 1988, camp residents represent between one-third and two-thirds of the total number of casualties. The Facts Information Committee documented 189 cases of injuries in the Occupied Territories in January, 107 of them camp residents.[31] In September the number of injuries as documented by another source was 963, 335 of them refugees from camps.[32]

Most of the injuries were inflicted by live ammunition, rubber and plastic bullets, but quite a high number were caused by beatings. Defense Minister Rabin announced on January 19 a new-old policy known as "the policy of beatings" when he declared that "the first priority is to use force, might and beatings." For the Israeli authorities, the new method is more effective than detention. A detainee, writes the *Jerusalem Post*, will be freed after eighteen days; he may then resume stoning soldiers. But if troops break his hand, he won't be able to throw stones for a month and a half.[33] The new policy was in no way new to refugee camps. The practice of beatings was, however, systematized and intensified. As soon as the policy was declared, the army attacked refugee camps, systematically beating whole families, as in Jabalia on January 18 and 19. The camp was then under curfew. At least sixty-four people, mostly women and children, required medical treatment, and two were hospitalized.[34] Similar actions were reported in the other refugee camps, particularly Beach Camp (Shatei'), Bureij, and Khan Yunis in the Gaza Strip and Jalazone, Balata, and Am'ari in the West Bank. Between January 19 and 26, UNRWA clinics in Gaza treated more than 120 refugees who had been beaten. The cases included a woman aged eighty, a man aged seventy, and children as young as four. At least twenty-four cases were referred to hospitals for further treatment. Between March 17 and 21, 163 people from Gaza camps were beaten, bringing the number of casualties among refugees in Gaza due to the beatings policy to 1,000.[35] The number had reached 10,242 by October 15, 1988.[36] The West Bank field office of UNRWA reported eighty-nine cases of beatings of camp residents between March 12 and 16. UNRWA records show a 20 percent increase in patient visits to UNRWA health centers.[37]

CURFEWS, SIEGES, AND RESTRICTIONS OF MOVEMENT

What characterized Israeli behavior toward camps, more than anything else, was the imposition of lengthy curfews. The intention was to isolate camps and prevent them from affecting neighboring regions. Camps have been in and out of curfews for most of the uprising, and curfews were clamped on for extended periods, forty-three days at stretch in the case of Jalazone. The army enforced curfews in camps very strictly. People were not simply confined to their houses; in most cases they were not allowed to use certain parts of the already small houses, like balconies or backyards. Food and medical supplies were cut off, and often during the current uprising a curfew has come to mean cutting water and electricity. This practice was first applied to Jalazone camp and then to other camps and curfewed localities. An Israeli soldier wrote in *Ha'aretz:*

I was in Jalazone. It had been under curfew for twenty days. At a certain stage the area commander, Avram Mitzna, decided that it was not right for us to be out in the rain while the Arabs were at home watching television. He wanted some symmetry, so he decided to cut off their electricity supply. It was considered legitimate because they have not learned their lesson.[38]

Troops also storm into houses during curfews, destroying furniture and food supplies, arresting youths, and beating and harassing the inhabitants. Inhabitants who managed to leave al-Dhesheh camp during the curfew of June 27 to July 6 reported that "troops had cut off the water supply since the first day, they screamed and shouted obscene and abusive words through loudspeakers, houses were stormed, residents were assaulted regardless of their age, some youths were arrested, residents are not allowed to leave to hospitals or to buy medication."[39]

On April 16 curfews were imposed on twenty camps simultaneously after severe clashes and were lifted on April 24.[40] During the month of July, the army imposed curfews on forty-six localities in the Occupied Territories; twenty-two of them were camps. The number of curfew days during that month was 198, 88 of them in refugee camps. The number of people affected was in the hundreds of thousands.[41]

Even when comprehensive curfews imposed on large areas were lifted, camps would often remain under curfew. The curfew imposed on the Gaza Strip after the shooting of two administrative detainees in Ansar 3 on August 16 was lifted two days later, while different Gaza camps remained under curfew until the end of the month. The curfew imposed on Nablus was also lifted on August 24, while neighboring Balata camp remained under curfew until August 30.[42]

Not a single refugee camp escaped curfews, which, combined with strikes and restrictions on travel, made life more difficult for the residents. Many found themselves unable to earn a living because they could not travel to their jobs in Israel and neighboring towns. Others lost their jobs. For example, in September there were about 500 breadwinners unemployed in Fawar and 200 in Jenin camp, while two-thirds of the Arrub laborers were unemployed.[43]

Curfews also started from late December to cause shortages of basic food supplies, particularly bread and milk, in certain camps, among them Jabalia, Beach Camp, Balata, and Jalazone. UNRWA responded by expanding the relief program to include more refugees,[44] and Palestinians all over the Occupied Territories formed popular committees to obtain food and deliver it to camps. Food supplies were often smuggled into camps and distributed from house to house overnight.

The UNLU responded by calling upon the people to offer moral and material support to curfewed and besieged camps. It also called upon UNRWA to expand food distribution to all refugees in the Gaza Strip and, along with the Red Cross, to provide medical and food provisions to curfewed and besieged localities in the Occupied Territories.[45]

DETENTIONS

The Israeli authorities claim that the number of Palestinian detainees during the first year of the uprising totalled 20,000, [46] while Palestinian sources estimate the number at more than 27,000.[47] It is hard to determine the percentage of camp residents among the detainees. They probably are the majority, as we know that all refugee camps have been raided more than once; in some of these raids hundreds of people were arrested, including children ranging in age from three to twelve.[48] The army brings in buses during the night, imposes a curfew, arrests the youths that they can find, and takes them away. On December 22, 1987, for example, one hundred youths were arrested from Jenin camp, and seventy other arrest orders were left for people who were not found in their houses. On March 17, one hundred more youths were arrested while the camp was under curfew.[49] On March 5, 1988, seventy people from Jalazone were arrested while the camp was under curfew.[50] Similar actions have been reported in all other camps. From May 1 to 7, 1988, refugee camps in Gaza were surrounded, the army went from house to house collecting the identity cards of the whole population, people were ordered to report to military headquarters, and many were then arrested and detained.[51]

DEPORTATIONS

Of the fifty-nine Palestinians who were ordered out of the Occupied Territories during the first year of the uprising, twelve were camp residents:[52]

Mursi Abu Ghweilh, 22	Kalandia	Student
Jamal Diab Lafi, 25	Kalandia	Journalist
Bashir Mohamad Hamad, 27	Kalandia	Worker
Husam Mohamad Khader, 27	Balata camp	Employee
Yusef Harb Odeh, 25	Balata camp	Student
Jamal Awad Zaggot, 31	Beach camp	Unionist
Ata Ahmad Hussein, 54	Beach camp	Engineer
Jamal Shafi Hindi, 30	Jenin camp	Student
Ayash Abdul Aziz, 30	Jabalia camp	Teacher
Jamal Ibrahim Faraj, 25	Dhesheh camp	Unionist
Tayseer M. Nasrallah, 27	Askar camp	Student
Abdul Hamid Al-Baba, 25	Am'ari camp	Student

They were accused of having organized and participated in the uprising in their own camps and in the Occupied Territories. The fact that more than 20 percent of the deportees are camp residents indicates that camps have succeeded not only in developing a local leadership but also in providing a leadership on the national level, in spite of the harassment that refugees have been subjected to during the past years of occupation.

HOUSE DEMOLITIONS AND SEALINGS

The military authorities stepped up the policy of house demolitions during the uprising. At least 145 houses were demolished during the uprising's first year.[53] In the camps, the army reversed its policy. In previous years they sealed houses partially or completely rather than demolishing them, probably because houses in the camps are UNRWA property. In the two years before the uprising, thirty houses in refugee camps were affected by this policy; fourteen of them were sealed completely and thirteen partially, and only three houses were demolished in Fawar camp.[54] On the other hand, most of the houses affected by the policy during the uprising were demolished. In Jalazone camp alone, thirteen houses were demolished, and in the process of demolishing these houses other neighboring houses were badly damaged. On December 7, 1988, the authorities demolished the houses of Ahmad Masud and his son Hafez from Jalazone. Seven other houses were badly damaged in the process of demolishing these houses. In past years, Israeli authorities used to demolish the parents' house only. In this case and in other cases during the *intifada* the house of a brother was demolished along with the parents' house. On August 24, 1988, the houses of Musa Gazaleh and his son Ahmad from Jalazone were demolished in retaliation for the throwing of a cocktail bomb by Musa's sixteen-year-old son Mahmoud. The authorities informed the family later that the house of the brother was demolished by mistake and that the army was willing to compensate them for it, which never happened.[55] In Jalazone also, Yusef Sha'ban, whose house was demolished on August 5, 1988, was brought from jail to witness the destruction of his house.[56] Demolitions usually take place late at night or very early in the morning after a curfew has been imposed on the camp. The occupants are given one hour to take out their belongings, and neighbors are not allowed to help; thus demolitions entail not only the destruction of the building, but of furniture and other household contents as well, especially because the hour is usually consumed in arguments between the owners of the house and the soldiers carrying out the order.

SOLIDARITY WITH CAMPS

The situation in the refugee camps deteriorated by late December 1987. Curfews, combined with strikes and restrictions on movement, left camp residents in need of outside help if the uprising were to continue. Palestinians in the Occupied Territories responded to the needs of the camps and to calls of the UNLU by forming popular committees to collect food and cash donations and deliver them to curfewed and besieged camps. Donations were channeled through popular committees in the camps and through UNRWA. Palestinians also responded by demonstrating and clashing with the Israeli army, and within a few weeks the entire West Bank and Gaza were inflamed with resistance, thus easing the pressure on the camps.

The Palestinians in Israel also responded by forming popular committees to raise funds from both Jewish and Arab communities to support the camps. These committees were working by mid-December 1987. The biggest outpouring of donations came to UNRWA from Palestinians in Galilee, the Triangle, and the Negev.[57] They also proclaimed December 21, 1987, Peace Day, general strike day in solidarity with the uprising.

On the international level, the camps of the Occupied Territories elicited a strong feeling of solidarity. Camp residents, who are usually suspicious of and somewhat hostile to foreigners, particularly Westerners, became accustomed to seeing foreign delegations every day. It seemed as if journalists had finally discovered the camps. Visitors included, in addition to media people, solidarity groups, high-ranking government officials, parliamentarians, and others, for example, the Italian president, Austrian foreign minister, Dutch foreign minister, former Danish prime minister, as well as parliamentary groups from Canada, the United States, Britain, Italy, Greece, Sweden, and Japan. The international community responded favorably to appeals for assistance from the Occupied Territories; $33 million had been pledged to UNRWA in cash or kind for emergency needs as of August 1988. Major contributors included the following: Italy, $9 million; Kuwait, $5 million; Iraq, $3.2 million; Qatar, $2.5 million; and Libya, $1.5 million.[58] This solidarity was certainly one of the factors that allowed the continuation of the uprising and at least minimally shielded camp residents from the full harshness of Israeli measures.

REFUGEES, UNRWA, AND THE UPRISING

UNRWA claims that it took extraordinary measures to cope with the uprising. This is true, but refugees are still disappointed and expect more, especially in the West Bank camps. On January 23, 1988, UNRWA began implementing an emergency relief program for refugees most affected by the uprising.[59] Refugees at the time demanded the expansion of food distribution to all camp residents who suffered from curfews, sieges, or strikes. The old love-hate relationship between UNRWA and refugees continues through the uprising, resulting in tension that has expressed itself particularly during food distributions. To deal with this, UNRWA abandoned some of its distribution centers and shifted operations to centers in neighboring towns; in other cases UNRWA asked the help of the national movement to distribute food in the camps.

On the other hand, Israel retaliated against UNRWA's efforts to help refugees by no longer paying port and transportation costs for commodities destined for UNRWA use in the Occupied Territories. According to UNRWA estimates, this signified additional costs to them of $800,000 a year, and this at a time of tight budget restrictions.[60] In fact, relations between Israel and UNRWA have never been good. There has always been tension between them on the working level, and this has intensified during the uprising. Many UNRWA employees were arrested, wounded, or deported, and many others were prevented from carrying out their duties. Agency staff, both local and international, were denied access to camps under curfew on numerous occasions.[61] The Commissioner General of UNRWA himself was denied entry to Jabalia camp on January 12, 1988. His visit to Dhesheh two days later was cut short when soldiers fired rubber bullets at a crowd surrounding him. The army also frequently blocks UNRWA doctors from reaching patients in need of care, and confiscates and delays ambulances.[62] In Khan Yunis, for example, soldiers threw to the ground milk powder that UNRWA intended to distribute.[63]

To help support area staff in the performance of their duties under these circumstances and also to help ease tense situations and prevent ill-treatment of refugees, UNRWA recruited new international staff on short-term contracts. Its field staff was further strengthened by temporarily posting international staff to the Occupied Territories from headquarters in Vienna and elsewhere.[64]

UNRWA also started a local and international campaign to collect donations. Some of these donations were handed to refugees as cash grants, and the rest as food supplies. As of May 16, 1988, UNRWA had managed to deliver more than 1.5 million kilograms of food, even though it was not allowed to distribute food in camps except when curfews or sieges were lifted.[65] The supplies included flour, milk powder, food parcels, bread, vegetables, and kerosene.

UNRWA's relief program usually consumes 10 percent of its budget. The uprising, UNRWA says, brought relief to the forefront again. The number of refugees listed as special hardship cases rose from 117,987 in 1987 to 135,357 in 1988.[66] UNRWA's health program, which is basically preventive in nature, had to deal with serious injuries from gunfire, rubber bullets, beatings, and tear gas. They kept some clinics in Gaza open around the clock and extended working hours in other clinics. They also organized special feeding programs and more than doubled their international staff in the Occupied Territories.[67] Were Palestinian refugees in camps impressed? Not at all; refugees will never settle for less than a homeland, and UNRWA will remain a symbol of their humiliation, regardless of its efforts.

CONCLUSION

From its historic origins, Israeli policy toward refugee camps aimed at removing them altogether. The attempt was made on several occasions, in the form of resettlement plans, housing projects, and transfers. These policies failed due to the refugees' resistance and unwillingness to cooperate with the authorities. Israel sought to solve the problem through harassment and collective punishment. The intention was to make life in camps intolerable, thus forcing refugees out of them. House demolitions and sealings seemed to be a logical action on the part of the Israeli government, which carried out this policy all through the years of occupation. In the early 1970s, for example, it demolished thousands of houses in the camps of Gaza, thus leaving tens of thousands of refugees homeless. They were then denied permits to rebuild in the camps. Some were resettled in the Sheikh Radwan housing project, others leased small plots of land away from the camps to build on, and the rest were dispersed throughout Gaza and the West Bank. Camps were attacked with an extraordinary range of measures throughout the occupation. They felt the burden of occupation more than any other area in the Occupied Territories, but refused to submit; the brutality that they experienced over two decades forged their spirit and enabled them to hold their ground in the face of Israeli attacks during the uprising. Refugees now can see the light at the end of the tunnel and will certainly proceed to reach it sooner or later.

NOTES

1. United Nations Relief and Works Agency, *UNRWA Quarterly Report*, Vienna: UNRWA, October 1-December 31, 1988.

2. Meron Benvenisti, *The West Bank Data Base Project* (Jerusalem: The Jerusalem Post 1987), p. 1.

3. UNRWA, *Report of the Commissioner-General*, Vienna, 1987, p. 24.

4. Interviews with refugees from Jalazone, Dhesheh, Am'ari, and Balata.

5. Her paintings were displayed at the Gallery of the Association of Artists-Gaza Strip, "Work of Children in Occupied Palestine."

6. al-Haq: Law in the Service of Man, *Demolition and Sealing of Houses as a Punitive Measure in the Israeli Occupied West Bank* (Ramallah: al-Haq, 1978), pp. 45–47.

7. "What Is UNRWA?" (Vienna: UNRWA, 1987).

8. Odeh Shehadeh and Basma Abu Swai. "Information Bank," unpublished report, Bir Zeit University Research Center, 1987.

9. Ibid.

10. UNRWA, *Report of the Commissioner-General*, 1987, p. 25.

11. Ibid.

12. Fahum Shalabi and Odeh Shehadeh, *Housing Conditions in the Ramallah Region* (Bir Zeit: Bir Zeit University Research Center, 1986), pp. 7–13 (in Arabic).

13. *Facts Weekly Review*, no. 18 (July 10–16, 1988): 7.

14. *Palestine Refugees Today*, no. 122 (May 1988): 2.

15. Facts Information Committee, Press Release no. 4, p. 1.

16. Penny Johnson, Lee O'Brien, and Joost Hiltermann, *Middle East Report* (May–June 1988): 6.

17. UNLU Communique No. 8, February 1988.

18. *Facts Weekly Review*, no.18 (July 10–16, 1988): 10.

19. *Facts Weekly Review*, no. 9 (May 1–7, 1988): 1.

20. Interviews with refugees from Shufat and Jalazone camps.

21. UNLU Communique No. 10, March 10, 1988.

22. *UNRWA News*, no. 147 (January 1, 1988): 2.

23. Ibid., p. 1.

24. Union of Palestinian Medical Relief Committees, *The Uprising: Consequences for Health* (Jerusalem: Union of Palestinian Medical Relief Committees, August 1988).

25. *Al-Quds*, December 9, 1988, p. 1.

26. Palestine Human Rights Information Center (Jerusalem), unpublished report, n.d.

27. Al-Haq: Law in the Service of Man, *Punishing a Nation: Human Rights Violations During the Palestinian Uprising, December 1987–December 1988* (Ramallah: al-Haq, 1988), p. 9.

28. *Al-Taliah*, December 8, 1988, p. 1.

29. *Al-Quds*, December 9, 1988, p. 1.

30. Palestine Human Rights Information Center, *Human Rights Violations Under Israeli Rule During the Uprising, December 9, 1987–October 9, 1988* (Jerusalem: Data Base Project on Palestinian Human Rights, 1988), p. 2.

31. Facts Information Committee, Press Release No. 6, February 2, 1988.

32. *Al-Ard al-Muhtalah*, no. 45 (September 1988): 190–99.

33. *Jerusalem Post*, January 20, 1988.

34. *UNRWA News*, no. 149 (February 1, 1988): 1.

35. *Palestine Refugees Today*, no. 22 (May 1988): 4.

36. UNRWA Summary Report 1988, p. 15.

37. *UNRWA News*, no. 166 (October 17, 1988): 1.

38. Ronit Matalon, "The Wild West," *Ha'aretz*, March 11, 1988. Quoted in *Report on the Violation of Human Rights in the Territories During the Uprising* (Jerusalem: Israeli League for Human and Civil Rights, 1988), p. 13.

39. *Facts Weekly Review*, no. 16 (June 27–July 2, 1988): 7.

40. *Facts Weekly Review*, no. 16 (June 27–July 2, 1988); no. 17 (July 3–9, 1988); no. 18 (July 10–16, 1988).

41. *Facts Weekly Review*, no. 24 (August 21–27, 1988): 9.

42. *UNRWA News*, no. 155 (April 28, 1988): 1.

43. *Facts Weekly Review*, no. 25 (August 28–Sept. 3, 1988): 15; no. 18 (July 10–16, 1988): 27.

44. *Palestine Refugees Today*, no. 122 (May 1988): 2–3.

45. See UNLU Communiqués No. 8, 10, 14, and 15.

46. *Al-Quds*, December 9, 1988, p. 11.

47. *Al-Taliah*, December 8, 1988, p. 1.

48. *UNRWA News*, no. 164 (September 15, 1988): 11.

49. *Facts Weekly Review*, no. 18 (July 10–16, 1988): 9, 12.

50. *Facts Weekly Review*, no. 3 (March 20-April 2, 1988): 14.

51. *Facts Weekly Review*, no. 9 (May 1–7, 1988): 1.

52. al-Haq, *Punishing a Nation*, p. 144.

53. Palestine Human Rights Information Center report.

54. *Demolition and Sealing of Houses*, pp. 45–47.

55. Interview with the family of Musa Ghazalah, Jalazone camp. August 28, 1988.

56. *UNRWA News*, no. 163 (September 1, 1988): 1.

57. *UNRWA News*, no. 149 (February 1, 1988): 1.

58. UNRWA, Press Release, August 22, 1988.

59. *UNRWA News*, no. 149 (February 1, 1988): 1.

60. *UNRWA Reports* 6, no. 3 (October 1988): 2.

61. *Palestine Refugees Today*, no. 22 (May 1988): 4.

62. UNRWA, Press Release, October 19, 1988.

63. Union of Palestinian Medical Relief Committees, *Emergency News Letter*, no. 4 (February 1988): 2.

64. UNRWA Summary Report, 1988, pp. 10–11.

65. *UNRWA News*, no. 156 (May 16, 1988): 1.

66. UNRWA 1987 Report, p. 25; UNRWA 1988 Report, p. 16.

67. UNRWA 1988 Report, pp. 10–16.

7

Jeep Versus Bare Feet

THE VILLAGES IN THE *INTIFADA*

Husain Jameel Bargouti

The Israeli occupation expresses itself in a state apparatus that rules an estimated 1.4 to 1.73 million Palestinians living in the West Bank and Gaza Strip.[1] This state apparatus consists both of regular army units and of about 70,000 armed settlers who came under the auspices of the military and established settlements after 1967 on confiscated Palestinian land. In addition, the secret state security agency, the Shin Bet, recruited a number of Palestinians to form an espionage network. This military branch of the state apparatus includes hundreds of Palestinian collaborators organized into isolated gangs called the Village Leagues whose members are armed and led by Israeli officers, and some 1,000 Palestinian policemen.

The "civilian" branch of this state apparatus consists of a governmental health system, a network of governmental schools, and offices for social affairs, taxation, car licensing, and so on. This branch in particular penetrates every cell of the Palestinian social organism.

These two branches are so interrelated that it becomes hard to differentiate between them. Somewhere between the military and the civilian branches stand the so-called appointed mayors, appointed village councils, and appointed village mukhtars, all of them mere state servants. They are supposed to perform civil functions on behalf of the Israeli authority, but some are members of the Village Leagues and/or well-known collaborators with the Shin Bet.

This state apparatus of occupation stands above Palestinian society as an alien force; but, paradoxically, it penetrates every cell of the Palestinian social organism through a labyrinth of bureaucracy without which Palestinians cannot get any official document and through a network of prisons for political activists—Palestinian cars in the West Bank are even given blue plates to differentiate them from the yellow-plated Israeli cars for "security reasons." This mutual alienation between the Israeli state apparatus and Palestinian society is most concretely expressed in land confiscation: about 52 percent of the total territory of the West Bank and Gaza Strip was confiscated in the period 1967–85, and the process is still continuing.[2]

The issue of the state was and continues to be the central issue of the political struggle throughout the uprising, whose goal is to sweep away the Israeli apparatus of occupation and replace it with an independent Palestinian one.

Insofar as the Occupied Territories are concerned, the Palestinian state apparatus consists of the four principal PLO-affiliated groups—Fateh, the Popular Front for the Liberation of Palestine (PFLP), the Democratic Front for the Liberation of Palestine (DFLP), and the Palestine Communist party (PCP)—as well as an infrastructure of resistance in the form of labor unions, popular committees, and so on, inspired or led by the same four groups.

The popular committees are particularly important insofar as the Palestinian state apparatus is concerned. Their first model was created in the early 1970s in the form of the voluntary work committees (VWCs). The Palestinian communists came up with the idea of helping villagers to harvest their crops, and the idea materialized in the form of the VWCs in which the communists, the diverse PLO factions, and independent individuals were involved.[3]

The organization of a work committee was simple, flexible, and efficient. Each member joined the committee by choice to work, expecting no payment. Members in a given locality elected a coordinator of activities, and these coordinators formed a new committee. On the top of this social pyramid emerged the Higher Committee of Voluntary Work in the West Bank and Gaza Strip. The VWCs were based on democracy, no bureaucracy: there were no headquarters, no official documents, no "orders," and no fixed plans which could not be changed at any moment by the volunteers directly involved in executing them. The simplicity, efficiency, flexibility, democracy, and diffused leadership of the VWCs have been sources of inspiration in the formation of the popular committees of the uprising.

Moreover, the VWCs were integrated into a nationwide organization encompassing cities, towns, villages, and refugee camps alike. There are about 450 villages in the Occupied Territories, fifteen in the Gaza Strip and the rest in the West Bank. No general population census has been taken since the 1967 Israeli census, but a study some years ago estimated that 64 percent of the West Bank population was living in villages, 26 percent in cities, and 10 percent in refugee camps; but only 11 percent of the population of the Gaza Strip was living in villages, 46 percent in cities, and 43 percent in refugee camps.[4] Thus, VWC penetration of villages was not a small achievement, especially in the West Bank.

The diverse PLO factions were able through these committees to implement political decisions on a national scale.

The experience of the VWCs in building such an infrastructure of resistance was indispensable in the formation of the popular committees of the uprising, which are essential constituents of the Palestinian state apparatus. One of the important manifestations, therefore, of the conflict between the Israeli state apparatus and the Palestinian state apparatus has been "the army versus the popular committees."

Nevertheless, the conflict has had a variety of forms; collective punishment is a form in which the army confronts a certain community as a whole and not the popular committees in particular; in the latter form, therefore, the mutual alienation between the Israeli state apparatus and Palestinian civil society as a whole is revealed. We can illustrate this mutual alienation by quoting an Israeli soldier, Jonathan Kestenbaum, who served in Qabatya in the West Bank. Qabatya had been under several weeks of continuous curfew when Kestenbaum began his stint there. The curfew, imposed from July 25 to August 20, 1988, was lifted for two hours every three days. Electricity had been cut off, access by journalists was forbidden, and crops were left rotting in the fields while people starved. Kestenbaum wrote:

As we reach the end of a night patrol, we spy a family bringing in a bucket of tomatoes. Suddenly our jeep springs into action as if the future of our country depends on it. We corner them and all are told to report to the commanding officer. They tell us they have no food and simply are starving to death and had no choice . . . a 16 year old-barefoot kid starts running away from us. In a chase, jeep versus bare-feet, the officer cocks his rifle and points at the kid from 10 meters away. I shout at him to stop—that's how "statistics" occur.[5]

The Uprising, December 9, 1987–January 31, 1988

The December 9, 1987, demonstrations in the Gaza Strip were essentially formed by the lower classes, especially the working class and petite bourgeoisie, although various ages, professions, and social groups participated on a broad scale.[6]

By December 18, 1987, the uprising had already spread to villages of the Gaza Strip such as Beit Hanoun, to a few West Bank villages such as Bani Naim in the Hebron area, and to Palestinian villages inside Israel proper such as Sikhneen and Kufr Kanna.[7]

The movement as a whole was becoming rapidly organized. The level of organization was so high that on December 21 a general strike was held in which the West Bank, the Gaza Strip, and the Palestinians inside of Israel proper participated. The Israeli government was not willing to admit to such an organizational achievement and insisted on the spontaneous nature of the "riots."

This insistence forced the military correspondent of the Israeli newspaper *Davar* to say: "They say in the radio 'local riots.' What local riots? I've seen how they are perfectly and completely organized."[8] Nevertheless, the Israeli government's denial of reality was somehow understandable. The uprising has thus far surpassed everyone's wildest imaginings.

The massive scale of the movement and the high level of its organization must not lead us to overlook its political program. The slogan of the demonstrators of December 9 was "We want a state, we want an identity." The uprising at its onset may therefore be described as a lower-class, nationalist, highly organized mass movement with a definite political program.

The army countered the uprising (throughout December 1987) with a combination of methods. Chief among them were killing, injuring, arresting, and imposing curfews. Isolating the areas of "riots" and clamping down on the "rioters" was the major tactic of the army. This tactic produced a new need: that of providing food for the isolated and suffering areas. Thus a higher level of social solidarity became necessary. Consequently, popular committees for food supply were formed in the first two weeks in several villages in the Nablus area, such as Beit Foureek, Beit Dajan, and Salem.[9] These committees collected, packed, and sent food to the nearby Balata refugee camp, which was the most volatile spot in the West Bank throughout December in terms of deaths and injuries. These committees gradually developed into specialized underground networks. The Israeli military apparatus, garbed in civilian clothes and called the civil administration, perceived the need to "calm down" the villagers by using a social stratum in the villages that was ready to "cooperate."

The Israeli state apparatus had recruited the Village Leagues in the late seventies from among a stratum whose history had been an extended moment of collaboration with every central authority. In nineteenth-century Ottoman Palestine, the Turks first introduced the idea of Village Leagues. Then the British organized leagues of their own on the coastal plain in the 1930s, and the Israeli and Jordanian states revived the same idea in the seventies. The well-known leader of the leagues, Mustafa Dudeen, from Dura village in the Hebron area, was a Jordanian member of parliament and a minister of defense prior to 1967, and collaborated with the Jordanians and Israelis simultaneously in the seventies. Blackmailing was a common method used by the Israeli state apparatus to recruit the leagues. Public rumors, for example, spread in the early 1980s about a certain village mukhtar in the north of the West Bank who had raped his own daughters. He became a league member when the Shin Bet used his fear of social scandal to blackmail him. However, the leagues, being extremely unpopular armed gangs and socially isolated, were the least suitable instrument to be used by the Israeli state apparatus to calm down a mass movement in the villages.

The other choices available to the Israeli state apparatus were village mukhtars and village councils. The Arabic term "mukhtar" means the "chosen one." Mukhtars were selected in nineteenth- and early twentieth-century Ottoman Palestine as representatives of the peasant class to the central authority, and vice versa. Chosen on the basis of seniority, property, age, and kinship, mukhtars derived their social power from these clannish relations and from their official status at the same time. Consequently, mukhtarship became a traditional symbol of power. However, social transformation leading to the decline of the peasant class was bound to lead to a corresponding decline in mukhtarship as well.

The gradual decline of the peasant class reached a critical turning point in the West Bank and the Gaza Strip in the period 1967–88. A section of the peasantry, unable to support itself through other means, turned to wage labor, especially in Israel. A Palestinian sociologist, Salim Tamari, noted, "We have today roughly 100,000 workers commuting daily from Camps, villages, and urban centers in the West Bank and the Gaza Strip to Israel, most of them going back to their villages in the evening."[10] Not all of these workers are wage laborers dependent solely on wages; for example, a certain number of them depend on family labor on their parcels of land as well, and therefore constitute a fraction of a specific transitional class, the semi-proletariat. The power behind the transformation of peasants into wage workers and semi-wage workers has been the development of capitalism in general and Israeli capitalism in particular. The expansion of trade, as a consequence of the Israeli economic annexation, in addition to the Israeli policy against Palestinian agriculture, forced a certain section of the peasantry to turn to trade by opening shops in villages and cities. Consequently, they augmented the commercial class. Furthermore, some peasants bought vehicles to transport workers and commodities, and joined the industrial-commercial section of the petite bourgeoisie. All in all, disregarding the mosaic of the social class structure, the peasantry was polarizing into either bourgeoisie or proletariat, notwithstanding all of the transitional shades that lie between these two poles.

The social base of mukhtarship therefore declined. Like any other social form that outlives its time, mukhtarship became a comic existence. A number of mukhtars, for example, are collaborators, league members, etc. Other mukhtars still believe in the traditional symbols of power in spite of changing social conditions. Nevertheless, comic characters as a whole have a role in the social drama of occupation.

Village councils are a relatively new phenomenon in comparison to mukhtarship. Traditionally, the peasant class was socially organized into clans and had no village councils. Village councils should be regarded, then, as elements of the modern bourgeois state apparatus that came into being with the development of capitalism. They are therefore similar in essence to the municipalities in cities and towns; however, insofar as some councils are elected, they represent the general public will before the central authority and, at the same time, the central authority before the public will. The appointed village councils and mayors, on the other hand, derive their social power solely from the central authority and are regarded by the population as collaborators and mere state servants. Both the elected and the appointed village councils, however, have a definite relation to the central authority and are expected to perform services on its behalf.

In the first week of January 1988 the military governor summoned the mukhtars and the members of village councils in Beit Nuba, Ithna, Beit Kahel, and other localities in the Hebron area to his headquarters. He asked them to "calm down" the uprising in their respective villages and to provide him with information concerning the identities and activities of the "rioters" and "agitators."[11] Needless to say, the elected councils were not ready to cooperate with the military governor against the uprising, and the appointed councils needed the army to protect them from a mass movement that was already hostile to them. For example, in May 1988 the army raided the village of Beit Fajjar following the resignation of the appointed village council, because "the military governor was not convinced that the resignation . . . was without public pressure to implement Communiqué No. 13" of the United National Leadership of the Uprising. The army besieged the village, cutting off the water supply and conducting house-to-house searches and arrests. When the inhabitants collected water fees in a public meeting, the military governor refused to accept the money unless the council was restored, and warned them not to hold such meetings.[12] Popular committees clashed with the army for months over the village council issue. Finally, on November 18, 1988, new headquarters for the council were officially opened by the army, only to be burned, two days later, by the popular committees.[13]

Every method used throughout December 1987 to quell the uprising failed. The uprising was thought to be a transitory phenomenon that would not last for more than a few days beyond January 1, 1988—the birth date of the Fateh movement. When the uprising intensified in January, the Israeli military authorities declared three "new" policies in an attempt to quell it. The Chief of Staff of the Israeli army, Dan Shomron, started to view curfews as a major weapon to be used against the uprising,[14] while his superior, Israeli Minister of Defense Yitzhak Rabin, declared his economic war and "bone-breaking" policies to put an end to it.

Israeli generals have had the unique habit of declaring a "new" policy after, rather than before, its application in reality. For example, curfews, the economic war, and the bone-breaking policies had been used in December 1987, but were not declared as policy until January 1988. To "declare," then, meant to apply an older policy on a wider scale. Curfews, for instance, were imposed on 300,000 Palestinians on January 16, 1988, and on more than 1 million on November 15, 1988.

Meanwhile the uprising was manufacturing its own general strategy, which came to be known as civil disobedience, that is, to liquidate as much as possible all the different manifestations of the Israeli occupation in general, and the Israeli state apparatus in the Occupied Territories in particular, through diverse means: defying military orders, the nonpayment of taxes, resignation of police, boycotting of Israeli products, nonwork in Israel, resignation of village councils, liquidating the espionage network, and so on.

However, the direct aim of the militia of the uprising throughout January 1988 was the imposition of a general commercial strike, while the Israeli army aimed at the exact opposite, forcing shopkeepers to keep their shops open. Gradually, the commercial class was forming merchant committees and joining the movement. The question of the commercial strike became a central issue for several months. However, imposing a commercial strike was almost impossible without cutting off public transportation.

There are more than one hundred Palestinian bus companies, seventy-one running one bus each, and the biggest running thirty-one buses, in addition to tens of thousands of private and public vehicles that link the different population centers (cities, towns, villages, and refugee camps) to each other.[15] Cutting off transportation was extremely important in order to paralyze commercial life and to impose a general strike throughout the Occupied Territories. In addition, the army moved freely on the roads to and from the villages, and this freedom had to be restricted as much as possible. The village militia erected stone barriers everywhere, cutting off all transportation, and removed the barriers at specific times only. Needless to say, villages became virtually isolated and, within this relative isolation, the village militia felt itself prepared to extend its civil disobedience further: several villages were declared "liberated zones" under the rule of the militia. The notion of liberated zones meant that the army could not enter them. Palestinian flags were raised continuously, and the social order was in the hands of the militia.

THE UPRISING IN THE VILLAGES: FEBRUARY 1–MARCH 3, 1988

By the beginning of February 1988, a well-known Israeli journalist, Ze'ev Schiff, noted in *Ha'aretz* that "some areas got out of the army's hands."[16] Within these circumstances, a summons to the military headquarters or to the Shin Bet offices was no longer obeyed, and the army had to storm the villages to arrest or "break the bones" of whoever was wanted. Gradually, the phenomenon of political refugees in their own homeland was becoming noticeable: thousands were sleeping in hiding places, in fields, and on mountains. "Wanted!" has been the war-cry of the army since then.

Furthermore, the governmental school system was collapsing. The West Bank student body, comprising about 300,000 pupils, had been highly politicized prior to December 1987. To close schools was tempting to the Israeli state apparatus, since a center of the uprising would be crushed; but the closure of schools meant a further liquidation of the Israeli state apparatus itself, of which the school system had been a cornerstone. Finally, the Israeli state apparatus turned against itself and, on February 3, 1988, the schools were ordered closed.[17] Gradually, popular committees for education emerged to counter this move.

Meanwhile, the popular committees were preparing to liquidate the espionage network as much as possible. The espionage network is an extremely hated manifestation of occupation. A few months before the uprising, the Fahmawi case terrorized the population. Fahmawi was a child of about fourteen when the Shin Bet recruited him. He finally confessed to the following: some years later, in cooperation with a hairdressing salon, he drugged, raped, and videotaped tens of girls; using the tapes, he blackmailed them to become spies. Furthermore, he participated in poisoning about 1,000 schoolgirls in the West Bank in 1983; the poison case was termed "mass hysteria" by the Israeli government at the time and wholly denied.[18] However, the Fahmawi case was a highly controversial issue; some Palestinians dismissed it as "false" and "doubtful" on different grounds. The author of this article cannot verify the charges, but it is useful in illustrating the public attitude of distrust toward the espionage network.

On February 9, 1988, a spy was killed in Biddo village.[19] However, the real explosion happened in Qabatya when a well-known collaborator was killed and his body was found hanging from an electric pillar—most likely because he had killed a child earlier. Consequently, the army raided Qabatya and injured eighteen people, and on February 25 a curfew that lasted for a few weeks was imposed.[20] The eyes of the Occupied Territories were on Qabatya. Although killing spies was an old practice, it was not a popular one in the uprising, which used a different tactic to cope with spies: repentance. In a public confession, the spy revealed his secret career with the Shin Bet and repented. Spies were repenting throughout March 1988 in a large number of villages such as Kufr Ni'ami, 'Aarrabih, and Bil'een.[21]

The reaction of the Israeli state apparatus to the attack against the espionage network was collective punishment. But, ironically enough, the Shin Bet was eager to create inner village divisions of the divide and rule type, that is, to turn the uprising against itself. How? By turning the espionage network against itself. Lists of names of spies were distributed in several cities, refugee camps, and villages. According to public rumors, 90 percent of the names were correct, and the rest were names of ordinary people and militia members. All in all, this tactic failed. Another tactic was to direct spies to commit sabotage, such as robbing shops and cutting down trees.

Communiqué No. 10 of the United National Leadership of the Uprising, released in early March 1988, called for attacking spies, nonpayment of taxes, boycotting Israeli products, and the resignation of Palestinian policemen working for the Israeli state apparatus. All of these demands were to be implemented as much as possible in the villages, and confrontations with the army were to be intensified. Consequently, the phenomenon of the liberated villages or zones spread. The Israeli newspaper *Ha'aretz* talked in the first days of March about "the army's reoccupation of villages."[22] On March 23, 1988, Israeli television stated that traveling from Bani Na'im to Al-Shiokh villages in the Hebron area required a special force, and that the demonstrators of Al-Shiokh and the nearby Sa'ir villages had turned them into "closed areas."[23] Meanwhile, a village council resigned in the Hebron area, as did the council of Al Mizra'ah Al Sharkiyeh.[24]

Civil disobedience was extended in March to include about 1,000 policemen, and by March 15, 450 policemen had either resigned or had been given unpaid leave.[25] Palestinian owners of public and private means of transport were the most eager stratum in the villages to support police resignations. They had been subjected to various police measures that constituted a continuous chase after them for insurance, licenses, traffic violations, taxes, and so on. Since a certain percentage of policemen were of village origin and still resided in villages, and given the nature of police service, which involved being present in public places, the militia of the villages was able to exercise public pressure on a number of them to resign.

The Shin Bet, pushing its spies toward more actions of sabotage, wanted to prove that chaos would reign without a police force, while the militia wanted to prove the exact opposite, that is, that a social order based on police was a form of chaos and that a higher form of order would reign without policemen. Consequently, popular committees were formed to resolve conflicts, regulate traffic, and so on. Since then the Occupied Territories (excluding East Jerusalem) have been functioning without a police force, and the crime rate has in fact declined.

THE UPRISING IN THE VILLAGES: APRIL 1–MAY 31, 1988

When a certain social form is withering away, the irony of history brings its internal contradictions out into the open. We have seen that the Israeli state apparatus had turned against itself (distributing the names of its own spies, closing schools, etc.). These measures were counterproductive, and the economic war of Rabin backfired as well.

By the ''economic war'' is meant the totality of economic measures taken by Israel with the definite aim of quelling the uprising. In April and May 1988, cutting electricity, water supplies, and telecommunications as a form of collective economic punishment of villagers became a common practice. On April 6, for example, water reservoirs and the solar-heating system in Deir Jreer village were damaged by army bullets.[26] Toward the end of April and the first week of May, ten villages, among them Beit Illo, Beit Soureek, Biddo, and Attirah, were informed of the intention of the military governor to cut off the water supply if disturbances continued. Electricity was cut off in Bidya, Yitma, 'Atteel, and other locations.[27]

The economic war deepened the economic crisis and accelerated the return-to-the-land movement among the semi-proletariat and the petite bourgeoisie. These two social classes, owning their own parcels of land and working them with family labor, could depend on their own produce: thus, they found a way to boycott not only Israeli products but working in Israel as well. The return to the land became fashionable even for the urban middle class. Amanda Hitchison noted that

university professors in Ramallah are growing vegetables in their flower beds. Villagers are planting abandoned land and learning . . . how to irrigate crops with perforated plastic juice bottles, and how to turn an old fridge into a chicken incubator, using a dynamo, bits of a car, and plenty of silver foil. . . . the movement has given a quaint twist to the warfare: armed soldiers guard village threshing machines; troops prowl past vegetable plots measuring the size of courgettes, and the pink hue of tomatoes.[28]

Popular committees for agriculture were formed to conduct such activities.

Nevertheless, the Israeli state apparatus refrained from declaring a total economic war, that is, the economic war remained within "limits." The Israeli coordinator for the Occupied Territories, Shmuel Goren, stated that the military and the civil authorities were cognizant that they could not continue the policy of economic suffocation, and that to continue such a policy could lead to an uncontrollable explosion in an unexpected place.[29] By May 1988 it was clear enough that the uprising could not be crushed: the Israeli state apparatus could use neither its military might nor methods of total economic war. The uprising, by the same token, could not defeat the Israeli army with stones and slingshots. A certain balance of forces prevailed: a highly developed and armed state was forced to invent stone-throwing machines—it went back to the "stone age," to use an expression of Yitzhak Rabin himself. The jeep's chase after the kid of Qabatya continued. The same Shmuel Goren, on May 14, 1988, coined a special term to designate such a chase that became an absolute dogma for a few months in the Israeli media: "relative calm."[30]

Relative calm meant, in fact, getting accustomed to injuries, prisons, deaths, military campaigns, and curfews.

The Israeli soldier, Kestenbaum, who served in Qabatya noticed

a kind of obscene competition among the standing army units to see who is the most feared. Nahal arrived for 3 hours of "support" as they called it. For one afternoon they ran about the town looking to impose the curfew and beating up anyone they could find. The Golani youngsters are particularly trigger happy and shoot at any provocation. . . . Among the soldiers a depressing routine of wild abandon. Everyone here makes up their own rules. The young officers see our job as some kind of game and their behavior ranges from callousness to pure sadism. . . . The reaction among the soldiers is frightening. They have almost become de-sensitized to the human misery around them.[31]

Another experience of an Israeli officer is revealing enough. He served in the Occupied Territories and registered his confession on a cassette that was sent by Israeli Knesset member Dedi Zucker to the military police. The officer said that he and his soldiers persecuted Arabs on the Jewish religious holiday, Yom Kippur. Stripping people of all their clothes and leading them to orchards, the soldiers tied them up and released dogs at them. They then chained and tied them to tree trunks for the entire night. The officer and his soldiers established a "private" prison surrounded by barbed wire for "drying the Arabs in the sun" and baking them. "You have to understand that the issue is about harsh conditions, severe cold in the night and dogs and unbearable heat in the day," the officer confessed. The story was revealed when the officer was interviewed by the Israeli newspaper *Yerushalaim* on October 7, 1988.[32]

THE UPRISING IN THE VILLAGES: JUNE 1–SEPTEMBER 30, 1988

Let us now have a look at the "limits" of the economic war up to September 1988. When the uprising started in December 1987 there had already been a deep economic crisis. The economic war of Yitzhak Rabin deepened this crisis and, consequently, the uprising escalated.

In the first four months of the uprising, the West Bank's gross domestic product declined by 29 percent, the rate of employment by 36 percent, and individual consumption by 28 percent, according to Israeli television on August 29, 1988.[33] Nevertheless, the Israeli state apparatus aimed at quelling the uprising through pushing the limits of Rabin's economic war further and further. The Israeli civil administration in the Occupied Territories, for example, used to channel part of the public money collected from different Palestinian social classes to about 4,000 needy Palestinian families, but this help was abolished as a form of economic war. On May 30, 1988, in a telegram asking the cancellation of this decision, an Israeli Knesset member, Jady Yetsib, described the decision as fighting the uprising through hunger.[34] To punish about 58,000 people who received medical services from the governmental health apparatus in the Occupied Territories, the fees for medical services rose and nonparticipants in government insurance (the majority) had to pay from 25 to 118 percent more for the same services.[35]

Pushing the limits accelerated more and more. For example, in the week of June 9–15, 1988, a total of 5,600 Palestinian trees were destroyed and 200 dunums of crops burned. A total of eighteen villages suffered the consequences of this week-long sabotage.[36] All in all, more than 100,000 trees, mostly olives, were destroyed in the first year of the uprising.[37] The economic collective punishment did not spare any social class or section of a class in the villages and in the entire Palestinian society. Nevertheless, the economic crisis hit the lower classes in particular.

The uprising is, as mentioned before, essentially a movement of the lower classes, especially the working class and the semi-working class. For example, a sample of 160 people killed between December 9, 1987, and October 17, 1988, reveals that 44 percent were wage-workers, 33 percent pupils, 5 percent university students, 5 percent housewives, 3 percent children below six years of age, 3 percent farmers, 2 percent office employees, 1 percent intellectual professionals, 2 percent craftsmen, and 2 percent merchants and other categories. In the Gaza Strip, a total of 137 were killed between December 8, 1987, and December 1, 1988; of these, 45 percent were wage workers, 29 percent students, 9 percent housewives, 7 percent craftsmen and merchants, and 10 percent children below the age of five.[38] Needless to say, housewives, students, and children do not form social classes in themselves—the majority of them belong to the working class, the semi-working class, and the petite bourgeoisie. All in all, the lower classes form the overwhelming majority of the cases. Furthermore, a sociological survey done on a sample of 3,196 prisoners registered in the files of the Union of Lawyers in the Gaza Strip shows that 1,605 were workers (employed and unemployed) and 983 were students.[39]

The top of the social class structure, that is, big capitalists and big landed proprietors and their political representatives, had their own political program: the so-called confederation with Jordan. In other words, their program, which consisted of annexing the Occupied Territories to Jordan, was (and continues to be) the exact opposite of the program of the lower classes, which consisted (and continues to consist) of the establishment of an independent Palestinian state in the West Bank and the Gaza Strip. The uprising was bound to come into open conflict with big capital and big landed property. The majority of the population was moving ahead with the independent Palestinian state program. By May 1988 it had become clear that sooner or later big capital and big landed property would give in. Finally, King Hussein was forced to sever legal and administrative ties with the Occupied Territories on July 31, 1988. Consequently, the confederation program was damaged.

This damage left the Israeli jeep face to face with the barefooted kid of Qabatya, that is, with the uprising. It became necessary for Israel to push the limits further in order to fill the so-called vacuum left by Jordan. Meanwhile, the uprising was gradually pushing the whole of the PLO to turn the collapse of the confederation program into a political victory, that is, into a clear and realistic political program in which the two-state solution was clearly expressed.

On September 10, 1988, the spokesman of the Israeli army declared a ''new'' strategy: the army was to besiege one or several localities at a time, and then sweep through the area with ''a very fine comb.'' This strategy was meant to quell the uprising through a systematic military campaign. As usual, the ''new'' strategy had been applied earlier, on September 6, 1988, in Qalqilya.[40] Following the declaration of the new strategy, the Israeli army carried out raids on several villages in the northern West Bank situated between Tulkarem and Jenin. In two days no less than thirteen villages were raided.[41] This policy has been fashionable since then. On October 9, 1988, a total of thirty-five villages were raided and ''combed.''[42] On October 19 more than twenty villages went through the same process. The economic war was pushed to new limits as well. Let us have a look at the dimensions of the economic war as a whole throughout the first year of the uprising.

The only comprehensive field study, done on a sample of eight villages, reveals the following: 95 percent of 2,000 dunums of vegetable crops and 60 percent of 2,000 dunums of cereal crops in Ithna village were destroyed; 80 percent of 1,650 dunums of the early plum harvest, 50 percent of 2,500 dunums of the late plum harvest, and 40 percent of 4,000 dunums of grapes, in addition to fifteen tractors, were destroyed in Beit Ummar village; 100 percent of 400 dunums of irrigated vegetables, 90 percent of 2,000 dunums of rainfed vegetables, 80 percent of 1,000 dunums of grapes, and 1 million seedlings were destroyed in Qabatya; 90 percent of 100 dunums of figs, and 100 olive trees were destroyed in 'Azzoun village; 80 percent of 2,000 dunums of melons, 50 percent of 2,000 dunums of irrigated vegetables, and 10 percent of 1,500 dunums of bananas were destroyed in Al'Oja village, etc. The total losses of the eight villages amounted to 2,399,800 Jordanian dinars, or about 7 million U.S. dollars.[43]

Nevertheless, pushing the limits of economic war further was needed. On September 8, 1988, the civil administration forbade farmers in the Halhoul area, where a considerable percentage of West Bank grapes is produced, from marketing their grapes in Jordan; about 15,000 farmers suffered major losses estimated at several million U.S. dollars.[44] In the Nablus area agricultural products were sold at 40–60 percent less than their cost due to diverse sanctions against agriculture.[45]

If we put aside the economic war, the September 6 military campaign against Qalqilya became, to a considerable degree, a model for the subsequent campaigns against villages. Two Israeli journalists, Joel Greenberg and Joshua Brilliant, gave the following account of the Qalqilya campaign:

The 25,000 residents of Qalqilya remained under curfew for the eighth consecutive day, as troops continued searching homes for suspected activists. Residents say the curfew had been lifted once for two hours, and there was a shortage of fresh foodstuffs and milk for infants. Electricity and water supplies had been periodically interrupted, and fruit trees and other crops . . . were being damaged because of lack of irrigation during the curfews, residents say. Phone links . . . remain cut . . . residents charged that the troops had broken into homes and damaged furniture, and converted the local high school into a makeshift prison, holding some 400 detainees.[46]

The Qalqilya campaign was quickly followed by similar ones against several villages, such as Kufr Sur, Kufr Zeibad, Kufr Jammal, and others.

The remote villages were targeted because they had been taken over by activists and turned into so called "liberated zones." Classes had been organized at local schools in defiance of a military closure, activists had blocked roads with rocks and searched incoming vehicles for Israeli products, broadcast communiques over loudspeakers, and interrogated and assaulted one person suspected of cooperating with [the Israeli] security authorities.[47]

The limits of the economic war, and the military campaigns as well, were pushed further toward damaging the olive season in October 1988. Different villages received threats that they would not be allowed to pick their olives. The warning was delivered to Azzawyeh village on September 4; on September 10 settlers burned 500 dunums of crops and trees, including 1,000 olive trees and 2,000 almond trees.[48] On September 26, 1988, the army delivered a clear message to Jayyous village: it imposed a curfew, rounded up all males over the age of fifteen, then took them to a nearby valley and delivered the message that they would not be allowed to pick their olives if "disturbances continued." Moreover, taxes were imposed on olive presses ranging between 500 and 10,000 Jordanian dinars. These taxes were sometimes higher than the yearly income from a typical olive press. Other olive presses were simply closed by military orders, such as the five olive presses of Bal'aa village.

Plastic bullets, introduced in August 1988, were a further military incarnation of "the very fine comb." Israeli Defense Minister Yitzhak Rabin summed up the point of plastic bullets at a press conference on September 27, 1988: "The rioters are suffering more casualties. This is precisely our aim."[49] Plastic bullets, according to *Hadashot,* an Israeli newspaper, are 70 percent zinc, 20 percent glass, and 10 percent hard plastic material.

THE UPRISING IN THE VILLAGES: OCTOBER 1–NOVEMBER 15, 1988

The collapse of the confederation program, that is, the program of big capital and landed property, left the program of the uprising as the only alternative for the solution of the Palestinian question. This latter program needs to be clarified. The PLO as a whole, from July 31, 1988, was moving toward adopting the two-state—Palestine and Israel—solution. The Israeli government felt that such a move on the part of the PLO would transform the uprising into an international political victory; thus, the uprising would be injected with new power, and it would escalate.

On October 19, 1988, newspapers reported that the Israeli security apparatus had been drawing plans to counter the new wave of the uprising. The new plans, in fact, were nothing more than pushing the limits of the economic war toward sabotaging the olive season, accompanied with military campaigns on a wider scale.

In the week of October 5–11, 1988, more than 50 villages were raided, a curfew was imposed on 27 areas, 334 people were injured, and 2 were killed.[50] By January, 1989, injuries in the Gaza Strip following the use of plastic bullets increased by 600 percent.

Burning and bulldozing olive trees, preventing villagers from picking olives, closing, raiding, and taxing olive presses, chasing villagers with helicopters and troops, imposing curfews, impounding agricultural machinery, and declaring olive-tree areas "closed military areas" were only some of the methods used to halt the harvest during the olive season. The case of Burka village (population about 3,500) is not a particularly unusual example of these methods: the only petrol station was ordered closed, a curfew was imposed, fifteen agricultural machines were impounded, picking olives was forbidden, food was banned from entering the village, including milk for children, and tens of youths were severely beaten.[51] The degree to which this economic and military war had accelerated from the Burka case in early October to November 15, 1988, is illustrated in the following example.

On October 7, 1988, the army raided seventy villages in a campaign that was meant to continue for several days.[52] However, about fourteen villages were not able to pick their olives until October 29, and this was far from a total economic war, that is, the economic war remained within "limits." The olive season, ironically enough, was the best in the last ten years, with an estimated surplus of 20,000 tons of olive oil. But Jordan, which had never forgotten the collapse of the confederation program, came to the help of Rabin, and on October 26, 1988, declared its intention of not importing West Bank olive oil. Jordan's political motivation was clear: it refused for a while even to allow olive oil to be exported via Jordan.

Meanwhile, a very unusual phenomenon occurred in Salem village: the militia of the uprising organized a military march, with uniforms and ceremonies, on October 3.[53] A similar parade had been organized in the city of Nablus. The military ceremonies among the militia members in several areas were a new phenomenon to the Israeli security apparatus.[54] The embryo of a popular army for the future state of Palestine had been born.

The climax of the October and November battle was reached when the PLO declared the establishment of an independent Palestinian state. On the day of independence, November 15, 1988, a curfew was imposed on more than 1 million Palestinians (in the entire Gaza Strip and thirty-one areas in the West Bank). All of the occupied state of Palestine was cut off from the external world, the entire Gaza Strip and the West Bank were declared a "closed military area," transportation between cities and villages was forbidden, and electricity was cut off in the entire Gaza Strip and most of the West Bank.[55] The army wanted to repress all possible forms of Palestinian celebrations of independence, and Palestinians were eager to dance. For a few weeks the battle raged between soldiers and "dancers." Nevertheless, December 1988 was the bloodiest month of the uprising: thirty-one Palestinians were killed and hundreds more were injured.

NOTES

1. Meron Benvenisti, in a press conference, October 18, 1988. Reported in *al-Ittihad*, October 19, 1988.

2. Dr. Samir Abdallah, "Data on the Occupied Territories," unpublished study, n.d., p. 1 (in Arabic).

3. Interview with Muharram Bargouti, former General Secretary of the Higher Committee of Voluntary Work Committees in the West Bank. Emile Sahliyeh puts it in the following terms: "[The voluntary work program's] original aim was to mobilize mass support for the communists," although "its activities were geared to economic development." *In Search of Leadership: West Bank Politics Since 1967* (Washington, D.C.: Brookings Institution, 1988), p. 106.

4. Sami Khader, "Illiteracy Among Palestinian Women: Realities, Effects, and Suggested Developmental Plans," *al-Katib*, no. 101 (September 1988): 55 (in Arabic).

5. Joel Greenberg, "A Soldier's Diary," *Jerusalem Post Magazine*, September 16, 1988.

6. *Al-Ittihad*, December 9, 1987.

7. Ibid., December 12/13, 1987.

8. Translated in ibid., December 23, 1987.

9. *At-Tali'a* (weekly), December 24, 1987.

10. Salim Tamari, "What the Uprising Means," *Middle East Report*, no. 152 (May-June 1988): 25.

11. *At-Tali'a*, January 7, 1988.

12. Ibid., May 5 and 12, 1988.

13. *Al-Quds*, November 21, 1988.

14. *At-Tali'a*, January 14, 1988.

15. Meron Benvenisti, *The West Bank and Gaza Atlas* (Jerusalem: Jerusalem Post Books, 1988), p. 36.

16. Translated in *al-Ittihad*, February 5, 1988.

17. *At-Tali'a*, April 14, 1988. See also *al-Ittihad*, February 4, 1988.

18. Information contained in an undated underground leaflet entitled "The Victim Confesses" (in Arabic).

19. *Al-Ittihad*, March 9, 1988.

20. Ibid., February 25/26, 1988.

21. Ibid., March 8, 1988.

22. *At-Tali'a*, March 7, 1988 (translation).

23. Ibid., April 1, 1988.

24. Ibid., March 10, 1988.

25. *Al-Ittihad*, March 15/16, 1988.

26. *At-Tali'a*, April 7, 1988.

27. Ibid., May 5, 1988.

28. Amanda Hitchison, "Palestine: How Does Your Garden Grow," *New Statesman and Society*, June 21, 1988.

29. *At-Tali'a*, May 19, 1988.

30. Ibid.

31. Greenberg, "Soldier's Diary."

32. Translated in *Ash-Sha'b* and *al-Nahar*, October 11, 1988.

33. Reported in *al-Nahar*, August 30, 1988.

34. *At-Tali'a*, June 9, 1988.

35. Ibid., July 21, 1988.

36. Ibid., June 16, 1988.

37. Ibid., December 8, 1988.

38. Ibid.

39. Rashad Madani, "Truths and Opinions on the Uprising," *al-Ittihad*, November 3, 1988 (in Arabic).

40. *Al-Bayader As-Siassi* (weekly), September 17, 1988, pp. 15–20.

41. *Al-Ittihad*, September 11, 12, 13, 1988.

42. *Al-Quds*, October 10, 1988.

43. *The Siege of Agriculture: Examples of Israeli Sanctions Against Agriculture in the Occupied Territories During the Palestinian Uprising* (Jerusalem: Jerusalem Media and Communication Center, October 1988).

44. *Al-Quds*, December 9, 1988. See also *al-Nahar*, September 16, 1988, and *at-Tali'a*, October 6, 1988.

45. *Al-Nahar*, September 28, 1988.

46. *Jerusalem Post*, September 15, 1988.

47. Ibid.

48. *Al-Quds*, September 11, 1988. See also *al-Ittihad*, September 17, 1988.

49. *Jerusalem Post*, September 28, 1988.

50. *At-Tali'a*, October 11, 1988.

51. *Al-Ittihad* and *Ash-Sha'b*, October 16 , 1988.

52. *Al-Quds* and *Ash-Sha'b*, October 8, 1988.

53. *Al-Ittihad*, October 4, 1988. Other marches were organized in Tamoun and Tamra villages; *al-Ittihad*, October 23, 1988.

54. *Ash-Sha'b*, October 20, 1988.

55. *Al-Quds*, November 16, 1988.

8

From Salons to the Popular Committees

PALESTINIAN WOMEN, 1919–1989

Islah Jad

One of the distinguishing features of the uprising is the spontaneous but organized role of Palestinian women, which has commanded admiration nationally and internationally. Women are in the forefront of popular demonstrations; they confront soldiers, save the men, rescue the injured, and inform merchants of strike days. The pictures of women and girls in the media, though representing only a small part of the intense role of women, have invited many questions.

Is this role new to Palestinian women? What precise part are they playing in the *intifada?* How do men and the United National Leadership of the Uprising (UNLU) regard women's roles? Does the participation of women reflect a new stage in the history of the women's movement? Are the political role and the sacrifices of women in the uprising going to improve women's social status and their political role in the future?

This chapter attempts to answer these questions, first placing women's activities in historical context. It is based on various sources, including published studies; interviews with old and young female leaders; publications of women's groups and associations containing their political and practical programs; women's yearly reports, magazines, and irregular publications (sometimes special issues); and their publications on national occasions and International Women's Day. Findings are also based on the author's personal witness to specific events. Unfortunately, both the negligence regarding women's roles and problems on the part of society at large, and Israeli repressive policies since 1967 in the area of research and publication, have led to a dearth of serious writings on Palestinian women.

THE EMERGENCE OF THE PALESTINIAN NATIONAL MOVEMENT AND WOMEN'S WORK

Women's activities in Palestine are relatively recent, since social conditions at the beginning of this century restricted their autonomous development. In farming communities, they were responsible for ploughing and planting the field, but also bore full responsibility for the children, kitchen, and laundry. There is a consensus in our sources that women worked more than men. The economic role of rural women gave them the experience of mixing with men and liberated them from wearing the veil, unlike city women. Yet women's important economic role did not improve their social status, since the attitudes, values, and traditions of Palestinian society at the turn of the century were condescending to them. In the presence of a patriarchal and reactionary society based on religion and its laws, women were prevented from inheriting the land, and their role was considered a part of housework. In the cities, women's status was much worse. Women had to stay home at age sixteen to be prepared for a husband who often had other wives. This resulted in the segregation of men and women in the cities, with the latter usually hiding behind a complete facial veil.[1] Nonetheless, interaction with the West, which intensified during the late nineteenth century, and the spread of governmental and Western missionary schools, brought women in cities and small villages into contact with the outside world. Christian families in the cities were the main beneficiaries, while women in rural areas rarely got an education. It is therefore small wonder that Christian middle- and upper-class women formed the nucleus of the first women's associations in Palestine, beginning in 1903. The associations were limited to charitable services. They did not have a program or a center but held their meetings in private homes, schoolrooms, and churches.

After World War I, a new stage of women's activity developed. With the dissolution of the Ottoman empire, Palestine came under a British mandate whose first goal was to secure a national homeland for Jews. This sparked the Palestinian national movement to come into existence, and it in turn gave birth to the Palestinian women's movement.

Under the British mandate, two major factors influenced the forms, development, aims, and limitations of women's work:

1. The focus on ending the occupation, a common trait of women's movements under occupation, unlike those in independent countries, where the struggle is for freedom within the society.

2. The leaders and members of the women's associations and the national movement under the mandate consisted of upper-class people in the cities.[2] The class nature of the Palestinian movement's vanguard at that time dictated the type of activities carried

out, which were charitable and humanitarian in nature. During that period some women in the cities participated in demonstrations on national occasions, such as the demonstrations of February 1920 and March 1921.[3]

Women protested alongside men against land sales to Zionists, the expulsion of peasants from their lands, and increasing Jewish immigration to Palestine. In August 1929, out of 120 Arabs killed by the British as they put down nationalist protests, 9 were women.

The first women's conference was held in Jerusalem in 1929; it was chaired by the wife of the Arab executive committee head, Musa Hatem al-Husaini.[4] More than 200 women attended, most of them wives and relatives of political leaders or notables, or rich women. The resolutions of the conference were similar to those of the Arab executive committee and included the rejection of the Balfour declaration and Jewish immigration. After the conference, the women drove out and demonstrated in their cars, roamed the streets of Jerusalem, passed by the foreign consulates, and stopped at the British governor's home. A delegation of women took off their veils, saying, "To serve our homeland we shall take off our veil!" and presented a memorandum with their demands.[5]

Although the creation of the Arab Women's Committee in 1929 marked a milestone of sorts, as it provided a framework for women's activities and contributed to developing the general awareness of its members, women were still not involved in the existing political parties due to sex segregation. Women went out in demonstrations surrounded by scouts for protection or in a single group marching behind men. Women's conferences and demonstrations increased after 1933, and notably during the 1936–39 revolt, but in general participation remained limited to upper-class women or students.[6] Women in the countryside helped in transporting weapons and food, and donated their jewelry to buy arms. Women hardly took part in the actual fighting, nor did they work as nurses, except in a few cases.[7] In 1948 the Jewish state was established in Palestine. Palestinians were expelled from 20 cities and 400 villages. At least 10,000 Palestinians were killed, while triple that number were wounded. Sixty percent of the Palestinians became homeless.

The wholesale destruction of a society led to a new phenomenon in 1949, that of refugee camps relying on donations for survival. One million people were involved. Three out of four Palestinians found themselves living in a state of poverty.[8] The majority at first lived on relief. Men tended to leave the camps in Palestine (the West Bank, including Jerusalem, and Gaza Strip) seeking work. Refugee camps thus became havens for women, children, and the elderly.[9] In that part of Palestine which remained outside the Jewish state, six charitable associations were established to meet the needs of an expelled and destroyed nation. Educating girls was a high priority, for it meant getting a degree and a better job than serving and sewing, the only jobs available for camp women. UNRWA also offered some services in teaching and opened training centers.

With the annexation of the West Bank by Jordan in 1950, Palestinian men and women formed the national movement in Jordan, and women became members in underground political groups such as the Jordanian Communist party, the Ba'th party, and the Arab Nationalist Movement. Nevertheless, these parties did not give enough attention to issues of women's freedom and emancipation. Out of fear of the prevailing traditional values, women members were asked not to challenge society. Women members had their own party cells, an extension of sex segregation in society. Women's activities were restricted to secretarial work, typing services, signing petitions, and delivering messages and communiqués.[10] Women members were either students, educated women, or relatives of male members. But the lasting consequence of women's work in political parties was the gradual emergence of experienced female cadres, who were to play a significant role in confronting the Israeli occupation as of 1967.[11]

Women's status in the Gaza Strip during the 1949–67 period was similar to that of women under Jordanian rule in terms of their bad economic situation and men's emigration. The area was at that time under Egyptian military rule, nondemocratic, though nationalist, in nature. Here too, then, women were the backbone of refugee camp life.

Some women participated in political parties in Gaza, whether the Palestinian Communist party (for example, Samira Saba and Mahba' al-Barbari, women communist leaders arrested in August 1952),[12] the Ba'th party (which as of 1954 included a women's section headed by May Sayegh), or the Arab National Movement. Some charitable associations provided services in refugee camps by opening nurseries, mother and child centers, and literacy centers, or by teaching simple skills such as sewing, weaving, and embroidery. By 1967 there were sixty-eight associations in Nablus, Jerusalem, Hebron, and Gaza. Most of them, however, were apolitical.[13]

The General Union of Palestinian Women (GUPW) was formed in 1965 as a consequence of the Palestinian conference in Jerusalem in 1964, which established the PLO. The GUPW was created as a mass organization to participate in liberating the homeland.[14] Due to the way it was formed and its membership, it continued the strategy of the charitable associations by "giving services to women."[15] It did not deal with social questions, since its leadership consisted of privileged, socially liberated women. Furthermore, until 1967 the PLO itself was not popular in nature. Although it was associated with some progressive Arab regimes, it lacked a clear program for resistance.

THE 1967 DEFEAT AND ITS EFFECTS ON THE PALESTINIAN WOMEN'S MOVEMENT

The 1967 defeat led to the occupation of what remained of Palestine, the West Bank and Gaza Strip. From the beginning Israel acted to destructure Palestinian society, with a view to integrating it into and subjugating it to the Israeli economic system. This policy resulted in socioeconomic changes that affected the family and, in turn, Palestinian women.

Women under occupation thus entered the labor market. They took up unskilled jobs at low wages in relation to those of Arab men, which were, in turn, lower than those of Israeli workers. Women also worked in the absence of any attempt to apportion housework between the sexes, which caused them psychological stress, in addition to the stress-provoking nature of the work they tended to find, which was temporary and dependent on the fluctuations of the Israeli market. Working women's oppression under Israeli rule was therefore threefold: as Palestinians, as workers, as women.

WOMEN AND THE PLO

The 1967 defeat transformed the PLO into a mass representative organization, which it has remained to the present time. Its program called for reliance on "the people in arms" rather than "Arab armies" for the task of liberation. Although such slogans lacked clarity, they helped focus on the need to organize various social categories, including women. But the Palestinian resistance organizations failed to establish an agenda for women as part of the overall agenda of the revolution. Certain slogans were formulated in lieu of such an agenda, for example, "Women will be liberated when society is" or "Men and women— side by side in the battle."[16]

In the Occupied Territories, women confronted the occupation through the channels of the charitable organizations and the General Union of Palestinian Women, both of which were linked to the Palestinian leadership embodied in the National Guidance Committee (established in 1967; disbanded in 1969). In the early days of the occupation Israel ignored women, since only a handful were actually imprisoned. However, by 1968 women prisoners totalled 100, mainly accused of contacting fedayeen, concealing weapons, incitement, or membership in armed organizations.

The National Front followed the National Guidance Committee in leading the Palestinian people in the Occupied Territories, in the wake of the defeat of the Palestinian armed resistance in Jordan in 1970–71. It consisted of active personalities and leaders, including one woman whose role was to coordinate the mobilization of women in resistance to occupation.[17] The Palestinian National Front (PNF) encouraged voluntary work projects in various areas. For the first time, young men and women worked together and discussed their problems. Women participated in armed struggle and airplane hijacking; they were tortured and imprisoned, thus changing the concept that women are weak creatures and undermining the concept of "women's honor."[18] The number of women enrolled and organized in political and military organizations in the West Bank and Gaza in turn led to an increase in the number of women prisoners, which had by 1979 reached 3,000.[19]

In 1975 and 1976 student organizations were created to organize men and women, such as the Palestine Student Union, the Committee of Secondary Students (in 1975), and the Union of Secondary Students (in 1976). The creation of these organizations led to more demonstrations and increased participation by women.[20]

The charitable organizations likewise organized women to demonstrate, sending them into the streets. But all these activities were sporadic and somewhat improvised, based as they were on national issues and slogans. Women's issues were looked down on as not worth considering. This may have been due partly to the de facto restriction of membership to middle-class women from the major cities, which limited their influence with the camp and rural women. The only relationship between activist women and the masses was in giving them assistance in cash and in kind. This was notably the case for the In'ash Al Usrah (Family Rehabilitation) Society in al-Bireh, which focused on distributing material for embroidery to village women. It likewise provided some medical assistance and vocational training. The main goal was to help women face their harsh conditions in the event of death, deportation, or imprisonment of the man. These services are doubtless important in the absence of a national authority. But by carrying out the PNF's directives and linking their work to the general struggle of women at a strictly "national" level, the charitable organizations were mobilizing women only sporadically and in a limited fashion.[21]

Although the PNF was progressively dismantled by Israel from 1974 to 1977, it fulfilled its function of directing and channeling protest activities. Several other factors also contributed to the mounting involvement of women in political resistance in the West Bank and Gaza Strip from 1975 to 1978:

1. Women were granted the right to vote for the first time in the 1976 municipal elections, through an Israeli military order amending the 1955 Jordanian electoral law, and enfranchising all people over twenty-one. Defense Minister Shimon Peres had made the mistaken calculation that Arab women would tend to vote conservatively. In fact, they voted heavily in favor of nationalist and progressive candidates.[22]

   With this revolutionary transformation of two dozen town and city councils, bringing a younger and far more progressive leadership to the forefront, work with the masses assumed a new dimension. Various municipalities organized work camps (most notably in the Bethlehem–Jerusalem–Ramallah–Al-Bireh area) that became breeding grounds for women activists.

2. In the mid and late seventies, nine colleges and community colleges (four- and two-year undergraduate institutions) opened, heavily attended by young women (who made up from 35 to 55 percent of various student bodies).

3. The election in 1977 of the Likud government of Begin-Shamir-Sharon led immediately to a significant escalation in repressive measures taken against the Occupied Territories and their inhabitants. As might have been expected, this palpably heightened repression led to greater determination and resistance, not least among women, many activists among whom were placed under house arrest. In the case of the charitable associations, the new Likud policy did some damage, since decision making was restricted to a few members, and their detention at home or in prison tended to paralyze the working of the organization. But student organizations, which included women among their cadres, elected their leadership democratically and in a decentralized manner.

They and the new women's organizations were able to escape some of the effects of the repression. The role of charitable organizations in relation to student and women's organizations therefore began to decline.

4. Some of the cultural activities of the mid-1970s dealt increasingly with women's issues. This was true of theatrical performances, magazine articles, and even entire books.

This sequence of interrelated developments throughout the 1970s finally resulted in the birth in 1978 of a new women's vanguard within the Palestinian national movement in the Occupied Territories.

THE EMERGENCE OF A VANGUARD FOR THE PALESTINIAN WOMEN'S MOVEMENT, 1978

The experiences of the Palestinian National Front, and the National Guidance Committee had shown the importance of public efforts to organize the masses. The mass organizations were associated with PLO factions; each one sought to strengthen its following. Labor unions, voluntary work organizations, and women's organizations were all duly factionalized. And while it is true that a single organization would have sufficed in each case, this partisanship did have the advantage of increasing the numbers of people organized, by appealing to the partisans of all the political groups. It was also much harder to destroy these new organizations than the old ones.

FIRST ATTEMPTS

For these reasons, and against the background of the intensity of national resistance in 1976, International Women's Day, March 8, 1978, was especially important. Some activist women held a meeting which resulted in the creation of the Women's Work Committee. It was largely made up of that generation of women who worked in political organizations and were not welcomed in the existing women's charitable associations. Despite their minor political role, the charitable organizations were concerned with preserving their position and power. The Women's Work Committee included the cadre of women who had emerged from various voluntary work camps, which proliferated especially after the 1976 municipal elections.

Although the Women's Work Committee was initially made up of active cadres without regard to political affiliation, soon enough a partisan power struggle emerged within its ranks. The only solution found was for each faction to establish its own women's mass organization, as was happening in other sectors, notably the trade unions. One therefore witnessed the successive creation of the Union of Palestinian Working Women's Committees (March 1980), the Palestinian Women's Committee (later the Union of Palestinian Women's Committees [March 1981]), and the Women's Committee for Social Work (June 1982). The division of the women's movement, which continues to the present, does not reflect differences in the agenda and goals of the different groups. Everybody's first goal is to involve the greatest possible number of women in the national movement. The achievement of this goal required flexible conditions of membership, such as attending meetings, the adoption of the organization's goal, and participation in decision making. This flexibility (contrary to the membership conditions of the charitable organizations) enabled women from different social classes to participate; thus, the women's movement was not restricted to middle-class women as in the past.[23]

The first goal of all these organizations is political. However, "emancipating Palestinian women" is an item in the agendas of all the organizations, specifically the left-oriented ones. Several demands are made in the quest for women's emancipation, such as equality with men in the form of equal pay for equal work, and various types of social protection for working women. What is meant by "women's social issues," then, takes the form of equality in general, dealing with union skills and qualifications. Accordingly, in the women's publications we find no mention of the laws that govern woman's status in society, or of the traditional values that still reinforce the tribal and patriarchal culture, especially for rural women. Many issues concerning gender are avoided.

The organizations have avoided such a discussion either because they actually believe it is not a priority in the period of national struggle or because they are afraid to open an internal front at a crucial time demanding the unity of all efforts to end the occupation.

In any event, there is a common and strong belief within the women's vanguard that the rising generation of Palestinian leaders cannot ignore the role of Palestinian women in resistance and that women are going to be liberated through a change in the laws. The leadership of the independent Palestinian state will, it is hoped, change the laws that govern women's status in society and thus liberate them.

The methods adopted by the women's groups do not differ in form from the charitable organization's methods. Some of these are establishing nurseries, training programs, literacy centers, workshops, and cooperatives. The major difference between the former and the latter lies in the people who supervise such projects and their awareness. Their level of political consciousness helps in transforming that of the participants and in giving them self-confidence through shared decision making, taking decisions by vote, holding elections, deciding on agendas in common, and so on. All projects undertaken by the women's organizations provide a permanent pool for various national or women's activities, whether in the village, refugee camp, or city. The project here is not a goal in itself but a means to achieve a future goal. Sometimes, especially during intense factional conflict, the increase in the number of these projects is taken as a measure of the strength of a given political faction. In spite of all these overlapping efforts, the number of organized women is still low, not exceeding 3 percent of the population.[24]

THE PALESTINIAN WOMEN'S MOVEMENT AND THE *INTIFADA*

Palestinian women have played a major role in the *intifada* since its beginning.[25] Many observers were surprised at this massive role. It was not new, however, for Palestinian women to take on a political role in society, especially in emergencies, as seen above. What was new, as will be discussed, was the scope and various manifestations of this role.

From the start, women of all ages and social classes took part in the demonstrations that broke out on December 9, 1987, throwing stones, burning tires, transporting and preparing stones, building roadblocks, raising Palestinian flags, and preventing soldiers from arresting people. These activities were most intense in poor neighborhoods in the towns, in villages, and in refugee camps. Women's actions were sometimes violent, and they were often involved in serious confrontations with the army.[26]

The role of women was duly acknowledged in leaflets distributed in Gaza in December 1987, which urged them to continue. With the spread of the *intifada* to the villages, towns, and cities of the West Bank and with the publication of the communiqués of the United National Leadership of the Uprising, women, like other sectors of society, were called upon to participate in different protest activities: "Oh people of martyrs . . . Oh revolutionary giants . . . Men and students . . . Our workers, peasants and women . . . the land shall be burned under the feet of the occupiers." The language of such appeals differs from that of the appeals issued by the National Committees or the Arab Higher Committee in the 1936–39 Palestinian revolt. The 1936–39 leaflets read, "Youngsters of Palestine, men, elderly people," without mentioning women. This evolution in the language reflects the importance of the present political role of women.[27] In contrast, the four women's organizations distributed a political leaflet on October 1, 1988, to protest the deportation of nine activists and addressed to "the heroic masses of our Palestinian people, the heroes of the great intifada . . . " without mentioning women except in the sentence "heroic masses of our people, your intifada has reached the whole world . . . and Palestinian women have thrilled with joy."[28]

Before March 8, 1988 (International Women's Day), the women's organizations did not have a clear agenda specifying the forms women's participation should take. It was left for the UNLU to call upon women as well as other sectors. Thus, each women's organization separately, or all four together, organized the activities called for by the UNLU, such as demonstrating and holding marches and sit-ins. The weekly average of women's demonstrations in the West Bank and Gaza Strip—as recorded through March 8, 1988—was 115 demonstrations, during which 16 women from different places were killed.[29]

THE FIRST COMPREHENSIVE PROGRAM

The first leaflet containing a comprehensive program and addressing women was distributed on March 8, 1988, by the four women's organizations and the charitable associations, signed "Palestinian Women in the Occupied Territories." The leaflet reads:

Our heroic women, mothers of martyrs, the imprisoned and the injured, their wives, sisters and girls. To all the Palestinian women in camps, villages and cities, who are united in their struggle and their political confrontation with repression and terrorism . . . to all our sisters in the battle where all hostile theories have been burnt . . . let our activists participate extensively in the popular committees in neighborhoods, cities, villages and camps. Let them participate in making programs to promote the intifada and support our steadfast people. Let us send representatives to collect donations and expose the various occupation practices. Let our working women participate in the unions and organize as workers; and step by step we'll achieve victory. Oh working women, join your fellow workers in boycotting work on strike days for you mostly suffer from racism and continuous oppression. Oh heroic teachers, our children's future is important; the occupying authorities have closed down all our educational institutions. Therefore, unite and confront the policy of closing the educational institutions, whose purpose is to produce an illiterate generation.

Mothers, in camps, villages and cities, continue confronting soldiers and settlers. Let each woman consider the wounded and imprisoned her own children. In the name of the great uprising, we ask you all to develop the concept of home economy by producing all food and clothes locally. This is a step in boycotting Israeli goods and paralyzing their economy. We can achieve this goal by going to the land, the source of goodness and happiness.

Two demands set forth by this program need to be discussed in detail: setting up popular committees and engaging in home economy.

The popular committees were seen by some as alternative institutions and by others as the infrastructure of the future independent state. And they helped to unite people, including women, who were to varying degrees active in the five principal ones: agriculture, education, food storage, medical, and guarding committees. In the towns women participated actively from the beginning, with variations based on qualifications and age. The one committee reserved for urban males, and young ones at that, was the neighborhood guarding committee, whose activities were especially required at night. In camps and villages, on the other hand, older and less educated women assumed an active role in the guarding committees.

Women were relatively most active (in some neighborhoods to the exclusion of men) in the education committees. For much of the spring and summer of 1988, they bore the brunt of organizing and carrying out neighborhood popular schooling, made necessary by months of military-ordered closures of West Bank schools. In this respect, of course, women were in fact continuing traditional practice, since they are largely entrusted with childcare and are in the majority at all levels of pre-university education. Housewives were likewise most assiduous among the population in attending committee-organized lectures given in homes, notably on health matters (especially first aid) but on a variety of other subjects as well. Young women in the cities also took an active part in the distribution of leaflets and added a cooperative and enthusiastic tone to work in general.

From these indicators, one can infer the extent, but also the limitations, of women's involvement in the popular committees, in the urban setting at least. But there is no indication from these elements that women's participation in decision making increased through the experience of the popular committees.

A preliminary conclusion regarding the urban popular committees is, therefore, that they were used more as means for maximizing the number of organized people than as instruments of social change. This explains why the committees were essentially limited to those who organized them.[30]

The participation of village and refugee camp women in popular committees took a different course from that of urban women from the start. In the camps, committees actually carried out the activities called for in UNLU communiqués more spontaneously than in the towns. Usually, however, meetings were held in a coffee shop or in the mosque, places where women rarely go. Despite the massive participation of refugee camp women in demonstrations, their involvement in committees was rare and indirect.

In the villages, committees similar in structure and function to those of the camps were formed. But there only men took part. Women and girls did not participate, although here too women took an active part in such mass activities as marches, demonstrations, and martyrs' funeral processions. Here too there was coordination with women's organizations, but mixed popular committees like those found in the cities were never formed.[31]

Overall, it may be concluded that a variety of popular committees played an important role in the *intifada* during the year 1988. But they were not new instruments through which the status of women was transformed. Their essential goal was to find new members for the mass organizations of each faction. Women's role in the popular committees became an extension of what it traditionally had been in the society: teaching and rendering services. In this respect it was difficult to distinguish between committees controlled by the leftist organizations (PFLP, DFLP, Communist party) and those controlled by the centrist Fateh. A woman's participation in decision making was the result of political affiliation and remained within the confines of the existing political balance. By the beginning of 1989, however, the four major women's committees joined together to form the Higher Women's Council. The council became the nucleus for coordination among its participant groups.

HOME ECONOMY

The second important demand made of the Palestinian people during the *intifada* requiring women's participation was the strengthening of home economy. The general connotation of the concept was self-reliance in the production of food and clothing and the return to the land. In implementing the demand, women's organizations in various cities worked directly or through popular committees to hold lectures on home economy. They also distributed publications discussing food storage and preservation and caring for plants and animals.

There is, if one looks at UNLU Communiqués No. 8 and 9 as well as publications of women's groups, some confusion as to the exact definition of home economy. In one instance it means taking steps toward boycotting Israeli goods,[32] in another measures to achieve "the highest levels of self-sufficiency in the face of the economic blockade imposed by the occupation forces."[33] In yet another context it is described as "the gradual return to the family farm, an economy of self-sufficiency led mainly by women."[34]

The UNLU entrusted to women responsibility for the success of the home economy movement. And various popular and women's committees endeavored to further one aspect or another of home economy.

The question then arises as to whether this particular woman's activity has a qualitatively new content, or whether it maintains her in her traditional social, economic, and familial role. In other words, is there, through the home economy movement, a new division of labor among the sexes, or is the role of women conceived according to the traditional and still prevailing gender division of labor, in which women's work is seen as unproductive?[35]

Two main types of cooperatives were established.[36] The first involves women in productive and income-generating projects outside the home. These cooperatives are run democratically, with women in control of production, management, and marketing. A second type encourages a variety of women to produce food at home, while the women's organizations market products and pass profits on to the women. The first type is qualitatively more advanced than the second, since its functioning is more truly cooperative and less oriented toward individual profit, and it helps bring women out of their homes. But one should not, as is sometimes done, take a mechanistic attitude regarding the virtues of women's work outside the house. Thus we read that "although women's work in the cooperatives [in Beitillo and Sa'ir, respectively Ramallah and Hebron area villages] has added new responsibilities for women, coming in addition to their housework, child-rearing etc., it has played an important role in transforming men's appraisal of women's work in general and housework in particular. . . . [Women's contribution to the family income] led to change in the traditional gender-based division of labor."[37] The fact of the matter is that such changes in the traditional division of labor, where they have occurred, have not been accompanied by a public critique of existing rural values. Setting up a women's production cooperative in the countryside does not automatically lead to changes in the gender-based division of labor, nor to an upward reevaluation by men of women's work. Political activists, although they are working women married to politically progressive men, continue to suffer from the existing division of labor. There is no congruity between their political or productive work and housework, which continues to be divided among women according to age and class, and not among men and women.[38] The theoretically highly developed political and productive role of women is not reflected in their social status.

A clear illustration of this gap is provided by events during the *intifada*, which gave great responsibilities to women activists. These required them to devote much time to physically and psychologically exhausting activities. In this context, women activists stood up and, for the first time in the history of the Palestinian women's movement, publicly criticized its long negligence of social issues.

It is difficult to argue that implementing home economy projects plays a progressive role in changing the status of women, unless it is associated with a change in existing values built on the gender division of labor. The present concept of implementing home economy is a qualitatively advanced one only through its connection to the *intifada*. It has value as a national demand, but there has been no attempt to imbue it with progressive social content.

OTHER QUESTIONS

Other demands on the March 8 agenda were restricted to women only.[39] One was that of gathering to prevent men from being arrested. Despite the continuity of this role from the outset, it had not previously been an organized activity. Women's teams were formed to prevent arrests. But an accurate assessment of this phenomenon would have to describe it as the momentary reflex of women who know the fate that awaits prisoners: the process begins with kicking and ends with death. Women, unlike men, are not targeted when they gather in the streets, even if they represent a target during demonstrations and confrontations.

One can thus trace an evolution in the image of "ideal women" from "ladies" at the beginning of the women's movement, to "men's sisters" with the emergence of the Palestinian resistance in the 1960s, to "martyrs' mothers" or "factories for men" in the 1970s. This last image is still popular, unlike the first. Emerging images of the ideal woman are in fact positive, related to the struggle, and no longer limited to "cries of joy" of the martyrs' mothers. We are here speaking of popular concepts, those of the poor in villages, refugee camps, and city neighborhoods.

The women's organizations likewise worked actively to involve women in demonstrations, tire burnings, and martyrs' processions in camps and villages. Clearly, Palestinian women played a key role in activating the street and in encouraging men to participate. It became difficult to go out in a demonstration without seeing women in the front lines. During all of 1988, continuous demonstrations would break out from the mosques on Fridays and from the churches on Sundays. Women would start the demonstrations, which became serious confrontations with the soldiers. Different female sectors of society participated, including students, workers, housewives, girls, and employees.

The political role of women in the demonstrations helped in weakening the concept of "women's honor." Often, when soldiers broke into homes in villages and camps, they tried to strip the women, cursed using foul sexual language, exposed their own or attempted to expose women's sexual organs, or threatened to rape the women in an attempt to humiliate them. There were even some individual cases of attempted rape.[40] The new and unexpected women's response, instead of the traditional covering of the face, was to hurl back the identical curses unabashedly at the soldiers. Many stories of this nature (not all of them necessarily true) circulated and became part of the *intifada* heritage, reflecting new values concerning women. Women occupied leading positions in decision-making bodies for the first time. In addition to a certain political vacuum due to imprisonments and the enormity of the task at hand, the length of the *intifada* and the continuously acquired experience in politics facilitated the new role of women. Still, there were some political activities of women that can only be seen as an extension of the traditional political role. These took the form of solidarity visits to the camps and villages, consolation visits to the families of the martyrs, collecting donations, or distribution of food to suffering families. Also the *intifada* brought about a greater degree of coordination among activist women in the form of the Higher Women's Council.

CONCLUSION

In this discussion of the role of women in the *intifada* we have seen that politically experienced people led the masses of women into becoming involved in resistance. Most women's organizations, as has been shown, have programs that call for a linking of national issues (ending the occupation) with women's liberation. At the same time, most discussions within the women's movement focus on gaining rights for working women and giving women skills so that they can be active and productive members of the society. There is even some discussion of daring issues such as divorce, guaranteeing women's income, and raising women's status in the family.[41] And yet there has been no "gender agenda" for the women's movement until now. This fact endangers the few rights obtained by women through their involvement in politics and the relative advancement of their role. It is all the more risky since the tendency is to postpone the setting of such an agenda until after independence has been achieved.[42] The assumption is that women will legally obtain their rights along with national independence.

Unfortunately, a study of the Palestinian national movement does little to justify that assumption, for a variety of reasons. First, the women's movement stemmed from the Palestinian national movement. Women's political participation is therefore dependent on the national movement, that is to say, on development—positive or negative—at the level of the leadership. The women's movement is divided into four organizations following the leadership of the national movement. The absence of social critique in the national movement, especially on the part of Fateh, which is its backbone, adds to the danger facing the women's movement.

A second inhibiting factor is the emergence of the Islamic forces, which strongly affect Palestinian political life in the West Bank and Gaza Strip, as has clearly been shown in the *intifada*. What is women's position in society in the programs of the Islamic forces? Women's position is in the home, in reproduction, and in the improvement of the quality of life, although women's education is not prohibited. We read in a document of the Islamic resistance group Hamas under the title "The Roles of Muslim Women": "In the resistance, the role of the Muslim woman is equal to the man's. She is a factory of men, and she has a great role in raising and educating the generations."

Because of the general strength of the Islamic movement in the area of social life, it is not going to be easy to change laws affecting women and family life in the event of independence, and it would be wrong to rely on a Palestinian government to change laws in recognition of the role of women in the resistance. The very fact that trust is placed in a future independent government is itself linked to the weak feminist consciousness of most women, raised to believe that gender division of labor is their natural duty.

Because of its roots in the national movement, the Palestinian women's movement was from the start characterized by its political work, that is to say, its concentration on national resistance while ignoring or avoiding issues of social change. The establishment of the women's organizations from 1978 on represented a qualitative step forward, since they devoted themselves to organizing women and encouraging them to be politically active. Bent on reaching large numbers of women, these organizations differed radically from the earlier charitable organizations.

Some of the leaders of these organizations, through their work in political organizations, had become aware of social issues; but they have not, in general, in their publications and speeches, focused on them. They believe that during the national liberation struggle they should focus on resistance and not open secondary fronts. Discussions nonetheless took place among members, making it difficult for them to adapt to obsolete values, notably marriage practices.

Then came the *intifada*, a supreme manifestation of popular resistance to the occupation due to its continuity and the participation of most classes, sectors of society, and ages, and of both genders. Spontaneously, women went out to participate courageously in resistance activities. Women's organizations, assuming their vanguard role within the Palestinian women's movement, organized and directed women's participation with an agenda of several points.

The program was popular, though imprecise. And the existing gender division of labor continues to place women at the lower end of the family hierarchy, even when they work inside and outside their homes. This reflects the continued low level of feminist consciousness within women's organizations and on the part of the UNLU.

Nonetheless, women play a crucial political role, even if it is a motherly one of saving demonstrators from soldiers. The point has been reached where it has become dangerous for men to participate in demonstrations or marches in the absence of women.

This in turn has led to the emergence of a new ideal of women as saviors rather than weak creatures needing protection. It has weakened traditional values and given women strength, self-confidence, and fearlessness in the face of killing, beating, arrest, and the threat of sexual assault. The new climate has helped the women's vanguard publicly to criticize restrictions placed on women's social life.

Will this trend be reflected in a new social agenda for the women's organizations? Or will the process be reversed if and when the confrontations diminish or come to an end? The answer to this question depends on women's awareness itself, an awareness that has penetrated the vanguard, where it continues to progress. It depends, ultimately, on whether that vanguard manages to formulate an appropriate agenda and communicate it to the masses of women.

NOTES

1. "The Women's Movement," in *Palestine Encyclopedia* (Damascus: Palestine Encyclopedia Committee, 1984), p. 212 (in Arabic).

2. Ibid., p. 211.

3. Union of Arab Women, *The Golden Jubilee* (Jerusalem: Union of Arab Women, 1980) (in Arabic).

4. Ibid.

5. Nahla Abu-Zu'bi *Family, Women and Social Change in the Middle East: The Palestinian Case* (Toronto: Scholar's Press, 1987), p. 21.

6. On May 14, 1936, 600 women students participated in a demonstration and called for the boycotting of Zionist goods. Ibid., p. 22.

7. Ghazi al-Khalili, *The Palestinian Women and the Revolution* (Akka: Dar al-Aswar, 1981).

8. Pamela Ann Smith, *Palestine and the Palestinians, 1876–1983* (London: Croom Helm, 1984), p. 137.

9. Ibid., p. 175.

10. Khadija Abu-Ali, *Introduction to Women's Reality and Their Experience in the Palestinian Revolution* (Beirut: General Union of Palestinian Women, 1975), pp. 44, 54–55 (in Arabic).

11. *Woman and Her Role in the United Arab Movement* (Beirut: United Arab Studies Center, 1982), pp. 216–17.

12. Ziad Abu-Amr, *Origins of the Political Movement in Gaza* (Akka: Dar al-Aswar, 1987) (in Arabic).

13. League of Arab States, *Women's Associations and Committees in the West Bank and Gaza Strip* (Tunis: League of Arab States, 1984) (in Arabic).

14. Maysoon al-Weidy, *Palestinian Women and the Israeli Occupation* (Jerusalem: Arab Studies Society, 1986), pp. 8–9 (in Arabic).

15. Interview with 'Isam Abdul-Hadi, chair, GUPW executive committee, *Revue d'Etudes Palestiniennes* 1 (1981): 82.

16. Al-Khalili, *The Palestinian Women*, p. 113.

17. Interviews with women leaders in the movement, December 1988. For detailed figures on women prisoners and martyrs during that period, see ibid., and al-Weidy, *Palestinian Women*.

18. Raymonda Hawa-Tawil, *My Home, My Prison* (London: Zed Press, 1983), p. 131.

19. Sonya Antonius, "Femmes prisonnières pour la Palestine," *Revue d'Etudes Palestiniennes* 1 (1981): 76. A majority of women prisoners were from left-wing organizations, while the largest group of male prisoners belonged to Fateh.

20. Moshe Ma'oz, *Palestinian Leadership on the West Bank* (London: Frank Cass, 1984), pp. 116–17.

21. Conclusions drawn from the analysis of annual reports of charitable organizations in the Jerusalem, al-Bireh, and Bethlehem areas covering the period in question.

22. Ma'oz, *Palestinian Leadership*, pp. 134–36. Four candidates for municipal office (out of 577) were women.

23. See Lisa Taraki, "Mass Organizations in the West Bank," in Naseer Aruri, ed., *Occupation: Israel over Palestine*, 2nd ed. (Belmont, Mass.: AAUG Press, 1989).

24. Union of Women's Work Committees, *The Development of the Palestinian Women's Movement* (Jerusalem: Union of Women's Work Committees, n.d.) (in Arabic).

25. Often deaths resulted. For example, two female martyrs fell in Balata camp near Nablus on December 11, 1987: Suheila Ka'ibi, seventy-five years old, with a bullet in the heart; and Sahar al-Jarmi, seventeen years old, with a bullet in the heart.

26. During the funeral on December 9, 1987, of the *intifada*'s first martyr, Hatem al-Sisi, a woman grabbed a soldier's gun and threw it to the ground.

27. Which nonetheless, and notably in the Gaza Strip, has to deal with deeply ingrained conservative values concerning women's activities. Cf. Susan Rockwell, "Palestinian Women Workers in the Israeli-Occupied Gaza Strip," *Journal of Palestine Studies* 14, no. 2 (Winter 1985): 130.

28. Their first joint statement.

29. Data based on *Towards a State of Independence: The Palestinian Uprising, December 1987-August 1988* (Jerusalem: Facts Information Committee, 1988). It is significant that the four women's organizations were the first mass organizations to form a permanent coordination committee, even before the *intifada*, in March 1987. This shows that partisan conflict among women's organizations is less intense than among the male-dominated ones.

30. See *The Conscience of the Intifada* (Popular Resistance Committees in the Occupied Territories), no. 4 (November 1988) (in Arabic).

31. Interviews with women and girls from villages, as well as village activists in women's organizations.

32. Statement on March 8, 1988, signed "Palestinian Women in the Occupied Territories."

33. UNLU Communiqué No. 12, April 2, 1988.

34. Adel Samara and Odeh Shehadeh, *The Economy of the West Bank and Gaza: From Restricted Development to Popular Protection* (Akka: Dar al-Aswar, 1988), pp. 59–61 (in Arabic).

35. The concept of home economy in fact predates the *intifada*. See, for example,

Muharram Barghouti, "Tanmiat al-Mafhoum Mutakhallif" (Developing the Concept of Backward), *al-Katib*, no. 78 (December 1986).

36. Seminar conducted by the four women's groups at the Ramallah offices of Bir Zeit University (the campus has been shut by military order since January 1988). See also Union of Palestinian Women's Committees, *The Intifada Continues*, special issue (March 1988) (in Arabic).

37. Eileen Kuttab and Khalida al-Ratrout, "The Women's Cooperative Experience— The Beitillo and Sa'ir Cooperatives," *Shu'un Tanmawiyya* (Development Issues) 3 (1988): 24–26.

38. "In other words, the woman outside is a leader, but not inside [the home]." Roundtable: "The Palestinian Woman's Struggle—Obstacles and Ambitions," *Shu'un Tanmawiyya* 3 (1988): 10–11.

39. See Union of Palestinian Working Women's Committees, *Women of the Intifada* (Jerusalem: UPWWC, March 1988); Union of Palestinian Women's Work Committees, *Newsletter* (Jerusalem), March 8, 1988, and June 1988.

40. Soldiers attempted to rape Samia Ibrahim Shir'a, eighteen years of age, in Jabalia camp on January 26, 1988. See National Information Committee, Gaza Strip, *Newsletter*, no. 6 (n.d.).

41. *Shu'un Filistiniyya* (Nicosia: Palestinian Research Center), no. 189 (December 1988).

42. See various publications by the women's committees over the years.

43. See, for example, the statement by the representative of the Palestinian Federation of Women's Action Committees at the debate on the Palestinian women's movement held at the offices of Bir Zeit University, January 1989.

9

Work and Action

THE ROLE OF THE WORKING CLASS IN THE UPRISING

Joost R. Hiltermann

The popular uprising in the Occupied Territories has highlighted the limits of the participation of the working class, such as it is, in the Palestinian movement's struggle for national liberation. Before the uprising, the main constraints on the Palestinian working class as a historic actor in the escalating struggle for national liberation have been: (1) workers' overriding need for a steady income to provide for families caught in an economic depression; (2) divisions in the labor movement and the unions' tendency to address national concerns over those of workers; and (3) the Israeli authorities' repressive measures, which were aimed at curbing organized activity of any type in the Occupied Territories. During the uprising, these constraints, with the exception of (2), were exacerbated, further limiting the role of the working class in resistance to the occupation. These issues will be addressed in an attempt to determine exactly what the role of the Palestinian working class has been in the West Bank and Gaza Strip during the first year of the popular uprising.

THE PALESTINIAN LABOR ECONOMY AND THE EMERGENCE OF A "WORKING CLASS" IN THE OCCUPIED TERRITORIES

From the outset of the occupation in 1967, the Israeli state pursued a policy of economically and administratively integrating the West Bank and Gaza, while keeping the Palestinian population deprived of any political rights.[1] As part of the policy of economic integration, the Israeli authorities allowed the entry of

Palestinian workers from the Occupied Territories into the Israeli economy in 1968. There were two conditions, however. According to Moshe Semyonov and Noah Lewin-Epstein, "workers would be required to obtain and carry work permits and could work only for the employer specified in the permit; and . . . both gross and net salaries of nonresident Arabs (including social benefits) would be equal to those of Israeli workers with comparable jobs and skills."[2]

To control the flow of workers, the government set up labor exchanges in the main Palestinian towns and villages. At the end of 1988, slightly over 46,000 workers from the West Bank and Gaza were employed in Israel through the exchanges, according to figures provided by the Israeli Employment Service.[3] An even larger number crossed the Green Line on a daily basis without the proper documentation. Accurate figures are difficult to obtain. Palestinian unionists estimate that an average of 120,000 workers from the territories were employed in Israel before the uprising; this figure may have been substantially higher during the summers, when Palestinian children helped in the harvests.

A number of control mechanisms were introduced by the authorities to ensure that only a particular type of worker would enter the job market, and only as many as would satisfy labor demand at any given time. Such mechanisms included the requirement that a job applicant present evidence of army service for certain jobs (which automatically excludes all Palestinians), the obligation of employers to hire "local workers" first (which excludes workers from the territories), and the function of labor exchanges to screen and limit applicants according to the needs of the economy and the interests of the Shin Bet, the Israeli internal intelligence service.[4] Through the labor exchanges, the Israeli state has been able to (1) control the wage level of Palestinian workers to ensure that they would not undercut Jewish workers, and (2) deduct sums from workers' wages for social security and insurance which in large part are not returned to them.[5] Through these control mechanisms, the Israeli economy's specific need for cheap, unskilled manual labor led to a heavy concentration of Palestinians in such sectors as construction and services (street cleaning, dishwashing, etc.), invariably at the bottom ranks of the ladder with Israeli Jews acting as managers. Thus Palestinian workers became the "hewers of wood and drawers of waters" of Israeli society.[6]

One-tenth of the population of the territories, representing more than 50 percent of the labor force, is continuously involved in work in Israel, according to official figures. In reality, the actual number of people with experience in Israel is much higher, as there is constant turnover. Most Palestinians employed in Israel are unable to hold jobs for any length of time. Most are legally considered day-laborers, which means that they have no automatic right to tenure and can be dismissed before employers are obligated by law to pay seniority benefits. The problem is pervasive among undocumented workers, the majority of whom move from job to job, especially in construction, or in agriculture during the harvesting season. They find work through relatives or friends who act as labor contractors, or are hired directly by Israeli employers and contractors at one of the various "slave markets," that is, informal labor markets that are situated at major road junctions leading into Israel from the West Bank and Gaza. A virtual reserve army of labor, these workers have played the role of a buffer for Israeli workers in particular and the Israeli economy in general at times of economic depression.

In the West Bank, the process of depeasantization in the rural areas has not been matched by a simultaneous process of urbanization. Lack of significant industrial development, in part caused by obstacles laid by the Israeli occupation, in addition to tight zoning policies, inhibited the twin processes of urbanization and industrialization typical of Western countries, and instead encouraged the migrant character of labor. Rather than being emptied of their populations, West Bank villages became dormitories for workers employed in Israel. In short, although peasants were depeasantized, they were not permitted to proletarianize.

If, therefore, we speak of a working class in the Occupied Territories, we are referring primarily to the casually and informally employed workforce of itinerant day-laborers and their families, living under a military occupation. They are a class to the extent that they are different from the other main social grouping in Palestinian society, the petit-bourgeois class of merchants, traders, and professionals. Subjectively, they see themselves as workers rather than as peasants, even if the village remains their home. They see as their adversary not just the owning classes, however, but also, and more significantly, the military occupation. In short, Palestinian workers in the Occupied Territories constitute a nascent migrant-worker class of predominantly nationalist orientation.

THE WORKING CLASS AND THE PALESTINIAN NATIONAL MOVEMENT IN THE OCCUPIED TERRITORIES

Palestinian workers' experience in the Israeli workplace both encouraged organization—because of the flagrant violations of the workers' rights and the lack of protection from the largest Israeli trade union federation, the Histadrut—and inhibited it because of military repression. The first Palestinian trade unions date from the Mandate period. Dominated by the Palestine Communist party, they survived the disaster of 1948, the subsequent Jordanian occupation of the West Bank, and the 1967 war. During the first years of the Israeli military occupation there was little organizational activity on a mass level. In Gaza, trade unions, never very significant, were outlawed, while those in the West Bank were harassed by the army and their leaders arrested or deported. In addition, the prevailing perception was that the occupation would not last long, reducing the incentive to create an infrastructure of services as long as the occupation continued.

In the early 1970s, however, this perception changed as it became clear that Israel was entrenching itself in the territories. A new realization emerged that Palestinians in the West Bank and Gaza would have to take their fate into their own hands and cease to rely on assistance, let alone liberation, from the outside. A new perception grew that there had to be a force that could counteract the actions of the occupier on a local level.[7] At the same time, the PLO became the driving force of the Palestinian national movement both inside and outside the Occupied Territories, gaining international legitimacy at the Rabat Conference in October 1974 and with Yasser Arafat's speech at the United Nations one month later. It adopted a new, transitional program, calling for the establishment of a "Palestinian national authority in any Palestinian areas liberated from Israeli control," the embryo for the future Palestinian state.

The drive behind mass organizing came initially from high-school and university students. By the late 1970s, many of those student activists who had completed their educational career continued their organizational work in the women's and labor movements. The trade union movement was infused with new energies as activists began to direct their attention to unionizing the migrant labor force. In 1979 the Workers Unity Bloc was set up as a new union framework, identifying politically with one of the leftist trends in the national movement. New frame-works emerged also from the other main political trends: the Progressive Workers Bloc, the Workers Youth Movement, and two smaller blocs. These blocs differed more in their political views than in their strategies for organizing workers. The period of the late 1970s and early 1980s was one of fierce competition among the various blocs to recruit the unorganized pool of laborers, especially those traveling daily across the Green Line.

The labor movement in the Occupied Territories thrived in the late 1970s and 1980s because of both the growth of a disenfranchised migrant labor force and the emergence of the PLO as the single representative and articulator of Palestinian national aspirations. To the extent that they were politicized at all, workers were imbued primarily with a nationalist rather than a socialist consciousness, although union leaders have espoused socialist views. Even these, however, are often inspired more by an affinity with the Soviet Union as a political ally of the Palestinians (i.e., nationalist considerations) than by strong ideological convictions. The Palestinian working class in the Occupied Territories, such as it was, thus became one of the pillars of the Palestinian national movement in the decade leading up to the uprising.[8]

THE ROLE OF THE WORKING CLASS IN THE POPULAR UPRISING

The First Stage: Mass Action

During the first chaotic months of the uprising, Palestinians took massively to the streets to protest the occupation, suffering high casualties as the army responded with live fire. Workers joined demonstrations as much as anyone else; given their relatively high numbers among the general population, it is no surprise that of all fatalities in the period December 1987-October 1988, approximately 50 percent were workers.[9] It is important to note, however, that during the initial month, when the formal unified local leadership did not yet exist, no specific calls were made on workers to take action as members of the working class, and at no point later, when there was such a leadership, were workers summoned specifically to demonstrate. To the extent that workers demonstrated and were killed, they participated in the uprising spontaneously as members of the general population.

With the emergence of the Unified National Leadership of the Uprising in mid-January 1988, special attention was paid to the role of workers in resistance to the occupation, and initially the working class was alternately exhorted to take specific actions and showered with praise for particular contributions made. For example, in Communiqués No. 1 and 2 (of January 8 and 10, respectively), the UNLU called on workers to participate in a general three-day strike planned for January 11–13. Communiqué No. 2 addressed the "valiant Palestinian working class," stating: "Let your arms of steel set to work to achieve the success of this strike by boycotting work during days of general strike." And it promised: "Your prominent role in this comprehensive uprising is the best answer to the threats and abuses of the occupying troops and will defeat the policy of racial discrimination and constant oppression." In Communiqué No. 3, issued on January 18, after the successful three-day strike, the UNLU devoted what is probably the longest paragraph of any of its communiqués during the first year of the uprising (except for the communiqué issued on the occasion of International Workers Day, May 1) to the role of the working class, even using a bit of Marxist phraseology to make its point:

To the Palestinian working class: Yes, the arms of steel have succeeded through their participation in the strike in stopping the machines in thousands of Israeli factories and workshops. Your role in this uprising is unique and special. Continue your strike against work in Israeli factories, oh heroic workers. We will not be frightened by the frantic threats uttered by the Zionist authorities, courts and employers, for in this uprising we have nothing to lose but our chains and the oppression and exploitation befalling us. Let us paralyze the machine of Israeli production because enhancing the Israeli economic crisis is one of our weapons on the road to achieving our right to return, to self-determination and to establish an independent national state.

The call on workers to stop working in Israeli factories has been repeated regularly since Communiqué No. 3. The call was modified, though: the leadership stopped short of asking workers to quit their jobs inside the Green Line; instead, they were requested only to stay away from work on general-strike days. At the same time, workers employed on Israeli settlements in the Occupied Territories were encouraged to find alternative employment (e.g., Communiqué No. 6 of February 3). In Communiqué No. 11 of March 19, workers were commended for observing this call.

Workers were lauded for other activities as well: in a communiqué on January 12 signed by the "National Forces in the Gaza Strip," the local Gaza leadership referred to a national committee of merchants in the Gaza Strip as having "hailed the efforts of volunteer blacksmiths who repaired locks broken by the occupation forces in their failed attempt to stop the strike." Popular committees organized metalworkers in West Bank towns as well to counter the army's violent attempts to force shops to stay open.

It is not clear, however, that organized workers' activism during the first weeks of the uprising went much beyond the few celebrated actions by volunteer blacksmiths. Generally, workers followed the calls of the UNLU to stay at home on strike days, although at times local activists enforced strikes by preventing busloads of workers from traveling to their jobs in Israel. Whether or not workers consistently and voluntarily boycotted work in Israel on strike days is therefore not clear. But it is clear that during the first months of the uprising, absenteeism in Israel was rampant. This was due not only to general strikes, but also to the frequent curfews imposed by the army on villages and refugee camps as collective punishment for demonstrations. In March 1988 the head of the Israeli Employment Service referred to the uprising as "traumatic" for the Israeli economy because of absenteeism, especially in the building industry and during the citrus harvest. Statistics showed that at that time only about 58 percent of the Palestinian labor force normally employed across the Green Line was coming to work to jobs in Israel, including Israeli settlements in the territories.[10]

Labor activists have suggested that large numbers of workers have switched from jobs inside Israel and on Israeli settlements to agricultural production in their own villages. For example, of the sixty to seventy people from the small village of Wadi Fukin in the Bethlehem area who used to work in Israel and on surrounding settlements, only fifteen continued to do so at the beginning of 1989. On the nearby settlement of Hdar Betar, Israeli workers had to be hired to replace the twenty Palestinians who used to be employed there before the uprising, while in the smaller neighboring settlement of Betar Illit, building activity was stopped altogether. According to residents of Wadi Fukin, the workers went back to tilling their land, which had previously been the domain of women and old men only.[11]

In response both to the high rate of absenteeism and to the uprising in general, the Israeli authorities instituted a number of economic punishments to exhaust the population and break its spirit of resistance. Among these measures was the threat to prevent Palestinian workers from entering Israel at all and to replace them with workers from southern Europe. For example, the director-general of the Ministry of Industry and Trade called on the Israeli government to make its policy on permitting foreign workers to work in Israel more flexible.[12] The threat was never fully carried out, underlining the degree to which Israel is dependent on cheap labor from the territories. Workers have been fired from their jobs, however, and there have also been temporary bans on labor from specific locations.

Absenteeism due to strikes and curfews triggered layoffs in several workplaces in Israel in the spring of 1988. To the extent that they were able, Israeli employers tried to replace their Palestinian workers with local hirees or workers from South Lebanon or southern Europe. To forestall being laid off and losing their income,

Palestinian workers therefore increasingly began to circumvent strike calls by staying overnight in Israel. Even though this is illegal under military orders that restrict Palestinians' access to Israel to daytime hours, the authorities closed an eye to this practice, as they saw it as a way of undermining the UNLU's sway over the population.[13] Although no precise figures are available on attempts to circumvent strike calls, interviews with unionists indicate that workers from refugee camps and nonagricultural villages (especially in the Hebron area) who have no alternative sources of income, as well as workers formally employed through the labor exchanges (i.e., those working in Israeli factories rather than on building sites or in the services sector), have been more likely to work on strike days than irregularly employed day-laborers or those who could revert to agricultural production on their own land for a living. The latter suffered economically, since the local market for agricultural produce is very limited, but because they on average did not suffer more than most members of the population, they accepted the reduction in their income, especially given the nationalist content of their action.[14]

At the same time, the army began to clamp down on those who were attempting to organize workers and enforce UNLU calls, the Palestinian trade unions in the West Bank and Gaza. A number of trade union offices were closed down by the army during the first half-year of the uprising. By the end of August 1988, at least twenty-four unions had been closed by military order, as well as one of the three labor federations in Nablus, which itself housed six local unions. Most of the remaining unions closed their own doors, fearing army reprisals. In addition, during the first wave of mass arrests in March 1988, detainees included a large number of union activists; by August at least thirty-eight top union leaders had been placed in administrative detention.[15]

Despite the repressive measures taken against trade unions and their leaders, trade union activity continued, but its form was adapted to prevailing conditions. According to one union leader, union activists went underground during the first weeks of the uprising, becoming members of local popular committees and strike forces. This transition went relatively smoothly because, in the words of the unionist, "unions had been harassed before the uprising as well, and unionists were therefore used to working informally. Unions were never bureaucracies. In Israel, for example, organizing in workers' committees was always done informally, and this simply continued during the uprising."[16] In the village of Yatta, for example, the local labor union, transformed into a workers' council shortly after the beginning of the uprising, was active in coordinating events in the village and used to "discuss the current situation, raise the political consciousness and press for the formation of popular committees."[17] One of the important functions of the popular committees was to classify workers according to their location of work and their economic needs, so as to determine which role each could and ought to play in the uprising. At the same time, the traditional work of trade unions—providing health insurance and legal aid, and negotiating contracts—was temporarily suspended.

The Second Stage: Institutionalization

The UNLU responded to the army's closure of trade unions by stepping up efforts to create alternative structures. Workers were exhorted to "expand their workers' committees in their factories and in their places of residence, in order to organize themselves and consolidate their role in the struggle" (Communiqué No. 13 of April 12). On the occasion of International Workers Day, the UNLU called on workers to organize themselves and "to work for the unification of the labor movement" (Communiqué No. 15 of April 30). Shortly thereafter, workers were urged to "complete the formation of unified workers' committees and to participate in existing unions" (Communiqué No. 19 of June 8). The rationale was clearly that as long as the proper structures were not in place, it would be impossible to support those workers who might be willing to strike but could not for lack of alternative income or for fear of reprisals by the authorities.

At the same time, demands on workers to boycott work on "Israeli projects" were softened, reflecting the UNLU's acute awareness of the difficulties faced, particularly by workers, as well as of the need for a continuing in-flow of money to keep the uprising going. So, whereas the UNLU insisted on the importance of workers boycotting Israeli settlements in the Occupied Territories (e.g., in Communiqués No. 13 and 14), it called on workers "not to waste opportunities for alternatives to working across the Green Line" (Communiqué No. 15). In Communiqué No. 16 of May 13, workers were urged to "intensify the boycott against work in Zionist settlements and to refrain from giving any services to the settlers."

However, if workers were to quit their jobs on the settlements, alternatives had to be available. The UNLU therefore called repeatedly on Palestinian employers in the territories to absorb these workers to the extent that they were able, and also not to fire workers or lower their wages in response to reduced sales. In Communiqué No. 10 of March 10, for example, the UNLU stated, "Factories are requested to lower their prices, not to lower their workers' wages, and to open only during authorized periods." And in Communiqué No. 13 of April 12, the UNLU called upon "the national manufacturing institutions to increase their production and to absorb more and more of our laborers. We also ask them to pay full wages during the days of general strike." In Communiqué No. 19 of June 8, the UNLU urged "employers to refrain from dismissing workers, increasing their work hours, or deducting strike days from their salaries," in response to growing attempts by employers in the spring to shift the economic burden of the uprising onto the shoulders of the workers. The UNLU toned down its implicit criticism of employers shortly thereafter, affirming in Communiqué No. 22 of July 21 that "factories may work at full capacity and during hours agreed upon between management and workers' committees. Workers' rights should be protected, especially if there is overtime work." This new position reflected a growing confidence on the part of the national leadership in the institutionalization of the uprising, such that a large degree of authority in handling day-to-day affairs could be devolved to the popular committees.

Throughout the first year of the uprising, the authorities saw their control over the population slowly slipping as Palestinians refused to pay taxes, observed general strikes, and generally avoided contacts with the institutions of the occupation, especially the civilian administration branch of the military government. The army responded with more arrests, deportations, and economic punishments. The labor movement was targeted along with all other grass-roots organizations. In April a deportation order was issued against 'Adnan Dagher, one of the leaders of the large and active Construction and General Institutions Workers Union in Ramallah and a member of the executive committee of one of the three trade union federations; he was deported on August 1. Five more union leaders were ordered expelled in the summer: Radwan Ziyada, the brothers Muhammad and Majed al-Labadi, and 'Odeh Ma'ali, all top activists in the Workers Unity Bloc, as well as Jamal Faraj, a unionist from Bethlehem.[18]

It continued to be difficult to establish how many workers had actually stopped working inside Israel and on Israeli settlements in the territories. Official figures at the end of 1988 suggested that there had been a 20 percent drop in the number of workers employed across the Green Line since the beginning of the uprising.[19] Settlers claim that despite absenteeism on strike days, Palestinian workers have generally continued to appear for work on their jobs in the settlements in the territories, despite UNLU calls on workers to quit.[20] Palestinian unionists have confirmed this, although they state that attendance varies from location to location.

In the late summer, the authorities began to target the infrastructure of the uprising, outlawing the popular committees by military decree on August 18. The definition of the term "popular committee" in the banning order was so vague as to allow the army considerable leeway in prosecuting anyone perceived as providing services on a mass level.[21] Despite the ban, however, the established mass organizations continued operating, exposing themselves to the usual level of harassment, including the arrest of their leaders.

Some of the trade unions remained active. One of the three labor federations opened offices in East Jerusalem (i.e., under Israeli law, where it enjoys a larger measure of protection), primarily to serve as spokespersons of the labor movement for trade union delegations and journalists visiting from abroad. On August 24, representatives of this federation, supported by the Rakah faction in the Histadrut, convened a press conference in Jerusalem to protest attacks on workers by Jewish extremists and repression of the unions by the army. Union leader Ibrahim Shuqair claimed, according to the *Jerusalem Post*, that "Israeli officials were doing everything possible to keep workers from organizing in the territories and demanding their economic rights."[22]

Despite the repression, local unions continued to work informally, operating on work sites rather than from a union office. There was also a growing preparedness to take on Palestinian employers for the latter's attempts to sack workers and reduce their wages. The first major action by workers at a Palestinian-owned factory since the beginning of the uprising took place at the Royal Crown Cola bottling plant in Ramallah in August. Workers organized in an impromptu workers' committee called for an end to exploitation and demanded basic rights. They were partially successful, gaining an eight-hour workday and agreement by the management to pay wages also for general-strike days called by the UNLU. However, the leader of the committee was promptly placed in administrative detention by the military authorities for a period of six months.[23]

In the fall, efforts to defend workers' rights in Palestinian workshops and factories increased. As one unionist explained, owners have claimed that because they are "national industries" it is imperative that they stay in business, even at the expense of the workers they employ. According to the same reasoning, workers are not supposed to strike to seek redress for their grievances, because that might result in the closure of the factory or workshop. Yet, the unionist said, agreements with owners can be reached, because "the bourgeoisie is happy as long as it stays on the safe side." Thus, workers may observe general strikes as long as they agree to work their regular forty-eight hours a week. On their part, owners continue to pay full wages. Such an agreement was reached, for example, between workers and management at the Beit Sahour Plastics Company, following mediation by unionists.[24]

In December, activists of the Construction and General Institutions Workers Union in Ramallah, which had been closed down by the army earlier in the year, went around the various places of employment in the Ramallah area to urge owners to accept a new collective work agreement adjusted to the exigencies of the uprising. The contract stated that the uprising had created new social conditions requiring a new basis for understanding between workers and management of factories and institutions. It proposed that workers and management should work together in a "spirit of understanding and cooperation . . . in the framework of national interests" to reach agreement on the following: stepped-up production in order to replace Israeli products with locally produced goods; dialogue between management and elected workers' committees; just wages per sector (specified in the contract); application of Jordanian labor law with regard to annual vacations, and so on; a ban on the dismissal of workers except under very strict conditions (specified in the contract); continued payment of wages despite absenteeism due to army-imposed curfews; fair negotiations between management and workers' committees over health insurance and provident fund; and the right of every worker to be a member in a trade union or workers' committee.[25]

The Third Stage: Retrenchment and Consolidation

In the fall of 1988, the Jordanian dinar, which is the currency used in the West Bank alongside the Israeli shekel, started a slide downward, falling as low as 2.2 shekels to the dinar (as opposed to the previous 4.9 shekels) in January 1989, but finally stabilizing in March at 3.2 shekels to the dinar. Because West

Bank salaries are paid in dinars, workers employed in the West Bank suddenly found that their incomes had been cut in half. This, in addition to declining production and growing unemployment, led to a severe economic crisis in January 1989. In response, the labor movement shifted its focus from nationalist concerns back to the strictly economic interests of their members.

In an attempt to cope with the economic downturn, the UNLU, in Communiqué No. 32 of January 9, addressed Palestinian employers as follows:

The UNLU urges owners of factories and national institutions not to deduct their employees' salaries on general strike days. We urge them to compensate their workers for the rising cost of living and the decline in the value of the dinar. We also encourage them to expand the ranks of their employees, and to cease from singling out activists for special treatment and dismissal from their jobs. These unfair practices will place their perpetrators in direct confrontation with the masses of the uprising and their watchful eyes.

In Communiqué No. 33 of January 24, the UNLU called on employers to raise wages by at least 40 percent and urged workers' committees to enforce this demand. The call was repeated in subsequent communiqués. The UNLU issued a special warning, in Communiqué No. 32, cited above, and Communiqué No. 34 of February 11, to employers not to fire unionists as unions resumed an active role in labor disputes on the shopfloor. In addition, in Communiqué No. 36 of March 16, the UNLU affirmed "the necessity of resolving labor disputes on a nationalist basis" and called for "the formation of national arbitration committees for this purpose."

Strikes erupted in several Palestinian and foreign institutions employing Palestinian workers in January. Employees at the United Nations Relief and Works Agency (UNRWA) organized a sit-in, a partial strike, and eventually a full three-day strike at the beginning of February to demand a recalculation of their salaries, whose value had deteriorated, according to the Union of UNRWA Employees, by 70–80 percent. The union accused UNRWA management of "making an unseen profit of about 50 percent off West Bank salaries as a result of the deterioration."[26] The union, representing 2,700 UNRWA employees, reached a temporary agreement with UNRWA at the end of March (with UNRWA conceding a 30 percent interim increment in salaries for March), pending the outcome of a study of salaries by a special UNRWA committee.[27] The 214 employees at the UNRWA-run Augusta Victoria Hospital in East Jerusalem carried out a two-day strike on February 22–24, and then continued with twice-weekly two-hour strikes to give force to their demand to be compensated for the fall of the dinar.[28] A similar interim agreement was reached between this union and the UNRWA as well.[29]

The economic crisis was exacerbated by a concerted Israeli policy to punish Palestinians in the Occupied Territories by economic means for their continuing resistance to the occupation.[30] Aware of Palestinians' dependence on jobs in

Israel, the authorities especially targeted the Palestinian workforce employed across the Green Line. Various means were used. For example, the Israeli National Insurance Institute (NII), which pays out pension payments, child allowances, and medical insurance to documented workers employed with Israeli companies (i.e., in Israel or on Israeli settlements), stopped payments to a number of Palestinian residents of East Jerusalem in the fall of 1988. In March 1989 it became clear that at least 1,470 residents were affected by the cutoff. In defense of the measure, NII director-general Mordechai Zipori stated, *inter alia,* that "as long as they don't boycott our allowances, they shouldn't boycott our taxes either," suggesting clearly political motives on the NII's part.[31]

In another measure, after almost twenty-two years of occupation the Israeli Employment Service in Jerusalem suddenly announced that it would start to "enforce the law" on employment of West Bank and Gaza residents in East Jerusalem in March, requiring them to be hired through the official government labor exchanges.[32] Unionists condemned the move, both because workers from the Occupied Territories receive only limited services, compared with Israeli workers, on the basis of the deductions made from their pay slips by the Employment Service, and because, in the words of one unionist, "demanding West Bankers to get work permits to work in East Jerusalem is an attempt to enforce the illegal annexation of the city to Israel."[33]

The authorities also continued to regulate the daily flow of labor across the Green Line. Many incidences of firings of Palestinian workers by employers, either as a result of absenteeism or in response to demonstrations in particular areas of the territories, have been reported in the Palestinian press.[34] On January 24, Defense Minister Yitzhak Rabin threatened that denying work permits to Palestinian workers might contribute to attempts to put down the uprising.[35] On February 24, a new measure was announced, requiring Gazan vehicle owners to obtain a sticker if they wished to enter Israel. Issuance of the sticker was made contingent on the owner having a "clean record." This meant that anyone who was found to have regularly committed "violations of public order" was ineligible to receive such a sticker. In response to questions, the military commander in charge of the Gaza Strip, Yitzhak Mordechai, declared, "I don't want to punish anyone, but to grant those who deserve it the privilege of working in Israel."[36]

Unfazed by army measures designed to break the back of the uprising by exhausting the population economically, the UNLU consolidated its hold over the Palestinian masses, including workers, through specific gains on both local and international diplomatic levels. Most important among these were the declaration of an independent state and the opening of a dialogue between the United States and the PLO. On this basis, the UNLU felt itself sufficiently strong to continue calling for workers to boycott Israeli institutions, among other actions. In Communiqué No. 31 of December 22, 1988 the UNLU called on Palestinians "to escalate the struggle for the eviction of Israeli institutions from the State of Palestine, beginning with banks, agencies, labor exchanges, and the like." In two examples, the labor office in the village of Attil was set on fire on January 10, 1989, and the labor office in Nablus was firebombed on February 19.[37] In Communiqué No. 33 of January 24, the UNLU urged workers to "boycott citrus-picking in Zionist citrus groves." In Communiqué No. 34 of February 11, the UNLU "renewed its call" to "all employees of the civil administration, auto licensing department, customs department and the police to resign from their posts and to join the ranks of the Palestinian people."

CONCLUSION

The role the Palestinian working class has played has been limited, reflecting the overriding importance of economic interests over nationalist concerns. At the same time, workers, organized in unions and workers' committees, have tried to comply with nationalist directives whenever possible. The role of workers as individuals therefore has been to carry out the instructions of the national leadership while continuing to bring home an income and support their families. In the words of one trade unionist: "The uprising equals life. This means that it is the task of workers to bring in money for others who are active in resistance to the occupation."[38] At the same time, the UNLU was careful, especially after the first heady months of the uprising had passed, to assume a realistic approach toward workers, making only demands that could be satisfied, and always gradually, while leaving room for flexible interpretation. The UNLU also emphasized the need for social peace between workers and Palestinian employers in order to make an effective united stand against the occupation. Generally speaking, the UNLU placed relatively few demands on workers; an analysis of UNLU communiques during the first year of the uprising shows the secondary role played by workers as compared, for example, with that played by the merchants.

As for the institutions of the working class, the trade unions, they continued to play their dual role of providing services to workers, to the limited extent that they were able, while mobilizing workers under the banner of Palestinian nationalism. Divisions that had wracked the labor movement in the 1980s were largely overcome during the uprising, if not on the level of the general federation, then at least in the popular and workers' committees active in neighborhoods and places of work. The UNLU placed the responsibility for directing the role of workers in the uprising with the popular committees during the early stages of the uprising, and later, when trade unions reemerged, with the unions. Many labor activists were forced underground in the face of army repression at the beginning of the uprising, reinforcing the informal structures that had been built in the previous years. As one unionist explained, union activity was continued informally, like all other activities in Palestinian society, including education:

This year has changed everything, and we will not return to where we were before. What has happened in Palestinian society in the last year has superseded what happened in the previous twenty years. The important question is how to continue our regular work, and the answer is that it has to be done informally. Everything is informal now, including education. The important thing is not the university, but the process of education: what the university can offer in terms of education despite its closure. For the union movement it is exactly the same.[39]

Despite their circumscribed role in the uprising, however, workers have given full emotional support to the active resistance by their friends and relatives, and indeed, in light of their relatively high numbers among the general population, have suffered casualties at a higher rate than any other social sector when caught in the army's line of fire. In that sense, and given the limitations put upon it by historic constraints, the Palestinian working class has played a significant role in perpetuating the popular uprising in the Occupied Territories.

NOTES

1. See Sheila Ryan, "Israeli Economic Policy in the Occupied Areas: Foundations of a New Imperialism," *MERIP Reports,* no. 24 (January 1974): 9.

2. Moshe Semyonov and Noah Lewin-Epstein, *Hewers of Wood and Drawers of Water: Noncitizen Arabs in the Israeli Labor Market* (Ithaca, N.Y.: ILR Press, 1987), p. 12.

3. *Jerusalem Post,* January 20, 1989.

4. See, for example, Emanuel Farjoun, "Palestinian Workers in Israel: A Reserve Army of Labour," *Khamsin,* no. 7 (1980); and Stanley B. Greenberg, "The Indifferent Hegemony: Israel and the Palestinians," draft chapter in a forthcoming book, provided by the author.

5. See, for example, International Center for Peace in the Middle East, *Research on Human Rights in the Occupied Territories, 1979–1983* (Tel Aviv: I.C.P.M.E., 1985), pp. 76–77, 94–96.

6. In the words of Semyonov and Lewin-Epstein, *Hewers of Wood,* p. 114.

7. See, for example, "An Interview with Rita Giacaman: Women, Resistance, and the Popular Movement," *Palestine Focus,* no. 24 (July-August 1987): 3.

8. For a detailed overview of the development of the labor movement in the Occupied Territories, see Joost R. Hiltermann, "Before the Uprising: the Organization and Mobilization of Palestinian Workers and Women in the Israeli-Occupied West Bank and Gaza Strip," Ph.D. dissertation, University of California at Santa Cruz, 1988.

9. These figures, calculated for the West Bank by al-Haq, the Palestinian human rights organization, are not exhaustive but approximate reality. During this eleven-month period, 104 workers were killed in the West Bank, as opposed to 101 nonworkers. Included in the category "workers" are the unemployed and self-employed, such as drivers and barbers, as well as teachers. Workers made up approximately 50 percent of the monthly casualty toll as well, except for March 1988, when twenty-eight workers were killed as opposed to sixteen nonworkers. Figures for the Gaza Strip can be assumed to be similar.

10. *Jerusalem Post,* International Edition, March 26, 1988.

11. Interview, March 18, 1989.

12. *Jerusalem Post,* December 15 and 22, 1987; January 12 and 13, 1988; March 1 and 4, 1988.

13. Interview with a Palestinian unionist, January 9, 1989.

14. Interview with activists, March 18, 1989.

15. Al-Haq, *Punishing a Nation: Human Rights Violations During the Palestinian Uprising, December 1987-December 1988* (Ramallah: al-Haq, 1988), pp. 318–9.

16. Interview, December 15, 1988.

17. "The Yatta Diary," in *Towards a State of Independence: The Palestinian Uprising, December 1987-August 1988* (Jerusalem: Facts Information Committee, September 1988), p. 30.

18. Al-Haq, *Punishing a Nation*, pp. 318–19.

19. *Jerusalem Post*, December 21, 1988.

20. Settlers were interviewed in March 1989 by Robert Friedman, a U.S. freelance writer, who permitted me to use this information.

21. Al-Haq, *Punishing a Nation*, pp. 322–23.

22. *Jerusalem Post*, August 25, 1988.

23. Memos written by the Interim Workers' Committee at the RC Cola Factory; also, al-Haq files.

24. Interview, January 9, 1989; see also the article on this subject by Muhammad Manasra in *al-Tali'a*, October 27, 1988.

25. Copy of contract obtained from Construction and General Institutions Workers Union, Ramallah/al-Bireh (December 1988).

26. Quoted in *al-Fajr Jerusalem Palestinian Weekly*, February 13, 1989.

27. Ibid. April 10, 1989.

28. Ibid. February 27, 1989.

29. Ibid. April 10, 1989.

30. See al-Haq, *Punishing a Nation*, chapter 7.

31. *In Jerusalem* (weekly special section in the *Jerusalem Post*), February 17, 1989; *Jerusalem Post*, March 15, 1989.

32. *Jerusalem Post*, February 14, 1989.

33. *Al-Fajr Jerusalem Palestinian Weekly*, February 6, 1989; February 19, 1989.

34. *Al-Tali'a*, July 14, 1988.

35. *Jerusalem Post*, January 25, 1989.

36. Ibid., February 26, 1989.

37. Ibid., January 11 and February 24, 1989.

38. Interview, January 9, 1989.

39. Interview, December 15, 1988.

10

The Revolt of the Petite Bourgeoisie

URBAN MERCHANTS AND THE PALESTINIAN UPRISING

Salim Tamari

> *Q.* Can you think of one major blunder you have committed (during the uprising)?
>
> *A.* Yes. Opening commercial stores by force. That was a mistake and we have learned the proper lessons from it.
>
> Defense Minister Rabin, Ha'aretz, April 22, 1989

Reflections on the *intifada* are permeated with the ideological predispositions of their writers. It evokes the parable of the blind men and the elephant: every perception reveals the perspective of the beholder. Because of its populist character, the social composition of the mass movement has lent itself to a multiplicity of interpretations. It has variously been assessed as the movement of the dispossessed in refugee camps (with the focus on the initial demonstrations in Gaza and the intensity of confrontations in the camps); as basically a rural insurrection (with the focus on the spread of the uprising to 88 villages in January 1988, and to over 200 by the end of February)[1] and as a witness to the leading role of workers in the national movement (highlighting the declining participation of Palestinian labor in Israeli firms and workers' commitment to strike days).[2] There has even been a suggestion, despite evidence to the contrary, about the leading role of professionals and academics in the uprising.[3] The breakdown of data about those killed, injured, and arrested in clashes with soldiers was used to buttress claims as to the "weight" of various groups involved in the rebellion:

predominantly refugees in Gaza, and predominantly workers and students from villages in the West Bank.[4] Most of these studies, however, say little about the process by which these groups became involved, or the relevance of their occupational identification ("women," "peasants," etc.) to their actual participation in the mass movement. Surprisingly, there has been a tendency to neglect the significance of the merchant community in general, and the role of urban shopkeepers in particular, in the consolidation of the uprising during the first three decisive months of its launching. One can only attribute this neglect to certain preconceptions about the "inert" conservatism of shopkeepers[5] and to the absence of a heroic image that businessmen can project opposite the "children of the stones."

Based on interviews with shopkeepers and merchant-activists, and on analysis of the clandestine leaflets of the mass movement, I will examine the crucial role played by this traditionally conservative class, suggesting that it was the only social grouping that appears to have acted cohesively in the consolidation of the uprising in its earlier phase (spring of 1988). In its later development, what is usually referred to as the "institutionalization of the uprising," merchants' associations—acting within the United National Leadership of the Uprising (UNLU)—determined the contours of the "economic war" between Israel and the resistance movement. The salient features of this confrontation were the successful boycott of Israeli commodities; the nonpayment of taxes; the pressure for the resignation of tax collectors and customs officials; and, to a lesser extent, the creation of an "alternative economy," based mainly on cottage industries. Finally, I will discuss the impact of the organizational crisis of the popular committees as it affected merchants' declining participation in the uprising as it entered its second year, and the emergence of differences between manufacturers, shopkeepers, and street peddlers.

A historical note is fitting in this prelude: fifty years separate the two prolonged commercial strikes that consolidated the two great Palestinian rebellions of our century, the 1936 revolt and the uprising of 1987–89. In both cases the participation of merchants in the national movement endowed the rebellion with a social weight and an urban character that would otherwise have diluted and fragmented its overall thrust. As in 1936, the urban general strike in 1987 preceded and set the tone for the spread of the uprising to the countryside. Then, as during the *intifada*, the primary objective of the colonial authorities in the initial stages of the rebellion was the dissolution of the general strike.[6] But there are significant differences between the two movements: merchants' participation in the 1936 rebellion involved a substantial degree of coercion,[7] while the 1987–88 strike was basically a *voluntarist* act. Moreover, the Palestinian political elite that led the 1936 rebellion—a combination of urban notables and the coastal commercial bourgeoisie—had been destroyed as a class by the war of 1948. That class has no hegemonic equivalent in the contemporary social structure of the West Bank and Gaza, its remnants having been dispersed among the professional and business strata of Jordan and the Gulf states. The current uprising was (and is) led by a strategic coalition of forces and social groupings that bear little resemblance to the elitist and semi-feudal character of the Higher Arab Committee of the 1930s.

BACKGROUND: THE PASSIVE AGENTS OF RESISTANCE

Merchants and shopkeepers have always constituted the passive side of resistance to the military authorities. Commercial strikes have been a primary weapon of protest by the national movement since 1967. However, those have been usually one-day affairs, in observance of nationalist memorials or in response to acts committed by the military government, such as the deportation of national figures or the punitive demolition of houses. They also were accomplished, in most cases, with a considerable degree of persuasion—to put it mildly—on the part of activists from the national movement.

The turning point was the imposition, in 1976, of the value-added tax (VAT) on all merchandise and services in the Occupied Territories as a means of financing the budget of the Israeli military government. In addition to being illegal by the terms of the Geneva Convention ("the occupier may not institute new taxes in the territory under its control"),[8] this tax was resented because merchants and manufacturers bore the brunt of its imposition. With the onset of the uprising merchants readily responded to UNLU calls for a total commercial strike and the nonpayment of taxes. Faced with a move for total civil disobedience and a sharp drop in revenue for its civil administration, the Israeli authorities responded quickly:

The granting of permits and licenses of any kind was made contingent on payment of taxes, among other required criteria (including obtaining a certificate of "good conduct" from the internal intelligence services, the Shin Bet). Such permits include, among others, drivers' licenses, travel permits, identity cards, birth certificates, permits to visit relatives detained [in detention centers], construction permits and import and export licenses.[9]

The forceful collection of taxes was used both as a means of revenue and as a method of subduing the rebellious population. The Jerusalem Arabic press daily reported the incursions of the "tax brigades." The following items were reported for an average day, covering events for November 23, 1988:

Last Wednesday the customs and tax bureau staff, accompanied by soldiers, raided the tailoring shop of Yusef Abdallah Shafiq and seized seven sewing machines whose value was estimated at 4,000 dinars [$8,000], for non-payment of taxes. A 1982 Renault belonging to Nasim Odeh was appropriated for the same reasons. A physician from Yatta [Hebron], Dr. Nayef Mahanbeh had his car seized; the condition for reclaiming it was the payment of 1300 dinars in back taxes. Tens of merchants in Khan Yunis were raided and their IDs confiscated. They were directed to reclaim them from the Military Government after paying the taxes imposed on them.[10]

The latter practice, of confiscating citizens' IDs for nonpayment of taxes, was later declared illegal by the High Court; nevertheless, the practice continued.

The human rights organization al-Haq detailed in its annual report the manner in which the army was used for these exactions:

Typically, a curfew would be imposed, and the army would enter homes impounding property or summon property owners to makeshift tax offices (usually schools) to present proof of payment for taxes. Al-Haq has documented confiscations of jewelry, vehicles and (occasionally exorbitant) sums of money, for example in the town of Beit Sahour at the beginning of July 1988. In addition, Palestinians have been stopped at roadblocks by police or army carrying lists; if their name appeared on the list, their car would be seized and returned only after the person had paid all outstanding taxes, as estimated by the authorities. In other instances, identity cards were confiscated and returned only after taxes had been paid.[11]

By the beginning of 1988 it became clear to the Israeli authorities that the December uprising was not limited in character or duration, as was the case in earlier outbursts. Defense Minister Rabin, who was quick to condemn the initial upheaval as the work of PLO inciters from the outside, announced a month later that "the disturbances reflect the tension that was building in the administered territories over 20 years and are not the result of Palestinian organizations' call to violence."[12] The Chief of Staff, Dan Shomron, boasted on a tour of Gaza on December 1987 that "under no circumstances will we allow a small minority of inciters to rule over the vast majority—a majority which is, in general, pragmatic and wants to live quietly."[13] A few months later he made an about-turn: " . . . there is no such thing as eradicating the intifada because in its essence it expresses the struggle of nationalism . . . *the participation of large number of civilians in violence has created what physicists call a 'critical mass.'* "[14]

The repressive measures listed above were thus leveled accordingly, not only to contain and isolate activists and inciters associated with the underground movement, but also to intimidate whole segments of the civilian population, including groups that had been—so far—immune. Mayors, mukhtars, heads of chambers of commerce, and leading businessmen and manufacturers had to spend hours under the sweltering heat, rubbing shoulders with youngsters summoned from refugee camps and peasants from curfewed villages asking for special permits to harvest their crops. Throughout 1987 and 1988 several prominent businessmen from Nablus and Ramallah were incarcerated for nonpayment of taxes, an unprecedented move.[15] The army developed a special preference for commandeering the Volvos, Audis, and Mercedeses of the rich (bearing blue West Bank licenses) to mount night raids against rebellious villages. They were often observed taking the vehicles afterwards for joyrides and returning them to their owners damaged and in need of major repairs.[16] Special yellow passes issued in the early 1980s for dignitaries and businessmen to spare them the humiliations of excessive searches at border crossings were now abolished.[17] The Israeli satirist Philip Gillon encapsulated the situation succinctly: "it is deplorable to treat the Arabs like dogs, and it is deplorable to treat dogs like Arabs."[18]

In short, the *intifada* witnessed the dethronement of the Palestinian bourgeoisie from the relatively sheltered niche they had managed to occupy over the last two decades. Thus a combination of increasing tax pressures and a shift in the perception of the military government, which now saw the urban middle classes as part of a hostile subject population rather than as part of a "pragmatic majority that wants to live quietly" (a shift that was itself brought about by the ascendancy to power, and the staffing of the military government, by extreme right-wing elements), engendered a self-fulfilling prophecy. It hastened the process of involving the shopkeepers as willful activists in the uprising.

WHO CONTROLS THE STREETS?

Within two weeks of the insurrection that marked the beginning of the uprising in the refugee camps of Gaza, Nablus, and Bethlehem, the battle lines shifted from street confrontations between youthful elements and border police toward a general commercial strike in the urban centers. This shift marked the transition of the uprising from its initial spontaneous (and volatile) character to one in which control passed into the hands of the clandestine United National Leadership of the Uprising. In this shift the cities of Ramallah, Nablus, and—earlier—East Jerusalem played a crucial role. The UNLU (comprising the four main factions of the PLO) began to direct and coordinate the daily activities of the popular movement through a network of popular, neighborhood, and strike committees, and now merchants' committees. The instrument for diffusing these directives was the serialized communiqués of the uprising (*bayanat*), as well as the occasional bulletins issued regionally by the popular committees.[19]

The battle for control over the streets of Jerusalem was the most protracted and, perhaps due to the centrality of the city in the Israeli strategy of control over the territories, the most crucial. It was sparked by General Sharon's transfer of his residence to the Old City of Jerusalem on December 14, 1987, with the onset of the major demonstrations in Gaza. A commercial strike commenced in Jerusalem and continued unabated for forty-one days, igniting a series of solidarity strikes in other West Bank townships, most notably in Nablus and Ramallah. The pattern that characterized the Israeli response to the Jerusalem strike established precedents for the behavior of the merchant community throughout the territories. This took the form of a cat-and-mouse game, which the Israeli press dubbed "the shopkeepers' war."[20] Throughout January and February 1988 merchants began to close their shops at 11 A.M. when soldiers would move in and force them to open their shutters. Activists of the strike committees would then engage the soldiers in a battle of stone throwing and compel the merchants to close the shops again. The scenario was reversed and the military authorities compelled the merchants to remain closed from 2 to 7 P.M. in response to a UNLU call for afternoon openings.[21] These confrontations turned into a contest of wills during January and February. The military authorities were determined to break the commercial strike as it became the most visible side of the by now institutionalized uprising. They may also have seen the merchants as the weak link in the organized national movement.[22] Soldiers began to smash the padlocks of striking merchants and leave the stores open overnight.[23] This last act boomeranged, however, as it generated unprecedented communal support. The *Jerusalem Post* reported at the end of January that control was slipping from the hands of the army: "Shopkeepers say members of the local metal-workers union have been repairing damaged shop doors free of charge, in one of the first signs of communal self-help to maintain the strike. There have also been reports of collections and donations of money and food for needy people, who have been deprived of jobs and wages by the prolonged shutdowns."[24]

Within a fortnight the initiative passed into the hands of merchants' committees in the Ramallah-Jerusalem area. Merchants' representatives held their first public press conference on February 2, 1988 in which they exposed the army's attempts at the forceful breaking of their strike and the widespread destruction of property.[25] In al-Bireh about 300 Muslim and Christian shopkeepers made a "blood oath" at the end of March in which they vowed not to pay their Israeli taxes.[26] Their act was saluted by the UNLU as a precedent to be emulated by other cities.[27] Significantly, the merchants also tied the ending of their commercial strike to national political demands: the annulment of unfair taxes, the ending of the deportation policy, the release of prisoners held during the December and January demonstrations, and the convening of an international conference to resolve the future of the territories.[28] On their part, the Israeli Merchants Association, in West Jerusalem, voiced their opposition to the forceful opening of Arab shops, apparently wary of the effects on tourism.[29]

Following the mass resignation of the Arab police force in March, at the behest of directives issued by the UNLU, street committees and popular guard committees were formed to protect shops forcefully opened by the army.[30] In Hebron bands of *shabab* were observed manning observation points on strategic rooftops following settler attacks on Arab cars and shops. They later began to set up barricades to prevent armed settlers from entering the town.[31] By the early spring the battle over the shops was won. The army and border police gave up interfering with storekeepers, and the directives of the United Leadership began to regularize opening hours. The commercial strike became the most visible daily feature of the uprising.

"TOWERS" OF THE *INTIFADA*

The victory of shopowners in the battle over the commercial strike marked a turning point in the formative phase of the uprising. It witnessed the ascendancy of the urban middle classes as leading elements in the confrontations with the Israeli army, and resolved for the first time during the two decades of Israeli rule the ability of the national movement to control the streets, *and sustain that control,* through the mobilization of the most self-conscious and individualistic sector of the urban population. The "war of the shops," in the view of a Palestinian historian, "brought the bourgeoisie into the fold, participating very fully and effectively in the uprising."[32] This occurred, in the analysis of one of the factions in the UNLU, when the uprising brought home the conclusion "to those segments of the bourgeoisie and the intelligentsia that it is impossible to continue coexisting with a 'liberal' occupation."[33]

This achievement would not have been possible without two essential ingredients: first, the willful involvement of the merchants in the uprising after a brief period of hesitation *and* intimidation; and second, a decision on the part of the national movement—and the UNLU in particular—to give priority to the demands of merchants (and manufacturers) within the tasks of the movement as a whole. Concerning the first factor, there is no doubt that the imposition of taxes, the manner in which they were collected, and the generalized contempt displayed by the Israeli army and civil administration toward the middle classes since the early 1980s (as discussed above) hastened the process of their revolt. This created a fertile atmosphere for the involvement of the merchants in the commercial strike. The shift in the attitude of the UNLU toward the merchants from one of patronizing exhortation, and on a number of occasions actual intimidation in the streets, to direct involvement was realized through the establishment of the merchants' committees—which became the instruments of incorporating shopkeepers and small businessmen as direct participants in the uprising. These changes can be clearly monitored from the regional communiqués of the national committees of the UNLU.

In an early political circular distributed by Fateh on February 20, 1988 ("second month of the people's great rebellion"), merchants were already identified as occupying "the paramount position [*makan al-sadara*] in support of the uprising" since the commercial sector has the power and the ability *to paralyze the economy* in a general strike.[34] Merchants are targeted for mobilization in the following manner:

1. Merchants should be organized around the nonpayment of taxes as *a matter of self-interest.* Otherwise a prolonged strike cannot be sustained.

2. Merchants should be assured that their stores will be protected against looting in case the army opened their shutters forcefully. The national movement should repair damaged shops, and provide guard duties [at night].

3. Striking merchants should be supported and non-striking merchants should be punished severely.

4. The strength of the general strike lies in its implementation. Hence the duration of the strike should *be restricted* and coordinated with all the regions through the national communiqués.[35]

This circular is remarkable for several reasons. First, it reflects the political weight accorded to the merchants by the largest of the political factions in the

UNLU, identifying them as the primary mass base of the rebellion, *before workers and farmers*. Second, unlike the communiqués issued by the UNLU for mass distribution, the *bayanat* of the uprising, it is completely lacking in any sentimental jargon; the political idiom used is concrete and straightforward, almost cynical. Finally, the circular reveals the pragmatic positions that guided the leadership of the uprising, from the onset, in determining the timing and extent of its directives in a manner that clearly distinguishes it from the leadership of the 1936 general strike.

In the actual carrying out of these directives, however, considerable pressure was used, depending on the region and the issues involved. In the first phase of the commercial strike (lasting from January to April 1988) the main issue was the boycott of taxes and the regularization of strike hours. In the second phase (beginning June 1988 and intensifying in March 1989) the main issue became the boycott of Israeli goods and the expansion of the home market for native products. A circular addressed to the merchants of Qalqilyah (a market town west of Nablus) by the "Qalqilyah Peoples Committee of the Uprising" (January 24, 1988) is typical of the patronizing stance that characterized UNLU circulars toward merchants in the first phase. After exhorting shopkeepers to "assume your share in the national struggle, and to be *with* the people rather than *above* the people," it then proceeds to warn retailers who raise the prices of basic commodities of dire retributions: first the spoilage of their wares, and then the burning of their stores.[36] This balancing of exhortation with intimidation also characterizes the first three national communiqués of the United Leadership, albeit with considerably more astuteness and sophistication. In Communiqué No. 1 (January 8, 1988) a commitment is made to "protect the interests of honest merchants from any attacks by the authorities."[37] Communiqué No. 3 (January 18, 1988) elevated merchants to prominence: "we salute you and salute your leading role in the making of our people's uprising," but the language is still condescending.[38] (This is just before the period, at the end of January, when the United Leadership intervened in the prolonged Jerusalem strike by making allowances for limited opening hours in the morning.)[39]

The turning point occurred in Communiqué No. 5 (early February 1988). This is the only national communiqué that is almost entirely devoted to merchants and businessmen. More significantly, its formulation clearly reflects the elevation of merchants to a decision-making position within the leadership of the revolt. In its preamble it glorifies the merchants by calling them "towers of the intifada . . . its guardians, the bearers of its message and continuity."[40] This formulation corresponded to the formation of merchants' committees in Ramallah, Nablus, and Jerusalem whose task was "the escalation and coordination of the commercial strike within each city [i.e., through the UNLU] and the protection of striking merchants from retribution."[41]

Immediately after the success of the commercial strike the committees began to push for a tax boycott, and—in the words of a merchant activist from al-Bireh—"there is no doubt that the tax campaign was spearheaded vigorously by the merchants' committees, acting on the basis of their self-interest."[42] At the institutional level, the merchants' committees were expected to replace the disintegrating chambers of commerce as the organizational framework for representing their concerns, but this attempt apparently failed.[43] The chambers of commerce (and in the case of the Nablus region, of industry and commerce) had acted over the last two decades as the bodies for representing the grievances of the small merchants with the tax bureaus and, with the dissolution of the nationalist town councils after 1981, as the main conduit between urban citizens and the military government. In the 1980s they also assumed the task of validating official papers for the Jordanian government (passport papers, birth certificates, etc.).[44] For this reason the chambers acquired the reputation of embodying a conciliatory, pro-Jordanian (but not collaborationist) leadership for the urban middle classes. Their demise therefore ushered in the collapse of these linkages with both Jordan and the military government. The failure of the merchants' committees to supplant them can be seen in this context not only as a failure of class representation, but also as showing the limitations inherent in *any* organs of the national movement performing an autonomous political function.

MERCHANTS IN RETREAT?

In August 1988 the Palestinian uprising entered an organizational crisis. While street confrontations were continuing unabated with the army, and while the commercial strike provided the backdrop for the "routinization" of the uprising, the *institutional* development of the *intifada* was not galvanizing around the popular committees, as anticipated by the United Leadership. "The danger of this period," wrote Rib'i al-Madhoun, "lies in the possible loss by the uprising of one of its distinctive features—namely, its mass character. It marks the regression of the movement to pre-intifada days when revolutionary action was concentrated in the hands of students and rebellious youth in specified regions."[45] Two main institutional failures that can be mentioned here were the inability of the popular education committees to create a sustained alternative network to formal schooling (with the closing of most schools and universities in the West Bank); and the failure of the agricultural committees and the domestic production committees to create the much heralded system of home production, based on cottage industries.

These issues reflected the general political malaise in the uprising itself. As the tempo of the movement was routinized and the popular committees were in retreat, the United Leadership sought to resolve the crisis by heating up street action confrontations.[46] At the root of the problem was the shift in the political strategy of the PLO after the declaration of independence in November 1988, when the leadership was seen as "investing" the political momentum created by the uprising in the search for sovereignty through a negotiated territorial settlement. Although this "investment" was acceptable in principle by the factions of the United Leadership—as evidenced by Communiqué No. 29 of November 20, 1988—it nevertheless created considerable controversy on how to proceed inside the territories.

Briefly stated, the controversy was highlighted in the internal debate about the nature of the campaign for civil disobedience *(isyan madani)*—generally seen by all political factions as the main instrument of mobilization *as well as* the strategic means of achieving total disengagement from Israel's political control over the West Bank and Gaza.[47] Commercial strikes, tax boycotts, the mass resignation of police and tax collectors were all seen as steps toward a cataclysmic moment of separation when the system of colonial control would disintegrate. A necessary condition for this objective was that civil resistance *exclude armed activities* (to avoid brutal liquidation by the army) and that mass participation be sustained through the organizational work of the popular committees.[48] As the uprising escalated its momentum it would enter into a new, advanced plateau when these (popular) organizational networks would constitute an *alternative power base* to Israel's colonial administration.[49] It was the inability of the popular committees to create this alternative power base that was now seen as the essence of the crisis in the leadership of the uprising.[50] In effect the diplomatic initiatives by the PLO to enter into a negotiated territorial settlement were seen as the new *alternative* strategy that would circumvent, rather than supplement, the political gains of the uprising.

In the ranks of the merchant community this crisis was exemplified in three issues: (1) the retreat in the campaign for the nonpayment of taxes, after some success; (2) the manner in which the boycott of Israeli commodities was carried out; and (3) the emergence of differences in the ranks of manufacturers, shopkeepers, and street peddlers *(bastat* owners).

The initial success of the tax campaign was no doubt connected to the resignation of tax collectors and Arab police officers in response to calls (and later threats) by the UNLU in March 1988.[51] In subsequent months, however, Israeli moves to take drastic measures against tax delinquents and the forceful collection of taxes (described above) eroded the resistance of the business community. Factory owners and other manufacturers in Ramallah and Nablus received "special dispensation," according to a prominent Ramallah accountant, from the United Leadership at the end of March 1988, to pay their taxes in order to keep their factories open and receive import licenses for raw materials.[52] The move was generally seen as necessary to sustain local industries and to expand the employment of workers laid off by Israeli firms. It nevertheless helped to create a schism ("and considerable resentment")[53] between manufacturers and shopkeepers, and ultimately contributed to the collapse of the tax campaign. Since big merchants and manufacturers paid the bulk of the aggregate taxes, the result was to minimize the losses for the Israeli treasury. By July 1988 it is estimated that 25 percent of the business establishments in the al-Bireh–Ramallah region (out of a total of 4,520 establishments) had broken ranks and paid their taxes, amounting to 80 percent of the total Israeli tax levy.[54] An even higher payment rate was reported in Hebron, Bethlehem, Jenin, Tulkarem, and Nablus—the latter often referred to as the "citadel of merchants."[55]

The second issue that confronted the merchant community in this phase was the boycott of Israeli commodities. The boycott campaign had already been addressed in some detail in the early communiqués of the uprising. The Fateh clandestine directive (February 20, 1988), quoted above, laid down the conditions for boycott as follows: (a) Palestinian manufacturers should improve the quality of their products, to be on par with equivalent Israeli items; (b) Arab products should not be priced higher than similar Israeli products; (c) local products should be diversified so as to provide the maximum possible replacement for Israeli goods.[56] Strike forces were directed in a number of UNLU communiqués to enforce the demands for boycott.[57] This was usually understood to mean spoilage of Israeli commodities after initial warning to the storeowners, but only if there was a local substitute for the item. The spoilage campaign was accelerated in the spring of 1989 and reached its zenith in March, when masked squads of the strike forces raided hundreds of shops in several towns and held public bonfires of the offending items. In Nablus excesses were widespread, and often no distinction was made between commodities that had Arab substitutes and those that did not; at least one shoe store was reportedly burnt down.[58] The bonfire campaign elicited widespread protests by merchants and the public at large and occasioned a reprimand of the strike forces by the United Leadership. In a rare directive issued by the UNLU to local committees, the roughing up of Nablus merchants was severely criticized, and they were commanded to treat violating shopowners in a more careful manner in future encounters.[59]

The third feature of the crisis was related to the uneven burden borne by shopkeepers in the conduct of the general strike, in contrast to the situation of manufacturers and street peddlers. There is now concrete evidence that Palestinian manufacturers, especially those who invested in food processing, soft drinks, sweets, cigarettes, pharmaceuticals, cleaning solutions, and other items involved in the boycott campaign, benefited considerably during the uprising.[60] Increased demand for Arab products, despite a substantial drop in the public standard of living, allowed many Palestinian manufacturers to have a virtual monopoly on the local market. For this they received a special dispensation from the United Leadership to extend their working hours, and even as mentioned to pay taxes, to the chagrin of many storekeepers who demanded, through their merchants' committees, that a more even-handed policy be applied.[61]

The problem with street peddlers was more acute. In the earlier days of the commercial strike petty street vendors, *falafel* stands, and small vegetable traders were allowed to sell their wares beyond strike hours in order to avail the public of emergency shopping facilities. It was also an economic safety valve that permitted an increasingly pauperized urban population a supplementary source of income in the form of "alley stores," As the uprising entered its second year, however, these enterprises mushroomed all over the country, blotting the urban landscape and diminishing considerably the already curtailed incomes of strike-bound merchants. More significantly, these peddlers threatened the integrity and the discipline of the general strike itself. It was in response to this last consideration, and under pressure from merchants' committees, that directives were issued calling for the regulation, then curtailment, of street peddling, charging strike forces with the task of enforcing this directive.[62] But the number of peddlers involved was apparently too large to control, and this measure could only be enforced during general strike days.[63] Subsequently, the friction with street vendors continued to be a matter of contention among storekeepers.

CONCLUSION

The Palestinian uprising marks the entry of the urban merchant community (and its stormtroopers, the shopkeepers) as active participants in the national movement. Until then this conservative community was used by the movement, with considerable reluctance on its part, in limited strikes to mark national days of protest and expressions of grievances. The use of taxes by the Israelis as a form of punishment, and the general humiliation of the urban middle classes, leading to their dethronement from their relative privileges, brought the merchant community to the forefront of confrontations with the army. They realized, in the words of a leading member in the chamber of commerce, that "co-existence with the Israeli presence was no longer feasible." And this was not a mere figure of speech. In the first four months of the uprising, shopkeepers were the single most decisive element in paralyzing the urban economy and in consolidating the populist character of the insurrection.

For its part, the clandestine movement leading the uprising became aware of the limitations inherent in relying excessively on volatile street demonstrations and stone throwing as instruments for the realization of its political objectives. The leadership also realized that it was incapable of organizing Palestinian workers to desist from working in Israel since the home industries could not sustain alternative employment for them. The commercial strike was seen, therefore, as an essential component for adding "class weight" as well as durability and urban depth to the uprising. The incorporation of the merchant community into the leadership of the revolt, through merchants' committees, received the blessings of both left and right factions of the UNLU.

A setback to this incorporation occurred as a result of the mishandling of the tax boycott campaign and giving special dispensations to manufacturers and big businessmen to pay taxes while pushing the shopkeepers to take the heat. But the main obstacle leading to the retreat of merchants (as well as other organized groups in the uprising) from the forefront of events was political, not tactical. It had to do with the inability of the popular committees engendered by the *intifada* to create an alternative power (and in some sectors economic) base to Israeli rule. This shortcoming was enhanced and fed by PLO political initiatives abroad, which were often seen (rightly or wrongly) as the *culmination* of political struggles in the Occupied Territories rather than as a supplement to them.

While the battle of the merchants constitutes part of the ebb and flow of the movement as a whole, it is a part that was decisive in the success of the uprising in its formative phase. Although merchants continue to exercise a visible role in the routinized features of the urban revolt, there is no doubt that the initiative is no longer in their hands.

NOTES

A modified version of this chapter was presented at the fourteenth annual symposium of the Center for Contemporary Arabic Studies at Georgetown University, May 4–5, 1989.

1. Samir Barghouthi, "Economic Preludes to the Uprising," *al-Ittihad* (Haifa), December 9, 1988 (special supplement).

2. Fayez Sarah, "The Social Structure of the Palestinian Uprising," *Shu'un Filistiniyya*, no. 189 (December 1988): 8–9.

3. "It can be said without hesitation that these confrontations [during the uprising] were led mainly by revolutionary intellectuals, and politicized nationalists drawn from the ranks of students, and academics"; Barghouthi, "Economic Preludes."

4. Ibid.; Rashad al-Madani, "Statistics on the Martyrs and Wounded of the Uprising in the Gaza District," *al-Ittihad*, April 21, 1989; see also Ronald Stockton, "Intifada Death Patterns," unpublished paper, University of Michigan, Dearborn, June 1988. The categories of "worker," "peasant," etc., used in these breakdowns should be used critically.

5. Rib'i Madhoun, *The Palestinian Uprising: Its Organizational Structure and Mode of Action* (Akka: Dar al-Aswar 1989), p. 32 (in Arabic).

6. It is curious that little attention has been paid, so far, to these parallels in writings about the *intifada*. This might be related to the coercive character of the general strike in 1936, as well as its failure to reach its economic objectives, namely, the paralysis of the Jewish economic sector. Y. Porath, the Israeli historian of the 1936 rebellion, contrasted the more radical nature of the 1987 uprising with the 1936 rebellion: "This is the first time that there has been a popular action, covering all social strata and groups. True, the refugee camps are the vanguard. But remote villagers and the urban population are also involved, active." *Jerusalem Post*, March 12, 1988. For his analysis of the general strike of 1936, see *The Palestinian Arab National Movement: From Riots to Rebellion* (London: Frank Cass, 1977), pp. 162–95.

7. Cf. Porath, *Palestinian Arab National Movement*, pp. 177–78.

8. Al-Haq: Law in the Service of Man, *Punishing a Nation* (Ramallah: al-Haq, 1989), p. 272.

9. Ibid., p. 281. These measures were subsequently given "retroactive legitimacy" through Military Order No. 1262.

10. *At-Tali'a*, December 15, 1985.

11. Ibid.

12. "Rabin: Violence in Areas Indicates a 20-Year Build-up of Tensions," *Jerusalem Post*, January 10, 1988.

13. *Jerusalem Post*, December 16, 1987; December 9, 1988.

14. "Shomron: Intifada Can't Be Eradicated," *Jerusalem Post*, January 1, 1989. Emphasis added.

15. Interview with O.A.J., owner of a construction materials store, Ramallah, February 19, 1989.

16. I am writing here of incidents personally observed on numerous occasions in the Ramallah-Bireh regions during the months of December 1988 through April 1989. Car owners were allowed to apply for compensation to their damaged cars; in most cases, however, the Ramallah police would not process these claims or would not respond to them. Similar cases were reported to me in Nablus, Jenin, Bethlehem, and Hebron.

17. Interview with A. F., a leading member of the Ramallah chamber of commerce, December 22, 1988.

18. "Arafat Puts on His New Keffiyeh," *Jerusalem Post*, December 16, 1988. Gillon was referring to the remote-controlled-detonation on live Israeli Defense Forces' dogs sent to the bunkers of Palestinian fighters in South Lebanon.

19. In the north, and in most villages, where the printing and distribution of leaflets was curtailed, minarets and portable loudspeakers were used to announce the directives.

20. See, for example, Joel Greenberg, "The Battle moves from the Streets," *Jerusalem Post*, March 18, 1988; and Joel Greenberg, "Abnormal Becomes Normal in West Bank," *Jerusalem Post*, January 26, 1988.

21. Andy Court, "The Battle of Salah e-Din Street," *Jerusalem Post*, May 4, 1988.

22. Interview with S. J., striking merchant and member of the Ramallah merchants' committee, January 4, 1988.

23. Facts Information Committee, *Towards a State of Independence: The Palestinian Uprising December 1987-August 1988* (Jerusalem: Facts Information Committee, September 1988) pp. 139–40.

24. Greenberg, "Abnormal Becomes Normal."

25. *At-Tali'a* (Jerusalem), February 4, 1988.

26. Interview with S. J., January 4, 1989.

27. UNLU Communiqué No. 12, April 2, 1988.

28. Ibid.

29. "Jerusalem Merchants Oppose Forced Opening of Arab Stores," *Jerusalem Post*, April 26, 1988.

30. "The Formation of Popular Guard Committees in the West Bank," *at-Tali'a*, March 17, 1988.

31. Ibid.

32. Mahmud Ibrahim, Bir Zeit University medieval historian, quoted by Judith Gabriel, "The Economic Side of the Intifada," *Journal of Palestine Studies* 69 (Autumn 1988): 205–6.

33. Palestine Communist Party, *Political Bulletin* (limited circulation), June 18, 1988, p. 17.

34. Fateh, [untitled] Political Circular No. 2, February 20, 1988, p. 17.

35. Ibid., pp. 17–18; emphasis added.

36. Qalqilyah Popular Committee of the Uprising, "A Communiqué to the Merchants of Qalqilyah," January 24, 1988, reprinted in *al-Intifadah: Basic Documents*, vol. 3 (Nicosia: Beisan Publications, 1988), p. 433.

37. UNLU Communiqué No. 1, January 8, 1988.

38. UNLU Communiqué No. 3, January 18, 1988.

39. Madhoun, *Palestinian Uprising*, p. 35.

40. UNLU Communiqué No. 5, (undated), distributed first week of February 1988.

41. Interview with B. S., owner of a tailoring shop and activist in merchants' committee, al-Bireh, February 19, 1989.

42. Ibid.

43. Madhoun, *Palestinian Uprising*, p. 35.

44. Interview with M. K., wood merchant and member of the chamber of commerce (Ramallah), March 3, 1989.

45. Madhoun, *Palestinian Uprising*, p. 77.

46. Ibid., pp. 77–78.

47. UNLU, "On Civil Disobedience" (limited distribution), May 21, 1988.

48. Ibid.; Nayef Hawatmeh, "Where the DFLP Stands," *as-Safir* (Beirut), reprinted in *Jerusalem Post*, April 18, 1989.

49. UNLU, "Civil Disobedience," p. 2; see also Popular Front, *Damir al-Intifada*, no. 5 (January 1989).

50. PFLP, Memorandum to Factions in UNLU (undated, probably mid-March 1989).

51. UNLU Communiqués no. 9 and 10, March 3, 1988, and March 10, 1988. See also Joel Greenberg, "Screws Turned on West Bank Collection," *Jerusalem Post*, February 18, 1988; and *Jerusalem Post*, March 3, 1988.

52. Interview with F. K., accountant and a prominent political activist, Ramallah, January 3, 1989.

53. Ibid.

54. Ibid.

55. Ibid.

56. Fateh, Political Circular No. 2 [untitled], February 20, 1988, p. 23.

57. For example, UNLU Communiqué No. 19, June 8, 1988.

58. Interview with S. M., Nablus money changer, April 10, 1989. The bonfire campaign was reportedly launched by one faction within the United Leadership.

59. UNLU, General Directive (undated; limited distribution, end of March 1989).

60. Hazem Shunnar, *Social and Economic Conditions During the Uprising* (Jerusalem: Passia, January 1989), p. 42 (in Arabic).

61. Interview with B. S., February 21, 1989.

62. UNLU Communiqués no. 19 and 25, June 8, 1988, and September 6, 1988.

63. A date was even set by the United Leadership, February 28, 1989, to eliminate the presence of street vendors (and roving money changers), but no concrete action was taken in that direction. Cf. UNLU Communiqué No. 36, March 16, 1989.

11
The Islamic Movement and the *Intifada*

Jean-François Legrain

For more than a decade, islamicism (a term taken to mean the political face of the Islamic movement) has been an integral part of the contemporary Arab world. While there is today increasing clarity as to its common matrix,[1] it finds expression in very different ways from one national context to another, and sometimes within a given state.[2] In the Palestinian case, the specificity of the political and historical context is such that one cannot see the Islamic movement there as a mere extension of the Egyptian experience or an appendix of the Iranian revolution, although some of its members claim the latter experience as a model. At the heart of that specificity lies the absence of a classical state structure as well as the exceptional strength of nationalist ideology, which in the Occupied Territories has never had to face the challenges of independence, making things more difficult for the political-religious alternative.

At the end of the 1970s, the very time when the PLO had managed to monopolize the political advantages of nationalism, the islamicists made their appearance and, playing on the contradictions of the PLO, proposed Islam as an ideological, political, and military alternative to its model of struggle.[3]

Contrary to many islamicist groups the world over, which sought state power as a prelude to re-islamicizing society, the Palestinian islamicists, such as the traditional Muslim Brothers, having analyzed the power relationship with the occupation, postponed until later the liberation of Palestine. They worked to resocialize the society along Islamic lines from the mosques, the universities (where they were to be found in large numbers with the massive arrival of students of refugee or rural origins), and the clubs. They declared puritanical values in opposition to the alleged corruption of the pro-PLO elites and of Israelis in general. The Muslim Brotherhood also played on conflicts of interest among various Palestinian sectors, allying themselves from time to time with Jordan or with Fateh, which had a stake in marginalizing the left in whatever municipalities, universities, unions, or social and charitable associations the latter were in the majority. The authorities were only too happy to favor such developments, which promoted inter-Palestinian dissensions.[4]

The two years 1986–88 saw the emergence in Gaza and the West Bank of an Islamic current of another type. In contrast to the Muslim Brothers, with which they had broken several years before, these new proponents of the jihad advocated the immediate resort to armed struggle. In 1986–87 they launched, in the name of Islam, a whole series of military operations against Israeli objectives, thus heating up the internal Palestinian front and making an essential contribution to the preparation of the general uprising of December 1987.[5]

Whereas it had been possible, in periods of "normalized" occupation, for the Muslim Brothers to favor re-islamization over the struggle against the occupation, the coming of the *intifada* forced them, on pain of losing all legitimacy, to translate into daily practice the radicalism of their discourse on the liberation of Palestine.

The remainder of this chapter will deal with the following questions: What does the term "Islamic Jihad" designate as applied to the group or groups which, under that name, participated in the outbreak and in various phases of the *intifada*? What is the Islamic Resistance Movement (IRM—better known today under its Arabic acronym Hamas)? What was, and is, its relationship to the Muslim Brotherhood? What was the contribution, at each stage of the *intifada* during its first year, of each of these groups and of the Islamic, as opposed to the Palestinian national, movement?[6]

THE ISLAMIC JIHAD

"Islamic Jihad" is a generic term designating a nebula of groups whose strategies sometimes diverge but which are united by a sense of belonging to the same political and religious movement.[7] Their political communiqués are usually signed "al-Jihad al-Islami" (Islamic Jihad), while their military operations are claimed by the Saraya al-Jihad al-Islami (Brigades of the Islamic Jihad). Several student organizations backed the ideas of the Jihad in Gaza and the West Bank. The group's communiqués, signed "Haraket al-Jihad al-Islami fi Filastin al-muhtalla," were regularly published abroad in London and Paris, then in Cyprus in the journal *al-Islam wa Filastin (IF)*, which also opened an office in Tampa, Florida.

The Military Operations of the Jihad, 1983–87

The claiming of military operations in the name of Islam on the part of the Palestinians under occupation is a relatively new phenomenon. True, the examples given by Sheikh 'Izz ad-Din al-Qassam in the 1930s and Hajj Amin al-Husseini throughout the period of the British mandate were never forgotten. But the first overt military act of the Jihad occurred in 1983, when a young Israeli settler was knifed to death by a commando that justified its act as a dictate of the "holy Jihad." In October 1984, in Gaza, a cell grouped around Sheikh Ahmad Yasin, president of the most important religious association close to the Muslim Brothers, al-Mujamma' al-Islami (the Islamic Grouping), was dismantled and its members sentenced to long prison terms for "illegal possession of weapons [which were never used] destined for acts of sabotage aimed at the destruction of Israel and the creation of an Islamic state." Sheikh Yasin was to be freed under the terms of the prisoner exchange between Israel and the PFLP-GC (General Command) in May 1985.

In 1986–87 a whole series of military actions was carried out in the name of Islam. The most important occurred on October 15, 1986, in the Old City of Jerusalem. A commando of the Jihad Brigades threw grenades at new recruits of an elite unit of the Israeli army at the Wailing Wall, killing one and injuring sixty-nine. A few days before, the Brigades had assassinated an Israeli taxi driver in the center of Gaza. Several waves of arrests followed, in both the West Bank and the Gaza Strip, but on May 18, 1987, six members of the Brigades escaped from Gaza's central prison and organized several armed operations, including the knifing to death of a military police captain on August 12. On October 1, 1987, in Gaza, three fighters of the Jihad Brigades were killed in an ambush set by the army (it is claimed that one of them died later under torture). On October 6, four other Jihad Brigades militants were killed in Shu-ja'iyya (Gaza) during an exchange of fire that resulted in the death of a Shin Bet officer. These events again resulted in numerous arrests, leading to the discovery of arms caches and the expulsion of Sheikh 'Abd al-Aziz 'Odeh, presented as the spiritual guide of the Islamic Jihad. Several large-scale demonstrations then broke out in the Gaza Strip; the Brigades claim the attack against patrols in northern Tel Aviv on November 22 and the killing in the center of Gaza of an Israeli on December 6.[8]

The Structure of the Jihad

The Palestinian Islamic Jihad, like other Islamic movements the world over, is imbued with the consciousness of making up an elite bearing a divine mission, which makes its political commitment an outgrowth of its faith. It considers that present-day Arab and Islamic regimes (with the exception of Iran) have returned to a state of *jahiliyya* (ignorance-barbarism prior to Islam) and calls for their overthrow by a popular revolution, which alone will reestablish God's rights. Unlike the traditional Muslim Brothers, who are mainly concerned with Islamic resocialization, the Jihad has, on the model of revolutionary Iran, made a political and military question, the Palestinian cause, a central religious focus for the entire Islamic world. Since Israel is the cutting edge of the West's general offensive against Islam, it is every believer's duty to struggle for its elimination. Although critical toward the PLO's policies—noninterference in Arab affairs; distancing itself from the Iranian revolution; abandonment of armed struggle as the only way to achieve the total liberation of Palestine—the Jihad considers dialogue with nonreligious nationalists essential in view of the fact that the common enemy is the Israeli occupier.[9]

Whereas the Jihad's ideology is well known through its various publications inside and outside the Occupied Territories, its origins and history remain problematic in view of the scarcity of primary sources, which are currently limited to its communiqués and to the rare interviews of Sheikh 'Odeh, and to secondary sources, including the Israeli judicial and military authorities. The Jihad made its appearance at the end of an evolution within the traditional Muslim Brotherhood. The critique of the priority accorded to re-islamization of the society through personal reform over the liberation struggle emerged among certain members of al-Mujamma' al-Islami in the late seventies. The Jihad was the result of one of the splits from the Brotherhood that occurred at this time within the Mujamma'. The intellectuals of the group, Sheikh 'Odeh, an instructor at Gaza Islamic University, and the pharmacist Fathi Shqaqi, both fascinated by the Iranian revolution, developed their theses through close contact with Egyptian Islamic radicalism during their studies in Zagazig. The May 1985 prisoner exchange between Israel and the PFLP-GC appears to be the key date in the passage from ideological to armed struggle. The Jihad Brigades benefited from advice and direct assistance on the part of former Popular Liberation Forces members imprisoned for their resistance activities in the early 1970s who had during their detention found their way back to Islam.[10] The Brigades would not, however, have been able to take action without the financial and logistical support of Fateh, thanks to the mediation of Abu Jihad, whose Amman office was open at that time.

The number of militarily active members of the Jihad was relatively small. In the absence of official statistics, one can reckon that in November 1987 about a hundred persons were incarcerated in Gaza, and about thirty in the West Bank, for "membership in the Jihad," without their necessarily having carried out any military activities. But its support among the population was considerable, and on the rise. In November 1986 the student council elections at Gaza Islamic University yielded a 69 percent score for the Islamic Bloc, close to the Muslim Brotherhood, while the Mustaqillun (Independents), who supported the Jihad, got 4 percent. One year later, the Islamic Bloc's vote fell to 60 percent, while that of the Jihad supporters rose to 11 percent.

The Jihad in the Uprising

By general consensus, the numerous military operations carried out in the name of the Jihad Brigades played an essential role in the process that led to the *intifada*. The Jihad continued to be very active at the beginning of the uprising "in the wake of the formidable popular insurrection which began in the first week of October following the martyr[dom] of the heroes of Shuja'iyya" (communiqué, January 15, 1988). A few months later the Jihad disappeared from the Palestinian scene, not to reemerge until the fall of 1988.

Organized Mobilization

Between December 10, 1987, and March 8, 1988, at least a dozen communiqués bore the signature of the Jihad or the Brigades.[11] From December 10, the Jihad exhorted the population to act against the occupation, and it was among the first organizations to call for mass actions under a particular slogan and on a precise date. The general strike it declared for January 9 (communiqué of January 8, 1988, reproduced in *IF*) was strictly observed. Its presence on the ground was so strong that Israeli observers considered it responsible for tracts distributed in Jerusalem by an "Uprising Leadership" that was still poorly understood.[12]

Its tracts, whether rhetorical or programmatic, did not refer to the Iranian revolution, but the idea of "Islamic revolution" recurs several times, as does the Libyan-inspired term *jamahiri* (mass-based), to describe the movement.

The Will for Unity with the PLO

At least during the first months of the uprising the Jihad stated its desire to work in concert with the PLO so as to intensify the struggle. Like the United National Leadership of the Uprising (UNLU), the Jihad Brigades renounced the use of weapons (only collaborators were threatened with death). While in their communiqué of January 29, 1988, the Brigades gave a series of instructions on ways of fighting the enemy (burning Israeli vehicles, attacking Israeli economic interests, refusing to pay taxes, eliminating collaborators), there was never any call to kill Israelis, civilian or military. In its press communiqué of February 3, 1988, the Jihad denounced articles in the British press according to which it was calling for military operations, stating its belief that Israel would be forced to "withdraw its military apparatus under the exclusive impact of the blood of the martyrs, the cries that 'God alone is Great' and the throwing of stones." This was the fruit of a deliberate choice, since the Jihad recalled that it was also capable of carrying out armed struggle when it found it necessary.[13] The will for unity was demonstrated even where its positions differed from those of the PLO.[14]

The Jihad and the UNLU

The constant preoccupation with stressing its identity in relation to the PLO, and its effective participation in the anti-Israeli struggle, have led many outside observers as well as a number of Palestinians, including leaders on the outside,[15] to conclude that the Islamic Jihad had joined the UNLU. The UNLU itself, however, never made any such claim, and the Jihad rejected it. The "important communiqué" of the National Leadership of the Uprising in Gaza (undated, early 1988) simply stated that it is "a large coalition of combat brought about by the intifada," made up of the main PLO forces represented in the Occupied Territories, Fateh, the Palestine Communist party, the PFLP, the DFLP, and "other patriotic forces, patriotic committees, . . . institutions, patriotic personalities and patriotic religious forces committed to the program of the PLO." This formulation obviously excludes the Muslim Brotherhood and others whose objectives diverge widely from those of the PLO. While stressing its solidarity, the Jihad negated its participation in the UNLU (communiqué of February 3, 1988). It is not clear whether or not certain individuals, members of the Jihad Brigades and also close to Fateh, may have agreed to associate themselves with the UNLU.[16]

Israeli Repression

In early March 1988, the Jihad seemed to disappear from the Palestinian political scene. The rapid and violent Israeli repression of its members, activists or simple sympathizers, doubtless explains this withdrawal. High-ranking leaders were deported from the Occupied Territories: Sheikh Abd al-'Aziz 'Odeh, April 11, 1988; Dr. Fathi Shqaqi, August 7, 1988; Ahmad Hasan Muhanna, December 14, 1988; Saïd Barakat, January 1, 1989. On the outside, military leaders were eliminated: on February 2, 1988, in Limassol, three of them died in a car-bomb explosion; on April 16, 1988, Abu Jihad himself, whose name had variously been mentioned, during the trials of Brigade members, as the Jihad's contact in Fateh and the PLO, was assassinated in Tunis. Numerous arrests were made, in continuation of a policy predating the uprising. All of this amounted to a severe blow to the organization, whose quasi-disappearance a number of people announced. Israel, however, continued periodically to announce the dismantling of Jihad cells.[17] Various local reports also speak of tracts being circulated.

Rejection of the PNC Decisions

The Jihad reappeared in the fall of 1988, announcing its break with the PLO, which was preparing for the nineteenth Palestinian National Council (PNC) meeting in Algiers. On October 10, "on the occasion of the first anniversary of the battle of Shuja'iyya," the Jihad Brigades broke with eleven months of common abstention with the UNLU from armed struggle and announced their resumption of military activities, claiming to have thrown a grenade against a military patrol in Sheikh Radwan neighborhood (Gaza). The Islamic Jihad, in a communiqué on November 11, 1988, reproduced in *al-Islam wa Filastin,* attacked "those who consider themselves the representatives of the Palestinian people," just as the PNC was preparing to accept UN Resolutions 242 and 338 as the bases for the PLO's participation in an international peace conference:

Oh masses of our Palestinian Muslim people! The Movement of the Islamic Jihad in Palestine proclaims in your name, in the name of your jihad, in the name of your struggle, in the name of your sacrifices, that that peace is sacrilegious, that that commitment is null and illicit, that the partition of the homeland with the enemy and the recognition of its legitimacy go against the divine order.

THE ISLAMIC RESISTANCE MOVEMENT (IRM)—HAMAS

For their part, the traditional Muslim Brothers could not remain outside the unfolding events. They thus broke with their long history of abstention from anti-Israeli mobilization. In Gaza, their individual participation from the beginning of the uprising is certain. As for their mobilization as an organization, it is a problematic issue, as will be seen.

The Ideology of the IRM

Ideological tenets of the Muslim Brotherhood were clearly perceptible in communiqués of the IRM from the beginning of the *intifada,* and their coherence was preserved throughout. In each of its tracts, the IRM devoted a good deal of space to ideological positions, setting forth in simple terms a historiography of the Palestinian question since the beginning of the century: the Islamic people has a consciousness of its duties before God in the defense of Palestine, God's blessed country and that of the prophets, eternal property (*waqf*) of the Islamic community. Enduring and courageous, it has never hesitated to shed blood again and again, but it was duped by Arab regimes and leaders, simple stooges of the atheist West and its regional representative, Israel. In 1988, as in 1936, the Arab leaders have become the instruments of surrender and defeat, being disposed, at the behest of the United States, to recognize Israel and thus legitimize usurpation. The PLO is never directly attacked by the IRM; never quoted, it does not exist. Implicitly however, the political initiatives of its leaders are constantly under attack.

The Various Phases in the Mobilization of the IRM

Whereas the IRM displays great ideological continuity, several periods can be distinguished, corresponding to clearly differentiated political practices, and leading to serious questions as to whether the authors of its very first tracts were the same as those of its later ones. The first year of the uprising is divided into three distinct phases where the IRM is concerned.

Participation in the Uprising

The first period begins with an undated tract and ends with the distribution on February 11 of the IRM's fourth communiqué. Signed by the Islamic Resistance Movement (*Harakat al-Muqawama al-Islamiyya*), a heretofore unknown organization, the first tract was a hymn to the courage of the people, to its endurance and to its faith in final victory. Without providing a detailed calendar for mobilization, it called in general for the continuation of the uprising. That first tract was undated, but from various indications it may be presumed to have been circulated around December 15, 1987. While this is clearly a very early date in the history of the written communiqués of the uprising, it does not, as the Muslim Brotherhood now claims, prove decisively that it was mobilizing even before the PLO-affiliated groups. This is because nothing proves that the first, second (mid-January 1988), and third (January 22, 1988) IRM communiqués were issued by the Muslim Brotherhood. Those communiqués in fact give no indication as to their authors' affiliations. On the contrary, their slogans remained vague and universal ("This is the voice of Islam! The voice of the entire Palestinian people!"—January 22, 1988). This ambiguity has been interpreted as a Muslim Brotherhood tactic designed to appeal to a much broader base at a time when the Islamic Jihad enjoyed much greater popularity. But the publication by *al-Islam wa Filastin* of two early IRM tracts, including the first one, suggests that persons close to the Jihad may in fact have been the founders of a movement which only in mid-February 1988 became the political expression of the Association of Muslim Brothers. Some writings (including of course those of persons and groups close to the PLO) claim that the Muslim Brotherhood as an organization was absent from the events of the first months of the *intifada*, and was then forced by the departure of some of its members and ever-stronger internal criticism to become involved later on.

Organizing the Uprising

The participation of the Muslim Brothers characterizes the second phase of the IRM's history, which begins with the fourth communiqué of February 11, 1988, in which the movement presents itself as "the powerful arm of the Association of Muslim Brothers" (a presentation that appears to have been contested by some in the IRM, since one version of the tract omits it). This period continued through May-June 1988. For the first time, the initials HMS (Harakat al-Muqawama al-Islamiyya: Movement of the Islamic Resistance) are used, which in the fifth communiqué become the acronym Hamas, a (non-Koranic) term signifying "zeal" or "enthusiasm."

This new stage witnesses the appearance of a precise mobilization calendar, including general strikes, fasting, or days of confrontation with the enemy. Hamas, like the UNLU, also gives instructions for the organization of the uprising in all aspects of daily life: appeals to merchants or landlords, including threats against those who do not comply, not to raise prices; warnings against those thieves who would try to take advantage of the mass resignation of Palestinian police; exhortations to collaborators to repent; appeals to the population to defend itself against settlers, and advice on security measures; appeals for a return to the land and development of domestic economy so as to ensure the greatest possible self-reliance. Traditional Muslim Brother themes are likewise found, such as "the role of the Holy City of Jerusalem and Palestine among Muslims" or "the perversion of the children of Israel." Religion is now placed at the service of the anti-Israeli struggle, which is depicted as the eschatological combat between good and Evil.

The mosques became the natural place for this social structuring of the uprising by Hamas, especially in Gaza. By mid-March, mosque committees were instructed to organize popular teaching to make up for the closure of schools and universities. They were also to see to the collection of the *zakat* (Muslim charity) and its proper redistribution among the poor and the victims of the uprising.

The political content of the communiqués from that period does not vary much from the outlines traced during the first stage: Hamas continues violently to denounce the Arab regimes, with their lip-service to American initiatives, a just and durable peace, an international conference, and so on. "Our answer . . . is as follows: no to peace with the Zionist entity" (March 13, 1988). Hamas, like the UNLU, mobilizes against George Schultz's various missions to the region and calls (simultaneously with the UNLU) for a general strike against his visit on February 24 and 25.

Despite differences on the final resolution of the Palestinian question, Hamas and the UNLU reached a good-neighborly *modus vivendi* in the streets. Hamas' unilateral call for a general strike on April 9 in commemoration of the 1948 Deir Yasin massacre did not lead to clashes on the ground, since Hamas had not attempted to impose a strike beyond its traditional areas of mobilization. The theme of national unity is a recurrent one, and the UNLU and Hamas together denounced Israeli provocations in the form of false communiqués,[18] car burnings, the attempted burning of the Gaza blood bank (a PLO stronghold), and so on. "The unity of our people in this phase constitutes the supreme objectives to which we are attached and over which we watch" (Hamas communiqué, May 6, 1988).

Directing the Uprising

The third mobilizing phase of Hamas begins in May and June. It is characterized by tension with the UNLU, at a time when the PLO is multiplying its diplomatic initiatives. The political themes continue as before, but Hamas, while denying that this is the case, presents itself more and more as the alternative leadership of the *intifada*. On August 18 it publishes a Covenant (*Mithaq*), a forty-page synthesis of its ideological stance, which Hamas intends to defend through popular mobilization.[19] Its communiqués are henceforth numbered, like those of the UNLU. Hamas takes advantage of this development by inflating the number of its tracts so as to strengthen its claim to an earlier commitment than that of PLO advocates. The communiqué of June 26 carries the number 24, whereas everything indicates that about fifteen Hamas tracts had by then been published. At the same time its mobilization calendar becomes heavier and takes priority over all else in the text. Beginning on August 2, 1988, its calls for general strikes are multiplied and become catalysts for tension with the UNLU, which increases after King Hussein's announcement on July 31, 1988, of the "severing of legal and administrative ties" with the West Bank.

The UNLU welcomed this development as a major achievement for the *intifada* and a ratification of the eighteenth PNC of 1987, which reinforced the authority of the PLO (UNLU Communiqué No. 23 of August 5, 1988). Hamas in this context decided to show its lack of accord with the PLO's claim of filling the political void alone by contesting the de facto prerogative of the UNLU and drawing up a calendar of popular mobilization. As of August 2, 1988, three days before the UNLU communiqué, Hamas called for a strike on August 9, the now-traditional monthly remembrance of the outbreak of the *intifada*, as well as August 14, the Islamic new year. The UNLU then chose dates at variance with those of Hamas, forcing the latter unilaterally to call for general strikes. This happened three times in a row (twice in August, once in September),[20] and in the three cases the Brothers, isolated, felt they had to respond to the challenge. Whereas on August 14 Hamas had limited itself to mobilizing the Gaza Strip, on August 21 and September 9 it decided to move beyond its traditional areas of influence and impose its strike call in the West Bank, using methods that included physical pressure. Clashes occurred in Nablus, Ramallah, Bethlehem, and Hebron. Only Jerusalem remained free of tension, since Hamas had not tried to impose its strikes there on merchants, virtually all of whom opened their shops.[21]

The UNLU and Hamas both issued repeated mutual denunciations coupled with calls for unity. For Hamas, "agents of the Jews tried to break the strike, but our people . . . made this occasion fail. . . . Let all know that the IRM is not against any of the children of our people but against the Jews and those who resemble them. It calls for patriotic unity" (September 5, 1988). For the UNLU, "the attempts of the last few days led by the Hamas movement, which is the wing of the Muslim Brothers, to impose its authority on the patriotic street and impose a general strike Sunday, 21 August, were perceived by the masses of our people . . . as . . . going against the patriotic calendar determined by its United National Leadership. . . . We have extended our hand and we extend it again, to any force which wishes to join in the patriotic task" (September 6, 1988).[22]

On the outside, moderation was the order of the day. PLO leaders minimized the significance of these contradictions,[23] while "summit meetings" were arranged between the parties.[24] An armistice was concluded, as shown by the fact that from September 17 to December 9, Hamas and the UNLU called for nine general strikes in common, Hamas choosing only two independent occasions,

October 29 and November 29. On the former date, the UNLU gave instructions by word of mouth to go along with Hamas' date, which became a common strike. The latter occasion, on the other hand, marks the anniversary of the 1947 UN Partition Resolution, and Hamas insisted on going its own way. Since the UNLU, following the decisions of the PNC, no longer saw any need to protest a resolution which, on the contrary, was now considered a basis for resolving the problem, Hamas found itself mobilizing for a strike side by side with the PFLP to mark their common, continued rejection of partition.[25] There was after that a renewed general convergence in calendars between Hamas and the UNLU.

The Political Offensive of the IRM

The progressive coordination in mobilization on the ground cannot mask profound political differences as to the future. On August 18, under the title "Palestine is Islamic from the sea to the river," Hamas had launched its offensive in the face of preparations for the nineteenth PNC meeting and denounced the temptation of negotiations. While Hamas never mentioned the PLO in its communiqués, its Covenant discusses it in a broader framework of an analysis of patriotic movements, which it casts in a highly positive light "as long as they do not owe their allegiance either to the communist east or to the crusader west. . . . The PLO is the closest of the close to the IRM. Father, brother, neighbor and friend belong to it. Can the Muslim remain a stranger to his father, his brother, his neighbor or his friend? Our homeland is one, our struggle is one, our destiny is one and our enemy is common. But . . . the PLO has adopted the idea of a lay state . . . [which] totally contradicts the idea of religion. . . . The Islamic nature of Palestine is a part of our religion. . . . The day the PLO adopts Islam as its rule for life, we will be its soldiers" (articles 26–27).

One of the Muslim Brothers' leaders, Sheikh Ahmad Yasin, also made contradictory statements during the same period, sometimes stressing the association's convergence with the PLO, at other times its divergence from it. The publication of the Covenant and outbreaks of inter-Palestinian street violence were played up in the Israeli media, which accorded a long interview on (state-owned) television to Sheikh Yasin. The PLO denounced this development, noting the relatively light repression to which the Muslim Brotherhood was being subjected by Israel.[26]

The PNC's decisions did little to change the course of events. The IRM continued to stress its own views while usually seeking to engage in joint mobilization with the UNLU. In a letter to the PNC, it claimed paternity for the uprising, stating that

Hamas was born of the establishment of total jihad . . . until the liberation of all of Palestine. It decided to launch the uprising on 8 December 1987 in order to attain this objective. All of the children of Palestine then stood by its side and continue to do so. . . . Do not err regarding the voices which call for peace with the assassins, at the very time when they occupy our land and persecute our people. . . . Brothers! We declare before you that the projects for so-called "provisional government," for a "declaration of independence," or a "government in exile" . . . are all nothing more than bait whose objective is to destroy the gains made by the intifada, a knife thrust into the back of the children of stones.

After having expressed this warning, Hamas returned to deliberately ignoring the PLO. The very name of the PNC is not to be found, nor is any reference to an independent Palestinian state. Hamas returned to denouncing its traditional enemies: the Arab regimes and their historic betrayal of Palestine (cf. communiqué 32 of November 21, 1988).

OF THE DIFFICULTY OF BEING SIMULTANEOUSLY PALESTINIAN AND ISLAMICIST

For Hamas, peace is an unacceptable option. It would mean having God surrender to Evil through negotiations with the incarnation of illegitimacy, Israel. This intransigence contrasts with the policies of the UNLU. Both Hamas and the UNLU broke in their mobilizing practices with the policy of the Jordanian-oriented notables of an earlier age. Both depersonalized their policies: decisions are made by an anonymous leadership, and the UNLU only very rarely mentions Yasser Arafat by name. The *intifada* is in this sense, both in its lay and in its religious wings, a fruit of the 1980s, after the charismatic Palestinian leaders in the Occupied Territories (such as the mayors elected in 1976) had been deposed, imprisoned, or deported. The politics of the *intifada* are marked by the practices of a decade when the society was being restructured through various unions and associations that imposed themselves even more deeply than its national leaders in defense of certain values. Mobilization was decentralized and transferred from restricted elites to a multitude of local leaders. This was most evident in the case of the followers of the PLO. The youth of the refugee camps for a time swept the intelligentsia of the Jerusalem-Ramallah-Bethlehem area aside to launch the uprising. In the longer run, and thanks to the diplomatic process, these personalities appear to be making a comeback.

Developments in the religious camp should be seen in similar terms. The prominent early role of the Jihad and the structural absence of the Muslim Brothers during the first months of the *intifada* represented a warning by a more radical base to the Islamic elites, one that was heeded, as can be seen by the Muslim Brothers' subsequent effective participation. In the beginning, it would appear that individuals or groups still belonging to the Muslim Brothers, but seduced by the ideas of the Jihad and carried away by the wave of the *intifada*, forced the leadership of the movement to adopt an offensive attitude toward Israel. In the second phase, the Brothers in turn played on the tensions between the pro-PLO elites linked to the outside and a determined internal base to challenge the UNLU, suggesting the importance of ties between the PLO and Arab leaders.

The Muslim Brotherhood no longer makes social re-islamization its top priority. In order to acquire broad political legitimacy, it has to show that it is an effective actor in the anti-Israel struggle. It has in this the very clear example of the Jihad, which in the course of a few months managed to obtain the unanimous support of the population.

The realities of the occupation and the absence of a state have meant that islamicists and nationalists often find themselves in ideological and political proximity, due to their Palestinian specificity. Whereas around the world, the Islamic movement has focused on challenging the states issued from decolonization, thus making antinationalism a key element of their ideology, the a-statism of Palestinians has led their Islamic movement to preach something close to the ideas of their "nationalist" rivals. Disillusionment with the Arab states has led both the Islamic movement and PLO supporters to preach a certain distancing from the Arabs and a concomitant "palestinianism." Arabism, for the rising Islamic and nationalist generation, no longer passes through any Arab capital, but through an attachment to the land and to religion.

With the *intifada*, the Islamic movement has asserted, perhaps for the first time with as much clarity, that patriotism (*wataniyya*) "is an integral part of the religious credo" (article 7 of the Covenant). While remaining ultimately Islamic in its inspiration, the current historiography of the Islamic movement in the Occupied Territories is almost exclusively Palestinian.

For a long time the Muslim Brothers have been convinced that the PLO's diplomatic initiatives will inevitably founder. The people will then, they believe, find themselves with no alternative other than Islam. For them to be able to pick up the leadership at that point, the Muslim Brothers must, so they feel, effectively participate in the anti-Israeli struggle. They do not, in case the Arafat-led PLO should falter, see any threat coming from a Marxist left, always suspected of atheism. Some also point to unbroken ties to Jordan and certain circles in Syria as giving the Brotherhood a chance of assuming national leadership in the event that the diplomatic line of Yasser Arafat should collapse.

Hamas has surely scored some points against the pro-PLO figures. It has not yet managed to acquire the overwhelming legitimacy born of resistance. Its participation is still doubted in the West Bank. But its success is genuine: it is an essential interlocutor for the majority nationalists, unlike the partisans of the rejection front, who are almost nonexistent and who are discredited by their close ties with Syria, considered responsible for the massacre of Palestinians in Lebanon.

Unity is one of the most effective weapons against Israel, and neither the nationalists nor Hamas will take the risk of abandoning it. In their struggle against the islamicists' quest for legitimacy through the rejection of all negotiations in the name of the religious obligation of liberating all of Palestine, the PLO supporters cannot permit themselves to combat the Muslim Brotherhood openly. Thus reduced to isolating Hamas on a case-by-case basis, the only guarantee of victory for the PLO lies in the rapid attainment of political results through diplomatic initiatives designed to realize the independent Palestinian state whose existence it has declared.

NOTES

1. R. Hrair Dekmejian, *Islam in Revolution: Fundamentalism in the Arab World* (New York: Syracuse University Press, 1985); Gilles Kepel, "Intellectuals et militants," *Lettre Internationale* 19 (Winter 1988–89); Olivier Roy, *L'Afghanistan, Islam et modernité politique* (Paris: Seuil, 1985); Emmanuel Siwan, *Radical Islam: Medieval Theology and Modern Politics* (New Haven: Yale University Press, 1985).

2. François Burgat, *L'Islamisme au Maghreb* (Paris: Khartala, 1988); Olivier Carré and Paul Dumont, *Radicalismes islamiques*, 2 vols. (Paris: L'Harmattan, 1985–86).

3. Jean-François Legrain, "Islamistes et lutte nationale palestinienne dans les territories occupés par Israël," *Revue Française de Science Politique* 36, no. 2 (April 1986): 227–47.

4. The toleration or even assistance granted by the occupation authorities is now openly recognized by the Israeli media. Cf., for example, Yehuda Litani (a journalist known for his intimate ties to the security apparatus), *Jerusalem Post (JP)*, September 8, 1988; Ori Nir, *Ha'aretz*, September 16, 1988 (article translated into English by the Israeli government).

5. Jean-François Legrain, "Les islamistes palestinians à l'épreuve du soulèvement," *Maghreb-Mashrek* 121 (July 1988): 4–42.

6. Answering these questions as objectively as possible has become all the more important since competing and contradictory historiographies are being created by the PLO (cf. the chronologies of *Shu'un Filastiniyya*) and the Muslim Brothers (cf. 'Abd al-'Aziz 'Odeh, interviewed in *al-Wahda al-Islamiyya*, April 29, 1988, reproduced in *al-Islam wa Filastin (IF*—Limassol), no. 5 (June 5, 1988): 4–6; Muhammad Nazzal, "Li-madha hadha al-tajahul li dawri-l-haraka al-islamiyya fi-l-intifada?" (Why this ignorance of the role of the Islamic movement in the *intifada?*), *Filastin al-Muslima, (FM)* March 1988, pp. 12–13; 'Abd al-'Aziz al-'Umri, "Man alladhin ash'alu al-intifada wa man alladhin yaqudunaha?" (Who initiated the *intifada* and who leads it?), *al-Mujtama'* (Kuwait), June 28, 1988, pp. 18–20. The islamicist historiography has been partially adopted by certain Israeli journalists. Cf. Sheffi Gabbai, "Hamas and the Uprising: The Mosques' Revolution," *Maariv*, December 16, 1988 (translated by the Israeli government).

7. "Al-Ard al-muhtalla tashta'il didd al-sahayna" (The occupied land catches fire against the Zionists), *al-Thawra al-Islamiyya* (London), no. 95 (February 1988): 40–43; Hala Mustafa, "Al-Jihad al-Islami fi-l-ard al-muhtalla" (The Islamic Jihad in the occupied land), *Qadaya Fikriyya* (Cairo), no. 6 (April 1988): 178–83; Israel: defense spokesman, "Islamic Jihad in Judea, Samaria and Gaza," reproduced in *JP*, February 3, 1988.

8. This last attack was also claimed by Fateh's Force 17.

9. Cf., for example, the manifesto of *Sawt al-Jama'a al-Islamiyya* (Gaza) 1 (October 1986); 'Abd al-'Aziz 'Odeh, *al-Fajr* (Jerusalem), August 23, 1987.

10. Interview with a leader of the Communist party, Gaza, December 1988; see also Wendy Levitt, "The Shadowy Face of Fundamentalism," *The Middle East*, November 1988, pp. 15–16.

11. It is very difficult to obtain Jihad tracts. Of the sixteen in my possession, I obtained

five (including two forgeries) in the Occupied Territories, while the others, apparently authentic, were published in *IF*.

12. *JP*, January 19, 1988.

13. Cf. 'Abd al-'Aziz 'Odeh, interviewed in *al-Wahda al-Islamiyya*, April 29, 1988, who states that "the present stage does not permit the use of arms because the people [are] in the camps and the streets."

14. Cf. communiqué of February 3, 1988.

15. *Democratic Palestine*, organ of George Habash's PFLP, March 1988, and *al-Hurriya*, organ of Nayef Hawatmeh's DFLP, September 18, 1988.

16. In March 1988, Sheikh Bassam Jarrar, a personality from al-Bireh close to various Islamic groups who was later imprisoned, noted that their profound divergences made it impossible for Jihad members to be in the UNLU, adding that "if there are any religious persons in the UNLU, they are all members of Fateh." In November 1988, Dr. Mahmud al-Zahhar from Gaza, close to Hamas, estimated that the Jihad had for the first few months participated in the UNLU and added, giving no reasons, that it had withdrawn around April 1988.

17. According to the Ministry of Defense, the Shin Bet, in October-November 1988, dismantled ninety-three "terrorist cells," three of which belonged to the Jihad.

18. Notably one by the "Palestine Communist Party," denounced by a Hamas communiqué, February 11, 1988, and by the PCP communiqué of February 14, 1988.

19. Dan Fisher and Dan Williams, "Islamic Group Calls Holy War Palestine Key," *Los Angeles Times*, September 5, 1988; Reuven Paz, *Ha-'imna ha-islamit umichma'utah 'iyyon rechoni utargum* (The Covenant of the Islamicists and its significance—analysis and translation) (Tel Aviv: Tel Aviv University, Dayan Center, 1988) (in Hebrew).

20. Hamas: August 9, 14, and 21; September 9 and 17. UNLU: August 9 and 22; September 8 (!) and 17.

21. Joel Greenberg and Joshua Brilliant, "Islamic Activists Lead Their First West Bank Strike," *JP*, August 22, 1988; Glenn Frankel, "PLO-Fundamentalist Rift Seen in Occupied Territories," *Washington Post*, September 6, 1988; Joel Greenberg and Joshua Brilliant, "Latest Leaflet Scores Split in Uprising Leadership," *JP*, September 7, 1988; Daniel Williams, "Rivalry to Control Uprising Grows," *Los Angeles Times*, September 10, 1988.

22. *Facts Weekly Review*, published clandestinely in English by circles close to the UNLU in Jerusalem, denounced Hamas, considering that Israel and the Western press were playing up the islamicists so as to brandish the specter of Islamic fanaticism. It attributed the entire responsibility for competing calendars to Hamas. *Facts Weekly Review*, no. 24 (August 28, 1988), and no. 25 (September 11, 1988).

23. For example, Yasser Arafat in an interview with *al-Ittihad* and *al-Khalij* (Abu Dhabi).

24. *Washington Post*, September 18, 1988.

25. It was in fact the second time this had occurred, the first being July 8, 1988.

26. As compared with what happened to the Jihad, this allegation is justified. Only one Muslim Brotherhood leader, Sheikh Khalil al-Quqa, was deported, while others, such as Sheikh Yasin and Mahmud al-Zahhar, are regularly interviewed as *Muslim Brotherhood* leaders on Israeli television.

12

The Revolutionary Transformation of the Palestinians Under Occupation

Jamal R. Nassar and Roger Heacock

The *intifada* resulted from the accumulation and festering of deep-rooted griev-ances that made the Occupied Territories a ticking time-bomb. The forces behind it had been at work since Israel's occupation began. While these forces, within the territories and abroad, gave the uprising its organizational and political con-tent, the occupier's behavior over twenty years gave it its very birth and, in retrospect, made its outbreak inevitable. This chapter will trace and assess these recent developments.

Within days after the first skirmishes and deaths in Gaza, the pro-PLO na-tionalist forces formed a joint command known as the United National Leadership of the Uprising (UNLU) and began to issue directives. The UNLU was made up of representatives from Fateh, the Popular Front for the Liberation of Palestine (PFLP), the Democratic Front for the Liberation of Palestine (DFLP), and the Palestine Communist Party (PCP). In Gaza they coordinated with the Islamic Jihad from time to time.

The drafting and distribution of leaflets is a classical method of the Palestinian political forces in the Occupied Territories. To the Palestinians under occupation, the leaflets of the UNLU, issued as numbered communiqués, were transformed into a sort of a biweekly legislative-executive-judicial document with the force of a constitution. Signed by the UNLU-PLO, the communiqués raised the slogans of a given period. These were rooted in the macro-political setting of Palestinian and world revolutionary history, and in the micro-political setting of the ongoing issues and challenges of the *intifada*.

From the very first communiqué, the tone set by the UNLU was unyielding in its confrontation of Israeli practices in the Occupied Territories and clear in its political vision. Communiqué No. 2, for example, issued on January 10, 1988, confirmed the Palestinian rights of "return, self-determination and the creation of our Palestinian state under the leadership of the Organization"; at the same time it asked the people "to struggle for the realization of the *intifada*'s basic and immediate slogans, which are represented in:

- an end to the iron fist policy, and to rule by the Emergency Law, including the immediate revocation of expulsion orders;
- forbidding the violation and defiling of the holy places, and [demanding] the removal of the terrorist Sharon from the old city of Jerusalem;
- withdrawal of the army from towns, camps and villages . . . and banning [their] firing on our unarmed people;
- dissolution of town, village and refugee camp councils that were appointed by the occupation authorities, and holding democratic elections for all municipal and village councils in the West Bank and Gaza Strip;
- the immediate release of all the prisoners of the *intifada* and the closure of Al Far'a, Ansar 2, Ansar 3 and Dhahrieh prisons;
- cancellation of the value-added tax, so arbitrarily imposed on our merchants;
- ending land confiscation and the erection of settlements, and the . . . provocations of the settlers;
- forbidding the invasion and closure of the educational, union and mass institutions, and banning the authorities' interference in their internal affairs. [1]

The determined tone, the realism of stated political goals, and the detailed and comprehensive list of short-term demands all contributed to propelling the uprising, its leadership, and the Palestinian issue onto the center stage of world politics. From the beginning, the UNLU had as clear a perception of the nature of the enemy as it did of its own people. Their communiqués helped them knit the Palestinians together by stressing grievances of various age, social, and professional groups (city, village, and camp dwellers, as well as religious groups, peasants, merchants, workers, and even students and educators).

The wisdom, pragmatism, and strong local and international appeal of those very first communiqués assured a favorable response from the international media and from most governments. They set the tone for the thirty UNLU communiqués issued during the *intifada*'s first year. They also demonstrated to an initially incredulous world that the Palestinian revolution had reached maturity in both the strategic and tactical fields.

UNLU communiqués were, from the first, the product of an ongoing interaction between the Palestinian national organizations on the inside and their leaders or colleagues on the outside. This important fact must be understood, as it undermines the superficial conventional wisdom prevalent in official circles in Israel, which assumed that the UNLU had either "replaced," "disobeyed," or "imposed itself upon" the outside leadership of the PLO. Israeli officials later reached a different conclusion and began to argue that the entire operation was under the control, after a very few weeks, of the PLO leadership in Tunis. Both of these views are expressed by the Israeli academic community and by the country's political elites.[2] Many international reporters also repeated such claims. In fact, the development and successive stages of the *intifada* cannot be understood, nor could they even be imagined, without the permanent and fruitful, if sometimes tense, interplay between the inside and the outside. In the words of George Habash, secretary general of the PFLP, there are "two fundamental poles to the Palestinian revolution (inside and outside), and it is impossible for one to cancel the other or to operate independently of it."[3] Clearly, the communiqués of the UNLU are the product of the interaction between these two poles. In fact, they have always been signed UNLU/PLO.

The most important result of the uninterrupted flow of UNLU communiqués, which seemed to embody the will of the majority of the Palestinians under occupation, was to fully mobilize the population for the first time. Whether they lived in camps, villages, or cities, the Palestinians of the West Bank and Gaza were mobilized to work for the goals of the *intifada*. By the beginning of 1988, the platforms, slogans, and approaches of the Palestinian political organizations had become those of virtually the entire population. A revolutionary transformation was thus accomplished. From 1967 to 1987 certain sectors of the society had adopted revolutionary political norms. The general population was progressively sensitized to these norms but largely inactive in pursuing their achievement. During that time, the occupation forces had effectively repressed these norms through the threat or application of all sorts of legal or illegal measures of punishment. But repressing behavior does not mean eradicating it. Within few weeks of the start of the uprising, the cry of tens of thousands of Palestinians, from the Egyptian border to that of Lebanon, from the Mediterranean to the Jordan River, had exposed the inherent weakness of repression. When the angry voices were seen to have a determined leadership, most of the population, of both sexes and all ages, joined the *intifada*, adopted its slogans, and espoused its aims. Such goals continued to be proclaimed in the UNLU communiqués: the uprising would continue until it brought about recognition of the Palestinian right to self-determination and an independent state, and the PLO's role as the sole legitimate representative of the Palestinians. Of course, the revolutionary transformation of the Palestinians under occupation did not reside in their acceptance of these goals, which a majority had espoused for well over a decade, but in their common decision to live in accordance with certain principles. Foremost among them is their rejection of a return to normalcy. In other words, the Palestinians under occupation have become actively determined to continue the *intifada* until their demands are met.

Other documented cases of the mass mobilization of a people have occurred in modern history. That in France between 1789 and 1794 is a case in point.

Other examples are the mass mobilization during the Chinese Cultural Revolution in the late 1960s and the Algerian revolution between 1954 and 1962. Such cases are not numerous, but all of them were based on an interplay of objective and subjective factors as well as on a balance of power between revolutionary and counterrevolutionary forces that was, at least temporarily, favorable to the revolution. The Palestinian *intifada* resembles these earlier models in some ways but is unique in others. Its uniqueness stems from the fact that whereas subjective conditions had reached the point where life was unbearable for the occupied, the balance of forces continued to be overwhelmingly favorable to the occupier; the role of organization, discipline, and will is thus relatively greater in the *intifada* than it had been in other cases.

This is perhaps the area where the political groups represented in the UNLU showed the most political maturity and revolutionary sophistication. In their mobilizing task, they were aided by the invaluable experiences of forty years of trial and error, pain, suffering, setbacks, and failures. Each of the four groups participated in hammering out the communiqués, which became biweekly. The first communiqués, were, in fact, issued in Gaza. Later communiqués were issued in the West Bank, but the Gaza leadership had the right to add strike days or special action requests for the Strip. In the Gaza Strip, the Islamic Jihad, a small but active group within the Islamic movement that has for years worked closely with Fateh, coordinated with the UNLU. Its role in the outbreak of the *intifada* was significant. But in time its leadership was arrested, expelled, or, in a few cases, killed.

As for the splinter groups in the Palestinian national movement outside the Occupied Territories, none has a significant following in the West Bank and Gaza and none participated in the UNLU. Thus, the *intifada* "has made it clear that, out of the alphabet soup of PLO groups, only the four main ones are organizations of any political significance, a fact that somewhat diminished the credibility of claims of fissiparousness."[4] This is not to say that other groups had no role whatsoever in the *intifada*. While Ahmad Jibril's Popular Front for the Liberation of Palestine-General Command (PFLP-GC) has only few members besides its salaried fighters in Syria and Lebanon, its activities may still have contributed to fanning the flames of the *intifada*. The PFLP-GC commando who flew on a hang glider into an Israeli military camp in late November 1987 is seen by many as one of the catalysts contributing to the eruption of the *intifada*. Al-Quds (Jerusalem) radio station, which broadcasts from Syria, was also significant, at least until it was jammed by Israel in January 1988, in keeping the initial momentum of the *intifada* going. Abu Musa's Fateh-Provisional Command has a small and dwindling student-based following. In addition, there are several small groups that have splintered off from the Communist party. Five groups, including the PFLP-GC and Abu Musa's, along with three others likewise known for their close ties to Syria, issued a communiqué in mid-February 1988 advocating vigilance in the face of "surrenderist" and "neoimperialist" tendencies within the PLO but coupled with tactical support for the UNLU and its directives. After the November 1988 Palestine National Council meeting in Algiers, these groups found themselves in complete disagreement with the declaration of an independent Palestinian state (November 15, 1988) and, even more so, with Yasser Arafat's speech before the UN General Assembly in Geneva (December 13, 1988). A spate of dissenting leaflets was found littering the streets in the days and weeks that followed, signed by the above groups. These leaflets rejected the Algiers decisions and the Geneva speech and labeled them treasonous. Yasser Arafat himself received the bulk of their verbal abuse. However, it is not clear whether these communiqués were the work of dissenting forces within the Palestinian ranks or of the Israeli secret services; the latter are naturally quick to seek opportunities for driving wedges within the Palestinian ranks.

Unlike the above splinter groups, the Muslim Brotherhood enjoys a limited mass following in the Occupied Territories. The Brotherhood, along with the Islamic Jihad in Gaza, had a role in the *intifada*. Traditionally, the Brotherhood had maintained ambiguous relations with the Palestinian national movement in general, and the PLO leadership in particular. Up until the outbreak of the *intifada*, the Muslim Brotherhood had decidedly favored religious over macro-political and macro-social programs. Prayer, relations between men and women, family life, and similar issues were its main preoccupations. And since its ideology foresaw the restoration of the Islamic Caliphate as a precondition for the liberation of Palestine, it did not often participate in mass demonstrations as called for by the pro-PLO groups. This is indeed one reason for the rise of the Islamic Jihad out of the ranks of the Islamic bloc, as an activist critic of the Brotherhood's relative passivity.

The *intifada*, however, transformed the Brotherhood as it entered into every corner of public and private life. Consequently, the Muslim Brotherhood appears to have done some self-criticism, or at least to have decided to adapt its strategy to new conditions. It issued dicta from its mosques and distributed communiqués signed "Hamas," which stands for Movement of the Islamic Resistance. Since 1988 Hamas has issued several dozen communiqués (about as many as the UNLU), in which the Islamic movement's political programs were set out, and which, for the most part, tended to call upon the people to follow the instructions of the UNLU. Beginning in late August 1988, however, some of the instructions were at variance with those of the UNLU. Serious strategic differences exist between Hamas and the UNLU. For one, Hamas trusts neither superpower and rejects the call for an international peace conference. It also rejects the partition of historic Palestine. The groups represented in the UNLU, on the other hand, all support the international conference and the creation of an independent Palestinian state next to Israel. As the debate on these issues intensified, so did the differences between the UNLU and Hamas.

The Israeli authorities, on their part, tried to exploit these differences by at least passively encouraging Hamas' line wherever it contradicted that of the

UNLU. On September 9, 1988, for example, Hamas enforced a general strike that had not been called for by the UNLU. In doing so, Hamas activists used strong-arm tactics, accosting shopkeepers and threatening to burn down their shops if they did not close immediately. These young Hamas men strode down the streets of Ramallah, for example, holding stones in their hands, and in full view of large numbers of soldiers who patrolled the streets or watched from rooftops without intervening. The same scenario was repeated on other occasions, such as the one on November 29, 1988, when Hamas militants repeated the Ramallah scene in Bethlehem. On the whole, however, it is clear that the strong-arm tactics adopted on occasion by Hamas were unpopular among the population, not just in Ramallah and Bethlehem, but also in Nablus and even in Gaza (two predominantly Islamic centers). As a result of this public disapproval, Hamas seems to have decided not to appear totally isolated and has returned to accepting the general strike calls of the UNLU. There still are occasions, however, when Hamas calls for and attempts to impose its own general strikes (such as on December 31, 1988).

Within the UNLU, on the other hand, each of the four principal groups, in concert with broader forces, participated in hammering out the biweekly communiqués. But each one also occasionally issued its own communiqués and leaflets, making its views, preferences, critiques, and perspectives known to the public. That is to say, there was never any tendency for the principal groups to melt into one another. Indeed, the decision jointly to coordinate *intifada* strategy never blunted broader differences, which arose on many occasions over a variety of questions. Examples of such differences include such issues as the pace at which the society should move toward massive civil disobedience, the frequency of general strike days, the slogans of the moment, and the question of carrying out *intifada*-related activities across the Green Line into pre–1967 Israel (such as burning forests or sabotaging machines). In very rare cases, these divergences even led to the failure to agree on a common platform for the communiqué. In late May 1988, for example, disagreement revolved around the number of general strikes to be scheduled for the month of June. Some favored moving rapidly toward massive civil disobedience by scheduling eighteen general strike days within that one-month period. Others, worried that they might overburden the people, suggested that there be only three such days. Before the compromise was reached and the number of general strike days set at seven from May 30 to June 28, several mutually contradictory "UNLU" communiqués were issued. But no faction overdramatized this situation, even as it was unfolding, or the fact that more than one communiqué was issued. Indeed, it has happened on more than one occasion that a corrective UNLU communiqué was issued when it was deemed that the original was, after all, in error. Such occurrances reflect a vital debate among the participants in the UNLU on strategies and tactics as well as on human capacities and limitations.

Divergences also arose following the Palestine National Council's meeting in Algiers, which had, in addition to unanimously proclaiming the Palestinian state, accepted UN Security Council Resolutions 242 and 338 by majority vote. The

PFLP and some independent members had voted against such acceptance. But at no point did the UNLU even appear to be falling apart. Agreement on Communiqués No. 29 and 30 was reached in principle, while slightly differing versions were in fact printed by the parties to the UNLU. It is clear now that the parties to the UNLU have come to the realization that the continuation of the *intifada* is more important than their differences on long-term objectives or ideology.

In this connection, it is important to understand the precise nature of the UNLU and its relationship to the popular movement in the Occupied Territories. On various occasions, going back to the early weeks of the *intifada*, Israeli Defense Minister Yitzhak Rabin, as well as the internal security services (Shin Bet), claimed that all of the members of the clandestine leadership of the *intifada* had been captured. Indeed, on one occasion it was claimed that the four leaders had been arrested as they sat drafting a UNLU communiqué. On March 25, 1988, for example, the front-page headline in the *Jerusalem Post* read "Authors of Leaflet–11 Arrested," and the story went on to quote Police Minister Haim Bar-Lev as saying that the arrested authors "belong to several Palestinian organizations."[5] It may have been true that the individuals involved in a given *intifada*-related activity, including the drafting of leaflets, were arrested and imprisoned or even expelled. But there were always others to replace those arrested. It is not just a question of the availability of cadres but relates to the nature of the UNLU itself. The UNLU is nothing more, and nothing less, than the personnel involved in the ongoing coordination between political groups in the territories. There is no centralized or personalized leadership of the *intifada* as distinct from the leadership of the four principal groups. The job of drafting communiqués rotates among cadres. Indeed, given the security risk involved, the groups sometimes agree not to act together for that purpose but leave it to two or even one of the four to produce a particular communiqué after the general thrust has been decided on in concert. This draft is then, if possible, circulated among the other groups for their comments and suggested changes.

In general, the individuals designated to write the communiqués are middle-ranking cadres, it being too hazardous from the point of view of security, and too touchy in terms of intergroup politics, to delegate top leadership for this task. But this does not mean that the UNLU is made up of cadres rather than top leadership, since this would be a contradiction in terms given the total identification of the UNLU with the PLO-affiliated groups, and given those groups' Leninist organizational bent (including the only non-Marxist one among them, Fateh). This apparent contradiction can only be understood by moving beyond a shallow, journalistic approach (which has offered the occasional interview with a UNLU "member") to the actual nature of the UNLU. The latter may be defined as the momentary embodiment of the coordination between the four groups (which, either singly or jointly, may also be consulting with other groups, such as Hamas). Since there is simultaneously a permanent form of mutual feedback between the four political groups and their grass-roots constituencies, it can be said that the UNLU, which is the momentary expression of a permanent coordinating process, represents a form of direct extraparliamentary democracy. The evolution of public opinion is reflected in the decision- and policy-making process via the political groups, through their individual leaflets, articles, or policy directives, and finds expression in UNLU communiqués.

At the same time, the UNLU is answerable to the PLO leadership via the groups' representatives on the PLO executive committee. All four groups have been represented on that committee since the seventeenth Palestine National Council session of April 1987. Organizationally, therefore, the UNLU is the concrete link, which had previously been more tenuous, between the Palestinian people in the Occupied Territories and the PLO leadership. This is one of the reasons why, by the fall of 1988, the time had finally become ripe for the declaration of a Palestinian state. The dynamics of this declaration had accumulated through eleven months of the *intifada* and its dual expression: the unitary mobilization of the Palestinian masses under occupation, and the operation of the UNLU. Through the common experiences of many months of uprising, the Palestinians had negated the twenty-year divide and rule policy of the occupiers, and the Palestinian state had de facto come into being in the Palestinian lands captured by Israel in 1967.

The declaration of an independent state, or a government-in-exile, had often been mooted over the years, but any earlier attempt would have been premature. That is indeed why it never came to fruition. But now the time was ripe. The Palestinian state was coming into being. And just as the *intifada* brought King Hussein to recognize, for the first time, that he could no longer lay claim to being the king of the Palestinians, it also, through its grass-roots organizations, the UNLU and the PLO, brought about the declaration of an independent Palestinian state—an enormous achievement for less than a year of the revolution of stones.

THE POPULAR COMMITTEES OF THE *INTIFADA*

The popular committees spawned by the *intifada* overlap with, but are different from, those that were born and flourished during the previous twenty years of occupation. The latter were the mass organizations identified with the four main political groups that existed in four distinct social areas: youths, students, women, and workers. In addition, there were committees active in medical and agricultural relief work. All of these groups covered the entire area of the Occupied Territories. The popular committees of the *intifada*, on the other hand, began to take shape in December 1987, particularly in the area of food relief. Food relief was very important in that the population had been taken by surprise by the extraordinarily long and vast curfews imposed, particularly on the Gaza camps, which resulted in severe food shortages. Neighborhood by neighborhood, village by village, camp by camp, food relief committees were formed. These committees began secretly to collect donations, especially of dry goods, and, even more secretly, delivered them to areas curfewed or besieged.

Meanwhile the preexisting committees continued and expanded their activities during the uprising, notably women's committees and those active in the medical and agricultural fields. They remained, however, identified with one of the four political groups. The *intifada*-spawned committees, created first by dire need and then in response to calls by the UNLU in January 1988, were designed to be non–party-affiliated or at least interparty activities. Great efforts were made to include political activists from the various groups, but also independent persons as well as both genders and various age groups. Most of all, they were organized at the neighborhood or even the block level in the cities and camps. In the villages, there might be one or more committees depending on the village's size.

Initial meetings of entire neighborhood populations were held starting in early March 1988, with children and adolescents in attendance. People volunteered for committees in each of five sectors: education, health, food storage, agriculture, and security. After the system had been set up, a follow-up committee was elected, made up of one member from each of the five committees and two or three other persons. By mid-May 1988, according to one account, there existed 45,000 such committees in the Occupied Territories.[6]

The neighborhood education committees set up a schedule for classes for their area. Classes were held for preschool through high school.[7] Volunteer teachers ran classes in homes, mosques, and churches. Teaching began by mid-March 1988 and continued for two and a half months until the end of May. During that time, the authorities prowled through the neighborhoods, trying to intimidate people so that they would not receive pupils in their houses. Some homes were even placed under surveillance by unmarked cars. But popular education continued unabated until the military authorities reopened schools in late May 1988. The Israeli action may have been prompted by their concern over the success of a grass-roots experiment that was potentially rendering the society educationally independent and giving it a radical form and content.

Health committees were formed of medical and paramedical persons living in a given neighborhood. Assisted by volunteers, they informed those living in the neighborhood of the identity, numbers, and addresses of health professionals and in which houses emergency first aid equipment was being stored. They also coordinated with the various inhabitants of the neighborhood. In many areas makeshift clinics were set up, and a massive, centralized blood-typing program was undertaken covering tens of thousands of people.[8] The neighborhood health committees also took it upon themselves to test and treat wells and water storage facilities in their areas.

Food storage committees collected money from each family and kept basic foodstuffs hidden in the neighborhood in sufficient quantity to ensure minimal supplies for one or more months. The emplacement of these stocks was known only to a handful of people, since the troops often destroyed any noncommercial stores they came across. The food storage committees also supervised the collection and delivery of foodstuffs to nearby or distant besieged areas at night, and distributed food supplies to families whose breadwinner lost his/her income as a result of the uprising.

The agricultural committees were joined by virtually the entire neighborhood. Throughout the spring and summer of 1988, these committees used every cultivable plot, no matter how small, to raise tomatoes, cucumbers, squash, corn, peppers, beans, parsley, and other vegetables. Besides tilling the soil, planting and distributing seedlings, fertilizing, treating for insects, and watering, the agricultural committees also worked on providing the necessary cages for egg-laying hens, chickens, rabbits, and even sheep for those in the community who had the room to raise them. Brochures explaining basic gardening were also distributed throughout the neighborhoods.

Each neighborhood had a security committee, which established procedures for dealing with common crime in the absence of the police force, whose Palestinian members had resigned en masse in answer to a call from the UNLU. In fact, the crime rate dropped considerably.[9] A second purpose of the security committees became its principal one: halting attacks on persons or property by rampaging settlers, which had become a regular occurrence.[10] Each neighborhood was mapped out and a team of young residents made responsible for securing each entrance in case of need. Within seconds of an agreed signal (usually the blowing of a whistle) hefty barricades could block the streets, so that if marauders should get in they would be trapped. In this way, for example, a "burglar," in fact a provocateur in the service of the authorities, was trapped in a store he had entered late at night, soon after the police had resigned. It is likely that the existence of the security committees helped put an early end to this type of Israeli provocation.

The follow-up committees oversaw the execution of projects undertaken by the various sectoral committees. They were responsible for vertical coordination with interneighborhood committees, as well as horizontal coordination with surrounding neighborhoods, all the way up to the municipal level.[11]

These committees have come to assume a role as intermediaries and judges between citizens, a half-traditional, half-modern role, both that of the *wasit* (intermediary) arranging *sullhas* (reconciliations) among angry parties and replacing the police and judicial system characteristic of a modern society. Their decisions are respected and followed, and are usually considered final.

Part of this role consists in ferreting out and pursuing collaborators. A sign of the radical rearrangement of social relations is the regularly increasing activity against collaborators, which has also historically marked experiences in rapid social transformations as well as liberation struggles directed against an occupier. Hundreds of collaborators have repented under pressure from the masses; dozens have been killed through the procedures set up by the committees and their strike forces; hundreds more have been deterred from filling the void and becoming collaborators.

Here too the *intifada* is half-way between the traditional and the modern system of justice. The collaborators are dealt with first in ways that are both traditional and humanitarian. They are shamed by visits to their families; their names are written on walls; stories circulate about them; unknowing persons are warned to stay away from them. Usually this is enough. They repent in the presence of a religious figure and representative sections of the society and the *intifada*, notably the *shababs* and the popular committees. Early in the uprising, they surrendered their weapons if they had any, which were then publicly destroyed or even turned over to the Israeli army or police. In more recent times, this has not occurred because weapons have not as readily been distributed by the occupation, in view of the unreliable nature of their local "men in the field."

In the case of those who fail to repent, further pressures are mounted against them, this time through the family and local notables. Most of the remaining known collaborators "resign" at this stage, having made a deal with the strike committees responsible for following up their cases that they will cease to collaborate if they are left alone. These collaborators are one step up in rank from the first group, which had quickly agreed to repent publicly, thus showing that they had never been sure of themselves in their collaboration. Those who make deals with the strike forces in the presence of only their families are more important in rank, and also more likely, if not carefully monitored, to return to their previous activities.

Yet higher in rank are the known collaborationist leaders, whether integrated into the police forces or Village Leagues or not. They are armed, have bodyguards, and are highly dangerous; their houses and headquarters are heavily fortified, and they represent local bastions of the occupation which in the present stage, given the balance of forces with the occupation, nobody even thinks of eradicating. (The other category of collaborators who are untouched are those who have managed to remain secret—deep penetration agents, as it were.)

Finally, if none of the previously outlined measures works, the unrepentant collaborators are condemned to death by a committee made up of representatives of all four political groups. In the case of the Islamic movement, collaborators are dealt with similarly but within and by the movement acting alone, unless the actions of the collaborator have specifically spilled over into the realm of activities of the national forces. It would appear that the procedure within the Islamic movement is less institutionalized, systematic, and methodical, and that it may give the collaborators in question more leeway to escape justice.

As can be seen, the procedure, like so much else within the process of institutionalization at work in the *intifada*, combines traditional and modern, or even revolutionary, elements. It plays a key role in deepening and broadening the mobilization of the society. It permits the leadership, cadres, and committees to work in greater safety and allows people in general to feel more confident about expressing themselves and acting against the occupation. It also corresponds to a heightened stage in the confrontation with Israel, for the latter is seeking ways to reestablish its damaged network of local information gathering and control.

As a result of the operation of this mechanism over a long period, Palestinian society has been further unified. The ranks of the passive or resigned have been decimated by the positive measures of the *intifada*; those of the minuscule but influential collaborating forces are reduced and on the defensive. In this way, the triple division of the society among those who accept the occupation, those who actively and hatefully reject it, and those who, while not accepting it, have chosen "steadfastness" as their behavioral norm, has broken down. The entire society is now for the resistance, and therefore the *intifada*. Those who are against it through their collaborationist activities are excluded from the society.

This exclusion of collaborators is rendered possible by the nature of the Israeli occupation and its perception by Palestinians. Even collaborators were never and could never have become convinced Zionists, proponents of Greater Israel, or even convinced advocates of Israeli occupation of Palestinian lands. They were—and are—individuals whose personality or behavioral vulnerability leaves them open to blackmail and manipulation by the authorities. They therefore lack any social or ideological legitimacy whatsoever in the eyes of their fellow Palestinians. Since they are on the defensive as a result of the incessant investigations and campaigns of which they are the targets, they are now much less feared.

This classic struggle against collaborators, agents of occupation, is therefore a significant factor in social mobilization during the *intifada*, giving the population the sense that resistance is effective and capable of dealing with even the most ominous challenges. That is why this struggle is one of the prime tasks of the popular committees and their strike forces. It goes hand in hand with the other, positive activities of the committees, designed to promote the well-being, health, and security of the people.

What is remarkable in this context, where the local police have resigned and the occupier's forces have made every effort to drive wedges between Palestinians through propagandistic but also violent means, is the profound social peace and the high level of security enjoyed by men, women, children, and the aged in their daily lives, something highly atypical of other, comparable historical situations.

In sum, the popular committees established a shadow administrative structure for a society that had decisively rejected the one in place for over twenty years. They therefore institutionalized and legitimized the *intifada* at the grass-roots level. Thus the key link between theory and practice was in place. They did not, of course, need to replace services by the public or private sector for indefinite periods. But each one in its own sphere proved that it was capable should the need arise. In this way, they prevented a possible onset of mass anxiety, especially in large villages, camps, and towns, where the threat of social disorganization might have been greatest.

Popular committees were most active from March through July 1988. When schools reopened at the end of May, when the planting season ended in late June, when Defense Minister Rabin declared the committees illegal and threatened their members with ten years' imprisonment in August, some of their activities were suspended, reduced, or more carefully hidden from view.[12] But the committees have proved their worth, and they continue to exist. Each neighborhood knows and has confidence in its own people and has identified experts in various essential fields. The inhabitants have been drawn closer together by the experience of mutual self-help and self-reliance, as well as semi-clandestinity. Many barriers based on gender, age, and religion have fallen. Committee members are turned to for advice, mediation, and encouragement. Their successful struggle to provide essential services remains indelibly marked in the popular consciousness, an essential element in the determination of the people of the *intifada*.

The popular committees are still active, albeit from the shadows. They now coordinate more closely with the political groups and thus with the UNLU. They pass on national guidelines and help establish priorities. They also act as strike forces to coordinate demonstrations and other actions against the military or even collaborators. In the vital field of food relief to besieged villages and camps, they still carry out the same tasks as before, under more dangerous conditions. It is fair to say that without popular committees, the *intifada* might have found itself short of breath by the early spring of 1988, since it would have depended much more heavily on the unmediated rapport between the masses and the UNLU. With them, there emerged a grass-roots structure that legitimized the *intifada*, strengthened the revolutionary transformation of the society, and guaranteed mass endurance into the indefinite future.

THE ROLE OF ISRAELI COUNTERMEASURES IN STRENGTHENING THE REVOLUTIONARY TRANSFORMATION

Within a year of the start of the *intifada*, cumulative, empirical studies were published that drew a clear picture of the nature and extent of Israeli measures taken to crush it.[13] What emerges from those studies is a deliberate and graduated policy of repression that has encompassed state terrorist measures, that is to say, the application by the Israeli government of deadly force against civilians in the pursuit of its political aims.

Like the activities of the uprising itself, such repressive measures had been practiced for a long time, but on a lesser scale. There is a wealth of documentation by Palestinian, Israeli, and international researchers of the planned use of techniques such as shooting, beatings, imprisonment without trial, torture, and deportations during the two decades of occupation preceding the *intifada*.[14] Such methods were used by the Israeli authorities in order to impress upon the Palestinians their subordinate status and in an attempt to promote emigration from the homeland.

But these recent reports show that there was a quantitative leap in, as well as an intensification of, the measures applied. Today, the quality of such measures has been transformed from "intimidation" to "terror," and state violence has become state terrorism. By ordering his troops to implement a deliberate policy of aggressivity, beatings, and bone-breaking, the Israeli defense minister was committing Israel to a terrorist policy, because some of these acts could only result in injuring or killing unarmed civilians. The same goes for the massive use of newer, more powerful tear gas at closed quarters, and most of all, shooting with live ammunition in crowded neighborhoods.[15]

This policy was intended to achieve the aim of putting down the uprising. Instead, as is usually the case when such measures are employed against a population, precisely the opposite effect was achieved. This was the case because the measures were both graduated and generalized, thus putting virtually the entire population at serious risk in most aspects of their private and public lives, and indeed, putting their very lives at risk. In addition to the measures taken in the streets of towns, villages, and camps, further beatings, sometimes deadly, teargassing, and even torture were carried out at the many detention centers where Palestinian suspects were housed. The *intifada* also led to the creation of new such prisons. From December 21, 1987, when the Dhahrieh prison was opened near Hebron, through the spring of 1988, dozens of temporary and permanent prisons and camps were opened, the most notorious being Ketziot or Ansar III in the Negev desert. Tens of thousands of people have been in and out of one or another of these detention centers since December 1987. Between five and fifteen thousand are detained in them at any given time. There are innumerable documented cases of psychological and physical torture as well as several confirmed cases of killings of prisoners, including two in Ketziot who were shot point-blank on August 16, 1988, by none other than the prison director himself. In its 1988 report, Amnesty International concludes that there has been a marked increase in reports of ''torture and ill-treatment of Palestinian detainees.''[16]

Figures for Palestinians killed during the uprising are not consistent. Palestinian figures are always higher than those provided by the Israeli government. But whatever numbers one uses, one finds that, in the *intifada's* first year alone, proportionally more Palestinians died (one person out of three to five thousand) than did U.S. soldiers in the decade-long military intervention in Southeast Asia. Whereas the latter were brought down while in possession of the full panoply of contemporary armaments, the Palestinians were totally disarmed, or felled with rocks or gasoline-filled bottles in their hands. And whereas the frightening losses suffered by U.S. troops hastened their final withdrawal, the behavior of the Palestinians cannot be altered by the killing of large numbers among them. On the contrary, since they are fighting in their rump homeland, the killings have only strengthened their resolve and brought the passive and the fearful into the fray. Teenagers who set out to confront the occupation forces in early December 1987 were progressively joined in the streets by younger and older generations, with women, children, and old people taking leading roles in many of the demonstrations. This phenomenon is, in part, directly related to the measures undertaken by the Israeli army as well as to the exemplary work done by

Palestinian mass organizations, most notably the women's committees. Simply put, Israeli repression triggered the mobilization of an entire population.

The repressive measures taken against the *intifada* went beyond the massive infliction of bodily harm. They were graduated downward to include economic sabotage of a direct or indirect nature. Examples of such economic measures include crop burnings and the uprooting of trees; prolonged sieges of villages (which prevented planting and harvesting); the explicit prohibition of harvesting and marketing; house demolitions; prolonged curfews; and heavy fines, imposed, for example, on motorists for such "violations" as not having enough oil in the engine, having an elbow protruding from the window, improperly adjusting headlight beams in broad daylight, and having dusty license plates, in addition to the full array of moving violations. Oftentimes, a driver received a number of citations for the same offense several times a day. Merchants also suffered heavy fines for nonpayment or late payment of taxes. Many saw their businesses sealed and their property confiscated. Even street vendors and vegetable market operators suffered the loss of their products as soldiers often dumped market stalls and crushed their produce.

Such measures were not new. All had been applied over the previous twenty years. What was new was their application at once, in intensive and unrelenting fashion. This resulted in the further intensification of a mobilization already present, and thus contributed in no small way to the revolutionary transformation of Palestinian society.

NOTES

1. Discussion of the communiqués is based on the editors' translations of those available in their own libraries.

2. See, for example, Tsvi Gilat, "The Leadership of the Uprising," *Hadashot,* February 12, 1988, pp. 35, 37.

3. George Habash, *Nahwa Fihmin A'amaq Wa-Adaq Lilkiyan Al-Sahyuni* (Toward a Deeper and More Accurate Understanding of the Zionist Entity), *PFLP*, 1988, p. 44.

4. Rashid I. Khalidi, "The Uprising and the Palestine Question," *World Policy Journal* 5, no. 3 (Summer 1988): 503.

5. *Jerusalem Post*, March 25, 1988, p. 1.

6. *New York Times*, May 15, 1988, p. 16.

7. In some neighborhoods adult education courses were offered, principally in foreign languages. It must be remembered that except for three hours per day, even people with jobs (except for those who commuted to Israel) were at home with time on their hands.

8. This program proved itself time and again in ensuing months, and saved a number of lives when, despite the absence of large blood banks, orderly and effective calls for donors of a given type were carried out, and a severely wounded and bleeding person operated on.

9. For a discussion of this, see Jonathan Kuttab, "The Children's Revolt," *Journal of Palestine Studies* 17, no. 4 (Summer 1988): 26–37.

10. Raja Shehadeh, "Occupier's Law and the Uprising," *Journal of Palestine Studies* 17, no. 3 (Spring 1988): 30–31.

11. The higher the level of the committee, the more "political" it was, i.e., the more it responded to and coordinated with the political groups.

12. When the West Bank schools were again closed down on July 21, 1988, the neighborhood schools had trouble resuming their functions in many areas. Schools, however, remained shut until early December. Universities were closed throughout 1988 and 1989.

13. Besides the studies already mentioned, see also Amnesty International, *Amnesty International Report, 1988* (London: Amnesty International Publications, 1988), pp. 239–43; and United States, Department of State, *Country Reports on Human Rights Practices for 1988* (Washington, D.C.: U.S. Government Printing Office, 1989), pp. 1376–87.

14. The use of the term "deportation" here is consistent with its usage by the Nuremberg Judgement and the Fourth Geneva Convention of 1949; the more accurate term is "expulsion."

15. Indeed, the announcement by the Israeli army in October 1987 that it was using trained snipers to pick off selected leaders of "disturbances" (i.e., demonstrations) swiftly led to the death of a student on the Bethlehem University campus in late October 1987. This was followed by the closure of the university and is seen as one of the many catalysts that precipitated the outbreak of the *intifada*.

16. Amnesty International, *Report 1988*, p. 240.

13

"Discontented People" and "Outside Agitators"

THE PLO IN THE PALESTINIAN UPRISING

Helga Baumgarten

The outbreak of the uprising sowed confusion in Israel among politicians and journalists alike: was it inspired by "terrorists" (Yitzhak Shamir)[1] and carefully "planned and coordinated in advance" (Teddy Kollek)?[2] Or was it "spontaneous" (Yitzhak Rabin),[3] with the PLO belatedly hopping onto the "bandwagon,"[4] "trying to fuel the flames" (Yehuda Litani, the *Jerusalem Post*'s Arab affairs specialist)?[5]

The Israeli occupation power clearly faced a dilemma: by blaming the "terrorists," the PLO, for the uprising, it would be able to delegitimize it; yet, by the same token it was acknowledging the central role the PLO played in the Occupied Territories.

In order to gauge the PLO's role in the uprising, it seems appropriate to leave the ideologically loaded field of the Israeli-Palestinian conflict in order to see how students of collective action and revolutions have evaluated the interplay of various actors. Let me quote here a remarkable passage from Barrington Moore's brilliant book, *Injustice*:

Once a critical mass of potentially discontented people has come into existence through the working out of large-scale institutional forces the stage is set for the appearance of "outside agitators." It is important to recognize the crucial significance of their role because social critics are inclined to minimize it for fear of carrying water to the mills of conservatism and reaction. . . . It is always an activist minority that promotes and promulgates new standards of condemnation. . . . The outside agitators do the hard work of undermining the old sense of inevitability.[6]

This conclusion is shared by Charles Tilly in his research on collective action in European history. He states that "the extent of a group's collective action is a function of the extent of its shared interests, . . . the intensity of its organization and its mobilization."[7]

After an analysis of the PLO's activities in December 1987, the crucial first month of the uprising, the history of the PLO and its specific features, as reflected in its relationship with the Occupied Territories, will be discussed. Based on the results of this analysis, PLO politics in the uprising will be traced up to the Palestine National Council's nineteenth session in Algiers, which on November 15, 1988, proclaimed the independent state of Palestine. In conclusion, an attempt will be made to evaluate the PLO's role in the uprising and its achievements so far.

DECEMBER 1987: THE CRUCIAL FIRST MONTH

An in-depth look at the PLO and its political activities in December 1987 seems to be the most promising avenue to arrive at a realistic assessment of its initial involvement in the uprising. PLO chairman and Fateh founder/leader Yasser Arafat was on an official visit to Kuwait when, on December 9, the uprising started in the occupied Gaza Strip. On the second day of the uprising Arafat embarked on feverish diplomatic activities in order to protect the Palestinian civilian population against the fierce Israeli military response to the mass demonstrations first in Gaza and then in the West Bank.[8]

More important for our purposes here, however, is Arafat's first uprising message to the Palestinian people in the Occupied Territories, dated December 10.[9] Again, as in his diplomatic offensive, he condemns Israel's "violent repressive and criminal campaign" against his people. But from this initial defensive argument, he immediately changes over to an offensive revolutionary rhetoric: "The fires of revolution against these Zionist invaders will not fade out in the face of their injustice, terrorism and occupation, until our land—all of our land—has been liberated from these usurping invaders."

Arafat clearly perceived the special character of the day-old uprising when he praised "the children of the stones in our beloved, holy country." And he is the first to use—if only indirectly here—the image of David and Goliath, which he takes away from exclusive Israeli propaganda against the Arabs by turning it upside down, with the Palestinian David now pitted against the Israeli Goliath: "Let those who are heavily armed know that our bodies are stronger than their iron and that this revolution erupted to achieve victory and to impose its victory despite all conspiracies and plotters." The idea behind the biblical image is then taken up and employed in a different context in Islamic religious discourse, when Arafat quotes a Qur'anic verse evoking Muhammad's first battle against the Quraish, the Battle of Badr, when, with only 300 men unexperienced in battle, he defeated the vastly superior Mekkan force of 1,000 men under the command of Abu Jahl.[10]

Most important, however, is Arafat's interpretation of the uprising, which he places in the course of recent Palestinian history, the history of the Palestinian revolution as fought by the Palestinian people under the leadership of Fateh and the PLO. For him, the children of the stones in the Occupied Territories are "the living example of what you and your revolution have achieved."

At the same time, Arafat stresses the unity of the Palestinian people, both inside and outside occupied Palestine: "We have pledged to you and to ourselves that we will not rest and that we will continue resistance until our homeland is liberated. We will do this together inside and outside our occupied land." From there Arafat goes on to state the political goal of both the Palestinian revolution and the present uprising as its latest manifestation and its climax: "We will extricate our right through our blood and souls—our right to the establishment of our free independent state on Palestinian territory with Jerusalem as its capital." And he concludes with a clear and outspoken declaration as to which territory this state should cover: "Let all of us struggle in closed ranks and side by side until the banners of freedom, the banners of Palestine, are hoisted on the Strip and the courageous Bank and also on the minarets and churches of Jerusalem."

Thus, Arafat's very first address to the Palestinian people in the uprising shows a clear perception of its main symbolic features: children, stones, the flag—symbols immediately taken up by Arafat and thereby reinforced and widely spread. Also, Arafat stresses the singular importance of the uprising and encourages the people in Gaza and the West Bank to continue fighting until victory, combining in typical Fateh fashion secular-revolutionary and religious-symbolic discourse, a blend tremendously successful in contemporary Palestinian history, because of its all-encompassing mobilizing power.[11] Judging from this speech by Arafat on December 10, 1987, it is hardly possible to maintain that the start of the uprising took him and the PLO leadership by surprise. Rather, it seems events in the Occupied Territories in 1987—above all in the Gaza Strip, which had witnessed almost an entire year of off-again, on-again popular demonstrations and confrontations with the army—had the PLO leadership in the diaspora waiting for what broke out on an unprecedented scale on December 9, 1987. Finally, one cannot help but read into Arafat's address that the uprising constituted what the Palestinian revolution since 1958 (foundation of Fateh) and certainly since 1965 (taking up of armed struggle by Fateh) had been about and what its leaders had tried to achieve over the course of years with Fateh and after 1969 with the PLO.

On December 13 Arafat, now in Baghdad, where he had called an urgent meeting of the Occupied Homeland Committee, for the first time called the uprising a movement of "unarmed resistance." By that date he had become absolutely confident that the uprising, which had spread all over the Occupied Territories, was to continue. The unarmed character of the uprising is stressed again a day later when Arafat reports on the escalation of events in the West Bank and Gaza and the declaration of a general strike in most cities: "They are facing the Israeli forces' bullets unarmed.''[12] And finally, in an interview with Radio Monte Carlo on December 21, 1987, Arafat focuses on this new way of fighting the Israeli occupation when he speaks of his "beloved, steadfast people, who are hurling stones and defying the most up-to-date American weapons with stones, with their bare chest and iron will.''[13]

There are, however, some discordant notes with respect to the question of "armed struggle" early in the *intifada*. Sana'a Voice of Palestine, citing a communiqué by the Palestinian Revolution Forces General Command (effectively under the command of Abu Jihad), stated on December 10 that Palestinians had used "incendiary bombs and hand grenades" in Jabalia camp the previous day.[14] The operation in question is that in which Hatem al-Sisi, the first martyr of the uprising, was killed by soldiers. According to the *Jerusalem Post*, "two petrol bombs" had been thrown at an army vehicle.[15] Petrol bombs or Molotov cocktails were in fact the main weapon used throughout the *intifada*. It is fruitless to speculate as to whether or not there was at that stage an internal debate in the PLO regarding the question of armed struggle in the *intifada*, given the lack of access to relevant internal documents. Suffice it therefore to mention that traditional military communiqués stressing armed action continued until spring 1988. The climax of the attempt to support the *intifada* with an escalation of armed struggle against and inside Israel was the ill-fated Dimona operation on March 7, 1988, which ended in the death of three Fateh guerrillas and three Israelis. At that point it was beyond any doubt that similar operations hardly meant any help for the uprising, and they quite possibly had the opposite effect.

At the beginning of the second week of the *intifada*, on December 17, Abu Jihad, head of the PLO's Higher Committee for Occupied Homeland Affairs and the man responsible inside Fateh for the West Bank and Gaza Strip, gave a remarkable interview in Amman.[16] Abu Jihad reported that the Palestinian people inside the Occupied Territories had begun to form popular committees (*lijan sha'biya*) in the camps, villages, and quarters of the cities and that committees had been formed to take care of the families of the dead and wounded. Abu Jihad went on to mention specifically the kind of weapons used in the uprising: stones, bottles, slings with iron balls, nails, and iron bars thrown on the streets to prevent the free movement of army vehicles, etc., that is, all nonmilitary "weapons" directed against the formidable Israeli military machine. Finally, he stressed the new quality that distinguished the *intifada* from all previous uprisings, namely, its all-encompassing character, with the active participation of students, workers, merchants, artisans, and intellectuals—the whole Palestinian people. The Fateh leadership outside the Occupied Territories was clearly aware of all of the characteristic developments of the *intifada* from the very first days; it considered them potentially successful and therefore supported and reinforced them.

But what of the other PLO-affiliated groups based outside the Occupied Territories and their interplay with the uprising? On December 11, 1987, the Popular Front for the Liberation of Palestine (PFLP) published in Damascus a declaration through WAFA, the Palestinian News Agency, on the occasion of the twentieth anniversary of the PFLP, asking for international action in defense of the Palestinian people in the face of the Israeli military occupation.[17] It also reiterated the goals of the PLO concerning a political solution of the Palestinian problem: an international conference as well as the right of return, self-determination, and the establishment of a Palestinian state on Palestinian territory. Dr. George Habash, founder and charismatic leader of the PFLP, went on record with a surprisingly cool and anticlimactic first statement on the *intifada* in an interview with Radio Monte Carlo on December 16: ''There is an occupation there. Therefore, it is only natural for our people there to confront such an occupation. . . . Our people's confrontation did not start just this past week. . . . Our people's struggle against the occupation will continue until the occupation is terminated and the Palestinian people are granted the right to self-determination.''[18] For Habash, at this point, the *intifada* was just one in the long chain of confrontations with the occupation. According to the PFLP leader, one of the most dedicated militants of the Palestinian cause, there had been many uprisings and there would be many more until the achievement of liberation. The sense of urgency found in Arafat's speeches and statements since December 10 is strangely missing here. However, at a press conference on December 21 at PFLP headquarters in Damascus, Habash begins to show signs of a changing perception: the singularity of the *intifada* is at last being recognized, and he is convinced that the struggle will continue until the occupation ends and the Palestinian people regain their right to freedom, self-determination, and an independent state.[19]

On December 24, in an interview with the Voice of the Mountain Radio in Lebanon, Habash for the first time described the uprising as the most important one so far. He affirmed that ''it represented the highest point of the Palestinian people's protest against Israeli occupation of the West Bank and Gaza Strip for more than 20 years.''[20]

The main features of the uprising for Habash were that it was widespread and had even expanded into the Israeli borders of 1948. ''The uprising is also characterized by its duration, the participation of various classes of people, and unity under the unified Palestinian political motto: No solution without liberation and no solution without granting the Palestinian people their full right of self-determination.''

The Democratic Front for the Liberation of Palestine (DFLP), for its part, made an official statement emanating from its Politbureau in Damascus on December 12, which was later published in its party organ, *al-Hurriyah*, on December 20, 1987.[21] The main focus of this statement, similar to the first PFLP declarations, was on the major PLO demands for a solution to the Palestinian problem: the right to return, self-determination, and an independent state. Again, along the same lines of the PFLP, but going more into detail, national unity, both in the diaspora and in the Occupied Territories, cooperation of all national forces and personalities, and unification of all institutions serving the masses in West Bank and Gaza were demanded in order to ensure the success of the *intifada*.

On December 24, Radio Monte Carlo interviewed Nayef Hawatmeh, the founder and leader of the Democratic Front, on the *intifada*.[22] According to Hawatmeh, all political energies of the PLO should now be concentrated on "the general uprising in the occupied territories so it can achieve its objectives." What is new in this interview, distinguishing it from the available documentary material on Fateh and the PFLP, is a detailed catalogue of short-term demands and goals of the uprising: "The departure of the occupation forces from the towns and camps and their replacement by a U.N. observer force to protect the inhabitants . . . cancelling the British mandate emergency laws which are based on administrative detention and the deportation of people from the occupied Palestinian territory," and cancellation of "the mounting taxes which the Israeli occupation forces and the Israeli state are enacting." The long-term objectives remained the right to self-determination, ending the occupation, and an international conference. These very demands were taken up three weeks later in the fourteen-point memorandum presented by Palestinian national personalities and community leaders in a press conference in Jerusalem on January 14, 1988.[23]

The evidence presented above clearly refutes the claim of many analysts of the uprising that the PLO, with its three main constituent organizations, only belatedly realized what was going on in the Occupied Territories and then jumped on the bandwagon. On the contrary, especially Fateh, the biggest and most influential resistance movement, not only acutely sensed from the very first day the historical relevance of what had erupted in terms of a popular revolutionary mass movement, but had been waiting and preparing for this moment. Clearly, Fateh's sheer size, its organizational capabilities, the whole apparatus at its disposal, its leadership of the PLO, its presence from the Gulf and Baghdad, via Amman, to Tunis, gave it an advantage over much smaller organizations like the PFLP and the Democratic Front.

An idea of the interplay of the PLO outside and the mass movement inside is given by an interview in the French newspaper *Le Monde* with Arafat in his operational headquarters in Baghdad on January 16, 1988:

The nerve center of the network was the telecommunications room, which, thanks to a relay station, is in virtually permanent contact with the Occupied Territories. Fax machines constantly spat out news, the latest reports from various sources, Palestinian and Israeli, carefully researched statements by Israeli officials, and reports on the situation in the field by activists. . . . Messengers constantly brought in telegrams, awaited orders and left again. . . . One thing is certain, . . . there are good channels of communication between the occupied territories and the PLO command. . . . The PLO undoubtedly seems to be controlling, if not always directing, this uprising in the occupied territories.[24]

Arafat in this interview stressed the fact that 70 percent of the inhabitants of the Occupied Territories were teenagers who all their lives had "lived under the

Palestinian Revolution's umbrella. This new generation knows only one leadership which is neither Jordan nor any other Arab country, but the PLO alone.'' And it is this generation and its presence in the Shabiba movement (youth group) on which Fateh bases itself in the *intifada* in the West Bank and Gaza Strip.

While inside the youngsters, the Shabab, and, it must be added, the Banat, the girls and young women on an equal footing, make use of the most archaic weapons to fight for their freedom, the outside, the PLO under the leadership of Fateh, is utilizing the most advanced communications technology available, including the fax machine, to lead the Palestinian uprising to political success and the realization of the dream of many decades, the establishment of an independent Palestinian state.

This analysis of the first month of the *intifada* started with Arafat in Kuwait. In a way Arafat's history of struggle had come full circle. He had founded Fateh in Kuwait in 1958–59, together with Abu Jihad, Salim al-Za'nun, and a number of other Palestinian migrants then working in the Gulf sheikhdom; in Kuwait the decision to take up armed struggle against Israel in January 1965 was made; and in Kuwait on December 10, 1987, Arafat for the first time addressed the Palestinian people who had risen up against the Israeli occupation in order to fight for self-determination. The following pages sketch Fateh's struggle for the liberation of Palestine, together with the contribution by the PFLP and Democratic Front, especially as it has impinged on the West Bank and Gaza Strip from 1967 until 1987.

THE PALESTINIAN NATIONAL MOVEMENT AFTER 1948

Fateh was founded in Kuwait in the late 1950s by a group of young Palestinian migrants who upon graduation from university in Egypt had come to the quickly developing Gulf sheikhdom, where they worked as professionals in the oil sector and the construction business, or as employees in the fledgling but rapidly expanding state bureaucracy.[25] Because of their influential role in Kuwait as well as their excellent connections with the ruling family (as doctors, teachers, advisors, etc.), they received almost from the start strong official support, support that widened and intensified after Kuwait gained its independence in 1961.

At the end of 1959 Fateh began to publish its first underground journal, *Filastinuna* (Our Palestine), in which it developed the outlines of its ideology and political program: a militant Palestinian nationalism with the primary goal of reestablishing a Palestinian identity and creating an independent Palestinian state on every piece of territory not occupied by the Zionist state:

An entity [*kiyan* in Arabic][26] is our legal right, as it is with all people in the world looking for freedom. . . . There are Arab parts of Palestine, where we must build an authoritative [*quiyadi*] revolutionary Palestinian national rule [*hukm*]. . . . This rule which we intend to establish is represented in an entity, the product of our people's consciousness and an outgrowth of the Disaster [*nakba* in Arabic, i.e., the establishment of Israel in 1948 and the concurrent exile of hundreds of thousands of Palestinians]. Only this entity will enable us to regain the self-respect and dignity that we lost.[27]

Fateh proposed this new ideology and program against the then hegemonic Arab nationalist ideology and program, and against its motto, "Arab unity is the road to the liberation of Palestine." Fateh postulated a slogan that turned all established ideas upside down: "The liberation of Palestine is the road to Arab unity."

Arab nationalism since the late 1950s had been under the uncontested leadership of Egyptian President Gamal Abdel Nasser, while its main Palestinian proponents were organized in the Movement of Arab Nationalists (harakat al-qaumiyin al-'Arab, henceforth MAN), founded in 1952 in Beirut under the leadership of a young doctor from Lydda, George Habash, who had earned his degree in medicine at the prestigious American University of Beirut (AUB) in 1951.

Both movements, Fateh as well as the MAN, which were later to constitute the main independent nationalist organizations within the PLO (the MAN with its follow-up organizations PFLP, founded in December 1967 under the leadership of Habash, and the DFLP, which split from the PFLP in February 1969 under the leadership of Nayef Hawatmeh), were thus created by Palestinians in the diaspora. Habash's MAN was in essence a radical-nationalist student movement aimed at profoundly changing the whole Arab world, modernizing and uniting it in order to enter well prepared and as an equal challenger another war against Israel, which had defeated the old traditional and underdeveloped Arab world in a first round of fighting in 1948.[28] Today, with the radical-nationalist discourse replaced since 1967—68 by a radical socialist and later Marxist-Leninist discourse, students still make up the bulk of the movement, with the addition of a substantial following among Palestinians in the camps in Lebanon, Jordan, and Syria. The leadership still remains in the hands of the old former American University at Beirut militants (with a petit bourgeois background and excellent relations with Palestinian and Arab trade and finance bourgeois circles in Lebanon and Jordan) turned professional revolutionaries. Fateh differs considerably in its social setup. Its core leadership group (Arafat, Abu Iyad, etc.) is constituted of former Palestinian migrants to Kuwait, the sons of petit bourgeois families hailing from the coastal area of Palestine (both cities and villages) who were forced to flee their homes in 1948, sought refuge in Gaza, and studied in the early 1950s at Egyptian universities. From its very start, Fateh, with its extremely homogeneous leadership core group, tried to mobilize as wide a social spectrum as possible within the Palestinian communities in the diaspora, reaching from Palestinian students at German universities to refugees in the miserable camps in Jordan.

It has always been Fateh's proclaimed goal to mobilize the entire Palestinian people, take over its leadership, and implement its political program of liberating Palestine, that is, establishing a Palestinian state. The leitmotiv "entity" or *kiyan* was soon replaced, however, by the new catchword or motto, armed struggle, *al-kifah al-musallah*, which became Fateh's main mobilizing myth, through and around which it politicized ever larger parts of the Palestinian people. It was not so much the taking up of armed struggle against Israel in January 1965 (made in retrospect the beginning of the Palestinian revolution and accepted as such by all organizations) that propelled Fateh into the limelight, but rather the battle of Karameh in March 1968 in the Jordan Valley, when Fateh's guerrilla force under the leadership of Arafat decided—in violation of the most basic rules of guerrilla warfare—to face a vastly superior Israeli army force attacking over the river. This act of historical defiance turned Fateh from an elitist and marginal underground movement into a mass movement, into the new Palestinian national movement.

The MAN, which between 1965 and 1967, after Fateh took up guerrilla warfare and before the June 1967 war, had argued very rationally and convincingly against the chances for success of guerrilla warfare against Israel, made a complete about-face after Karameh.

In the years that followed, however, it was the Fateh leadership that assigned to armed struggle its appropriate role, as a tactic to be used in a well-defined place and time. The PFLP, on the other hand, tended in the years after Karameh to view armed struggle as the be-all and end-all of the liberation process. This paralyzing "fixation with the idea of armed struggle as the only revolutionary form," this obsession to express itself "almost entirely in military terms," was to be one of the most fateful mistakes of the Palestinian left.[29]

How did all these developments reflect themselves in the West Bank and Gaza Strip, especially after 1967, when Israel occupied these last remaining parts of Mandate Palestine?

Right after the June war, Arafat tried to start an armed insurrection in the West Bank, an attempt that was to end in complete failure.[30] The MAN, too, had dispatched some of its militants back into their West Bank hometowns, where they were to start patient underground work to mobilize and organize the population for embarking on an armed revolution. Their attempt, too, was to lead to nothing, at least in the short run.

From then on—with the exception of Gaza's guerrilla war until 1971—Palestinian armed struggle became the almost exclusive domain of the Palestinians in the diaspora: in Jordan east of the river until 1970–71, then in Lebanon until the Israeli war in 1982 against the PLO, which ended in the PLO's spectacular withdrawal from Beirut by boat.

What had been the reasons for the failure of both Fateh and the PFLP in instigating an armed Palestinian insurrection against the newly established Israeli military occupation in 1967? A variety of factors come into play here, the decisive one probably being the history of severe and at times violent oppression of independent political expression and activity among Palestinians under Jordanian rule. The Jordanian security service had done a thorough job: all the relevant security files after 1967 fell into Israeli hands and enabled the Israeli security forces to begin their turn of oppression in unbroken continuity.[31] To this must be added the almost impossible task of "outsiders"—and Arafat was an outsider in the West Bank's traditional society, not unlike the returning MAN/PFLP students who immediately fell prey to the deeply rooted network of collaborators taken over almost intact by the Israeli occupation—wishing to build up trust and to organize in the climate of fear, distrust, and confusion that reigned in the West Bank in the summer and fall of 1967. The experiences of Che Guevara in Latin America are the parallel case in a totally different environment.

From then on, struggle in the newly occupied Palestinian areas developed according to its own dynamics, and it did so, under the conditions of an oppressive if subtle occupation, very slowly. Two structural features of the occupation, however, reinforced over time the ties between Palestinians inside and those in the diaspora: Israeli deportations of political and community leaders, and labor migration to the oil states in the Gulf. Thus, the Occupied Territories became more and more receptive to influences from the outside. And it proved to be historical developments on the outside that had the most decisive effects on political developments inside: the bloody defeat of the guerrilla movement in Jordan in 1970–71 and its expulsion from the Kingdom, and, only a few years later, the recognition of the PLO as the sole legitimate representative of the Palestinian people by the Arab summit conference in Rabat in 1974, as well as its acquisition of observer status at the UN.

The Jordanian war against the Palestinian resistance in 1970–71 also marked a decisive turning point in limiting the influence of the Hashemite monarchy among the Palestinian population under occupation at large to a relatively well-delineated group of pro-Jordanians, while the man on the street identified with the fedayeen.

Developments from 1970 to 1974 thus allowed the Fateh leadership to embark on the long road of political and diplomatic struggle for the establishment of a Palestinian state next to Israel, that is, for a goal short of total liberation of Palestine, a struggle that continues to this very day.[32] Only in 1974 did Arafat and his colleagues deem it possible to pronounce this goal both among Palestinians in the diaspora and inside the Occupied Territories.

Nevertheless, the legitimacy granted the Fateh leadership in 1974 was deemed so precarious by Arafat that, until the beginning of the *intifada,* he refrained from spelling out clearly and unequivocally that the Palestinians had realized that they had to settle for a state next to Israel, however bitter their feelings remained about the historical injustice done to their people.[33]

Developments both inside and outside the Occupied Territories finally forced the Palestinians to resign themselves to this position. One bloody defeat after another of the armed resistance movement in the diaspora: Jordan, 1970–71; Lebanon, 1973, 1976; and finally the major war of Israel against the PLO, 1982; the massacres of Palestinians in the camps in Lebanon, starting with Tell ez-Za'tar in 1976, then Sabra and Shatila in 1982; the series of camp wars instigated by Syria and led by its local allies and stooges, first Amal, then the Fateh rebels; thousands of dead and countless wounded, many of them maimed for life—all this amounted to an argument much more forceful and convincing than theoretical discussions against continued guerrilla warfare and in favor of a political solution to be imposed on the intransigent Jewish state.

The major energies of the armed Palestinian organizations in the diaspora had been spent in resisting the attempts of one or another Arab regime (most notably the Syrian and the Jordanian) to place the PLO under its tutelage. Meanwhile, the Israeli occupation was becoming ever more oppressive, particularly after 1977 (see Chapter 3), while mobilization in the Occupied Territories, spurred from within and from without, went on apace (see Chapter 3).

It was precisely the interaction between the process of mobilization and the growing threats to Palestinian nationalism both inside and outside that finally made Gaza and West Bank Palestinians embark on the uprising. Two more developments have to be mentioned here to complete the picture: first, the conscious attempts by the Fateh/PLO leadership to mobilize all classes and sections of the Palestinian people under occupation, from traditionally pro-Jordanian mayors (a policy giving rise to tremendous strains between national leaders inside and outside),[34] merchants and industrialists (all groups never addressed by organizations like the PFLP and the DFLP), and professionals, to the most oppressed class in the camps in the West Bank and Gaza Strip, thereby continuing a tradition it had successfully inaugurated at the outset of its history in Kuwait.

Second, Israel's shortsighted occupation policy, with its outrageous imposition of taxes illegal according to international law, contributed its part to Fateh's success in mobilizing the merchants by producing a classical tax revolt along the pattern of "no taxation without representation." Add to this the achievement of national unity among the major PLO organizations (Fateh, PFLP, and the Democratic Front),[35] imposed on them by the unrelenting attacks of Syria and its Palestinian stooges (Fateh rebels, PFLP-GC) on all organizations who wanted to maintain Palestinian independence, and the stage was set for the outbreak of the *intifada*.

THE PLO AND THE FIRST YEAR OF THE *INTIFADA*

This analysis of the first month of the *intifada* and the major PLO organizations' role in it has led to the conclusion that the PLO was from the very start involved in the unfolding events in the Gaza Strip and in the West Bank. The last part of this chapter follows the PLO's political activities and its underlying policy through the first year of the *intifada* in order to evaluate the relationship between "inside" and "outside" in this historical period.

Any revolutionary upsurge, if it wants to keep its momentum, is in need of organization and leadership. Barrington Moore quite aptly pointed to "the brief and fragile nature of revolutionary upsurge" and focused on the eminently important distinction between crowd and party—a distinction that captures precisely the problems the Palestinian political organizations were facing during the first few weeks of the uprising.[36]

According to Moore's historically informed analysis,

a revolutionary crowd is something very different from a revolutionary party. Where the party is enduring, or tries to be, the crowd is ephemeral. . . . A major purpose of the revolutionary party is of course to serve as a strategic avantgarde at the moment of crisis, to lead the crowd to strategic targets at the right moment. . . . A leader from the outside with an acute feel for the sentiments of the audience can persuade and sway a crowd, suggest new targets, and the like. . . . On the other hand, such a powerful leader generally has to share most of the crowd's sentiments and is therefore as much its prisoner as its leader.[37]

Here we have in a nutshell the tasks that Fateh, the PFLP, and the Democratic Front had to live up to if they did not want to lose the—possibly—last chance to achieve some of the goals of Palestinian nationalism. They had to create the conditions to allow the *intifada* to continue; they had somehow to integrate in their own organizational framework the scores of new leaders that were emerging; they had to bring into play the political program of the PLO in a way that would respond to both "the crowd's sentiments" and the "new target" the leaders outside knew had a chance of being achieved considering the changing balance of power the *intifada* was bringing about.

It would seem that all through January 1988 there were feverish activities on the part of all organizations—including the Palestinian Communist Party (PCP), which is not dealt with here as it is not one of the historical diaspora resistance organizations—to establish an overall leadership over the disparate movements and crowds that constituted the *intifada*, in order to ensure its continuity and even escalate it by giving it a clear programmatic perspective.

As supported by all sources (the leaflets distributed in the Occupied Territories, press statements and interviews of PLO leaders, as well as the publications of the organizations involved: *Filastin al-Thaura, Saut al-Bilad* [Fateh], *al-Hadaf* [PFLP], and *al-Hurriya* [Democratic Front]), the PLO outside and the *intifada* inside considered themselves united, two sides of the same coin:

Our people's continued uprising is new evidence of the people's interaction and unity with their organization, the PLO, on all levels. . . . The revolution's generation is leading the uprising inside the occupied homeland, raising the PLO's flag, and chanting pro-PLO slogans to stress the organic cohesion between our people and the leader of their national struggle and their sole legitimate representative, the PLO.[38]

The various activities in support of and participation in the *intifada* from the outside were first the focus of the three-day special session of the PLO Central Council in Baghdad on January 7–9. On January 9, at the end of the meeting, an official statement was issued stressing the unity of the Palestinian people and its struggle inside and outside as well as its united stand behind one program:

the liberation of Palestine from Israeli occupation, the right of return, self-determination, and the establishment of an independent Palestinian state.[39] It also called for the speedy convening of an international conference in order to achieve a just solution to the conflict in the Middle East. The Central Council finally decided

to form a higher committee, in addition to the Executive Committee, to follow up all uprising affairs and developments. This committee shall be formed by the PNC Presidency, the Central Council Secretariat, the Occupied Homeland Affairs Committee, and representatives of the Higher Military Committee. This committee shall be in open session, and a working committee, for everyday affairs, shall stem from it.

In addition to various measures to ensure steady and sufficient financial support for the *intifada,* the Central Council specifically stressed the need "to bolster the popular and national action committees in all positions of confrontation in occupied Palestine—in camps, villages, towns, universities, institutes, schools, institutions, popular bodies, and other positions of popular struggle" as the main structure on which the *intifada* was built.[40]

Every meeting of a PLO body or a committee of one of its constituent organizations in the days and weeks to follow issued similar statements until by the beginning of February things began to consolidate: it was clear by then that the uprising would be led by a united leadership, the UNLU, and by early March the group to make up the leadership—Fateh, PFLP, Democratic Front, and PCP—had managed to settle their remaining differences. Both the Palestinian people under occupation with its UNLU and the PLO outside were determined to continue the uprising until the achievement of their overriding goal, the establishment of an independent Palestinian state. All were agreed that this was a struggle the Palestinians were waging on their own and independently, whether or not they received support from outside friends. This was articulated in a declaration by the PLO Executive Committee on February 3: "Just as the beginning of our revolution [in 1965] had depended on the vanguard and the arms of our sons, history is now repeating itself in the difficult circumstances facing the Palestinian march."[41]

While the support of the Palestinians in the Occupied Territories for the PLO was and is overwhelming, all rivals or enemies of the PLO nevertheless used the uprising either to win back some support for their political line or, in a purely negative fashion, to limit the influence of the PLO.

Ahmad Jibril, head of the PFLP-GC, a member of the anti-PLO Salvation Front with its headquarters in Damascus, and a long-time weapon against Arafat in the hands of the Syrian regime of Hafez al-Assad, counted on his presumed popularity in the Occupied Territories after the success of the hang glider attack in November 1987 perpetrated by a GC guerrilla who had killed six Israeli soldiers. Accordingly, the PFLP-GC on January 1, 1988, began to transmit a test program on a new clandestine Radio al-Quds, "the Palestinian-Arab radio on the road of liberating the land and the people,'' hoping to mount a serious challenge to Arafat's leadership of the PLO.

Jibril had been correct in his assessment that such a radio station would within days gain overwhelming popularity, and it is probably no exaggeration to claim that hardly a Palestinian household existed where this station was not listened to, with its Palestinian nationalist songs and, starting some time later, its information on events on the ground. However, and here Jibril's attempt at undermining Arafat's leadership totally backfired, among Palestinians in the West Bank and Gaza al-Quds was considered their station, the Palestinian people's radio, and was thus thought to be directed by the PLO, which accordingly harvested all the support generated by its broadcasts. The very moment Jibril tried to impose his and the Syrian regime's political line through the station by attacking the PLO and its alleged ''plots, compromises and sellouts aimed against Palestinian aspirations,''[42] he was criticized and rejected both inside and outside.

On January 25, 1988, on Baghdad Voice of the PLO, Radio al-Quds was for the first time officially attacked because of its ''campaign of disinformation and distortion of facts, placing the names of our strugglers in lists it claims as being those of the enemy agents in the heroic Gaza Strip.''[43] And on February 11, Baghdad Voice of the PLO broadcast an appeal by the UNLU to Radio al-Quds:

We appeal to those managing the al-Quds radio to refrain from making this radio of theirs produce a major discord in the voice of the uprising . . . to take into account that the functional and pragmatic methods pursued by those who are behind this radio do not serve the voice of the uprising. . . . We remind the respected radio . . . to broadcast in full, without any omissions or deletions, any of the statements of our uprising . . . it selects.[44]

But the decisive blow against al-Quds came from Israel, which started to jam the clandestine radio station in mid-February, thus unwittingly removing a potential challenge to the unity of the *intifada* and its unequivocal allegiance to the PLO under Arafat.

Israel tried in different ways, old and new, to limit the influence of the PLO and the freedom of action of its militants, irrespective of the organization to which they belonged. Deportations on a large scale were begun on January 13, 1988. On March 15 international phone lines to the West Bank and Gaza were cut, and a few days later (March 20) Fateh's Shabiba youth movement was banned. Then restrictions were imposed on the free movement of money over the bridge from Jordan in an attempt to cut off PLO financial support for the Palestinians under occupation in their campaign of civil disobedience. In a next step, the freedom of the press was severely curtailed with the closure of the Palestine Press Service, which had become the major source of news for the entire foreign press, at a time when the Israeli military spokesman had either become silent or unreliable.

Israel's attempt at hitting at the heart of the *intifada* came with the assassination of Fateh's second in command, Khalil al-Wazir (Abu Jihad), cofounder of Fateh with Arafat and his closest associate over the years, who had been responsible for the "Western Sector," that is, the West Bank and Gaza Strip. Obviously, Israel considered his role in the *intifada* of such overriding importance that it had decided to embark on a major terrorist operation, fully aware of the international condemnation that would follow.

The attempt, however, backfired. On the day of Abu Jihad's assassination the uprising experienced a new, unprecedented escalation all over the Occupied Territories, and April 16 entered the history of the *intifada* as its bloodiest day. Arafat addressed a speech to the Palestinian people on the death of Abu Jihad, accusing Israel of having killed him in the belief that

with their crime they could affect the course of our people's revolution, uprising and gigantic march. . . . They did not know it will be a furnace that will kindle the fire and entrench the uprising. . . . Abu Jihad, we will keep our pledge and oath . . . the revolution will continue . . . until the Palestinian flag flutters on the walls of Jerusalem. . . . Let us escalate our revolution and our blessed uprising. Let us scorch the earth under the feet of the occupiers.[45]

And the *intifada* did continue with unbroken strength, in spite or because of all attempts to subdue it (see Chapter 12). It had obviously crossed a line from which there was no way back, and every attempt to increase oppression only became oil on the fire of the uprising.

This was also to be the fate of King Hussein's decision to cut off ties with the West Bank on July 31, 1988. It is too early to attempt a comprehensive interpretation of Hussein's renunciation of sovereignty over the West Bank and his call on the PLO to assume responsibility for it. But one might venture to make the (plausible) assumption that this was one last desperate attempt by the Hashemite monarch to demonstrate to his all but lost constituency in the West Bank that only he was capable of providing for their needs. Hoping to corner the PLO by suddenly imposing vast new responsibilities on it, with huge pressure expected to be exerted by the thousands of civil servants and teachers who had suddenly lost a major part of their livelihood, the King played a daring game and lost it all. For it was Hussein's political withdrawal from the West Bank that laid the groundwork for the major political achievement of the *intifada* as a result of the political and diplomatic efforts of the PLO: the declaration of Palestinian independence.

Violence during the *intifada* was kept at a low level, with the militants refraining from the use of firearms. Mass demonstrations and acts of civil disobedience proved their superiority over armed struggle in the particular conditions of the Palestinian liberation struggle. Still, the issue of armed struggle remained a major bone of contention, above all among the PLO organizations outside. The Fateh rebels and the PFLP-GC held it up as their main weapon of criticism against the PLO leadership. But the PFLP and the DF also opposed some of

Arafat's political moves by (abortive) attempts at guerrilla raids across the border into Israel, claiming thereby to preserve the revolutionary essence of Palestinian struggle. It seems that, again, at least parts of the Palestinian left sacrificed all to the golden calf of armed struggle when measuring the degree of revolutionary commitment by the number of fedayeen operations, instead of focusing on the positions of power they doubtless held inside the Occupied Territories and which were major assets in struggles over a particular political line. Once again, as many times before in the history of Palestinian nationalism, Arafat proved the more successful mass leader and politician.

As the *intifada* went on, cooperation between inside and outside, between the UNLU and the PLO, obviously intensified and deepened. It seems plausible to argue that some sort of division of labor developed, with the PLO leadership outside engaging in political and diplomatic activities at a high level, while popular pressure on the ground was kept up through the *intifada*; or, looking at it the other way round, endowed by the *intifada* with new political strength and international weight, the PLO leadership could again, and with renewed confidence after the defeat of 1982, enter the international political arena and work for the achievement of Palestinian national goals, foremost among them the establishment of an independent state.

Arafat and his new political-diplomatic leadership troika (with Bassam Abu Sharif, a former PFLP leader gone over to Arafat, and Yasir Abed Rabbo, the second in command in the Democratic Front and a member of the PLO Executive Committee) from early on in the *intifada* were clearly determined to achieve the utmost political capital from the popular uprising. Their first political move, the attempt to establish a government-in-exile, proved abortive, with no consensus reached. They then embarked on intensive rounds of both Arab and international negotiations, in which, backed by wide Palestinian, Arab, and international support, a number of decisive steps could be taken to bring the Palestinian people closer to a Palestinian state.

At the beginning of June, after Arafat's official visit to Moscow in April and on the eve of the extraordinary Arab summit (June 7–9) in Algiers, the situation was deemed right to float a first serious trial balloon with Bassam Abu Sharif's position paper, "Prospects of a Palestinian-Israeli Settlement."[46] And it proved to be this paper, coming from Arafat's entourage, that set in motion a series of events leading to the Nineteenth PNC in Algiers in November 1988.

What was the PLO's position according to Abu Sharif's paper?

We want to go to the international conference as a liberation organization and as the sole legitimate representative of the Palestinian people to negotiate with our enemies, to negotiate with the Israelis. . . . The superpowers and the permanent members of the Security Council should participate in the international conference to guarantee the security and safety of all regional states, including the independent Palestinian state.[47]

Criticism on the part of the PFLP was formulated in a very cautious and statesmanlike manner by Dr. George Habash.[48] Similar statements were issued by the Democratic Front. Radio al-Quds, not surprisingly, called it "a crime against the Palestinian question," as it "ignored the charter and all PNC resolutions,"[49] and "an assertion of the overall non-nationalist and capitulatory policy represented by Arafat and the deviationist Arab forces."[50]

What gave the document the decisive push, however, was the favorable reaction coming from the Occupied Territories. According to a poll conducted by the East Jerusalem weekly *al-Bayadir al-Siyasi,* prominent Palestinian nationalists supported Abu Sharif's paper.[51]

The next step was more of a coincidence, an extremely lucky one in retrospect, with on the one hand King Hussein's unilateral cutting off of ties with the West Bank and the concomitant relinquishing of sovereignty over Palestinian territory, and on the other hand Faysal al-Husseini's arrest by the Israeli occupation and their publication of a document allegedly found in the offices of the Arab Studies Society led by al-Husseini: a document containing a Palestinian declaration of independence.[52]

Preparations for the establishment of a sovereign state had reached a mature enough level so that the Palestinians could take up Hussein's gauntlet. A declaration of independence was circulated underground as a proposal to be put by the *intifada* to the upcoming emergency session of the PNC, which would decide upon it.

When the Nineteenth PNC convened in Algiers on November 12–15, 1988, all the organizations that had been in Algiers for the Eighteenth PNC (April 20–25, 1987)—Fateh, PFLP, Democratic Front, PLF (Palestine Liberation Front), and PCP—participated in and supported the Palestinian declaration of independence. Virtually unanimous support was forthcoming from the Occupied Territories. The PNC, with its declaration of independence and only a few weeks later the start of a PLO-U.S. dialogue, demonstrated as clearly as could be the union—difficult at times, but never broken—between the Palestinians in the diaspora and the Palestinian people under occupation.

Arafat's political advisor Hani al-Hasan was one of the first to point out where the Palestinians had arrived: "We are aware that each liberation movement begins as a revolution and looks forward to reaching a phase in which state establishments will be entrenched. Such [an] entrenchment process proves the success of liberation."[53] As a result of the struggle of their national liberation movement, taken up in the 1950s from the diaspora, and as a first result of the *intifada*— still continuing—the Palestinians have reached the doorstep of the phase referred to by al-Hasan. While this represents a victory of a broad nationalist coalition of different political forces and social classes under a distinct bourgeois leadership, both inside and outside, it remains the task of the left to continue in the vein of its social-revolutionary tradition to give the future Palestinian state a truly democratic content. The power basis for this future struggle is being laid right now, not least in the popular committees of the *intifada*, and the left would be well advised to focus all their strength on this immense task.

NOTES

1. *Jerusalem Post,* December 15, 1982, p. 1.

2. Ibid., December 19, 1987, p. 2.

3. Ibid., December 25, 1987, p. 4.

4. Ibid., December 18, 1987, p. 20.

5. Ibid., December 20, 1987, p. 1.

6. Barrington Moore, *Injustice: The Social Bases of Obedience and Revolt* (White Plains, N.Y.: M. E. Sharpe, 1987), pp. 472–73.

7. Charles Tilly, *From Mobilization to Revolution* (Reading, Mass.: Addison-Wesley, 1978), p. 84.

8. Algiers Voice of Palestine, December 10, 1987, quoted from Foreign Broadcast Information Service [FBIS]—Near East Section, FBIS–87–238, December 11, p. 2.

9. Baghdad Voice of the PLO, December 10, 1987, quoted from FBIS–87–239, December 14, 1987, pp. 5–6. Reprinted in the Arabic original in *Filastin al-Thaura,* no. 679 (December 17, 1987): 6.

10. *The Holy Quran,* Al-Anfal (The Spoils), verse 7.

11. On this point, see Nels Johnson, *Islam and the Politics of Meaning in Palestinian Nationalism* (London: Kegan Paul International, 1982).

12. Manama WAKH, December 14, quoted from FBIS–87–240, December 15, 1987, p. 6.

13. Quoted from FBIS–87–245, December 22, 1987, p. 3.

14. Quoted from FBIS–87–238, December 11, 1987, p. 3.

15. *Jerusalem Post,* December 10, 1987, p. 1.

16. "Events 2: The Uprising," in *Filaston Al-Thaura Book* (Nicosia, January 1988), pp. 199–200 (in Arabic).

17. Ibid., p. 195.

18. Quoted from FBIS–87–242, December 17, 1987, p. 3.

19. Radio Monte Carlo, December 21, 1987, quoted from FBIS–87–245, December 22, 1987, p. 5.

20. Quoted from FBIS–87–249, December 29, 1987, p. 3.

21. *Filastin al-Thaura Book,* pp. 195–96. Also published in Arabic in *al-Hurriyah,* December 10, 1987.

22. Quoted from FBIS–87–248, December 28, 1987, pp. 6–8.

23. *Journal of Palestine Studies* vol. XVII, no. 3 (Spring 1988): 63–65.

24. *Le Monde,* January 16, 1988, pp. 1–2, quoted from FBIS–88–013, January 21, 1988.

25. For this and the following argument, see my unpublished Ph.D. Thesis, Berlin: The Free University of Berlin, 1985: "The Rise of the Palestine National Movement 1948–68: A Comparative Study of Ideology and Politics of the MAN and of Fatah." For the special role of migrants in Palestinian nationalism, see my articles "Migration and Diaspora-Nationalism," in press, Paris, and "Labor Migration and New Political Movements," in press, Berlin.

26. *Kiyan* covers a wide range of meaning from identity via entity to state.

27. *Filatinuna*, November 11, 1960. My translation.

28. This MAN argument is based on Constantine Zurayk's seminal "The Meaning of Disaster," published in Arabic in 1948; available in an English translation, Beirut, 1956.

29. Eqbal Ahmad, "Yasir Arafat's Nightmare," *MERIP* 119 (November-December 1983): 18–23; quotation from p. 21.

30. See the detailed description in Ehud Yaari, *Strike Terror: The Story of Fatah* (New York: Sabra Books, 1970), pp. 125–50.

31. This becomes obvious from Amnan Cohen, *Political Parties in the West Bank Under the Jordanian Regime, 1949–1967* (Ithaca, N.Y.: Cornell University Press, 1982).

32. See Helena Cabban, *The PLO: People, Power and Politics* (London: Cambridge University Press, 1984), and Alain Gresh, *The PLO: The Struggle Within: Towards an Independent Palestinian State* (London: Zed Books, 1984).

33. See my "The PLO, Its Struggle for Legitimacy, and the Question of a Palestinian State," *Jerusalem Journal of International Relations* 9, no. 3 (1982): 99–114.

34. See Ibrahim Dakkak, "Back to Square One: A Study in the Re-emergence of the Palestinian Identity in the West Bank 1967–1980," in A. Scholch, ed., *Palestinians Over the Green Line: Studies on the Relations Between Palestinians on Both Sides of the 1947 Armistice Line Since 1967* (London: Ithaca Press, 1983), pp. 64–101, which takes a very critical position toward the perceived hegemonial approach of the PLO in the West Bank; also Abdul Jawad Saleh (Mayor of al-Bireh), *Israel's Policy of De-institutionalization: A Case Study of Palestinian Local Governments* (London: Jerusalen Center for Development Studies, 1987). See also the same author's "Abu Ammar's Biggest Mistake Was Gambling on the Americans," *MERIP* 119 (November-December 1983): 26–28, 36.

35. See the relevant documents in *Journal of Palestine Studies* 16, no. 4 (Summer 1987): 189–204.

36. Moore, *Injustice*, p. 482, note 6.

37. Ibid., pp. 480–81.

38. Baghdad Voice of the PLO, Arafat in airport on the uprising to the PLO Central Committees, January 8, 1988, quoted from FBIS–88–006, January 11, 1988, p. 8.

39. Baghdad Voice of the PLO, quoted from FBIS–88–007, January 12, 1988, pp. 8–10.

40. Ibid.

41. Algiers Voice of Palestine, February 3, 1988, quoted from FBIS–88–023, February 4, 1988, p. 4.

42. Radio al-Quds (clandestine), January 26, 1988, quoted from FBIS–88–017, January 27, 1988, p. 5.

43. Baghdad Voice of the PLO, January 25, 1988, quoted from FBIS–88–016, January 26, 1988, p. 9.

44. Baghdad Voice of the PLO, February 11, 1988, quoted from FBIS–88–029, February 12, 1988, p. 4.

45. Ibid., April 18, 1988, quoted from FBIS–88–075, April 19, 1988, p. 3.

46. Reprinted in *Journal of Palestine Studies* (Autumn 1988): 272–75.

47. Interview with Abu Sharif in *Journal Palestine Studies* 69 (Autumn 1988): 237–239.

48. "He said no official in the PLO has the right to express views that run counter to the views agreed upon by the PNC. He criticized Abu Sharif's declaration about the PLO's readiness to make concessions in favor of any leadership chosen by the people of

the West Bank and the Gaza Strip. He said: The PLO is the sole representative of the Palestinians.'' Radio Free Lebanon, June 18, 1988, quoted from FBIS–88–118, June 20, 1988, p. 5.

49. Quoting Khaleel al-Fahum, the former PNC speaker, gone over to the Fateh rebels. Radio al-Quds, June 20, 1988, quoted from FBIS–88–119, June 21, 1988, p. 6.

50. In the words of a PFLP-GC spokesman; ibid.

51. The poll was reported about in *al-Hamishmar*, June 26, 1988, p. 2, quoted from FBIS–88–123, June 27, 1988, p. 35.

52. Reprinted in *Jerusalem Post*, August 12, 1988, p. 10.

53. Kuwait al-Anba, August 28, 1988, p. 21, quoted from FBIS–88–169, August 31, 1988, p. 8.

III

REGIONAL AND INTERNATIONAL REACTIONS

14

A Symmetry of Surrogates

JORDAN'S AND EGYPT'S RESPONSE TO THE *INTIFADA*

Ghada Talhami

No two states in the Arab world can rival Jordan's and Egypt's record of involvement in the Palestinian issue. Several historical and geopolitical considerations converged to transform the southern Syrian and Egyptian lands into an integral strategic zone. Egypt's historic vulnerability on its northeastern flank and Jordan's recently acquired vulnerability on its western flank guaranteed continued military and political engagement with the Palestinians. As the Egyptians sought to shore up their defenses along the flat Sinai landmass and the Jordanians to maximize control over the fertile Jordan Valley, wars became inevitable. A certain kind of international diplomacy that sought the constant readjustment of relationships also developed. This forced the Egyptians and the Jordanians to anchor their regional and pan-Arab policies to their Palestinian policies and to avoid the appearance of denying their Palestinian responsibilities.

These historical and geopolitical considerations, moreover, were transformed into legal relationships with the creation of the state of Israel and the liquidation of the British Mandate over Palestine in 1948. Jordan's control over eastern Palestine, legitimized and formalized in the Jordanian Constitution of 1950, and Egypt's administration of Gaza, which remained unassimilated to the very end, posed inevitable threats to irredentist Palestinian sentiments. With the demise of the General Government of Palestine (*hukumat 'umum Filastin*) in 1948, resulting from the connivance of the Great Powers and their Arab allies against this new Palestinian entity, nothing was left of the Palestinian political apparatus. Subsequently, Israel's strategy and that of the Powers revolved around circum-

venting the Palestinians by negotiating with their Arab surrogates. Even when
the wars were fought in the name of the Arab people of Palestine, settlements
were reached with their self-appointed representatives.

Thus, it should be no surprise that the issue of self-representation was always
regarded by Palestinians as the cornerstone of their political case. A much
contested issue, the question of who speaks for the Palestinians, has forced the
PLO in particular to sharpen its argument via-à-vis the international community
and to hone its tactical policy vis-à-vis its Arab sponsors. The question of
legitimacy, however, topped the PLO's agenda in times of regional peace only.
In times of severe regional crisis and the outbreak of serious conflicts elsewhere
in the Arab lands, the PLO was confronted with the preoccupation of the Arab
states with issues other than the Palestinian cause. This was particularly true
when the Iran-Iraq war expanded and all eyes were riveted on the Gulf region.
Unlike Lebanon's civil war, which inevitably called into question the Palestinian
presence in that country, the Gulf war did not possess any relevance to the
Palestinian issue. Instead, what the war accomplished was to strengthen the hand
of those Arab states who feared any change in the Arab-Israeli status quo. But
for those to whom the status quo of the 1980s was greatly disadvantageous,
terminating the Iran-Iraq war was more than just a necessity of preserving the
unity of the Muslim world. No single Arab entity desired an end to the Arab-
Israeli status quo of the 1980s more than the PLO. Having lost the Lebanese
theater of operations, having failed to sustain the PLO-Jordanian dialogue, it
now faced the dismal reality of the limited nature of the Arab attention span.
As long as the Iran-Iraq war continued, no Arab head of state, particularly of
the moderate states with access to Washington, was willing to consider the
implementation of the Arab consensus on the Arab-Israeli conflict. Thus, when
the Arab summit meeting of November 1987 convened in Amman, the Palestine
question was placed at the bottom of their agenda. The Arab League of States
broke its previous pattern of obligatory emphasis on the Palestine question by
allowing the Gulf states to monopolize the meeting with their own security
problems. The PLO was left to savor the crumbs of the Arab table. The League
pursued two long-term goals, namely, the rehabilitation of Egypt and maintaining
a unified Arab front toward the war. The latter was considered to have a salubrious
effect on the Palestinian issue, bringing the Arab states closer to a unified Arab
position on the Arab-Israeli conflict as well.[1]

Arab League meetings, for all intents and purposes, have become a barometer
of the pan-Arab mood of the region. By the time the Arab foreign ministers'
meeting took place in Tunis on January 24 and 25, 1988, the Amman picture
had changed drastically. Not only was the Palestinian issue placed at the top of
the agenda, but the PLO's standing as being solely responsible for the affairs
of the occupied Palestinian lands was reaffirmed. What had changed between
November 1987 and January 1988 was the outbreak of hostilities between Arab
civilians and Israeli soldiers beginning in December 1987. The *intifada* was
recognized at that meeting as a major development, and funds were pledged by

all Arab governments.[2] The Arab-Israeli status quo had suddenly shifted, and in the aftermath of this change the Arab states took notice and the PLO embarked on a serious reassessment of its relationship to Jordan. Indeed, the first outcome of the *intifada* was a drastic change in the Jordanian-Palestinian balance of forces in the West Bank. This was soon reflected in the altered political outlook of these two entities and their adoption of novel tactics on the international scene.

But while the PLO has always felt the need to align its policies and diplomatic moves with Jordan in the past, other alignments of forces suddenly seemed possible. Jordan's condition for resuming its talks with the PLO has always been the latter's acceptance of U.S. requirements and demands. This came down to sharing the task of Palestinian representation with Jordan, as well as accepting UN Security Council Resolution 242. The *intifada* facilitated the emergence of a new sponsor, one that would not succumb to American pressure as readily as Jordan. What made this shift in alignments possible was the *intifada's* increasingly anti-Jordanian position and its audible pro-PLO tone.[3] Of particular significance here was the *intifada's* call for the resignation of the Palestinian members of the Jordanian parliament. This demand was embodied in Communiqué No. 10 of the Unified Command of the Uprising. This call, in March 1988, so rattled the Jordanians that the PLO representative in Amman, 'Abd al-Razzaq al-Yahya, was summoned for an explanation.[4]

Developments such as these provided an opportunity for the PLO to avoid the Jordanian straitjacket. Egypt now loomed as the most logical alternative to Jordan, particularly in its capacity as a channel to Washington. Relations with Egypt, however, had also deteriorated to a dangerous level just prior to the *intifada*. With an eye on the Egyptian scene, the PLO began to hammer out a unified position in order to avoid exclusive reliance on Jordan.[5] Jordan's position in the West Bank, it was soon revealed, had been deteriorating for years. The *intifada* was no more than the final dramatic blow to the Jordanian foundation, already riddled with holes. Nowhere was this more apparent than in the economic sphere. Jordan's economic position in the West Bank had deteriorated badly in the wake of the 1967 war, due both to Israeli fiscal policies and to Jordanian fear of financial risk-taking. Due to Israel's own peculiar economic condition, the West Bank was steadily integrated in the Israeli economy, first via its import practices, then via its job market. The integration of Arab labor from the West Bank into the Israeli market developed early in the occupation. By 1971 fully one-third of all West Bank workers were employed in the booming Israeli sector. West Bank males, responding to an upturn in the Israeli economy, abandoned ancestral farms to the labor of women and children. Even though the Israeli economy began to decline in 1973, West Bank workers continued to supply 8 percent of the Israeli labor force.[6]

Israel was also successful in reversing the West Bank's trade patterns. The West Bank became a captive market for the Israelis, with 90 percent of its imports being Israeli-made or going through Israel. This did not mean the elimination of trade relations with Jordan but rather confining this trade to agricultural produce. At the same time, West Bank industrial imports using Israeli raw materials were not permitted into Jordan. The Jordanians contributed to this dependence on the Israeli economy through their own banking policies. Closed in the aftermath of the 1967 war, Arab banks in the West Bank were permitted to reopen a few months later. The banks refused and are still closed, since the alternative course, namely, operating within the Israeli banking system and under Israeli supervision, was fraught with complications.[7]

Thus, while Israel was deliberately making the West Bank and Gaza dependent on its economy in order to arrest the development of pro-PLO and pro-Jordanian sentiment, Jordan was letting things slide. This is not as puzzling as might appear at first and must be seen in the context of Jordan's overall Arab diplomacy. Although Jordan always professed its openness to the idea of a peace settlement and a resolution of the conflict in a manner compatible with the rights of the Palestinians, it was not averse to the maintenance of the post–1967 status quo. This became very clear after the failure of Jordanian-PLO efforts to come to terms on the matter of a joint peace conference delegation. To the Jordanians, the risks involved in negotiating a peace settlement, especially without Palestinian participation, became greater than the risk of living with the status quo. A certain *modus vivendi* operated among the West Bank, Jordan, and Israel, which, in the Jordanian view, was quite manageable. The economic relations of Jordan and Israel continued, and the long border has been eerily silent even as battles raged between Israel and Arab states to the north and south. Contacts between King Hussein and Israeli leaders were made with regularity. The situation in the West Bank may have become intolerable for its own inhabitants, but not for the Jordanian regime.[8]

Indeed, to pursue a diplomatic course leading to a peace conference and the restoration of the West Bank either to Jordanian or PLO hands was considered dangerous for Jordan's own delicate ethnic balance. The creation of a Palestinian state in the West Bank or the restoration to Jordan of that area could feasibly provoke Jordan's Palestinian majority. Yet, out of fear that the West Bank was being slowly annexed to Israel through the policy of settlement building, Jordan initiated an effort to coordinate future moves with the PLO. Negotiations to develop a joint position regarding the peace strategy began in 1985. But the negotiations ground to a halt when the PLO balked at the thought of accepting Resolution 242 and when a member of the PLO's higher command was accused of masterminding the *Achille Lauro* hijacking. The essence of Jordan's strategy was still the same, nevertheless. In this episode, as in several before it, Jordan demonstrated its willingness to indulge in any risk-taking, preferring to let the PLO bear the brunt of responsibility for the peace process. Again, the status quo seemed preferable to a hazardous course that might threaten the country with isolation.[9]

The *intifada* forced Hussein to react and initiate some necessary moves of his own. Because the Camp David Accords stipulated that autonomy be granted to the West Bank and Gaza, any subsequent plans for Jordanian-Palestinian federation designated Gaza's future destiny within that federation. Hussein's silence in the face of West Bank and Gaza violence was, therefore, intolerable.[10] As was shown earlier, the West Bank Palestinians quickly displayed their allegiance to the PLO, and this organization, in turn, asserted its independence from Jordan. All of a sudden, the PLO's main constituency emerged as that of the West Bank and Gaza, which soon eliminated the PLO's dependence on Arab states. The PLO's lack of bases in the front-line states became less significant as the entire West Bank and Gaza turned into a PLO base.[11]

Realizing that the West Bank had changed forever, Hussein finally issued a declaration extricating himself from the West Bank and asserting the PLO's legal responsibility to the area based on the Rabat Summit Resolution of 1974. Explaining the timing of the declaration, Hussein reminded his subjects of Jordan's quasi-trusteeship status over Palestine by quoting the unity resolution of the two banks of April 1950, which affirmed "the reservation of all Arab rights in Palestine and the defense of such rights by all legitimate means—without prejudice to the final settlement of the just cause of the Palestinian people, within the scope of the people's aspirations and of Arab cooperation and international justice."[12] Hussein stated that he was now bowing to the will of the Palestinian people, based on Jordan's longtime commitment to the Palestinian right of self-determination "on their national soil." This commitment, he added, was actually made two years before the Rabat Resolution. Jordan was never oblivious to the Palestinian national will, he claimed, since, the unification of the two banks was accomplished upon the request of Palestinian representatives in 1950.[13]

Israeli reaction to this Jordanian move was generally mixed, ranging from disbelief to a feeling of betrayal. Some commentators recognized that the move forced Israel to redefine its political choices, since now "a bridge has disappeared." By his act of withdrawal, Hussein has forced Israel, in effect, to choose between unilateral action or negotiating with the Palestinians. Unilateral action as such, whether amounting to partial withdrawal, as is favored by the Labor party, or to autonomy and effective annexation, as is favored by the Likud party, will have local and international repercussions. Labor's course might bring about the eruption of West Bank violence, and Likud's course might cause international criticism, hence both parties' need for Hussein. Only Jordan's participation in a negotiated settlement will ward off unwanted participation of the PLO and legitimize either one of these two Israeli solutions. But since the King has removed himself from the Arab-Israeli conflict, the Israelis immediately feared the inevitability of negotiating with the PLO.[14]

Other Israelis fretted over the legal ramifications of Jordan's move. Some, like Eli Natan, a former Jerusalem District Court judge, argued that even if the separation became a firm act based on the repealed unification law embodied in the Jordanian Constitution of 1950, it did not free Israel to alter the status of the West Bank. The Camp David Accords prevented Israel from following a unilateral course of action where the Occupied Territories were concerned. Others, such as Yoram Dinstein, one of Israel's top international law experts, insisted that Israel's status in the territories was no more than that of a "belligerent occupier." This, he went on, will not change as a result of Jordan's action, but will simply force Israel to face the Palestinians at the negotiating table. Only Jordan, in that case, has legal title to the West Bank, and as such has it within its power to make the Palestinians the new legal sovereigns. Dinstein's insistence that "title belongs to Jordan," which diverges sharply from the official Israeli view claiming sovereignty for Israel (by virtue of its 1967 "defensive" action resulting in occupation), also implies that Jordan has the right to dispose of the West Bank in any manner possible. Jordan has the option to negotiate with Israel, according to this view, or cede the area to the Palestinians. That, in Dinstein's view, was the meaning of the "Jordanian option." Both Dinstein and Natan, however, agreed that Hussein has not committed himself to the ultimate act of separation.[15]

Without the *intifada* and its real expression of hostility toward Hussein, this step would never have been possible. Its immediate outcome was the suspension of Jordan's financial obligations toward 24,000 West Bank civil employees. Jordan did not, however, revoke the Jordanian passports of its citizens on the West Bank.[16] The PLO immediately met this challenge by issuing an Executive Committee order instructing West Bank civilian employees to remain in their positions and pledging to assume the full Jordanian financial burden. The PLO also prohibited the alteration of any West Bank laws until the proper Palestinian legal authorities have looked into the matter.[17] PLO experts, such as Nabil Ramlawi, the PLO's representative to the UN Headquarters at Geneva, jubilantly welcomed the Jordanian decision. He asserted that the Palestinian natural right to sovereignty superseded any other legal rights that accrued to non-Palestinian authorities.[18] The PLO nevertheless denied its intention to banish Jordan totally from the negotiating process, insisting all along that Jordan's long border with Israel and its sovereignty over a large number of naturalized Jordanians of Palestinian origin necessitated its inclusion in the peace talks.[19] There was no denying, however, that the Jordanian-PLO relationship had changed dramatically and that the umbilical cord had been severed. This development, more than any other, prompted the PLO to intensify its relationship with Egypt.

Heir to another kind of Palestinian involvement, Egypt was also forced to reexamine its Palestinian obligations in the light of the *intifada*. The Egyptian withdrawal from the center of the Arab-Israeli maelstrom as a result of the Camp David Accords has been almost complete. What the *intifada* demonstrated was that constructive involvement in this issue, rather than the usurpation of the PLO's role, will be most beneficial to Egypt. The desire to see Egypt swing its weight behind the Palestinians was also an increasingly dominant theme among the PLO leadership itself. In an interview conducted just before the *intifada*, Chairman Arafat reiterated his conviction that Egypt should have a big role in a future international peace conference. Egypt, he said, is more important than Jordan not only because of its legal responsibility for Gaza, but because the Camp David Accords prohibit changing the status of the West Bank without

Egypt's approval. Although recognizing the complications introduced by Camp David, Arafat emphasized Egypt's regional significance based on its central location and tremendous human potential. Arafat added that the PLO was definitely behind the readmission of Egypt to the Organization of the Islamic Conference and that he himself was personally in favor of Egypt's return to the Arab League of States.[20]

The process of rehabilitating Egypt had actually started before the *intifada*. A difficult and tortuous process, it had to contend with the legacy of the Camp David Accords and the degree of insensitivity that Egypt had displayed in the past toward the Palestinians. One of the highlights of that period, which thoroughly alienated Arab public opinion, occurred during the 1977 Mena House talks. It was there that Egypt hoisted three flags, those of the Egyptians, Israelis, and Palestinians. Israeli delegates refused to begin the talks while the Palestinian flag fluttered over their heads, and the Egyptians were forced to lower all three flags. Even as the Palestinians made their intention not to participate in the talks very clear, the Egyptians felt that this symbolic gesture was needed. Israeli intransigence in this instance contributed greatly to Egypt's isolation in the Arab world and its relegation to the status of a pariah state.[21]

Egypt's position in the Arab world in general began to improve with the 1981 succession of Hosni Mubarak to the presidency. Mubarak has achieved almost the full restoration of Egypt to the center of Arab politics without sacrificing the Camp David Accords. His efforts were beginning to show results largely because of the Iran-Iraq war and his successful effort to keep Israeli-Egyptian relations on ice. Egypt's participation in the 1987 Arab League meeting in Amman was punctuated by a concurrent Egyptian arms exhibition in the same capital that interested the weaker Arab Gulf states immensely. Following that meeting, the United Arab Emirates, Iraq, Morocco, Bahrain, North Yemen, and Saudi Arabia restored full diplomatic relations with Egypt. Almost ten years after Anwar Sadat's visit to Jerusalem, Egypt was almost totally rehabilitated. Ostracism continued on the part of Syria and Libya, both of which led a serious effort to block Egypt's reentry into the Arab League of States.[22]

Egypt's policy toward the Palestinians has also improved, although many complications have developed along the way. Much of Egypt's diplomacy in the 1980s aimed at eliminating differences between Jordan and the PLO in an effort to force the emergence of a unified Jordanian-Palestinian negotiating team.[23] This strategy served Egypt well by enhancing its constructive pan-Arab role without necessarily endangering the Camp David Accords. The strategy did not simplify the peace process, however. As Arafat correctly pointed out in 1987, while Egypt's participation in a future peace conference is assured, the Camp David Accords will be hard to nullify or reconcile with the outcome of the peace talks.[24] Not that Israel was in agreement on the issue of Palestinian representation. Both the Shamir and Peres cabinets before 1987 refused to go along with the Egyptian notion of a Palestinian-Jordanian joint delegation. Criticism by the Palestine National Council in Algiers in 1986 had actually targeted

Egypt's special relationship with Israel. This criticism, in turn, narrowed Egypt's peace options. Egypt retaliated by ordering the closure of Cairo's PLO offices in April 1987.[25] But by November 1987 the PLO's Cairo office was opened again, and by January 1988 Mubarak was once more playing the role of the middle man between Washington and the PLO. It is interesting to note that Mubarak's first effort since the beginning of the *intifada* called for a six-month halt to the violence. The PLO considered this to be a miscalculation on his part but did not criticize him.[26] Soon the PLO began to take the initiative and to define a new role for Egypt.

Egypt's readiness to get reinvolved in the Arab-Israeli conflict, nevertheless, did not materialize overnight. Several factors propelled the Mubarak regime on this course. First, there was a tendency by the Egyptian public to blame the country's economic stagnation on the Camp David Accords. Rising unemployment and the decline of the Suez Canal revenue, both resulting from the shrinkage of Persian Gulf economies, have strained the reserves of the state. Public reaction to these adverse economic developments was colored by their peace expectations. Although stunned by the reaction of Arab regimes to the Camp David Accords, they seriously believed that other Arab states would follow suit and normalize relations with Israel. Yet Egyptians of all shades of opinion, save the Islamic movement, never recommended that Egypt withdraw from the Camp David Accords. Egypt's significant opposition groups, including the Wafd party, never expressed such a view. But most of the opposition did counsel keeping the Camp David peace on ice, if for nothing else than to strengthen Egypt's tie to the Islamic and Arab worlds. Thus, the Egyptian view was that of a static peace, while the Israeli view envisaged an active peace. Israel kept searching for means to bring others into its orbit, while Egypt went on trying to minimize its contacts with the Israeli state. This does not mean that Egypt can afford to stand by while the Arab-Israeli dispute festers. Egyptians are committed to a peaceful solution, if for nothing else than to see this issue removed from their list of priorities.[27]

There is common agreement that not only were the Egyptians tired of the general Arab unwillingness to adopt a peace initiative, but that Sadat's opposition grew not in response to his overall peace strategy but to his failure to achieve democracy at home.[28] In other words, Egyptians were anxious to turn to pressing domestic issues, but the inflamed Palestinian issue would not allow them to do so. Egypt's desire to be readmitted to the Arab League of States, the highest act of legitimation, could not be achieved while the Egyptian-Israeli peace treaty remained valid. Yet to revoke or abrogate this treaty would be tantamount to a declaration of war.[29]

Egypt's dilemma in the post–Camp David era hinged on finding a way to reintegrate itself in the Arab world short of revoking the Camp David Accords and declaring war on Israel. A partial answer to this dilemma was provided by the Taba controversy. The resort's value to Egypt was not measured in financial or economic terms but in its significance for Egypt's national pride, honor, and international standing.[30] Egypt's willingness to submit the dispute to arbitration was a test of Israel's goodwill. The Israelis, on their part, recognized the importance of complying with the decision of the International Court in order to avoid straining the special relationship with Egypt. A *Jerusalem Post* editorial stated this clearly: "Paradoxically, but thankfully, it may be Taba, the miniscule enclave itself and the settlement reached over it, that could now force a fleshing out of the cold, bare bones of the peace treaty with Egypt. The time has arrived for progress on the normalization which Israel demanded, and Egypt accepted, as part of the arbitration deal. With Israel moving out of Taba, it is up to the Egyptians to reciprocate by showing their good faith."[31]

The Taba decision, on the other hand, came as a boost to Egypt's standing in the Arab world and a vindication of the Camp David settlement. The significance of Egypt's restoration of some of its territory through arbitration and Israel's submission to an international verdict in a matter concerning a treaty partner has not been lost on the Arab states.

Thus, the *intifada*, coming on the heels of Taba, proved to be Egypt's golden opportunity. Egypt could finally play the role of a mediator, criticize Israel publicly, and if successful, exercise a moderating influence over the PLO. Once the *intifada* resulted in a new direction for the PLO, and once a new Palestinian peace offensive was mounted, Egypt seized the opportunity. Mubarak began to play the role of Arafat's chief advisor and mouthpiece in Washington, and the Arab world was treated to the spectacle of a polished diplomatic offensive on behalf of the Palestinians. Egypt seemed to bask in a glow similar to that enveloping it during Nasser's best pan-Arab days. But the new Egyptian-Palestinian relationship was in great contrast to the familiar pattern of the past. Egypt did not represent the Palestinians, and the Palestinians were not absorbed into Egypt's larger Arab policy. Egypt's goal this time emerged as that of facilitator, not representer, and therein lies Egypt's special appeal to the Palestinians. Unlike Jordan, which found it psychologically and legally difficult to disengage from the Palestinian issue and the future of the West Bank, Egypt claimed only the rights of an interested friend and sponsor. The advantages accruing to Egypt from this unexpected convergence of Egyptian and Palestinian interests were enormous. Egypt emerged as the major sponsor and champion of Palestinian rights and as their advocate in Washington. Moreover, sponsorship of the Palestinian cause was, as always in the Arab arena, the greatest legitimizer of errant regimes. Egypt, it appeared, had finally discovered the perfect antidote to Camp David.

Jordan, on the other hand, suffered as a result of the slow disintegration of its system in the West Bank. Unable to recognize the devastating impact of twenty-one years of Israeli administration on the West Bank, Jordan lingered on. The parallel rise of Palestinian nationalism and legitimacy has finally driven the point home to the Jordanians. But unlike Egypt, Jordan's multiple associations with the Palestinian issue precluded a radical shift of position to suit the conditions of the *intifada*. Sponsorship of the Palestinian cause was always problematic for Jordan and was bound to unleash a flood of accusations and misunderstandings. Therefore, separation was the only viable alternative.

As for the PLO, the *intifada* proved to be more than just a counteroffensive in the historic and deadly duel between Palestinians and Israelis. The *intifada* was a desperately needed development, freeing the PLO from years of dependence on Arab operational theaters. Once the staging ground of the Palestinian offensive moved inland to the West Bank and Gaza, the Israeli sword was no longer hanging over Egypt's and Jordan's heads. Israel was no longer capable of pursuing the policy of massive retaliation of the 1950s and 1960s against these two entities without incurring the wrath of world public opinion. Not only would this policy be indefensible in the eyes of the world, the use of excessive force against the civilians of the West Bank and Gaza was found to be equally reprehensible. Although the civilian population under occupation suffered and continues to suffer the agony of a slow-paced rebellion, the diplomatic and political windfall of this development was incalculable. Much of this diplomatic windfall, it should be noted, altered the balance of power between the PLO and the Arab confrontation states. For the PLO, revising the old arrangements with Egypt and Jordan was now possible, as was forging new relationships, finally ending the Arab trusteeship phase in favor of total Palestinian independence.

NOTES

1. Lamis Andoni, "The Gains and Losses of the PLO," *Middle East International*, no. 313 (November 21, 1987): 4–5.

2. Lamis Andoni, "Solid Arab Backing," *Middle East International*, no. 318 (February 6, 1988): 7–8.

3. Lamis Andoni, "Jordan and the PLO: Changing Tactics," *Middle East International*, no. 318 (February 6, 1988): 12.

4. Lamis Andoni, "Leaflet(s) No. 10," *Middle East International*, no. 321 (March 19, 1988): pp. 9–10.

5. Andoni, "Jordan and the PLO," p. 12.

6. Arthur R. Day, *East Bank/West Bank: Jordan and the Prospects for Peace* (New York: Council on Foreign Relations, 1986), p. 112.

7. *Ibid.*, pp. 112–115.

8. *Ibid.*, pp. 121, 131.

9. *Ibid.*, pp. 133–136.

10. *Ibid.*, p. 127.

11. Lamis Andoni, "A Year of the *Intifada*: Lessons for the Arab States," *Middle East International*, no. 340 (December 16, 1988): 9.

12. "Speech by King Hussein of Jordan Renouncing Claim to the West Bank and Gaza, July 31, 1988," *American-Arab Affairs*, no. 25 (Summer 1988): 195.

13. Reference here is to the Jericho Conference of 1950, where Palestinian dignitaries proclaimed their wish to be united with Jordan. No independent historian takes this incident seriously as laying the legal framework for the unification of the two banks, since what remained of Arab Palestine after the Israeli conquest was already under Jordanian military

control. Delegates to this conference were also not elected but carefully selected by the Jordanian regime.

14. Erwin Frankel, "Without Hussein," *Jerusalem Post*, International Edition, (August 20, 1988), p. 5.

15. Elaine Ruth Fletcher, "Whose West Bank Is It Really?" *Jerusalem Post*, (August 20, 1988), p. 3.

16. Lamis Andoni, "Hussein Throws Out a Multiple Challenge," *Middle East International*, no. 331 (August 5, 1988): 3.

17. "Qarar siyasi Filistini" (A Sovereign Palestinian Decision), *Filastin al-Thawra*, special issue, no. 728 (December 11, 1988): 39.

18. "Al-haqq al-tabi'i yasbaq al-qanuni" (Natural Rights Supersede Legal Rights), *Filastin al-Thawra*, special issue, no. 728 (December 11, 1988): 77.

19. "Lays fi al-muntasaf wa la ala al-hamish" (Not at the Center, Nor at the Periphery), *Filastin al-Thawra*, special issue, no. 728 (December 11, 1988): 39.

20. "Interview with Yassir Arafat," *American-Arab Affairs*, no. 23 (Winter 1987–1988): 4–5.

21. M. Cherif Bassiouni, "Reflections on the Arab-Israeli Peace Process and Its Future Prospects," *American-Arab Affairs*, no. 21 (Summer 1987): 56.

22. Tom Porteous, "Quasi Respectability," *Middle East International*, no. 313 (November 21, 1987): 6–7. Actually, these same governments kept their embassies in Cairo at full staff despite the severance of relations after the signing of Camp David. Only the ambassadorial rank remained vacant. See note 23.

23. Chaim Shur and Liora Barash, "Mohamed Bassiouny: We Must Move Quickly," *New Outlook* 28, no. 4 (April 1985): 8.

24. "Interview with Yassir Arafat," p. 5.

25. Tom Porteous, "A Meeting, but Not of Minds," *Middle East International*, no. 305 (July 25, 1987): 7.

26. Carol Berger, "Rebuff for Mubarak," *Middle East International*, no. 318 (February 6, 1988): 8.

27. Gaby Warburg, "Not on Their List of Priorities," *New Outlook* 30, nos. 11 & 12 (November/December 1987): 13–15.

28. Abd Elsattar Eltawila, "Ten Years Later: The Mood in Cairo," *New Outlook* 30, nos. 11 & 12 (November/December 1987): 9.

29. Porteous, "Quasi Respectability," p. 7.

30. Warburg, "List of Priorities," p. 15.

31. "Taba Back to Original Size," *Jerusalem Post* (March 11, 1989), p. 24.

15

The *Intifada* in American Public Opinion

Fouad Moughrabi

The Palestinian uprising, known as the *intifada*, erupted in early December 1987. Since then, hundreds of Palestinians have been killed and thousands have been wounded. The events were, until recently, amply covered by the American media. No less than eight nationwide public opinion surveys have been conducted in the United States to gauge the impact of the events on the American public and especially on the American Jewish public.

A careful look at the results of these polls reveals some significant shifts in public perceptions. Some of these shifts reinforce previous perceptions, and some are new. Some are likely to be ephemeral, while others are likely to be constant, based on already established trends.

What is most striking about these surveys is the fact that they show a wide gap between what the American public thinks and what the American government does. Indeed, the public's perception of events, of actors, and of the issues is consistent with the international consensus, while the U.S. government's position reflects an extremely narrow base among the American public. U.S. policy tends to be more reflective of the interests of some of Israel's supporters in the United States and of the positions articulated by the Labor party in Israel.

The polls also show a significant shift in the opinions of key segments of the American public, namely, those of opinion leaders. As the level and quality of information about the region increase, the opinions of the educated, well-informed, more affluent segments of the population become more critical of Israeli policies.

This chapter will summarize the key findings of these surveys and examine the gap between public perceptions and government policy, the relationship between information and attitudes, the shift in the perceptions of opinion leaders, and the question of whether these shifts are constant or ephemeral.

KEY FINDINGS

Images of Israel and the Palestinians

With the exception of two surveys, one conducted by Penn and Schoen for the Anti-Defamation League, and the other conducted by Martilla and Kiley for the American Jewish Congress (AJC), all other surveys conclude that Israel's image in the United States has been tarnished by its handling of Palestinian unrest in the Occupied Territories. Gallup's survey of February 14, 1988, reveals that more than four Americans in ten (43 percent) consider Israeli tactics too harsh and that about a third of Americans (30 percent) view Israel less favorably. Polls by the *Chicago Tribune* (April 26, 1988) and the *Los Angeles Times* (April 1988) also confirm the erosion of public support for Israel.

Timothy McNulty of the *Chicago Tribune* (April 26, 1988) sums up the results of the *Tribune* survey by saying, "In the current conflict with Palestinian demonstrators in the occupied West Bank and Gaza Strip, Americans again are registering negative attitudes toward Israel that were first noted during the 1982 war in Lebanon and again at the disclosures of Israel's involvement in the Iran-Contra affair." This survey reveals that 38 percent of those who follow events say that their opinion of Israel has diminished in recent months. College-educated voters, usually more favorable to Israel, are now more likely than others to say that their opinion of Israel has declined. Fifty-five percent of the college-educated express less favorable opinions of Israel. The *Los Angeles Times* survey (April 12, 1988) confirms these findings. In his description of the results, Robert Scheer writes, "The fact that 42 percent of Jews and more than half of non-Jews at least in part blame unacceptable Israeli actions for the erosion of support for Israel in the United States might have serious implications for future U.S.-Israel relations."

By contrast, the Penn and Schoen survey (January 20–24, 1988) conducted for the Anti-Defamation League and the American Jewish Congress study done by Martilla and Kiley, Inc., in April 1988, both claim that public sympathy for Israel is still very high among Americans and that it has eroded hardly at all as a result of Israel's handling of the Palestinian uprising. Both surveys were done to counter the perception of a decline in pro-Israel sympathy. However, a closer look at the data from both questionnaires reveals a more complex picture. While it is true that pro-Israel sympathy is still relatively high among the respondents, significant majorities are also quite critical of Israeli practices against the Palestinians and supportive of the Palestinian demand for a homeland. In the Penn and Schoen survey, 36 percent of respondents think Israel's response to the uprising too harsh, and 33 percent think the Palestinians are demonstrating because they have "legitimate grievances." Furthermore, 49 percent of the respondents say that the United States was right to vote for a United Nations resolution condemning Israel for its decision to deport nine Palestinians, and a majority favor a negotiated settlement that includes the PLO among all the other parties to the conflict.

The American Jewish Congress survey of registered voters concludes that "American support for Israel remains steadfast. . . . If anything, the trend data indicates Israel's fundamental position with the American people has been strengthened during the past few years." In an understated manner, however, the report adds, "There are several survey findings which indicate impatience with—and disapproval of—recent Israeli government activity." The AJC survey shows that the majority of the public (especially the opinion leaders) endorse an independent Palestinian state and the participation of the PLO in peace talks. These positions are not seen as necessarily anti-Israel.

At the same time that public sympathy for Israel has been eroding, a pro-Palestinian sympathy factor has begun to emerge. This pro-Palestinian sympathy applies to the Palestinians in general and not to the PLO. The latter is still viewed negatively among the American public, which nonetheless endorses its right to participate in peace negotiations.

The 1982 Gallup survey for the Chicago Council on Foreign Relations reveals for the first time the emergence of a pro-Palestinian sympathy factor among the American public:

While the public sympathized with Israel over "the Arabs" by 48 percent to 17 percent, they supported Israel over "the Palestinians" by a lesser margin, 40 percent to 17 percent. Opinion leaders were even more sensitive to the difference in terminology. Their support for Israel over "the Arabs" (51% to 19%) dropped to 42%–26% for Israel over the "Palestinians."[1]

Timothy McNulty confirms this trend in his analysis of the *Chicago Tribune* survey of April 1988:

In surveys conducted in previous years, Americans were asked whether their sympathies were with Israel or with the Arab states in the Middle East. Opinion was overwhelmingly in favor of Israel. . . . It is a measure of how much more difficult the current situation is for Israel, in terms of American public opinion, that the margin in Israel's favor is much narrower where people are asked to choose between the Israelis and the Palestinians.[2]

The *Los Angeles Times* poll (March 26-April 7, 1988) shows a significant increase in pro-Palestinian sympathy as opposed to pro-Arab sympathy. For the non-Jewish sample, support for Israel over the Arabs (50%–12%) changes dramatically in the case of support for Israel over the Palestinians to 36%–25%. Perhaps even more significant is the finding that among the Jewish sample, support for Israel over the Arabs (83 percent–4 percent) changes to 56 percent–17 percent in the case of Israel over the Palestinians.

Table 1
**SHIFT IN AMERICAN SYMPATHY (1978, 1981, 1982, 1988) GALLUP
(PERCENT)**

Israeli Position

	More	Less	Same	D/Know	Total
Feb. 1978	27	34	19	20	100
July 1981	29	37	18	16	100
Aug. 1982	32	41	15	12	100
Sept. 1988	24	51	10	15	100

Palestinian Position

	More	Less	Same	D/Know	Total
Feb. 1978	___	___	___	___	___
July 1981	22	36	21	21	100
Aug. 1982	28	40	18	14	100
Sept. 1986	39	27	15	19	100

Question: "Compared to a year ago, would you say you are more
sympathetic or less sympathetic to the Israeli/Palestinian question?"

Source: George Gallup, *The Gallup Opinion Index*. Princeton: The Gallup Organization, February
    1978–September 1988.

Table 1 shows the decline of pro-Israeli sympathy and the increase in pro-
Palestinian sympathy between 1978 and 1982.

The AJC (April 1988) study confirms the appearance of a long-term trend
showing an increase in pro-Palestinian sympathy: "Increased support for the
Palestinians is particularly evident among those who are the most well-informed
about the region." Sympathy for the Palestinians has increased by 7 percent
among the general public, by 11 percent among the well-informed, and by 15
percent among the college-educated. By contrast, sympathy for Israel has declined by 21 percent among postgraduates, by 17 percent among college-educated
men, by 14 percent among high-wage earners, and by 16 percent among the
well-informed. What is obvious here is that, given the results of more recent
polls, the emergence of a pro-Palestinian sympathy factor is not simply a passing

phenomenon. The facts of Palestinian homelessness, the events in Lebanon (June 1982), Israel's role in the Iran-Contra affair, and the impact of the continuing Palestinian uprising seem to have contributed to the shaping of a new set of perceptions of the key antagonists in the conflict.

Support for Palestinian Statehood and a Negotiated Settlement

The recent polls confirm already existing support for Palestinian statehood and for a negotiated settlement that includes the PLO along with all other key actors in the conflict. A Gallup survey (February 26-March 7, 1988) asked a nationwide sample if they "favor or oppose the establishment of an independent Palestinian state in Gaza and the West Bank." Of those who were aware of events in the region, 41 percent favor an independent state, while only 23 percent oppose the idea. College graduates (46 percent) are more likely than high school graduates (28 percent) to support Palestinian statehood.

The 1982 Chicago Council on Foreign Relations study had already discovered a two to one majority in favor of an independent state for the Palestinians in the West Bank and Gaza.

The proportion of the American public favoring the creation of a separate, independent Palestinian nation grew from 29 percent in October 1977 to 41 percent in July 1982. Indeed the 1982 figures show an almost two-to-one margin (41% to 21%) in support of a Palestinian state.[3]

Another October 1982 nationwide survey conducted by Decision/Making/ Information of Washington, D.C., revealed that 65 percent of the sample agreed that "there will be no peace in the Middle East until the Palestinian people have self-determination and their own state on the West Bank and Gaza." Only 29 percent disagreed and thought that such a state would be a threat to Israel's security. In the same study, 55 percent agreed that the Palestinians are entitled to have a state of their own based on the provisions of the 1947 UN Resolution, and 50 percent disagreed with President Reagan's decision to rule out an independent state for the Palestinians.[4]

In 1985 the Survey Research Center (SRC) of the University of Michigan discovered in a nationwide survey that 54 percent of the respondents agreed that a Palestinian state is needed for peace, while only 26 percent thought such a state would be a threat to the security of Israel.[5]

Questions that use the word "homeland" instead of a "separate, independent state" yield somewhat larger percentages. The 1986 study of the Chicago Council on Foreign Relations finds that 68 percent of the respondents favor a "Palestinian homeland on the West Bank" and only 32 percent oppose it.[6] A Yankelovich Clancy Shulman survey conducted between January 27 and 28, 1988, for *Time* (February 8, 1988) reveals that 56 percent of the non-Jewish sample favor "a Palestinian homeland in the occupied territories" and only 17 percent oppose the idea. Interestingly, when respondents were asked if they favor "more autonomy for the Palestinians in the West Bank and Gaza," the percentage of those who favor this option drops to 35 percent, while 33 percent oppose it.

The ability of the public to discriminate between "autonomy" and "homeland" should not be hastily dismissed. It is true that, in response to questions about the future of the Occupied Territories, about statehood, autonomy, or a homeland, the category "don't know" or "not sure" tends to be relatively large, indicating uncertainty. However, among respondents who are informed and who express an opinion, the distinction between autonomy and homeland appears to be fairly consistent. The *Los Angeles Times* survey of April 1988 confirms the results of the Yankelovich *Time* (February 8, 1988) survey. Thus, respondents are more likely to favor "giving the Palestinians a homeland of their own in the occupied territories of the West Bank and the Gaza Strip" (50 percent–18 percent) than giving them "more autonomy" (33 percent–26 percent).

The AJC (April 1988) study suggests that "neither 'issue leaders' nor the general public distinguishes between the terms 'homeland' or 'state.' On balance, responses to questions which were identically worded, except for alternating these phrases, produced statistically insignificant differences." This poll discovers that while the general public is almost evenly split (43 percent vs. 42 percent) on the question of favoring an independent Palestinian state on the West Bank, the well-informed support this option by a two-to-one margin (56 percent–30 percent). Postgraduates believe the Palestinians are right in wanting to establish a homeland/state by margins of 51 percent to 21 percent; college-educated men favor this option by 52 percent to 22 percent and high-income people by 49 percent to 21 percent. Furthermore, the well-informed are more likely (55 percent–39 percent) than the general mass public to believe that a Palestinian homeland/state is a precondition for peace. Almost identical results were obtained by the author in the 1982 Decision/Making/Information study as well as in the SRC (1985) study.

A large majority of respondents (63 percent) in the *Los Angeles Times* survey favor an international Middle East peace conference which includes all the parties to the conflict. Forty-seven percent favor it strongly and 16 percent favor it somewhat.

Similarly, 52 percent agree that "in order to bring peace to the Middle East, we (the U.S.) should be willing to talk to all parties involved in the conflict, including the PLO." Response to this question is important given the fact that its exact wording offers the official Israeli and U.S. government position by stating: "Some people say that the United States ought not to negotiate with the Palestine Liberation Organization—the PLO—because they are terrorists and they refuse to recognize the right of Israel to exist." Only 34 percent of the respondents do not think the United States should negotiate with the PLO, presumably because the organization is linked in their minds to negative characteristics. An earlier *Los Angeles Times* survey (June 3, 1987) asked respondents the exact same question about PLO participation. Fifty percent agreed that the United States should talk to the PLO.

The Gallup survey of February 26-March 7, 1988, asked respondents the following question: "As you may know, the United States does not currently deal directly with the PLO. Do you favor or oppose direct talks between the U.S. and the PLO as a way to help resolve the conflict over Gaza and the West Bank?" Fifty-three percent were in favor and 26 percent were opposed. An even higher percentage (58 percent) were in favor of direct talks between Israel and the PLO. In this case also, as the level of awareness and the level of education increase, much higher percentages tend to favor direct talks between the United States and the PLO (60 percent among college graduates) and between Israel and the PLO (72 percent among college graduates).

The *Chicago Tribune* survey done by Peter Hart simply asked respondents if they favor "direct negotiations between the United States and the PLO," without linking these negotiations with overall peace. The question referred to "suggestions people have made for dealing with the current situation in Israel." Thirty-nine percent favored direct negotiations between Israel and the PLO. This is roughly the same percentage of the sample who think the PLO should "publicly recognize Israel as a condition for negotiations between Israel and the Palestinians."

The *Los Angeles Times* survey (April 1988) asked respondents whether they think "Israel should give up the occupied territories in order to preserve its Jewish integrity," or whether the Arabs should be " 'transferred' out of the occupied territories," or whether the "Israelis should try to come to some sort of accommodation with the Arabs in the occupied territories." The overwhelming majority (56 percent) favor some sort of accommodation with the Arabs, while small percentages choose the other options.

U.S. Aid to Israel

Israel receives nearly $4.3 billion a year in economic and military assistance from the United States. This vast subsidy, which amounts to an average of nearly $1,500 per Israeli man, woman, and child, goes in the form of grant assistance.

Traditionally, Americans have approved giving Israel economic and military aid in spite of a generally negative predisposition toward giving aid to other countries. Furthermore, Americans have been reluctant to cut off aid to Israel as a means of pressuring it to compromise, preferring instead such options as reducing aid or suspending it temporarily.

American public opinion is now more inclined to favor cutting aid to Israel as a result of the latter's handling of the Palestinian uprising. Cartoons have appeared in major newspapers linking the Israeli crackdown to U.S. taxpayers' money at work. In other words, the call for reducing or cutting aid to Israel is no longer a taboo in American public discourse.

The Yankelovich *Time* (February 8, 1988) survey reveals that 45 percent of the public think the United States should "cut aid to Israel because of its actions against the Palestinians." Only 32 percent oppose it. Gallup discovers that a plurality of Americans (41 percent) think that U.S. aid to Israel should be decreased (19 percent) or stopped altogether (22 percent) as a consequence of that country's handling of Palestinian unrest. One-quarter (24 percent) say that the level of aid should remain the same, and 7 percent favor increasing it. The *Los Angeles Times* survey (March 26-April 7, 1988) asked respondents if they think the U.S. government "should step up its military aid to Israel, or keep it at about the same level, or do you think the government should cut down military aid to Israel?" Eight percent of the non-Jewish sample said that aid should be stepped up, 47 percent thought it should stay the same, and 34 percent thought it should be cut down. The *Chicago Tribune* survey of April 21–23, 1988, has 44 percent of the public favoring the reduction of U.S. aid to Israel as a way to pressure the latter into addressing the problems of the Palestinians, and 37 percent opposing it.

The Opinions of American Jews

"American Jews," says Arthur Hertzberg, "are losing some of their illusions about Israel and are being forced to think about the real Israel. However, they remain predictably committed to its security."[7] Hertzberg's conclusions are based on a review of the results of a major poll conducted by the *Los Angeles Times* (March 26-April 7, 1988), which included a substantial Jewish and non-Jewish sample. What follows is an analysis of the responses of the Jewish sample, using, as a frame of reference, a 1986 poll conducted by Steven M. Cohen on behalf of the American Jewish Committee.[8]

The majority of American Jews favor "strong U.S. support for the government of Israel" (*Times*, 1988) and "proclaim a deep sentimental attachment to the country and a concern for its survival" (Cohen, 1986). However, Cohen discovers that a surprising number of American Jews show a good deal of ignorance about Israeli politics and society. For instance, only 34 percent knew that Menachem Begin and Shimon Peres do not belong to the same party, and not even a third knew that only Orthodox rabbis can perform Jewish marriages in Israel. Another surprising discovery in Cohen's study is that only 27 percent consider themselves "Zionist," the majority of whom (53 percent) define the term to mean belief in "the centrality of Israel to the Jewish people."

Twenty-seven percent of younger Jews said they felt equally or more sympathetic to the Palestinians as compared to 17 percent of older Jews. A quarter of younger Jews have a worse opinion of Israel as a result of recent events, and one-fifth of older Jews disagree with the Israeli government's rationale for the disturbances, preferring to describe them as "acts of civil disobedience" rather than "war" against the government of Israel.

Orthodox Jews express the highest level of attachment to Israel. Among Con-

Table 2
ISRAELI vs. PALESTINIAN/ARAB SYMPATHIES (1988)

	Orthodox	Conserv.	Reform	Non-Aff.	Non-Jews
Israel vs. Palestinians	85:3	74:8	69:11	56:17	36:25
Israel vs. Arabs	87:1	87:2	91:1	83:12	50:1

Source: Cohen, 1987

servative Jews levels of attachment to Israel are evenly split between the higher
(43 percent) and the moderate (41 percent). The lowest level of attachment exists
among Reform and nonaffiliated Jews.

In sharp contrast to the 47 percent of non-Jews who feel that Israel's unacceptable actions are responsible for its poor image in the United States, the
majority of American Jews (52 percent) blame Israel's poor image on "public
relations" problems. However, a significant number of Jews (28 percent) blame
it on unacceptable Israeli actions, and 14 percent think it can be ascribed to
both. Robert Scheer concludes his analysis of the *Los Angeles Times* survey by
saying, "The fact that 42 percent of Jews and more than half of non-Jews at
least in part blame unacceptable Israeli actions for the erosion of support for
Israel in the United States might have serious implications for future U.S.-Israeli
relations."

The Israeli invasion of Lebanon was amply covered by the media. This was
followed by the Iran-Contra revelations, the Pollard spy case, and the coverage
of the Palestine uprising. Four in ten non-Jews say that they formed their first
impression of Israel following such recent events. Fifteen percent said that their
impression was formed "within the last several months," 9 percent as a result
of the June 1967 war, and 31 percent said that they "always knew" their attitude
toward Israel. On the other hand, 59 percent of Jews say that they "always
knew," while 22 percent date their first impression to June 1967, 7 percent to
the Lebanon war, and 5 percent to "several months ago."

The rise of pro-Palestinian sympathy factor among non-Jews is reflected to a
lesser extent among the Jewish sample. Table 2 shows that nonaffiliated Jews
are more likely to sympathize with the Palestinians (17 percent) rather than with
the Arabs (12 percent).

Where do American Jews stand on the key issues that divide Palestinians and
Israelis? What areas of consensus are there and what possible areas of difference?

A majority of American Jews favor "some sort of accommodation with the
Arabs in the occupied territories." Orthodox Jews are almost evenly split between
those who favor accommodation (40 percent) and those who favor "transfer,"
a term that reflects Rabbi Meir Kahane's platform, which calls for evicting the
Palestinians from their homes. The majority also favor Secretary of State George
Shultz's plan for an international peace conference, although most of them do
not accept the idea of Israel giving up the Occupied Territories in exchange for
Arab recognition of Israel. Most American Jews prefer a formula whereby the

Table 3
TERRITORIAL COMPROMISE (percent)

	Agree	Disagree	Not Sure
1986	29	36	35
1985	30	44	26
1984	43	37	20
1983	40	36	25
1982	31	52	17
1981	41	41	18

Question: "Israel should offer the Arabs territorial compromise in Judea
           and Samaria (the West Bank) in return for credible guarantees
           of peace."
(Source: Cohen, 1987)

Palestinians receive "more autonomy" in the Occupied Territories. On the crucial question of a "homeland of their own," only nonaffiliated Jews tend to favor it (40 percent). All the others reject this option to varying levels, the Orthodox most intensely (66 percent), followed by the Conservative (48 percent) and Reform Jews (44 percent). Only a third of the Jewish sample would favor a "homeland" for the Palestinians.

Table 3 shows the evolution of opinion among American Jews. The most recent figures (1986) show an almost clear split among American Jews. One-third are willing to endorse territorial compromise in return for peace. Another third disagree, and the rest are not sure. In response to the question "I firmly believe that God promised the entire land of Israel—including Judea and Samaria—to the Jewish people," an almost identical split occurs among American Jews, with 33 percent agreeing, 33 percent disagreeing, and 34 percent not sure. However, a majority (48 agree, 21 disagree) agree that "Palestinians have a right to a homeland on the West Bank and Gaza, so long as it does not threaten Israel."

The *Los Angeles Times* survey shows that the majority of American Jews do not think the United States should negotiate with the PLO. This is consistent with Cohen's figures. By contrast, nearly 52 percent of non-Jews are willing to have the United States negotiate with the PLO.

Furthermore, the majority of American Jews think the press has made the Palestinians look better than they are. By a wide margin, American Jews say that they are upset by television pictures that show Israeli soldiers using physical force against Palestinians. Most of them, however, do not endorse New York mayor Ed Koch's call for banning the press from areas of Palestinian disturbances.

The American Jewish community is not monolithic. Opinions cover the full range of issues from the extreme right to the left liberal. Only about 15 percent are "convinced, undeviating hardliners."[9] The majority (56 percent) consider themselves Democrats, and 17 percent view themselves as political moderates. A majority of American Jews reject the Likud hard-line position and identify more with the Labor Party in Israel. The *Los Angeles Times* survey asked respondents a rather interesting question: "As a Jew, which of the following qualities do you consider most important to your Jewish identity: a commitment to social equality, or religious observance, or support for Israel, or what?" The majority (50 percent) said that social equality is most important, 17 percent pointed to religion, and another 17 percent said that support for Israel is very important. Perhaps this is why nearly 42 percent of Jewish respondents feel that there is "an element of racism involved in the attitudes of Israelis toward Arabs."

The fact that a majority of American Jews value social equality considerably more than support for Israel is significant for several reasons. In the first place, the conflict between Israel and the Palestinians has entered a new stage. With Egypt at peace with Israel, and with most Arab countries willing to arrive at some accommodation, Israel's position is secure. The old theme that Israel's basic survival is at stake now sounds unbelievable. Not only is Israel secure from Arab threats, it is also an awesome military power. More important, however, most Israelis feel that survival is no longer an urgent issue. The debate that has been going on in Israel focuses not so much on the question of security as on the nature of the state. The question is whether Israel will be a democratic state at peace with its neighbors or a state with a Jewish majority and an oppressed Arab minority, which will be in a condition of perpetual siege. This means that the manner in which the Palestinian question is resolved will determine the nature of the state of Israel, its relations with the region, and the prospects of peace or continued warfare.

The Palestinian uprising has forced an acceleration and a sharpening of the ongoing debate among American Jews about their relation to the state of Israel and their views of a possible settlement of the conflict with the Palestinians. American Jews are now in a state of confusion. They support Israel and its right to security, but they are uncertain which Israel to support. It is difficult for American Jews, the majority of whom have contributed to the struggle for civil rights and social equality in the United States, to be seen supporting a state that oppresses another nation in a manner similar to that of the much despised white regime in South Africa.

THE U.S. GOVERNMENT VERSUS THE PUBLIC

In the month of March 1988, Palestinian resistance and Israeli repression were at their highest levels. Seventy Palestinians were killed during this month, nearly double the number of casualties in the previous months. Then Secretary of State George Shultz came to the region with the following set of proposals: (1) the convening of an international peace conference in April to be attended by the five permanent members of the Security Council. This conference would not have the authority to impose any decisions on the parties; (2) negotiations would be conducted bilaterally between Israel and each of the Arab parties participating; (3) the Palestinians would be represented within a Jordanian-Palestinian delegation; (4) negotiations would commence May 1, 1988, based on UN Security Council Resolutions 242 and 338; (5) a timetable for negotiations includes two stages. In stage one, arrangements for a three-year interim settlement are to be reached within six months and to be implemented three months later. In stage two, negotiations will be held on a final settlement to be completed within one year; (6) a withdrawal of the Israeli army from the populated areas to strategic locations; and (7) general elections on the West Bank and Gaza Strip.

Central to Shultz's proposals are the following explicit and implicit key points: a solution is to be based on UN Resolutions 242 and 338, which call for the trading of territories for peace; the outcome should be some form of autonomy for the Palestinians in the West Bank and Gaza in conjunction with Jordan. This means no Palestinian state and no self-determination for the Palestinians. Finally, the Shultz plan calls for negotiations over only parts of the West Bank and Gaza and eliminates the possibility of return to the June 4, 1967, borders. The international conference is proposed as a ceremonial occasion that permits the parties to hold bilateral negotiations. The PLO will not be represented during these negotiations.

Secretary Schultz's position is consistent with official U.S. policy since the signing of the Camp David Accords. It reaffirms the principles spelled out earlier by President Reagan in his September 1, 1982, initiative.

On other related matters, the U.S. government has elevated the U.S.-Israel special relationship to its highest levels. Aid to Israel was significantly increased. Strategic cooperation between the United States and Israel was enhanced based on the Memorandum of Agreement signed between the two countries. Requests for the sale of military equipment by various Arab governments have been frequently rebuffed by a Congress easily swayed by the pro-Israel lobby. Normally pro-American governments such as Jordan and Saudi Arabia began to doubt loudly whether it is possible, given the special U.S.-Israel relationship, for the United States to mediate the Palestine-Israel conflict.

Differences between public sentiment and government decisions are not new in the United States. Such gaps characterize views on Central America and South Africa and relations with the USSR, among others. In the case of the Middle East, the public endorses the idea of an independent Palestinian state, while the

U.S. government refuses to consider it. The public overwhelmingly approves the holding of an international conference with PLO participation, while the government wants to merge a non-PLO Palestinian delegation with a Jordanian delegation. A majority of the public think U.S. aid to Israel should either be kept at the same level or cut off completely given Israel's handling of Palestinian unrest. The U.S. government has increased military and economic aid allocations to Israel every year. Finally, the majority of the public view Israel's handling of the *intifada* as too harsh; they strongly disapprove of Israel's policy of deportation, and they seem to think that there is an element of racism in the manner in which Israel deals with the Palestinians. By contrast, U.S. government reaction to Israel's behavior has been lukewarm criticism.

The gap between public perceptions and policy decisions is not new. Back in 1982, the syndicated columnist Philip Geylin assessed several surveys and noted "an increasing awareness on the part of the American public that the old, pro-Israel, pro-Arab formulations don't work. It reflects a real and growing public awareness of a legitimate Palestinian grievance. And it suggests a public sensitivity to the intricacies of the so-called Arab-Israeli struggle that may well be running (not for the first time) ahead of the familiar Washington reflexes."[10]

The U.S. government position therefore appears intransigent and anachronistic. The diplomatic language used reflects conditions that prevailed in the aftermath of the June 1967 war and appears to ignore changes in the region that have occurred in the past twenty-one years.

The official position was reflected in the statements of both presidential candidates. Vice President George Bush and Governor Michael Dukakis came out against an independent Palestinian state, for strengthening relations with Israel, which is viewed by both as a strategic ally, and for a settlement on the basis of UN Resolutions 242 and 338 that excludes the PLO.

Perhaps the most striking difference between public and official perceptions came during the Democratic National Convention in July 1988. Endorsed by Jesse Jackson's campaign, a resolution calling for Palestinian self-determination was discussed but not voted on. James Zogby of the Arab American Institute spoke in support of the resolution. Senator Daniel Inouye and Representative Charles Schumer spoke against the resolution. However, a poll of the delegates conducted by the *Los Angeles Times* and Cable News Network between July 18 and 21, 1988, revealed that the majority of delegates in fact endorsed the plank. Fifty-nine percent of the delegates thought that U.S. military aid to Israel should be kept at the same level, or cut off altogether (36 percent). Seventy percent of the delegates favored giving the Palestinians a homeland in the Occupied Territories. Thirty-seven percent of the delegates had an unfavorable view of Israel, and 47 percent had a somewhat favorable view. Seventy-six percent thought the Middle East is an important issue, and nearly the same percentage (79 percent) thought Jesse Jackson could not be accused of anti-Semitism.[11]

It therefore appears that the opinions of the delegates to the Democratic National Convention in fact reflect the prevailing sentiments of the American public.

These opinions are not reflected in the platform of the Democratic party. Instead, the standard pro-Israel position as articulated by the pro-Israel lobby finds its way into the platforms of both parties. Only Jesse Jackson articulated positions on the Middle East that are close to the prevailing range of opinions among the American electorate.

OPINION LEADERS

A major shift in public perceptions has occurred among the well-informed segment of the American population. On nearly every question, sharp differences separate the attitudes of the general public and those of college graduates and the more affluent respondents. The American Jewish Congress study notes this phenomenon and reports:

Many foreign policy issues and the Israeli-Palestinian conflict, in particular, are ones which are more likely to be intensely debated within these kind of well-informed leadership circles than among the public at large. Thus, it makes good sense to pay special attention to the attitudes of these key subgroups; they are the people who are likely to have the greatest impact on the Israeli-Palestinian debate in the United States.

In the Gallup survey of March 1988, 35 percent of the general public favor the establishment of an independent state for the Palestinians in the West Bank and Gaza, 23 percent oppose, and 42 percent do not know. Among those who have heard or read about the conflict (79 percent), the number of those who favor such a state goes up to 41 percent and the number of people who do not know decreases to 36 percent. Those who oppose a Palestinian state (23 percent) remain constant, probably because they feel strongly about it and because they cluster around what is known as the pro-Israel lobby. As the level of education increases, so does support for Palestinian statehood. College graduates (50 percent) are more likely to support a Palestinian state than high school graduates (31 percent).

The AJC survey done by Martilla and Kiley in April 1988 confirms this trend. This survey finds that 43 percent of registered voters favor an independent state for the Palestinians and 42 percent oppose it. However, 51 percent of the college graduates favor it and 34 percent oppose it. Here again, as the level of education increases, support for Palestinian statehood also increases (53 percent for and 37 percent against). Fifty-seven percent of the well-informed favor a Palestinian state and 36 percent oppose it. Similarly, 55 percent of the more affluent (over $50,000 a year) favor it and 34 percent oppose it.

An earlier assessment of the impact of education on attitudes toward Middle East issues suggested that as educational accomplishment goes up, those who favor either side tend to be more convinced in their beliefs.[12] The obvious key factor in this case is the kind of available information on the conflict. Until 1981 coverage of events in the Middle East tended, with few exceptions, to be more favorable to Israel. Since Israel's 1982 invasion of Lebanon, however, coverage began to be more objective. It was no longer taboo to criticize Israel in public.

In 1982 a poll conducted by Decision/Making/Information for the author was designed to test what happens to attitudes when respondents are given publicly known, factual information about the conflict between Israel and the Palestinians. With each refinement of the question and the presentation of new information, a narrowing down occurs. A small minority of the population (20–25 percent) are adamantly pro-Israel. The remainder are not strongly committed to their positions and appear willing to change in the face of new information.[13]

Coverage of the Palestinian uprising was quite extensive for several months. By March 1988, however, Israel began to clamp down on access by Western reporters to the events unfurling on the West Bank and Gaza. Nevertheless, coverage continued until early in the summer of 1988, when it began to trickle down to an occasional story. By and large, editorial opinion in nearly all major newspapers was critical of Israel's handling of the *intifada*. It is obvious, then, that the extent and the quality of the coverage had a significant impact on well-informed opinion in the United States.

The opinions of mass publics tend to be ephemeral. By contrast, the opinions of key segments of the attentive public are more durable. In the future, it is quite likely that new information about the region will be filtered through a frame established as a result of the coverage of events that occurred in the area since 1982. The new frame is definitely less one-sided (pro-Israel) than the old frame.

CONCLUSION

The *intifada* has solidified a trend among the American public that has been evolving since the late 1970s and in particular since the summer of 1982. American public opinion still sympathizes more with Israel than with the Arabs. However, in the conflict between Israel and the Palestinians, the latter receive considerably more sympathy than do the Arabs in general. The rise of this pro-Palestinian sympathy factor among Americans translates into support for an independent Palestinian state on the West Bank and Gaza, and for PLO participation in peace negotiations.

As the levels of information and of education increase, so does support for the Palestinians. This is not seen by the majority as necessarily anti-Israel. In other words, there is increasing support for both sides in the conflict and, more important, support for a peaceful settlement.

The striking shift in the opinion of key well-informed segments of the American public means that the debate in the United States about the Palestine-Israel conflict will be much less one-sided than in the past, when a pro-Israel consensus prevailed. The shift in the opinion of the well-informed is likely to be durable.

Policy makers still lag behind the informed public on this crucial issue. The gap between public attitudes and the official position on the Middle East is still fairly wide. However, it is more likely to shrink now that opinion leaders are expressing an increasing awareness of the basic issues of the conflict.

NOTES

1. *Los Angeles Times,* April 12, 13, 1988.

2. *Chicago Tribune,* April 26, 1988.

3. John Rielly, ed., *American Opinion and U.S. Foreign Policy* (Chicago: Chicago Council on Foreign Relations, 1983), p. 21.

4. F. Moughrabi, *American Public Opinion and the Palestine Question* (Washington, D.C.: International Center for Research and Public Policy, 1986).

5. Ibid., p. 3.

6. John Rielly, ed., *American Opinion and U.S. Foreign Policy* (Chicago: Chicago Council on Foreign Relations, 1987), p. 23.

7. Arthur Hertzberg, "The Illusion of Jewish Unity," *New York Review of Books,* June 16, 1988.

8. Steven Cohen, *Ties and Tensions: The 1986 Survey of American Jewish Attitudes Toward Israel and Israelis* (New York: American Jewish Committee, 1987).

9. Hertzberg, "Illusion of Jewish Unity," pp. 6–11.

10. *Washington Post,* December 2, 1982.

11. *The Return,* September 1988.

12. Shelly Slade, "The Image of the Arab in America: Analysis of a Poll on American Attitudes," *Middle East Journal,* 35, no. 2 (1981): 143–62.

13. Moughrabi, *American Public Opinion,* p. 12.

16
The European Community and the Middle East Conflict

Jean-Paul Chagnollaud

In order to understand the current position of the Twelve that make up the European Community (EC), it is important to step back and take a broad look at its attitude toward the Middle East conflict over the past few years.

Today, ''something'' is happening in Europe: public opinion and government positions are changing and it seems the intention is there to play a greater role on the Middle East scene. For some, like France, it is after all merely a continuation of what has been a long tradition, but for the European Community as such, such a role is quite new. This could be an early sketch outlining what one day might become a foreign policy.

It has taken the European countries years to define a common position on the Middle East conflict. Since the establishment of political cooperation, they have not truly attempted to go beyond a diplomacy of words to take what could be qualified as an active diplomatic initiative. But from the end of 1988, there have been clear signs that the Twelve now want to move from declaration to action.

Looking back on their very divergent policies of the 1960s, there was little ground for a common stand on the part of the Europeans. To cite only one example at the time of the 1967 war, the Belgian foreign minister expressed his concern with ''protecting the existence of Israel,''[1] while General de Gaulle, speaking for France, stressed that ''whichever State used weapons first would not gain approval, let alone support.''[2]

One could hardly expect a unified Community stand in the absence of a structure that would enable the Europeans to compare and confront their respective attitudes. The possibility came in 1969 with the decision to establish a form of institutional political cooperation with the aim of harmonizing different points-of-view. The year 1970 saw the first meeting of foreign affairs ministers. Two concerns dominated the debates: a project for a conference on Europe's security and the Middle East.

From that time on and within that framework—which has improved with time—the Six (later the Nine, Ten, and Twelve) progressively built up, not a policy but rather a common stand, in three major stages: 1973, 1977, and 1980.

- The November 6, 1973, Brussels Declaration defined the principles upon which a negotiated peace settlement should be based. The declaration notably condemned the acquisition of territories by force, and insisted on the need for Israel to put an end to the occupation of territories it has held since 1967. It also called for the respect of sovereignty, territorial integrity, and independence of all the countries of the region as well as for their right to live within secure and recognized borders. More important still, the declaration also stressed that the establishment of a just and lasting peace will have to take into account the legitimate rights of the Palestinian people.

- The June 29, 1977, London declaration stressed two essential points: (1) the Palestinian people's right to a homeland and (2) that they should participate in negotiations in "an appropriate manner."

- The June 13, 1980, Venice declaration reiterated these provisions and went one step further, insisting on the need for "a global solution to the Arab-Israeli conflict."

For the first time, the Europeans insisted on the importance of the international guarantees that the UN Security Council could provide, in which the "Nine are prepared to participate in the framework of a global settlement . . . including in its implementation in the field." This was also the first time they mentioned the PLO by name, saying that it "will have to be associated with the [peace] negotiations." They also expressed certain reservations regarding Israel's policies: "The EEC will not accept any unilateral initiative designed to change the status of Jerusalem." The declaration also stressed that the EEC members were convinced that the Israeli settlements constituted a "serious obstacle to peace in the Middle East."

This eleven-point document should be considered as the reference on Europe's position. It was also the basis for the latest notable European declaration (Brussels, February 23, 1987), which called for the "convening of an international conference under the auspices of the United Nations with the participation of all the parties concerned."[3] The document also features a new and significant initiative: the Twelve considered that there was a need to improve the living conditions of the population in the Occupied Territories, with particular regard to their economic, social, cultural, and administrative affairs. With the declaration came the announcement of a decision to grant aid to the Palestinian population of the Occupied Territories and give preferential access to the Community market to certain products from these territories.[4]

It took fifteen years, but Europe has managed to adopt a precise and balanced joint position on the Middle East. Without going into details, one might also mention the many declarations issued by the Community in response to specific developments—from the 1973 war to the 1988 uprising, including, notably, Camp David, the Lebanon war, or the annexation of the Golan Heights.

The European Parliament has also endeavored to adopt a coherent position: on two occasions during the past decade, the Parliament has passed resolutions in the wake of reports presented by parliametarians (the 1983 Penders and the 1985 Charzat reports).

The position of the European Parliament was in line with that of the governments, though it did go one step further toward the Palestinians; the second resolution, adopted in 1986 after the Charzat report, notably stipulates that any "negotiated settlement must respect the right of existence of all the States of the region including Israel, as well as the Palestinian right to self-determination, with all that this implies." Although the declaration does not actually use the word "state" with regard to the Palestinians, it clearly cannot be interpreted in any other way: what is "implied" is, in due course, a state.

The PLO is mentioned in this resolution as follows: "The Palestinian people and the PLO will have to be associated with the [peace] negotiations." The European Parliament makes no statement on the representativity of the PLO, but is unambiguous in saying that the Palestinians will have to participate in negotiations "with the understanding that it is up to them to choose their own representatives."

One must not underestimate what has been achieved nor the considerable efforts that have been deployed for the sake of furthering political cooperation. But this cannot obscure the fact that although the Community has succeeded in developing a diplomacy of words, it has failed to engage in a diplomacy of action.

What is holding the Community back? While this is by no means an attempt to produce an exhaustive answer, several elements may shed some light: some are related to the specific nature of the conflict, while others concern the European Community itself.

Among the first one must cite: (1) the reactions of both Israelis and Palestinians; (2) the hegemony of the role played by the United States; and (3) the obsessive presence of terrorism.

1. Many Israelis are convinced that the change in Europe's attitude is purely a result of pressure and the threat on supplies from the oil-producing countries. Some argue that the first European declaration was adopted shortly after the Organization of Arab Oil Exporting Countries (OAPEC) brandished a concrete threat. Here, chronogical evidence is unavoidable: a total embargo was imposed on the Netherlands on October 20, 1973; on November 6, the Nine issued their declaration.

The question here is not whether the Israelis are right to uphold this argument;

the fact is that they insist on using it constantly. To quote only one example: shortly after the Venice Declaration, Israel's Ambassador to the EEC wrote, "One would hope that such submission in the face of the oil ultimatum will not be there under the guise of the role Europe proposes to play in the Middle East."[5]

Constant reiteration of this argument is obviously not without design: it is a means of preempting and disqualifying an approach that is based on principles that Israel rejects outright. For the Israelis, there is quite simply no question of withdrawing from the territories it occupies, of negotiating with the PLO, of reconsidering the question of Jerusalem, of dismantling the settlements, etc. A case in exercise point was the visit in 1980 of Gaston Thorn, then acting President of the Council of Ministers, to the Middle East. He had a particularly tense meeting with Menachem Begin, who described the Venice Declaration as a "recipe for the destruction of Israel." More recently, in April 1988, the director for political affairs at the Israeli Ministry of Foreign Affairs stressed in particular that "the Community's role must remain first and foremost an economic one."

On the Palestinian side, the PLO would like a European commitment to the search for a settlement to the Middle East question. And yet the PLO has not always been easy on Europe. For example, in a speech in Geneva in September 1987, the Director of the PLO President's Cabinet said: "Western Europe carries a moral and political responsibility in the creation of the Palestine Question. Balfour, Sykes, Picot are only a few of a long list of imperial Statesmen who were determined to destroy the Palestinian people."[6]

Although he welcomed the change in Europe's position since 1980, he nevertheless deplored its lack of clarity on both the representativity of the PLO and on the question of the national rights of the Palestinian people. He added that "Europe has not shown necessary courage . . . [to] commit itself further in the Middle East for fear of Israeli or American pressure."

Paradoxical though it may seem, Palestinians and Israelis do agree on one point: Europe is too pusillanimous. One side sees Europe as fearful of going against American interests, while the other says it dares not displease Arab oil producers. Such tenuous credibility makes it difficult for Europe to play a determining role.

2. The hegemony of the role played by Washington constitutes another very substantial obstacle and raises a major question: Can the Europeans take any sort of initiative in the Middle East without U.S. approval—not to mention an initiative that might go against the United States?

The balance of power, the interests at stake, the degree of involvement in the region, strategic considerations, the strength of the pressure apparatus—all these elements contribute to make what amounts to a very narrow path indeed. The 1956 Suez expedition was a turning point: the great powers of the time learned their lesson the hard way and came to the realization that their political autonomy in this region was well and truly over. It sufficed "Le Grand Frère," as the French say (supported on this occasion by the Soviet Union), to speak out for the military contingents—or forces, as they were seen to be at the time—to be promptly withdrawn.

the military contingents—or forces, as they were seen to be at the time—to be promptly withdrawn.

As time wore on, at every critical period in the tormented history of this conflict, the Europeans were seen to leave the Americans with a completely free hand. The same is true today; one need only consider the Shultz Plan.

Admittedly, one must neither neglect nor forget that some European countries— France, for one—have tried to shoulder some of their own responsibilities. But these efforts have invariably been met with hostility on the part of the United States—witness 1982, when France and Egypt submitted their draft resolution to the United Nations.

One may also point out here that the Venice Declaration came at an all-time low for the United States, embodied by President Carter who, tangled up as he was in the Teheran hostage affair, was incapable of imposing his view of the Camp David agreements. But when President Reagan came on the scene, the Europeans immediately pulled back.

While the United States favors partial agreements on Israel, Europe wants a global settlement that takes into account the legitimate interests of all the parties involved in the conflict. Make no mistake, the two cannot be reconciled, at least for the time being. Yet the Europeans cannot or do not want to take on the risk of such a profound disagreement with an ally of such political, economic, and military importance.[7]

3. Finally, the last factor: terrorism. If Europe has failed to react, it is also because it was placed on the defensive. For the past decade, it has served as the chosen theater for a long series of Middle East–inspired terrorist attacks.

Europe was the scene of several anti-Semitic attacks: against synagogues in Paris (October 1980), in Vienna (August 1981), in Brussels (September 1981), against a Jewish restaurant in rue des Rosiers in Paris (August 1982), and in Rome (October 1982), to quote but a few examples.

Equally, Europeans have been chosen as hostage in Lebanon since 1985. This extremely painful and distressing situation prompted the Europeans to protect themselves first and foremost; they elaborated a concerted antiterrorist policy. Yet all the while, they remained perfectly aware of the deep-rooted causes of these attacks. This led the Ten to declare in December 1985 that only a just, global, and lasting settlement ''could put an end to the climate of tension in the region [the Middle East], which is at the origin of these acts of violence and terror.''

Above and beyond the elements that are linked to the conflict, others are specific to Europe itself. First, to state the obvious, priority does not lie with the problems requiring political cooperation. By definition, the political energy of the Community is largely spent on dealing with economic questions—the very basis of the Community's existence—all the more so as 1992 draws nearer. Looking at things from that fundamental angle, the Middle East question seems as far removed as it is insoluble.

Second, although the Community proved extremely efficient in preparing the conference on security that was crowned by the 1975 Helsinki agreements, the situation today is quite different. It seems deeply divided on the options concerning its own security, particularly since the December 1987 Washington Treaty. How should Europe organize its defense after the implementation of the possible mutual removal of Soviet and U.S. strategic weapons known as the "double zero option" within the Atlantic Alliance? Or by building its own independent system?

Given that the Europeans have not come up with a single answer on such vital questions, can they be expected to take political risks on a hypothetical peace settlement in the Middle East?

Third, it may also be legitimate to question the limits of political cooperation, regardless of the substantial efforts deployed in its name. The fact is that the European declarations are only the fruit of a whole series of compromises. Though painstakingly put together, they do not bind the states, who retain their own individual vision of the problem, their own ideological affinities, their own economic networks. One may question the real worth of a joint declaration when confronted with the implications of daily political and economic realities.

Why should West Germany stick its neck out on the Middle East and endanger its economic ambitions? Why should Great Britain adopt a policy that may jeopardize its privileged relationship with the United States? There are plenty of other examples to demonstrate that a joint European declaration can in no way overrule all manner of weighty national considerations.

Besides, newly established governments could easily adopt a new line, a policy different from those laboriously sewn together within the framework of the Community's political cooperation. A typical example is the position adopted by France after June 10, 1981, when François Mitterrand took power. President Mitterrand had previously expressed support for the Camp David agreements; his later options were a logical follow-up that ignored the 1980 Venice Declaration in which the Community spoke out in favor of an international peace conference. It was not until 1987 in Brussels that Europe reaffirmed its support for the proposed international conference. Apart from some partial reactions along the way, this prolonged silence (1980 to 1987) is easily explained by the fact that it took President Mitterrand until 1985 to come round to the idea.[8]

Europe's difficulty in initiating wide-ranging action based on the principles outlined in the course of political cooperation meetings cannot obscure its will to establish a privileged relationship with the West Bank and Gaza.

In October 1986, the European Commission in Brussels, headed by Jacques Deoors, adopted a series of important measures in favor of the Palestinian population of these territories: (1) to provide financial support, in particular to small employment-generating projects; and (2) to give produce from these territories preferential access to the EEC under a regime similar to that granted to other Mediterranean trading partners involving duty-free access to the EEC market for industrial produce and preferential treatment for certain agricultural products.

The implications of this decision are not purely economic; as the Commission itself stressed at the time, the decision was also political and showed the "Community's will to reinforce and ensure the continuity of the action it has undertaken in favor of the Palestinian population in the Occupied Territories."

And this was precisely the reason why the negotiations between Israel and the commission were so problematic. The Israelis did not want to see these products reach the European market without their labels on them. It was not until summer 1988 that an agreement was finally concluded that allowed the Palestinians to set up their own marketing networks (certificates of origin are to be issued by Palestinian chambers of commerce and the products are to be labeled according to where they are produced: Jericho, Gaza, Hebron, etc.).

In order to secure this result, the European Parliament had to act upon its newly acquired power by deferring the ratification of the three proposed additional protocols to the 1975 EEC-Israel agreement. The 1987 protocols covered European loans to Israel and the extension of preferential treatment to other Israeli goods.

The ratification of the protocols came up before the European Parliament on several occasions in the course of 1988. The question was repeatedly removed from the agenda. With this, the majority of parliamentarians intended to protest against Israel's repressive practices in the Occupied Territories. The two questions thus became linked: there would be no question of ratifying the protocols if Israel continued to obstruct the export of Palestinian produce to the EEC.

Both the initiative itself and Europe's reaction are revealing and lead to at least two contradictory conclusions: on the one hand, this underscored Europe's concern for the problems in the Occupied Territories and the Arab-Israeli conflict in general, but on the other, it was a clear indication of the limitations of what Europe does, or can do.

The fact that Palestinian oranges may be sold on Europe's market under advantageous conditions is highly appreciated by the Palestinians themselves, particularly by those who see it as one step forward in a more ambitious economic context. Nevertheless, one cannot help but contrast Europe's enormous historical responsibility for the tragic situation in the Middle East with its political potential and its ability to take effective action today: they remain on a very modest level, though some might once again argue that this is only the beginning of a much more important process.

Seen from this angle, it is quite clear that the *intifada* has resulted in a significant change of attitude in Europe; with the uprising now over two years old, the answer to the questions it raises are not always clear.

For the whole of 1988—until December 15—the Twelve had adopted a wait-and-see policy and generally stuck to previous positions. Several important meetings that took place over this period led to little more than cautious treading, with most positions aligned on the smallest common denominator.

In Bonn on January 8, 1989, the Twelve foreign ministers were "deeply concerned by the deterioration of the situation'' in the Occupied Territories; they stressed the importance of an international conference under United Nations auspices and "exhorted" Israel to "fully respect Security Council Resolutions 605 [1987], 607 [1988] and 608 [1988] as well as the August 12, 1949 Geneva Convention on the protection of civilians in time of war." The Twelve later again expressed their concern regarding events in the West Bank and Gaza but went no further than to deplore and regret various Israeli policies. A political initiative for concrete action was not forthcoming.

Such a reserved attitude—which actually fell short of previous declarations— appeared particularly lackluster in the wake of the historic decisions adopted by the Palestine National Council in its November meeting in Algiers. The Twelve merely paid tribute to the "positive steps" taken by the Palestinians, although some countries, notably Spain, Italy, and France, were in favor of a more forceful welcome of the PNC's efforts at moderation.[9] Foreign Minister Roland Dumas of France actually described the declaration as "pretty feeble."

Toward the end of 1988 it looked as though, come what may and regardless of new developments, Europe was determined to keep a low profile. The impression was confirmed in early December at the Rhodes Summit, in which the European heads of state decided not to send their foreign ministers to Geneva to hear Yasser Arafat at the United Nations.[10] This is not to say that the decision was entirely unanimous: certain countries (again, Spain, Italy, and France) did wish to be represented at the foreign minister level, while others intended to send only their ambassadors to the United Nations. A compromise was eventually reached: as acting president of the Council of Ministers, Greek Foreign Minister Karolos Papoulias was to speak on behalf of the Twelve, while individual countries were to send their permanent representatives to the UN.

Then came the sudden and spectacular U.S. decision to open a dialogue with the PLO. The Reagan administration's surprising about-face carried considerable impact: all of a sudden, the United States indicated to the rest of the world that, after all, the Palestinian organization had a right to be heard in the international community. The U.S. decision signified that the PLO was one party among others and that it was no longer possible to reduce it to the status of a nebulous, outlaw terrorist group. This did nothing more or less than to legitimize in some way the Palestinian leadership and therefore, implicitly, the political claims it embodies. A real taboo was suddenly lifted, regardless of the outcome of these discussions, which at this point have barely reached the preliminary stage. In a matter of days, many of those who had never dared speak openly to the PLO suddenly discovered unsuspected sources of courage.

To put the European Community in that category would be excessive, but the fact remains that it was only after the American move that it decided to take action and meet Arafat. On December 19, the EC foreign ministers announced that they would engage in contacts with the PLO, Israel, and the United States in a bid to further the idea of an international conference for peace in the Middle East.

It must be said that the Europeans had considered this initiative before Washington made its move. Nevertheless, they had never succeeded in reaching an agreement on the subject, owing, notably, to Britain's opposition. This had in fact led France's Minister for European Affairs Edith Cresson to say that "it is a shame that owing to Mrs. Thatcher's refusal, we were unable to take an initiative in early December at the time of the Rhodes Summit, because now, we are way behind the United States."

The Europeans soon made up for lost time. In early January a troïka of three European foreign ministers (Spanish, French, and Greek),[11] set off on a short but intensive tour of the Middle East, having previously met Arafat in Madrid. At the end of the tour, a meeting of the Political Cooperation of the Twelve was held on February 14 in the Spanish capital. Foreign Minister Fernandez Ordonez of Spain declared that after a long "absence" from the Middle East scene, Europe "had regained the position it has by duty to occupy." For his part France's Roland Dumas stressed that "the Community has progressed from a policy of declarations to a policy of effective action by making direct contact with the parties concerned."

Such active involvement on the part of Europe is unprecedented. But one cannot expect too much from this first move. Its supporters stress that the aim was merely to listen to and understand the position of each party involved regarding the possibility of an international conference. It is perhaps because their ambitions were modest that the Europeans were not too discouraged by the rather chilly welcome they received in Israel, Syria, and even Jordan. Hosni Mubarak and Yasser Arafat were the only ones to have truly appreciated the European initiative.[12] Needless to say, Europe has a long way to go before it can leave a significant mark in the region. Nor can one expect to become a political heavyweight overnight in a tormented and long-neglected region. Of this Europe is perfectly aware, hence its extreme caution. This is going to take time—and a tremendous amount of political will.

It would be a mistake to rely solely on the results of the EEC's political cooperation to appreciate Europe's role in the current situation. In general, it now seems that the Europeans have genuinely grasped the true dimensions of the Middle East conflict. Though they vary widely in the degree to which they are committed to solving the problems of the region, the European countries now have a clear notion of the roots of the conflict and what is at stake.

Countries like France, Spain, and Italy now seem determined to act according to their capacity and contribute to establishing the peace process, without necessarily having to wade through the constraints of the political cooperation procedure. In Paris—where the status of the PLO office has been upgraded to that of a general delegation—considerable efforts are seemingly under way to help turn the notion of an Israeli-Palestinian dialogue into a reality. Some of these initiatives are discreet, if not secret, while others have clearly been made public since the beginning of 1989. In Rome, Bettino Craxi has put forward a plan according to which the Occupied Territories would be placed under European administration until the advent of a political solution. At the same time in Madrid, Spain's leaders have clearly decided to make this problem one of their top foreign policy priorities.

Meanwhile, countries that traditionally held back have lately been seen to adopt clearer positions. This is the case with the Netherlands, but perhaps more notably with Britain, whose Prime Minister Margaret Thatcher called upon Israel to "respond to the PLO's peace initiatives."

Another important pointer to this ongoing deep political change is the European Parliament. Its positions are first and foremost a reflection of the different political parties and therefore, by extension, of public opinion in Europe. The last resolution it passed in 1988 is particularly revealing. The lengthy eighteen-point text notably stated that any "solution implies the creation of a defined territory for the Palestinian State, which would guarantee Israel's right to live within secure and internationally recognized borders." The Parliament also "called upon the Twelve to recognize the PLO as a Palestinian government in exile."

It now looks as though the Europeans have fully understood the nature of the conflict. Gone are the days when all they saw in the smoke and thunder of gunfire was the tragic proof of the complexity of a region where the last thing to do was to get involved. Today, at last, it seems they are prepared to take action to help build peace in the region. Alone and together, the countries of Europe have the means and the capacity to do it. The question that now remains is whether they will seize an exceptional opportunity to assume the role that history commands them to play.

NOTES

1. Declaration of June 6, 1987.

2. Declaration of June 2, 1967.

3. D. Chevallier, "L'Europe pour la paix au Moyen Orient" (Europe for peace in the Middle East), *Le Monde Diplomatique,* December 1987.

4. On this question, see D. Sigaud, *"La CEE et les Territoires Occupés"* (The EEC and the Occupied Territories), *Le Monde Diplomatique,* August 1987.

5. S. Minerbi, "Israel et L'Europe," *Politique Etrangère,* June 1981.

6. S. Musallam, "Europe and Peace in the Middle East," *Journal of Palestine Studies,* vol. 17, no. 2 (Winter 1988).

7. D. Moisi, "L'Europe et le conflit Israélo-Arabe" (Europe and the Arab-Israeli conflict), *Politique Etrangère,* December 1980.

8. A. Chenal, "La Politique française au Maghreb et au Proche Orient" (French policy in the Maghreb and the Middle East), *Cosmopolitiques,* no. 5 (December 1987).

9. The text of the November 21, 1988, Brussels declaration is as follows: "The Twelve attach particular importance to the decisions adopted by the PNC . . . which include positive steps towards the peaceful settlement of the Arab-Israel conflict."

10. Yet, in a communiqué dated November 30, 1988, the Twelve criticized the U.S.

decision to deny Arafat a visa, saying, ''The Twelve believe that in accordance with the Headquarters' agreement and the opinion of the Legal Counsel of the U.N., Mr. Arafat should be allowed to address the U.N. Assembly in New York.''

11. Respectively, Fernandez Ordonez, Roland Dumas, and Theore Pangalos.

12. Cf. a conversation quoted by *Le Monde*, February 14, 1989, at the time of the meeting between the European troïka and the Egyptian president: ''Here is Europe, Mr. President''—''Ah! At last!''

IV

IMPACT ON THE MAIN PROTAGONISTS

17
The Third Factor
IMPACT OF THE *INTIFADA* ON ISRAEL

Azmi Bishara

More than a year after the outbreak of the uprising, polls taken in Israel indicated new tendencies in public opinion there. According to one organized by the Institute for Applied Social Research, 30 percent of those questioned support negotiations with the PLO in the wake of Yasser Arafat's declaration in Geneva, as against 13 percent in 1978. Another poll, taken by Minah Zimah, shows that 54 percent of the Israeli public supports negotiations with the PLO under certain conditions. In a poll organized by the same institute in March 1987, 45 percent of the participants rejected the notion of withdrawal from any part of the Occupied Territories "in return for peace with the Arabs." In January 1989, only 35 percent maintained that position, while 48 percent agreed with the principle of returning all or parts of the Occupied Territories. Most instructive is the fact that the idea of a Palestinian state is still accepted by only 20 percent of respondents in various polls.[1]

Long before the United States agreed to open a dialogue with the PLO, Israeli officials had repeatedly declared that the obstacle to negotiations with the PLO was neither its rejection of UN Security Council Resolution 242, nor its non-acceptance of Israel's right to exist, but the conclusion that such negotiations would lead to the creation of a Palestinian state. A Palestinian state in the West Bank and Gaza is the main question facing Israeli society as a result of the uprising. But this question does not appear answerable before two other subsidiary questions have been resolved: (1) Has the occupation become a losing proposition, socially, politically, and economically? and (2) Is there sufficient force in Israel to sustain the occupation even if it is a losing proposition?

The official Israeli reaction to the shifts in the declared policy of the PLO only confirms this analysis. That reaction took several forms: (1) the refusal to negotiate with the PLO under any conditions whatsoever; (2) the claim that the acceptance of U.S. conditions for entering a dialogue was fraudulent (a claim that can in fact not be verified rationally, but only empirically); (3) adding supplementary conditions to the ones fulfilled by the PLO, for example, that it should first give up the right of return of the refugees (that is to say, that it should speak out against numerous UN resolutions); that it should cancel the Palestine National Charter; or that Israel and the United States should wait a supplementary period of time until they have been able to evaluate the seriousness of PLO claims to having renounced terrorism (that is to say, transforming the whole issue into a debate on the definition of terrorism).

The relationship between the uprising and its goal, self-determination and a Palestinian state, is mediated by various factors. The uprising activates these factors to produce a new constellation, which increases the likelihood of a Palestinian state emerging. Three main elements are decisive in this process: the Palestinian and Arab factor, the international factor, and the situation in Israel.

The subject of this chapter is the third factor; more specifically, the political influence of the *intifada* on Israel during its first year. Because the process is still unfolding, our purpose will be to outline tendencies, possibilities, and probabilities, not to give definitive, static results.

FIRST REACTIONS

The first reactions of the Israeli establishment and establishment media were characterized by the following:

1. A focus on the spontaneity of the uprising. This relied on a number of assumptions, some of which corresponded to political objectives, and others of which were a direct result of prejudice regarding Arab political culture. The main assumptions were the separation between the PLO and the Occupied Territories and the notion that the uprising was an emotional sort of action that could not be dealt with politically. Moshe Arens, Minister for Arab Affairs at the time, for example, concluded from these assumptions that the solution is not a political settlement but a matter of contacts and relations with the residents of the Occupied Territories.[2] We are, on the other hand, offered no clue as to why this is the correct approach, nor what is meant by contacts. The second assumption proceeds from a prejudice that often modifies first reactions regarding the irrational nature of Eastern people: hence the uprising is pictured as the result of a car accident.[3] The people, in other words, would normally endure occupation and humiliations; their revolt against them seems further to illustrate their irrational mentality.

2. A focus, in the beginning, on religious movements (often confused with religious motivations), something that blends in with the ideas concerning spontaneity and irrationalism.

3. The Israeli right derived the uprising from "Israeli weakness" and "excessive democracy," a logic that makes it possible, whatever conditions may be, to claim that had repression been more intensive, there would have been no revolt.

4. The idea that the uprising emerged from despair. The latter would have been due both to the immediate reaction to the Amman Arab summit one month before (losing hope in Arab regimes was here confused with total despair), and to the general failure of terrorism. Yitzhak Shamir and other right-wing Israeli politicians consider Palestinian political action a continuation of terrorism as long as its goal continues to be Palestinian self-determination.

After the second week of the uprising, as it became clear that the *intifada* represented a qualitative change in the mode of resistance to occupation, Israeli comments became more sophisticated. Moreover, many Israeli beliefs and prejudices found themselves refuted by uprising-related phenomena, forcing commentators to pay more attention to the organizational factor, to the nature of the relationship to the PLO, to the distinction between various religious movements, and so on. The approach to the Palestinians as people began to be more differentiated and more sophisticated.

The first new interpretive twist was that the uprising was a propaganda campaign. After the media were banned from reaching areas of intensive action and repression, this claim did not stand up. It survives only through settlers and right-wing politicians, who accuse the mass media of being directly responsible for the continuation of the uprising.[4] Preventing reporters from reaching certain areas did not stop the uprising, but allowed harsher measures to be taken, especially after the third month.[5]

The second type of new interpretation, which still has partial currency, was the hope that the uprising might give rise to a new Palestinian leadership that "qualifies" for negotiations with Israel. This interpretation has its political parallel in Israeli government proposals to hold elections in the Occupied Territories.[6] Certain Israeli analysts, such as the journalist Ze'ev Schiff, continually stressed this alleged turn and regarded every development on the ground as its verification. Even improvements on the uprising's organizational level were viewed as evidence of the strength and sovereignty of the local element,[7] and the draft Palestinian declaration of independence found in the Arab Studies Society's offices in Jerusalem, alleged to have been the work of Palestinians under occupation, was taken to indicate greater independence from the PLO, regardless of its contents:

Is it not wise on our part to encourage differences between both wings of the PLO? Why not deepen the difference between the PLO in the territories and the PLO outside, if they represent conflicting interests? Those who desire a dialogue with a local leadership should be interested in that; those who are not interested should also exploit such a situation.[8]

The Israeli security establishment, on the other hand, believed that the uprising was a local initiative, but that the recognized leadership was that of the PLO. Amnon Shahak, head of military intelligence, announced that "the only leadership in the territories is that of the PLO; there are local leaders, and when we arrest one of them, others take his place. These may struggle for their status in the Palestinian leadership in ten years, for now the leadership is the PLO."[9]

Discussions in the Israeli establishment concerning the emergence of a local leadership did not simply stem from the possibility of conducting negotiations with them, but also from simple practical desires such as obtaining the information necessary for suppressing the uprising. Although this establishment is well informed, and although it has taken a variety of harsh measures against activists, the uprising seems to be continuing. And the constant updating of details does not seem to help the Israeli establishment in solving the riddle of relations between the PLO on the outside and the PLO on the inside, and the relationship between local and national mechanisms of the uprising.

The third interpretive turn, which still prevails, is the claim that the uprising is a form of war. It is not lack of precision or naïveté that led people like Yitzhak Beily,[10] Yoram Peri,[11] and Ron Ben Yeshai[12] to use the term "war." Even before the uprising, representatives of the Israeli right claimed that acts of violence on the part of the army or settlers in the Occupied Territories were to be considered in the framework of war circumstances.

The commanders of the three regiments stationed in the Occupied Territories admitted in a television program, "Moked," on April 17, 1988, that they explain the events to their soldiers in terms of "a decisive war on the Israeli principal line of defense." In fact, not a single Israeli government has defined the West Bank and Gaza Strip as the main line of defense. This political-military doctrine echoed by the officers is in fact the doctrine of the radical right wing in Israel. An example of how this concept haunts Israeli military commanders is found in a lecture by the chief of staff. He explained to his soldiers that their mission "is not a total war . . . in war you occupy and destroy targets but here we are the authority; an authority cannot destroy its subjects. We are responsible for many aspects of their life, but we should maintain law and order." In the same lecture he stated that "it is a war between two communities that has been going on for a long time, and will probably continue for a long time in the future."[13] Clearly, the Israeli soldier who is speaking here belongs to one of the communities. The neutrality of keeping law and order was cancelled by the very next statement. He represents one side in the "war" he conjures up.

Calling a civil revolt against foreign occupation a war between two communities was not the exclusive discovery of the Israeli chief of staff nor of right wing politicians. The thesis stems from the Zionist left. Meron Benvenisti derived it long ago from his more general thesis concerning the "gradual and irreversible annexation" of the territories. The fact that the uprising has torn Benvenisti's thesis to pieces in no way alters his paternity of the "war between two communities" thesis.

The concept of "war" found its way into the Israeli civil and military system and consequently governs the attitude toward the media. Uri Oren, a member of the administration of the Israeli Broadcasting Authority, asserted that "the mass media in general, and television in particular, create events and design realities. This is clear in the news coverage of wars and their results. . . . We are also in a state of war in order to prevent the establishment of a Palestinian state, a war that touches on our existence. All Israelis prefer a reality with no Palestinian state."[14] (One notes, of course, the confusion between a matter of existence and a matter of preference.)

On February 23, 1988, Defense Minister Yitzhak Rabin presented a report to the Knesset Security and Foreign Affairs Committee in which he described the uprising as follows: "The disturbances in the Territories are a continuation of the Lebanon war, in which Israel committed a grave error by making war against the Palestinians, because such a war can never lead to a framework for political negotiations." Regarding ways to overcome the uprising, he stated: "Victory over the disturbances in the Occupied Territories is not reached through [the disturbances'] total elimination, but by reducing them to the extent that they won't affect the political decisions Israel faces. There is a common interest in that for both those who support the idea of Greater Israel and those who support territorial compromise."[15] (It might be useful to note here that Rabin himself seems not to have learned from what he termed the "great error," since he advocates—and practices—its perpetuation.)

Right-wing circles disagree with Rabin on the impossibility of totally eliminating the uprising. Their message is more simple: the uprising could be totally crushed, and life must be made more difficult for the Palestinians, that is, the policy should be more convincing to them that they should leave. There is therefore a significant difference regarding Rabin's repressive measures in the Occupied Territories, but only regarding their ultimate purpose. The more moderate wing of the Israeli establishment regards them as mere security measures, while the more extreme elements see them as intended to destroy Palestinian culture. In his summary of various devices employed against the uprising, Ron Ben Yeshai regards "the economic measures to be the most effective."[16] Ze'ev Schiff and Yitzhak Beily, both considered liberal within the Israeli spectrum, made a number of recommendations for crushing the *intifada*[17] (recommendations endorsed by Rabin the same day Schiff's article appeared): (1) Limiting access of foreign journalists to the territories; (2) predicating permission for Palestinian workers to enter Israel on the existence of calm; (3) reducing restrictions on opening fire against demonstrators; (4) banning the export of agricultural products from the territories to Jordan; (5) carrying out mass arrests of organizers of protest actions, even if the number exceeds several thousand (this was the logic that led to opening the Ansar 3 detention camp).

The latest stratagem devised by the security departments was increasing the number of border police in the Occupied Territories, for their "efficiency" and experience surpasses those of regular army troops.[18] The reasoning involved has it that the largely Druze and oriental Jewish border police better understand the "mentality" of the Arabs and can better control them than the army. (Developments on the ground, including the Nahalin massacre and the alarming monthly statistics, quickly disproved the "better control" theory put forward to justify the use of border police.)

The uprising has in fact engendered an unprecedented and comprehensive dispute over the strategic importance to Israel of the Occupied Territories. Hundreds of generals and other senior officers made their contributions to the debate, in dozens of interviews and symposia. The military dispute was widely used in the election campaign by the major parties. There are basically three contending military doctrines:

1. The Occupied Territories constitute the most important factor in the defense strategy of the next war. They must therefore be kept under Israeli control even if this rules out peace. Peace with the Arabs would at any rate not be on the agenda, so Israel should adopt Henry Kissinger's theory that "no war" is a better situation for Israel than peace agreements. This doctrine is best represented by Yehoshua Sagi, a former head of military intelligence.

2. There should be a withdrawal from some or most of the territories, under specified security arrangements. This doctrine covers a wide range of variants and political positions, including "autonomy" and confederation with Jordan. The military doctrine is represented by Uri Or, former commander of the central region, and Ben Gal, former commander of the northern region, as well as other supporters of the Labor party (most of the senior officers are in this category).

3. The territories are a security burden; they threaten internal security and increase the likelihood of war. Officers who support this doctrine do not object to negotiations with the PLO and the establishment of a Palestinian state, along with security arrangements, should this be the only solution. Their outstanding representative is Yehoshafat Harkabi.[19]

Organizations like the Committee for Peace and Security, to which more than 130 senior officers belong, obscure the limits between the second and third doctrines. The focus of the officers' dispute is security, and it does not relate to Palestinian interests or to the dictates of international law. Hence the dangers of discussing the future of the Occupied Territories on the basis of military categories, very similar to the dangers of discussions centering on demographic categories. Both are subject to simplification and vulgarization. The first nurtures a military mode of thinking, the second contributes to a racist culture, and both contribute to the prevalence of a right-wing ideology.

ZIONIST PARTIES

The uprising directly influenced Israeli political parties, and in some cases even their political programs. In the election of November 1, 1988, the Palestinian question was the focus of debate, although immediately after the results were known, the issue of the religious parties came to the forefront of public interest, in what was actually a superficial controversy. The deepest division splitting Israeli society even during the elections was the Palestinian issue. Prime Minister Shamir justified breaking his promises to the religious parties on the basis that the threat of a Palestinian state necessitates a united Israel (Labor and Likud).[20]

If one looks at all Israeli election campaigns since 1949, it is found that the Palestinian issue was never before first on the agenda. Although objectively it has been the most important issue for Israeli society, subjectively this was not the case. It was placed in third or fourth place on the agenda, even where it interacted with the question of peace with the Arab world. In fact, the polarization process engendered in Israel by the uprising displayed the limits of the country's political parties which, rather than facing the society's vital, existential questions, which it will have to do sooner or later, avoided them. The more the uprising and its political effects advanced (Nineteenth Algiers PNC decisions, statements by the chairman of the PLO Executive Committee, U.S.-PLO dialogue, international diplomatic moves), the more Israeli society split, particularly regarding two basic issues: negotiations with the PLO, and recognition of the Palestinian right to self-determination, including the establishment of an independent state, that is, the future of the Occupied Territories.

If one adopts the Israeli manner of illustrating party divisions, one clearly sees that polarization has taken place within each bloc.

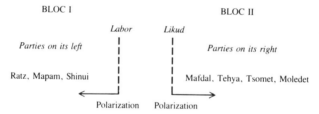

In the Likud, some groups have moved closer to the positions of Tehya, while others have shifted toward the right wing of Labor. Similarly, in the Labor camp some groups have shifted toward the positions of Mapam and Ratz, and others toward the Likud. In other words, the polarization process in each bloc has created a new center of the Israeli political spectrum, which includes groups from both Likud and Labor that do not differ regarding the refusal of negotiations with the PLO and the establishment of a Palestinian state, but at the same time refuse to annex the Occupied Territories. This new center formed the basis for eventual agreement on creating a new national unity government. The "new right" comprises groups from Likud, the Mafdal (National Religious party), Tsomet (a secular right-wing party), Tehya (the classical Greater Israel party containing religious and secular elements), and Moledet (which calls for the "transfer" of the Palestinians). They all favor the annexation of the Occupied Territories and refer to Jordan as the Palestinian state. They also reject the Camp David autonomy plan and want to harden living conditions in the Territories until the Palestinians leave. These groups include the settlers' lobby, and led the Likud to insist upon and obtain a provision in the coalition accords for the establishment of forty new settlements in the next four years in the Occupied Territories.

The "new left" among the Zionist parties includes groups from the Labor party, Mapam, and Ratz (the Citizens' Rights movement). They accept the principle of negotiations with the PLO under certain conditions and the idea of withdrawing from most of the Occupied Territories. They also accept the principle of partition.

The uprising was the key factor that led to the drawing of the new Israeli political map. This will be seen where the four units are concerned: "new right," Likud, Labor, "new Zionist left."

Where the right-wing groups are concerned, they gave a clear-cut answer to the questions insistently raised by the uprising: suppressing it regardless of the degree of force required, increasing settlements, annexation, and "persuading" Palestinians to emigrate. In all of these regards, there is no difference between the secular extreme right and the religious extreme right. A new phenomenon on the right was the establishment of Tsomet by Rafael Eitan (of "drugged cockroaches in a bottle" fame), the former chief of staff, and Moledet under the leadership of Rahbe'am Ze'evi. Both of these parties are secular, and their leaderships originate from Labor Zionism and its military bodies such as the Palmach. The political-ideological message of these two parties is not religious mysticism (as in the case of the right-wing religious parties), but a pragmatic answer to practical necessities and a natural continuation of the Zionist project in Palestine with its "eternal war" against the Arabs. Rafael Eitan, for example, in a speech delivered on April 6, 1988, stated the following: "Both the Likud and Labor face the same danger, due to their belief that they must find a solution, instead of saying: there is no solution, solutions are over with. . . . Transfer [of the Palestinians] is not practical because it is rejected by the super powers. So we should exploit the Arabs' anxiety regarding the future, we should own all the empty lands and encourage new births and new immigration."[21] As for the uprising, the solution is very simple: a bullet in the head of every stone thrower.

Moledet differs through its open call for transferring Arabs. Contrary to the prevailing belief, this party does not depend for its electoral strength on the supporters of Rabbi Meir Kahane's Kach movement. Its supporters come from a wide ethnic and geographic spread in Israeli society. True, its electoral score was higher in the settlements than in the country as a whole, but its highest score anywhere was achieved in Kibbutz Beit Gobrim, where it got 45 percent of the votes.[22] Both parties rely on right-wing forces. Such forces have always existed in Israeli society, but it was the atmosphere of the uprising that contributed to their crystallization. Together they got four seats in the Knesset, while Tehya lost two for a total of three, and Kach was not allowed to participate. In other words, the number of seats held by the extreme right in the 1988 Knesset (without counting the Orthodox religious parties) is seven seats, or 6.5 percent of the votes. If one adds Mafdal (the National Religious party), the total is twelve seats and 10.5 percent of the votes.

As for the Likud, before coming to power in 1977 its position was to annex the Occupied Territories. But realism came to prevail with its assumption of governmental responsibilities. Thus it shifted its position to maintaining the status quo. Begin's autonomy plan, adopted by the Camp David Accords and the Egyptian-Israeli peace treaty, represented an internal Likud compromise between the impossibility of annexing the territories and the refusal to withdraw from them. The Likud relies on one basic strategy: direct negotiations with the Arabs, combined with the anticipation of their results: "peace for peace," as Shamir likes to say. It is inexplicable that the Likud should so harshly attack Labor's so-called Jordanian option, when this is part of what the Likud means by direct negotiations. In fact, direct negotiations have been going on with Jordan for a long time, mired in part by Israel's rejectionism.[23] Although the uprising has negated the possibility of clinging to the status quo, the Likud has not basically changed its program. Worthy of note in this regard are two articles by Ariel Sharon in March 1988, as the Labor party was beginning to yield to U.S. pressure in the form of the Shultz initiative. In these articles Sharon drew the line beyond which no American pressure could push Israel. According to him, most of the points are common to Labor and the Likud: (1) Jerusalem united is the capital of Israel; (2) the Jordan River will remain forever Israel's secure eastern border, guarded by the Israeli army; (3) no military force will be allowed to enter the West Bank of the Jordan River, be it a UN or any other international force; (4) Israel is responsible for the internal and external security of all of the "land of Israel" west of the Jordan River; (5) there will be no foreign sovereignty in what he called "Judea, Samaria, and Gaza"; (6) there will be no Palestinian state west of Jordan; (7) the refugee question should be part of any solution; (8) the Golan Heights are an integral part of Israel; (9) the Arabs of the Occupied Territories should maintain their present (stateless or Jordanian) nationality and should be given relatively wide authority to administer their internal affairs without interference.[24]

Even if the Likud has not changed its political program, it would be a mistake to assume that it has not been affected by the uprising. During the uprising, for example, some Likud members proposed granting "unilateral autonomy," that is, without waiting for a peace treaty, after the holding of elections in the Occupied Territories.[25] They reject the idea of annexation and propose to leave open the sovereignty question. Among these figures are leading Likud members like Moshe Arens and Dan Meridor. Yet other groups within Likud, which reject the unity government, call for the immediate annexation of the Occupied Territories. During the build-up to the elections, for example, Ronnie Milo proposed that should the "national camp" emerge victorious, it would be possible to envisage passing the necessary legislation annexing the territories.[26]

The position of the Likud was clearer than that of Labor in the elections: it rejected all proposals. Shamir declared that it was not a question of borders but of existence,[27] either all of Israel or no Israel at all. Furthermore, according to the Likud, there was no partner for peace on the Arab side, a claim constantly repeated by Benjamin Netaniahu, Israel's former ambassador to the UN.[28] If Israel shows enough self-confidence, so the Likud argued, and if it drops any idea of an international conference, the Arabs will creep to the direct negotiating table.[29] Under no circumstances, and here all Likud factions agreed, should there be any type of negotiations with the PLO.[30]

The forty seats (30.8 percent of the popular vote) that the Likud achieved were not the direct result of its political positions. The supporters of Likud are among the least ideological sections of Israeli society. In order to market itself, the Likud relied on what it symbolizes: appeal of a general nature to the Sephardic Jews, against the defeatist Labor party, which had treated them with contempt and discrimination; stressing the Labor party's squandering of economic resources through its control of unprofitable projects; yes to peace, but from a position of strength, hence the need first of all to bring an end to the uprising. This "businesslike" and "realistic" language found a wide audience.[31]

The lack of ideology among Likud voters does not mean that there will be a change in its positions. It would be wrong to confuse the nonideological quality of Likud supporters and the total indoctrination of the leadership. True, the Likud constituency would not be the main obstacle in case the leadership were to change its position. But the lack of ideological firmness at the base is not a sufficient premise for change. In some ways, it makes it an even easier prey for the demagogy of the leadership. In the words of the Israeli researcher Sammy Smooha (who draws the wrong consequences from the premise, however), "Most Likud supporters are oriental Jews who are devoid of any ideological commitment to greater Israel and whose backing of the Likud has little to do with national security and foreign policy."[32]

As for the Labor party, it seems to have been most confused of all by the uprising. It has to defend itself against the right, which accuses it of surrenderism through its apparent willingness to be drawn into an international conference (an adventure seen more dangerous than the status quo), and against the left, which accuses the Labor party's Rabin of carrying out the Likud's policy in the Occupied Territories.

Its official line is still close to that of the original "Allon plan" with regard to the Occupied Territories. The latest incarnation of that plan was that put forward by Labor party generals (hence its name, the "generals' plan") and presented to Israeli voters before the December elections. It calls for an Israeli withdrawal from areas of "heavy Arab concentration," placing the bulk of the Israeli army in the territories on the Jordan River, demilitarizing the Occupied Territories, installing an early warning system, etc., and maintaining the Jordan Valley and Jerusalem under Israeli sovereignty. This military plan complements the political plan proposed by Shimon Peres and Yitzhak Rabin at a press conference.[33] The plan called for holding negotiations with a joint Jordanian-Palestinian delegation in the framework of a nominal international conference and elections in the Occupied Territories six months after the return of calm (i.e., the cessation of the uprising). Included in the plan was the promise never to withdraw to the 1967 borders and not to remove the settlements. After the elections, Peres renewed his proposal to hold elections in the Occupied Territories upon the cessation of the uprising.[34]

In fact, the internal crisis over the Jordanian option within the Labor party goes back to the beginning of the uprising and even before. But pressure increased with King Hussein's administrative "disengagement" from the West Bank, with the hawks following Rabin in proposing measures resembling the Likud's autonomy proposal,[35] and doves like Abba Eban, Yossi Beilin, Ha'yim Ramon, Avraham Burg, and Ezer Weizmann proposing negotiations, albeit subject to strict conditions, with *any* Palestinian party.[36] At this point, internal polarization became clear and strong, since the proposal of the party doves does not in fact differ from those of Mapam or Ratz, and makes it possible to negotiate with the PLO.

After the elections, the plan for an international conference (or "umbrella") was dropped by Labor, and it was made clear that negotiations with the PLO were out of the question, so that its platform became very similar to that of the Likud. The increasing activity of Labor doves, particularly after the United States began its dialogue with the PLO, was paralleled by an increase in the activity of the hawks.[37] Rabin, for example, rejected any possibility of the return to 1967 borders, saying that he would never accept it even if this prevented peace.[38]

On the other hand, certain Likud factions began to draw closer to Labor party hawks. Even Ariel Sharon, who appears most hostile toward Labor, began proposing the *partial* annexation of the West Bank and Gaza Strip, following the Allon plan,[39] and employing the Labor party's demographic argumentation. Rabin, in his analysis of Sharon's proposal, found that, over and above differences over the mere distinction between important or unimportant areas from the security point of view, it was very close to the Labor party's mode of thinking.[40]

Labor's election campaign was, propagandistically speaking, an extension of its previous arguments based on the "demographic threat," or the fear that the Arabs would eventually become the majority if Israel insisted on keeping all of the Occupied Territories. The expressions used to drive home the notion of a demographic threat were racist and designed to frighten Israeli Jews in the face of the high Arab birthrate and other such phenomena. The problem, in addition to its use of racist imagery, with the brandishing of the Arab demographic threat is that it can have the opposite effect to that intended, that is to say, the frightened voter can take refuge in programs advocating "transfer" and not in territorial compromise. At the very least the argument justifies a form of apartheid in the minds of many, who come to feel that, since the territories must be kept for security reasons, and because of the demographic threat, both the Palestinian lands and the Palestinian people must be kept under strict control.

The 1988 elections created a new, tripartite political map in Israel. This is apparent from the overlapping positions of the Labor right and the Likud "left" on a number of issues, as shown above, and the creation in this way of a new political center, which forms the basis for the national unity government. Its purpose is to block the uprising and resist potential international pressure. The model I suggest, which describes the emergence of three Zionist groupings in the country, differs from that found adequate until the recent past, as exemplified by the analyses of Israeli sociologist Yohanan Peres. For him, the Israeli political map is characterized by duality and balance between the Labor and Likud camps, based on a balance of birthrates among eastern and western Jews, respectively the basic constituency of Likud and Labor. According to that model, the function of the parties to the left of Labor and to the right of Likud and the orthodox religious parties is to "absorb or neutralize small differences."[41] This classical model no longer provides a sufficient explanation for political behavior of the parties, because it fails to explain the current process whereby Labor and Likud are moving closer, while other groups move from Labor to the Zionist left and from Likud to the extreme right. As for the non-Zionist religious parties (Agudat Israel, Shas, and Degel Hatorah), they place political issues further down on their agendas while adapting their position to the prevailing right-wing atmosphere. Within the context of this tripartite polarization, Labor's share of the votes dropped to 30 percent—thirty-nine Knesset seats—from 34.9 percent in the previous elections. The size of this drop is largely explained by the fact that Mapam did not run with Labor this time.

On the Zionist left, significant changes occurred within Mapam and Ratz due to the uprising. For the first time since the seventh Knesset, Mapam ran independently of the Labor party. Having left the Labor alignment in 1984 because of Labor's participation in the first national unity government, it gained three seats in 1988, based on 2.5 percent of the vote. During its party conference, which took place four and a half months after the outbreak of the uprising, on April 28, 1988, it amended its program to state its readiness to negotiate with the PLO and a recognition of the Palestinian people's right to self-determination, predicated on the PLO's renunciation of terror and recognition of Israel.[42]

As for Ratz (the Civil Rights movement), it likewise amended its political program as a result of the uprising along the same lines as Mapam's.[43]

Before the uprising, the Israeli Communist party and the Progressive List for Peace were the only parties that called for a two-state solution and for recognition of the PLO. Under the impetus of the uprising, Ratz and Mapam moved close to this position. Only since December 1988 can it be said that there is a significant left-Zionist camp that calls for the establishment of a Palestinian state.

FROM PROTEST TO DIALOGUE

Contrary to expectations, a broad radical protest movement, similar to that which developed during the Lebanon war of 1982, did not emerge. (Given the uprising's explosive potential, one cannot rule out dramatic events that would change the situation.) One widespread explanation for this is the very low level of Israeli casualties suffered as a result of the *intifada* as compared with Israeli losses in Lebanon. This explains part, but not all, of the phenomenon.

The most famous Israeli protest movement, Peace Now (Shalom Akhshav), emerged after Sadat's visit to Jerusalem in 1977, among reserve officers of the Israeli army. Its goal was to put pressure on the Israeli government to make concessions and not lose the chance for peace with the biggest Arab country. It organized mass activities in 1978–79 in the wake of Sadat's initiative. No similar mass protests took place following the Palestinian peace initiative in late 1988. The problem with such protests is that they of necessity focus on the question of oppression in the Occupied Territories and as such they force the Israeli public to face up to the Palestinian issue and the historical accumulation of contradictions bound up in it, going back to the genesis of the state. Such protests, when they occur, are therefore outside of the "national consensus," and their function is to create a new national consensus, which is a very difficult task.

The uprising's impact on the Israeli protest movement was more rapid and intense than in the case of the political parties. Dozens of protest groups emerged,[44] most of them local or confined to specific professions: university professors, students, lawyers, psychologists, soldiers, and so on. Their activities were confined principally to the big cities of Tel Aviv, Jerusalem, and Haifa. Their constituency is middle class and intellectual, and many of their members are active in more than one group.

The program of these groups goes from the adoption of a clear political line (as in the case of Stop the Occupation, a coalition of left groups calling for negotiations with the PLO and a two-state solution, or Ad Kan, a movement of Tel Aviv university professors seeking the same end)[45] to a general activist approach concentrating on a specific issue, such as human rights violations in the Occupied Territories, to calls for specific actions (as in the case of Yesh Gvul (There Is a Limit), which promotes the refusal to serve with the army in the Occupied Territories). The activities of the groups usually take the form of information campaigns, protest actions, the circulation of petitions, demonstrations, and specific solidarity actions after particularly harsh measures have been taken against a village or refugee camp.

The largest protest movement is Peace Now, which contains supporters of left-Zionist parties, notably Ratz and Mapam, as well as elements of the Labor party. Its political aim is to convince Israelis as to the necessity of compromise in the quest for peace with the Arab world, but its leadership did not invest any great effort in defining the essence of this peace, nor were principles like self-determination for the Palestinians among its objectives. Until the outbreak of the uprising, Peace Now hoped that the Labor party would succeed in promoting a Jordanian or a Palestinian-Jordanian option without having to negotiate with the PLO. The participation of the Labor party in a common government with the Likud from the post-Lebanon war period to the *intifada* kept the movement away from the streets, and it was characterized by passivity and silence.

With the *intifada* and the decline of the Jordanian option, Peace Now found itself in an organizational-political crisis. The uprising made it clear that peace (and certainly that peace "now") was predicated on a willingness to face the Palestinian issue and deal with the Palestine Liberation Organization. Many former activists, who could not wait for the movement to adjust, and in the face of atrocities committed by the Israeli occupation during the uprising, acted within smaller, more radical groups such as the Twenty-First Year of Occupation.

The George Shultz initiative seemed to provide a way out of the crisis for Peace Now. Despite its vagueness, the initiative was rejected by Prime Minister Shamir. Demonstrations against the government thus became possible without saying anything new beyond "Yes to Shultz." But the uprising remained and the Shultz initiative was forgotten. The questions remained the same. Almost a year after the beginning of the uprising, on November 29, 1988, Peace Now made its major policy shift, calling for negotiations with the PLO.[46] Ongoing moves in U.S. policy strengthened this turn by Peace Now.

In addition to Peace Now, other protest movements carried out activities before the uprising, such as Yesh Gvul, which is made up of soldiers refusing to serve in the Occupied Territories. This group faces a major challenge, for it has chosen to attack the occupation through one of the most hallowed institutions in Israel, the army. The number of soldiers refusing to serve in the Occupied Territories was over 200, and dozens of them went to jail for periods of five to six weeks, some of them several times. The number of soldiers refusing to serve in the Occupied Territories is in fact much higher, because many of those who refuse are never ordered to do so. Dai la-Kibush (Stop the Occupation) is another movement that existed before the *intifada*. It unites members of the left in the cities, including members of the Communist party, the Israeli socialist left, the Progressive List for Peace, and independent persons. It is a continuation of the Committee for Solidarity with Bir Zeit University and the Committee Against the War in Lebanon. Its program is clear and includes the evacuation of the Occupied Territories, negotiations with the PLO, and a two-state solution. It intensified its activities during the uprising, attracting new elements, but never developed into a mass movement.

With the movement on the part of the Zionist left toward positions of the more radical left, particularly regarding peace negotiations, an important debate began over elements that distinguish various movements on the left, notably with respect to political culture. It was in fact the radical left that had drawn Zionist elements gradually toward its positions, which were based on principle rather than circumstance or fear, and included solidarity, dialogue, the right to self-determination, and so on. What continues to distinguish the left is that, while it initiated a process others have now joined, it has not received the media coverage. The difficulty in this regard stems also from the Palestinian side, since it tends currently to seek more after partners in dialogue than partners in struggle.

Moreover, the political settlement called for by the Israeli left has now been accepted by the PLO leadership, and the left in Israel is hesitating as to whether its task is currently to bring more and more sectors within the Zionist left and center to accept the opening of a dialogue with the PLO (a task that is not so complicated, especially after the shift in the U.S. position) or to concentrate on protest and solidarity actions, seen as important for the continuation of the uprising, because they help to set limits on Israel's capacity to carry out oppressive practices.

The dialogue between the Israeli left and the PLO is of a totally different nature from future PLO negotiations with Israeli governments. The dialogue has led to concessions from only one side, the Palestinians, since the Israeli left cannot make concessions on behalf of Israel. The dialogue should more accurately be called solidarity or joint action. Dialogue and negotiations both take place on the basis of different national positions, while joint action and solidarity try to overcome national limits, pointing to a future that surpasses national boundaries established by political settlements.

Is the Israeli left going to concentrate on dialogue or on protest and solidarity activities? The discussion still goes on.

NOTES

1. *Ha'aretz,* February 7, 1989; February 8, 1989.
2. Moshe Arens, "Implications of the Intifada," *Ha'aretz,* April 6, 1988.
3. This was a frequent explanation of the outbreak of the *intifada* in Israel, based on the December 8 killing (intentional or unintentional) of four Gaza men by a truck driven by an Israeli, which smashed into their car.
4. A claim often reiterated by Ariel Sharon.
5. Bumper stickers with the words "People against the hostile media" were distributed throughout Israel.
6. A proposal made by Rabin in a meeting with Palestinians. Cf. *Yediot Aharonot,* May 31, 1988.
7. Ze'ev Schiff, *Ha'aretz,* June 8, 1988; July 27, 1988.
8. Ze'ev Schiff, *Ha'aretz,* August 10, 1988.
9. Lecture delivered at an international conference of the Washington Institute for Middle East Policy. Cf. *Ha'aretz,* June 30, 1988.
10. Yitzhak Beily, three articles in *Ha'aretz,* May 13, 14, 15, 1988.
11. Yoram Peri, four articles in *Davar,* March 12, 13, 14, 15, 1988.
12. *Yediot Aharonot,* February 23, 1988.
13. *Ha'aretz,* July 15, 1988.
14. *Ha'aretz,* November 22, 1988.
15. *Ha'aretz,* February 24, 1988.
16. *Yediot Aharonot,* September 11, 1988.
17. *Ha'aretz,* March 13–15 and 21–22, 1988.
18. *Ha'aretz,* November 4, 1988.
19. *Ha'aretz,* June 12, 1988; June 22, 1988; September 11, 1988; Y. Harkabi, *Fateful Decisions* (Tel Aviv: Am-Oved, 1986), pp. 49–78.

20. *Yediot Aharonot*, December 21, 1988 (Shamir's speech to the Likud).

21. *Ha'aretz*, April 7, 1988.

22. Dr. Gideon Bigger, *Ha'aretz*, November 15, 1988.

23. Yossi Melman, *Shotfot Oyenet* (Hostile Occupation) (Tel Aviv: Ha-Haraot-Goraliyog, 1987).

24. *Yediot Aharonot*, March 7 and 13, 1988.

25. Dan Margelit, *Ha'aretz*, August 28, 1988.

26. *Yediot Aharonot*, June 2, 1988.

27. Akiva Ildad, *Ha'aretz*, April 7, 1988.

28. *Ha'aretz*, May 23, 1988.

29. Cf. Shamir's statements in *Ha'aretz*, October 18, 1988.

30. Interview with Shamir, *Ha'aretz*, March 11, 1988; interview with Minister Moshe Nissim, *Ha'aretz*, July 29, 1988; statement by Minister Moshe Katzav, *Ha'aretz*, August 15, 1988.

31. Ya'ir Sheleg, *Ha'aretz* weekly supplement, August 15, 1988.

32. Sammy Smooha, "Internal Divisions in Israel at Forty," *Middle East Review*, Summer 1988, p. 32.

33. *Ha'aretz*, October 18, 1988.

34. Lecture by Shimon Peres before the Jeane Kirkpatrick forum, December 12, 1988, at Tel Aviv University.

35. This was the proposal made by some Labor ministers to replace the Jordanian option, and brought forward by Ya'cob Tsur, who is close to Rabin. *Ha'aretz*, May 17, 1988.

36. *Ha'aretz*, August 11, 1988; *Hadashot*, August 21, 1988; December 21, 1988.

37. *Ha'aretz*, August 1, 1988.

38. *Yediot Aharonot*, October 26, 1988.

39. *Ha'aretz*, August 18, 1988.

40. *Ha'aretz*, August 24, 1988.

41. Yohanan Peres, "Stalemate: Structural Balance in Israeli Politics," *Middle East Review*, Summer 1988, p. 41.

42. *Ha'aretz*, May 6, 1988. See also Mapam's party program.

43. Ratz party program.

44. Special issue of *Politica* (no. 22). Forty-six protest groups are mentioned.

45. *Ha'aretz*, November 18, 1988.

46. *Ha'aretz*, November 29, 1988.

18

Palestinian Elites in the Occupied Territories
STABILITY AND CHANGE THROUGH THE *INTIFADA*

Ali Jarbawi

Ever since the start of the *intifada,* there has been a flow of journalistic, academic, and political analyses of various social and political groups in the Occupied Territories, and of the changes within their structure and respective influence as a result of the uprising. Analyses have also focused on the evolving relationship between these groups and the Palestinian leadership abroad. Their conclusions have varied, depending partly on the outlook of their authors.

The broad consensus is that the *intifada* strengthened PLO elements in the Occupied Territories and strengthened ties between the leadership on the inside and on the outside. A second view has also evolved, however, particularly in Israel, where expectations, or rather hopes, have been raised that a local leadership, distinct from the PLO, was evolving and would eventually crystallize, taking the initiative based on their realization that "disturbances and violence are useless," and enter into direct negotiations with Israel. Defense Minister Yitzhak Rabin was the first to expound this view.[1]

Yet another interpretation emerged. Most notably in academic circles within the United States, the conclusion was reached that changes wrought by the *intifada* have led to a fundamental shift in the relationship between the local leadership and that of the PLO abroad. According to these analyses, the uprising is led by a new, young generation that is highly pragmatic politically, and which, while continuing to be linked to the PLO, enjoys considerable political freedom of action.[2] These predominantly Western analyses did not share in Israeli hopes regarding the emergence of local independent negotiators. They did not shed doubt on the patriotism of this local leadership. Instead they ascribed to it greater independence than reality would warrant. This distorted perception may possibly have been the result of the great distance separating the authors from the events they describe. The underlying political consideration may have been the suggestion that there was a potential schism between the local leadership and the PLO abroad in case the latter were to fail to adopt a ''realistic and moderate line.'' It seems relevant here to note in passing that these views were propounded prior to the November 1988 PNC session in Algiers.

In fact, the latter two interpretations are fallacious and not difficult to refute. Contrary to Israeli hopes, it can clearly be seen that no local ''negotiating'' leadership separate from the PLO on the outside has emerged, nor has the *intifada* paved the way for its emergence. The opposite has in fact occurred. The *intifada*, with its stress on unity and national renaissance, has ruled out the emergence of such a leadership. How in these times would an independent ''negotiating'' leadership appear, when in the times of greatest distress and division after the PLO's expulsion from Beirut, Israel's dream of separating the Occupied Territories from their political leadership abroad failed to materialize? The analysis of the position of the United National Leadership of the Uprising (UNLU) shows, on the contrary, that the UNLU sees itself as the local political and activist arm of the PLO. UNLU communiqués illustrate tight coordination between the inside and the outside, and show absolute support for the PLO abroad.[3] Even when differences arose among faction members of the UNLU inside, these were reflections of differences among the political groups both locally and abroad.

In order to illustrate the above propositions, I shall, in what follows, begin by describing the various elements of the political elites in the Occupied Territories prior to the *intifada*; I will then examine shifts within and among these elites in the course of the uprising and evaluate the prospects for future developments in their internal and mutual relations. It will thus be possible to reach concrete conclusions as to the status of the local elites in relation to the PLO leadership abroad, and therefore their potential for becoming autonomous actors in regional political developments.

COMPOSITION OF THE POLITICAL ELITES IN THE OCCUPIED TERRITORIES PRIOR TO THE *INTIFADA*

Prior to the *intifada,* and more precisely since 1982, the political elite in the Occupied Territories was composed of the leading elements of three major groups that together covered the entire political map: the national forces, the pro-Jordanian personalities, and the Islamic forces.[4]

The National Forces

The national forces in the Occupied Territories are made up of the political elements that support the PLO as represented by one or another of its factions, in addition to Palestinian national factions currently outside the umbrella of the PLO.[5] As a result of their commitment to the Palestinian cause, and over and above ideological differences that separate them, they are the forces that enjoy the widest popular support. Their elite in turn consists of three groups: the organizational leadership, the "public figures," and the independents. The organizational leadership consists of the leaders of various national factions in the West Bank and Gaza, and includes students, trade unionists, and representatives of various professions and associations, in addition to the factional leaders detained in Israeli prisons.[6] The organizational leadership of the national forces is considered the backbone of the national elite and the mainstay of the political process in the Occupied Territories. It derives its power and its legitimacy from four sources:

1. Its organizational ties with the leadership abroad.[7] This opens a direct channel of communication between the two sides, through which they exchange information and come up with decisions. In addition, the support it gets from the leadership abroad, which gives it legitimacy among the people in the Occupied Territories, gives it executive power over its cadres and supporters.

2. The location of this leadership at the summit of a hierarchical structure representing the various factions that cover the cities, villages, and camps of the West Bank and Gaza Strip. This guarantees the support of followers and supporters all over the Occupied Territories and gives it the ability to penetrate the social structure, enabling it to mobilize wide support from all sectors of the society.

3. Continuity. The organizational leadership is the only leadership within the national forces that has the mechanisms to form itself again without the need for time or ideological transformations. The hierarchical structure provides leaders for these organizations from top to bottom. If leaders disappear as a result of imprisonment or deportation, they are automatically replaced by leaders from the level immediately below. This arrangement ensures internal unity and continuity, decreasing the chances of internal struggle.

4. The prestige born from its long history of struggle against the occupation. Most of the elements of this leadership have long been in confrontation with the occupation, which has used various means against them, including town arrest, imprisonment, and deportation. This increases respect for them on the part of broad sectors of Palestinian society in the Occupied Territories and abroad. It is widely believed among politicized circles in the Occupied Territories that most of these persons have come to hold leading positions as a result of hard work. This fosters their legitimacy and increases their influence on political events in the territories.

But these same four factors that contribute to their legitimacy also restrict their effectiveness in certain ways. The organizational leaders need to clear their positions and decisions with their own leaders on the outside. Furthermore, given that the PLO is an umbrella organization consisting of various factions, they must spend time and energy coordinating with each other within the Occupied Territories and organizing their relations with the other factions. And Israeli repression, ever present, forces these leaders to make their moves under cover while constantly avoiding the political limelight. This means that the organizational elites, who are often unknown to most people, do not enjoy the popularity that would otherwise go with their functions.

That kind of public notoriety, along with support for the PLO, has since 1982 essentially been restricted to the second of the national forces' three elite groups, the public figures. They emerged as a result of internal and external factors: the Likud governments' harsh policies, which presided over the removal and deportation of leading elected mayors and the breakup of the National Guidance Committee in 1982,[8] and Israel's invasion of Lebanon, which resulted in the dispersal of Palestinian fighters and the PLO in various Arab countries, as well as the latter's decision to seek political rather than military solutions to the Palestine question. These two factors propelled the latter-day public figures to the fore, and most of them are characterized by political "pragmatism."[9]

The public figures are composed of a mix of traditional and "new" figures, all of them supporting the PLO. The mainstream national leadership has always seen the importance of ensuring the support of traditional notables in the Occupied Territories, all the more so after the summer of 1982 and the decision to seek a political solution. At the time, there was a hidden struggle for influence between the PLO and Jordan, and support for the former on the part of the notables meant lessened support for Jordan.[10] However, because the PLO was fearful lest the vacillating loyalties and narrow self-interest of traditional elites might cause them to desert the national cause, it also promoted new persons as public figures, persons whose loyalty was guaranteed, since they enjoyed no independent power base other than loyalty to the PLO. They were drawn from the universities, unions, cultural bodies, and news media in the Occupied Territories. Because these figures lacked the advantages of the traditional leaders and the prestige of the organizational leadership, they were entirely dependent for the preservation of their status on total loyalty to the PLO leadership abroad. In exchange for loyalty, the PLO leaders abroad guaranteed balance among the public figures inside and overall support for them.

The first task given the public figures was to direct Palestinian public relations in the Occupied Territories. In this task they were aided by four factors:

1. Their moderation and pragmatism in the eyes of the West, of Israeli public opinion, and of the military occupation.

2. Their ability to speak the language of the Western media, which made them welcome sources of information and wisdom for Western diplomatic representations. Some of them were used as vehicles for passing sensitive communications concerning the political process in the region.[11] In time, the public figures came to form the "national forefront."

3. Their ties to the PLO outside, which made them reliable sources for Israelis and Westerners.

4. Their presence on the inside, which made them a necessary ingredient for any solution to the conflict.

All of these factors helped the public figures to build a wide communications network inside Israel and in the West, both of whom have been keen to promote such "moderate" figures.

It is important at this stage to note that although these figures became popular outside the Occupied Territories, particularly in Israel and the West, they did not generally enjoy broad support on the inside. It is therefore impossible to think of them as a coherent group, or as a representative leadership in isolation from the PLO abroad, since their positions are entirely derived from the latter and they have not built up a popular constituency in the Occupied Territories.

The third category among the national elites, the independents, is made up of nonhomogeneous personalities with respectable social status, such as physicians, lawyers, university teachers, big merchants, and farmers. Their common denominator is support for the PLO as sole representative of the Palestinian people. Unlike the organizational leaders and public figures, they have no organizational ties with any PLO factions. Their influence is therefore limited to giving nonbinding advice to actors and decision makers. On the other hand, they are usually able to analyze the situation without factional bias. They stress unity in times of crisis, and their significant contribution to the national movement resides in their ability to reduce internal tensions.

After 1982 and prior to the *intifada,* there were periods of stress in relations among the elements of the national elite. Internal factional splits between organizational leaders marked the period, as well as criticism on their part of certain public figures. The independents, in turn, were accused of being inconsistent and incapable of holding a steady political line. Nonetheless, the three elements managed to coordinate broadly and to maintain an acceptable degree of harmony in the face of ongoing Israeli repressive measures and the challenge of the Islamic movement, through their common support for the PLO.

The Pro-Jordanian Figures

The pro-Jordanian figures belonging to the political elite in the Occupied Territories come from a common socioeconomic background. They belong to the upper half of the society and thus have similar political views. Many of their social and economic interests are in Jordan, and in order to preserve them they believe it necessary to associate Jordan with the effort to end the occupation. They have therefore adopted the "Jordanian option" as a formula to resolve the conflict. They fear that an independent Palestinian state would shatter the traditional social structure that so markedly favors them.

Most of the pro-Jordanian figures come from the ranks of the traditional leaders who were supported by Jordanian officials controlling some of the public institutions in the West Bank, such as the Awqaf (Islamic Trust) department or the health and education departments. They were also supported by newer figures who had been able to build their political presence as a result of Jordanian aid for their institutions. For historical reasons, they are mainly centered in the West Bank, though the Gaza Strip in time witnessed the emergence of similar figures.

Since its annexation of the West Bank in 1950, Amman sought to strengthen its hold by reinforcing the patriarchal structure of the society through personal ties rather than institutionalized relationships as the only basis for political participation. The notables of West Bank extended families were linked individually to Amman, and their personal loyalty was guaranteed by their receiving certain posts and benefits. Their role was to ensure the regime's interests among their followers, while representing the latter before the regime. Amman was thus able to secure its control over the West Bank by supporting these local, traditional "representatives" whose loyalty was ensured, while obstructing the possible formation of a modern, institutionalized Palestinian political infrastructure, which would have eroded the power of the Hashemite regime in the Occupied Territories.

None of the developments that from their point of view were unfavorable resulted in terminating the role of the pro-Jordanian elites prior to the *intifada,* from the September 1970 war against the Palestinians in Jordan, through the various phases of consolidation of the national forces, to the increasing absorption of the Occupied Territories' economy into that of Israel.

Jordan maintained its hold on the Occupied Territories and the influence of pro-Jordanian figures there through a variety of direct and indirect means, which can be grouped in six categories:

1. The distinctive relationship between Jordan and the West Bank, which was legally and administratively part of the Hashemite kingdom. All public institutions in the West Bank were linked to Jordan, and most government officials received salaries from Amman. In addition, the Occupied Territories have strong demographic, geographic, and economic ties with Jordan; Jordan is the main gateway to the Arab world for the people and exports of the Occupied Territories; and there are many Palestinians in Jordan tied by kinship and work relations with people in the territories.

2. Jordan's policy, aimed at consolidating the principle of Jordanian participation in efforts for a settlement of the Palestinian question. This policy led it to enter into public and secret agreements with the PLO, aimed at preserving its right to represent the Palestinian people under occupation. In furtherance of this aim, Amman applied various kinds of pressure based on its ties with the Occupied Territories, and involving the policy of "giving and withholding" toward the Palestinians under occupation. Financial aid and export facilities were the two arms of this policy, and they were given or withheld based on loyalty.

3. The patriarchal structure of the Jordanian regime. The use of this structure rather than institutionalized relationships by Amman gave the pro-Jordanian figures their power and influence. Personal contacts, mediators, and favoritism are the acknowledged bases for doing business with Jordanian officialdom.

4. The above three elements gave rise to a fourth one, namely, the use by Amman of the pro-Jordanian figures as mediators between itself and the people of the Occupied Territories. They became the official "agents" in the policy of "giving and withholding." It was necessary to approach them in order to pursue one's interests in Amman. To fulfill this function, they relied on their presence in the Jordanian parliament and in the highest positions of the administrative system, development committees, and agricultural cooperatives.

5. Israeli leniency toward these figures. This gave them considerable freedom of expression and movement, and even of political organization. Israel shared Jordan's interest in finding a political solution through the implementation of some version of the "Jordanian option," and therefore gave these figures ample opportunity for consolidating Jordanian influence in the Occupied Territories.

6. Their socioeconomic background. Since most of the pro-Jordanian figures are members of large families with high economic status, they were able to maintain the support of many people of the old generation who have a vested interest in clinging to traditional structures. Contrary to the national public figures, who are centered in cities, where many of them have their roots, pro-Jordanian figures often come from the countryside and reside in villages, which helped them consolidate their status and strengthen their influence.

As can be seen, most of the elements that helped pro-Jordanian figures maintain their influence do not relate to them as individuals or to general acceptance of their method of operation. Their strength was not based on a wide popular base but on their role as mediators between Amman and the population of the Occupied Territories. Support for these figures is therefore restricted to a small group of people with limited influence on the political process. National circles in fact regarded their role and their overall political views as digressing from the national consensus.

The Islamic Forces

The Islamic forces are composed of three active political movements in addition to groups that restrict their activities to religious preaching. The latter include movements such as At-tabligh wa-dda'wa, At-takfir wal-hijra, and As-sufiyun (the Sufis). The Islamic political movements are essentially composed of the Muslim Brotherhood, the Islamic Jihad, and the Islamic Liberation party (see Chapter 11).[12]

The political elite of the Islamic forces in the Occupied Territories is made up of the organizational leadership of the three political movements, in addition to a small number of politically independent religious figures. The organizational leaderships are divided into traditional elements, represented by the old generation of the Muslim Brothers and the Islamic Liberation party on the one hand, and new elements, which make up the Islamic Jihad and which have emerged within the Muslim Brotherhood and the Islamic Liberation party. The activism of the traditional leadership predates the occupation, and it therefore wields a great deal of influence, further heightened by social standing and economic power. True, part of the leadership in the West Bank is of lower-middle-class background and works in the educational field and in the Waqf, but the rest are upper-middle-class merchants and landlords.[13] Their status made it possible for them to create a wide network of relations with various social groups. In the Gaza Strip, on the other hand, most religious leaders, who belong to the Muslim Brotherhood, hold government, religious, educational, or UNRWA jobs, and come from the poorer strata of 1948 refugees. The educational sector in particular is for them a suitable environment for preaching and organizing.

The second category is that of the new and less experienced leadership. The Islamic Jihad's leaders are drawn from this group. It is more educated, more dynamic, and interacts more with other political forces. It is in close contact with organizational cadres through its activities in mosques, schools, associations, and universities. In this way it has also secured for itself a grass-roots following. Most of this category of leaders are of poor to middle-class origin, but have been able to rise through education, which has opened the doors of the upper middle class: many are physicians, lawyers, engineers, university teachers, and businessmen, as well as religious figures.

It is widely believed that the underground Islamic Jihad has a central command that functions mainly in the Gaza Strip. It seems to have drawn its leaders partly from secular elements, partly from former Muslim Brothers, and partly from elements of the Popular Liberation Forces belonging to the Palestinian Liberation Army and now in Israeli detention centers. The leadership of the Muslim Brothers in the Occupied Territories does not, on the other hand, have a central command; rather, it has local commands. The Gaza organization of the Muslim Brothers is therefore not linked to that of the West Bank, which is in turn divided into separate regional leaderships. Nonetheless, it would appear that strong coordination takes place. Yet one must assume that the lack of central command means that there is no overall leader for the movement in the Occupied Territories, and that important decisions are taken by consultation and agreement among the various local leaderships.

As for the independent religious leaders, they are marginal compared to the Islamic organizational elites, but they form a supporting element. They have respectable social positions and contribute to the general consolidation of the Islamic line while supporting the national Palestinian effort. They have thus become efficient mediators among Islamic and national forces in general, and between the Muslim Brothers and Fateh in particular.

The power of the organizational leaderships of the Islamic political movement is drawn from various factors, which can be summed up as follows:

1. The religious expansion witnessed in the Middle East over the years since the mid–1970s, which culminated with the victory of the Islamic revolution in Iran.

2. The prevalent Islamic cultural background of the Occupied Territories, particularly strong among the lower half of the social strata centered in camps and, to a lesser degree, in villages, which have thus become breeding grounds for the Islamic movements.

3. The moral and material support they (and especially the Muslim Brothers) receive from various external powers including, it is believed, Jordan and Saudi Arabia. In addition, Israel encouraged their political activities, on the assumption that any increase in their influence must be at the expense of the PLO.

4. The tight organizational structure of Islamic political movements in the Occupied Territories. These leaderships are ideologically committed cadres, and this guarantees compliance with their decisions. The amir of a certain group of Muslim Brothers, for example, enjoys absolute obedience from his followers whatever orders he may give.

5. The efficient institutionalized structure controlled by the conservative religious leaders, which spread over all parts of the Occupied Territories and which includes the Islamic Waqf departments in the West Bank and the Islamic Mujamma' in Gaza, in addition to mosques, Islamic societies and clubs, private and religious schools and institutions of higher education, and the *zaka* (alms tax) committees. This net of institutions gives the organizational leaders of the Islamic political movements in general, and the Muslim Brothers in particular, considerable power and influence.

Factors that weaken the influence of the religious leadership, in particular the more traditional Muslim Brothers and Islamic Liberation party, derive from the following:

1. Their downplaying of the national factor in the Palestinian problem and nonrecognition of the PLO as the sole legitimate representative of the Palestinians, the nonadoption of armed struggle as a means for liberation, and even, until shortly before the *intifada,* their refusal to resist the occupation while constantly confronting the national movements. This led to doubts among wide sectors of the population regarding their true intentions, since the majority of Palestinians, including religious elements, refuse to separate religious from national questions. The Islamic Jihad, which reconciled the two issues, is the exception to this rule and gained instant respect from Palestinians.

2. The stern point of view of the conservative religious movements regarding personal behavior of individuals in society (in matters of women's dress and general role in society, for example). This was coupled with the willingness by certain extremists to use force to implement their demands, and resulted in widespread opposition to the Islamic movement.

3. The lack of public personalities. Many of the popular traditional leaders are unqualified for public work under current conditions. As for new religious leaders, they are still building their public presence in the Occupied Territories (in the case of rising personalities in the Muslim Brotherhood). The leadership of the Islamic Jihad has no public influence, given its underground work. This lack of public figures makes it difficult for the religious movement to influence sectors of the population outside of their traditional strongholds.

4. Internal disputes are another weakening factor for the organizational leaderships of the Islamic political movements. These encompass ideological disputes between the organizations and methodological differences between traditional and new leadership

within the movement. At another level, disputes arise within the Muslim Brotherhood due to the lack of an overall leader for the movement within the Occupied Territories, which gives rise to internal strife and splits.

THE EFFECTS OF THE *INTIFADA* ON THE POLITICAL ELITES IN THE OCCUPIED TERRITORIES

When the *intifada* started, this new wave of Palestinian protest appeared similar to previous ones.[14] There was no external reason to believe that it was profoundly different. But this time, the Palestinian masses exploded and nothing could hold them back. The Palestinian political leaderships, when they realized the qualitative difference between this and previous uprisings, moved rapidly, in accordance with their various elements' strength and positions on the national question, to exercise control over people and events as much as possible.

Through this period of flux, shifts occurred in the balance of power within and among the various elite blocs. Two things should be clarified at the outset. First, the *intifada* did not spawn new political forces that did not previously exist.

Second, there has been no fundamental shift in the balance of power among political forces in the Occupied Territories, in particular between the national and religious blocs, where the balance has continued to weigh in favor of the former. As for the pro-Jordanians, the *intifada* affected them negatively, although this may turn out to have been a temporary phenomenon as they await the opportunity to resume their place on the political stage.

The National Forces

The organizational leaderships of the national forces were quickest to comprehend the unique nature of events and best equipped to control their course. This was due to their long struggle and commitment to resistance, their hierarchical infrastructure, and their broad influence among the masses. At the same time, the masses themselves had matured, through twenty years of occupation measures, and were now prepared to accept discipline under the leadership of the national forces. The organizational leadership of the Islamic Jihad in the Gaza Strip coordinated with the organizational leadership of the national forces in leading the *intifada* after it had begun, through its initial stages.

At the beginning, local cadres of the national forces, as they had in previous periods of protest, found themselves in the midst of the protest movement. And, again in accordance with previous practice, the various local factional leaderships began to coordinate among each other to guide the movement. (Such coordination was made possible by the decision of the Eighteenth Palestine National Council, held in April 1987 in Algiers, to bury differences. Indeed, coordination had been practiced ever since that time.)

By the beginning of January 1988 a national leadership on the inside existed.

Although Communiqué No. 1 of January 8 carried the signature of the "Palestinian National Forces," No. 2 of January 10 was already signed by the "United National Leadership of the Uprising" (UNLU).

Because the UNLU was made up of the organizational cadres of the Occupied Territories' main Palestinian factions, it introduced itself as the field command of the PLO in the Occupied Territories. The factions of the national movement found their prestige much enhanced by their ability to coordinate among one another and with the PLO leadership abroad. Factional strife was driven down to lower levels within the organizations, and was focused primarily on competition in the creation of popular committees and regarding which group was most active in the struggle. Meanwhile the leaders evinced "coalition tolerance" toward one another. And the UNLU's communiqués (thirty-one during the first year, or about two per month) became the leadership's "concealed presence" in every home.

With the passage of time, the UNLU increased its hold on the masses, repeatedly demonstrating its wisdom by not demanding the impossible from them, but expressing to a great degree their hopes and capabilities.

This image of the UNLU in the Occupied Territories as a unified, firm, effective, and credible body, even where exaggerated, has undeniably increased the status and influence of the organizational leadership. Its members have, due to the *intifada*, ceased to be tools in carrying out decisions made abroad, and have become more independent in planning the struggle program. The presence of those leaders in the heart of events has added to their authority and even occasionally led them to take instant decisions in the face of accelerating events. This has also increased appreciation for them on the part of their factions in the Occupied Territories and abroad.

Nonetheless, the nature of the leadership's ties with their factions abroad has not changed. The central command of each group—which for all but the locally directed Palestinian Communist party is abroad—remains the sole ultimate authority. And the commitment of the organizational leadership to the central decisions of their leaders abroad has remained as strong as ever.[15]

There is no possibility that the organizational leadership might become a local leadership as distinct from the PLO, or even parallel to it, given its strong factional commitment. On the contrary, developments have actually strengthened the links between the two sides.

On the other hand, the growing status of the organizational leaderships has led to changes in their hierarchical structures that are likely to have a significant effect in the future.[16] These changes are essentially due to the types of efforts made by the authorities to suppress the *intifada*. Israel has done its best to destroy structures and organizational networks, for example by outlawing the Shabiba movement and popular committees, and by closing down national institutions such as universities, trade unions, media centers, and societies, for long periods. Measures such as limiting the influx of funds and cutting phone links overseas for a year were designed to contribute to the same purpose, as were arrests and deportations. As a result of these last two measures, leaders have been temporarily or permanently lost, with some negative effects on performance, but with significant increased effectiveness and speed in the replacement of lost cadres. Automatic mechanisms were put in place to fill vacancies and preserve organizational structures. As a result, new elements have continuously risen from the bottom toward the top. These new elements are younger than the previous ones, closer to and more representative of the base.

Another more general attempt by the authorities to suppress the *intifada* is represented in collective punishments. The organizational leaderships are seriously affected by curfews and by certain areas being declared closed military zones. These measures have repeatedly interrupted communications with local leaderships. On the one hand, lack of communication reduced the degree of coordination and excluded local leaders from the decision-making process. But on the other hand, it boosted the status of these leaderships within their areas, for, given the necessity of self-reliance, they became the only authority on the local level.[17]

The rise of new elements within the organizational leadership of the national forces is bound to continue as long as the *intifada* goes on. As a result, internal change will continue to take place. A full analysis of this process of leadership formation is impossible until after stability once again prevails. One final point must be stressed in this regard. As a result of the clandestine nature of their operations, the power of the organizational leaderships will not necessarily be reflected in the personal status of the leaders concerned. Such individuals do not achieve personal notoriety until after national objectives have been achieved.

Contrary to the organizational leadership, many of the "public figures" did not view the *intifada* as a golden opportunity they had always sought. Rather, it was a new and strange situation threatening to undermine their political future. The activities of these figures are situated at the public relations level, and they flourished during a period when the masses were dormant. Moreover, the relationship between them and the people they were supposed to represent was never strong. They rarely addressed their own people or explained to them the results of their meetings with foreign dignitaries or Israeli leaders. In fact, the public figures never believed in local Palestinian capabilities, nor did they think that such a strong and continuous uprising would ever occur. This derives from their "realism" and the assessment that all important cards are in the hands of foreign powers. Hence their emphasis on opening dialogue with Americans, Europeans, and Israelis in the attempt to explain, persuade, and beg, hoping that in this way some positions might be modified and the conflict thus ultimately resolved. That is why they were justified in feeling apprehensive as to their political status and private interests when the *intifada* started. In the previous period these figures had contacts with some organizational leaders, especially those who supported the mainstream PLO leaders abroad. This meant that, when the *intifada* started, they lacked contacts with and support from the other organizations involved in the uprising, particularly the leftist forces of the UNLU.

Doubts prevailed among grass-roots national forces and in the general population regarding the right of these public figures to play a national role in the name of Palestinians, given in particular that they had no record of struggle and no ties to the masses. From the issuance of the first UNLU leaflet, it was stated by the organizational leaderships that "no voice rises above the voice of the *intifada*." This made it clear to the public figures that they faced a totally new challenge, and that they must submit to a reality that demanded certain efforts to adapt if they were to survive politically.

During the first months of the *intifada* things were difficult for the public figures. They could not of course claim to be leading the *intifada*, although some of them tried to.[18] The organizational leaderships of the national forces had invested their entire lives in the national struggle. They would never allow others to lead the *intifada*, especially after full coordination had begun within the UNLU. At the same time, the public figures were not in a position to bear the responsibility for leading the *intifada*, since that would subject them to the authorities' measures.[19] Furthermore, they lacked both the public support and the organizational means for leadership.

At the public relations level too, the public figures at first lost out. Prior to the *intifada*, foreign and Israeli media were virtually restricted to them. But with its outbreak, foreign journalists went out in search of the "real leaders" of the uprising all over the Occupied Territories. The base from which information was drawn widened, which resulted in breaking the monopoly previously held by these figures.

But despite this loss in status, it never looked as though the public figures were going to fade away, first of all because they were never the targets of the *intifada*, and second, because they felt that if they waited long enough, public protests would subside, giving them renewed leverage. In the meantime, they spoke out in favor of the *intifada* and even gave advice to national leaders.[20] Yet, at the same time, they used their channels of communication with the leaders of the PLO abroad to urge them to exploit the *intifada* politically and diplomatically. This shows the view held by these figures of the *intifada* and their opportunism. For them the uprising is nothing but a natural, mechanical, and random event, which will eventually end when the energy of the Palestinians under occupation is exhausted. It therefore in their eyes becomes necessary for the PLO to exploit this historic opportunity to break the political deadlock before the *intifada* ceases. Their expectation was that, once the *intifada* had begun yielding political results, they could return to the center of political and diplomatic activities.[21]

This is in fact what began to occur after several months, notably with Jordan's severance of legal and administrative ties to the Occupied Territories (July 29, 1988) and, especially, with the alleged seizure by the authorities of a Palestinian declaration of independence in the East Jerusalem offices of the Arab Studies Society. This document, by including some of their names among those proposed for inclusion in a future Palestinian parliament, guaranteed their status.[22] When their political positions became those of the PLO through the decisions adopted by the Nineteenth Algiers PNC, the public figures had regained their entire legitimacy.

As for the national independents, their status did not undergo drastic changes, in comparison with the public figures. Their position was not based on their being independents in a highly polarized context, but on their respectable positions in the traditional Palestinian social structure, since the *intifada* is not a revolution aimed at achieving social change. Their contribution to the *intifada*, since they are from the educated sector, was essentially in acting as a think tank and generating ideas that found their way to the UNLU. This process played a significant part in guiding decision making during the first months of the uprising.[23] But as the *intifada* moved toward the political stage, the independents gradually resumed their previous role, from which at any rate they had only partially deviated.

The Pro-Jordanian Figures

The *intifada* pulled the carpet out from under the pro-Jordanian figures. From the beginning it implied a shift in the relationship between the Occupied Territories and Jordan. In the past, Jordan sought a role for itself in any settlement by competing for influence with the PLO, particularly through its institutional ties with the West Bank. The pro-Jordanian figures had profited from that competition and used it as a power base.[24]

And in fact, with Jordan's cancellation in February 1986 of the February 1985 agreement with the PLO, the pro-Jordanian figures had enjoyed some of their best times since the beginning of the Israeli occupation. Jordan and its local representatives used various means at their disposal, but especially economic ones, in competing for influence with the PLO and assuring the success of the so-called Jordanian option for peace. In its attempt to "improve living conditions" in the Occupied Territories, Amman announced an increase in financial support, notably for employees on the Jordanian government payroll. In August 1986, Jordan announced the initiation of a new five-year development plan through which $3 billion would be invested in the Occupied Territories. For the implementation of this project, Jordan obtained the right to reopen the West Bank branches of the Cairo-Amman Bank, which had been closed since the beginning of the occupation. Specialized regional development committees were formed in the Occupied Territories. Financial aid was extended to city and villages councils, as well as for the establishment of the Jerusalem-based *An-Nahar* newspaper. This was a golden opportunity for pro-Jordanian figures to consolidate their status and broaden their influence. They seized it, with support from Israel, which had always sought a division of tasks between itself and Jordan. The pro-Jordanians were accorded broad freedoms in establishing institutions, obtaining finances, moving back and forth to Amman, and holding meetings.

Just as they were in the process of thus strengthening their status, the *intifada* broke out. Suddenly, and contrary to their every expectation since February 1986, their political future was under threat. From the beginning, the *intifada* carried the clear message that every attempt to neutralize the PLO was rejected.[25]

King Hussein's July 29, 1988, announcement, and the immediate implementation of the decision (cutting financial support, cancelling the Jordanian nationality of West Bankers, etc.) was a recognition that a totally new situation had been created. The severing of ties meant the end of the Jordanian option, and it neutralized pro-Jordanian figures in the Occupied Territories. These had no choice but to adapt to the situation, lightening its effect as much as possible. Some found refuge in their socioeconomic position, while others took refuge in some of the leftover institutions of the Jordanian development plan. Some decided that they had learned the lesson once and for all, and began to maneuver to secure a niche for themselves by trying to join the national caravan.

The Islamic Forces

The Islamic Jihad, as mentioned above, had had a significant effect in increasing mass preparedness in the period leading up to the uprising. It also contributed to mobilizing in the streets during the first weeks in Gaza. But as the *intifada* developed, Israel used all of the measures at its command to crush it. This came at a delicate time, for the organization had not yet accomplished the process of transforming itself from an elite into a mass organization. And due to its small size, the Islamic Jihad was unable to absorb the authorities' blows while continuing to play a major role in the uprising. The leadership that replaced imprisoned, killed, or expelled members seems to have decided to remain dormant while the organization rebuilds itself.

As for the traditional leaders, particularly those within the movement of the Muslim Brotherhood, they were at first embarrassed by the invalidation of their theses regarding the primacy of personal and religious over national considerations. The masses had spoken otherwise, and there was a distinct possibility that the Brotherhood's leaders faced a coup d'etat by disgruntled followers.

The outstanding role played by the Islamic Jihad and the void left by its disappearance, as well as the incessant probing of the international media, eager to highlight the role of religious forces in the *intifada,* offered the Muslim Brothers the chance to regain their lost influence. But the traditional leaders faced a significant threat from within their movement even as the movement itself regained some lost ground by participating in *intifada* activities as the Islamic Resistance Movement (Hamas). New leaders who had proved themselves in the streets challenged their positions.

On the one hand, the traditional leaders had to respond to the pressures from within and below, in order to maintain their influence during the *intifada*. But on the other hand, they did not want to commit themselves and the movement to a new official policy that would divert the movement from its traditional course in ways that could harm them if the new policies were displeasing to those that supported them financially.

The solution finally chosen represented a wise compromise. The traditional leaders attempted to obtain maximum advantage for both themselves and the movement. They officially and retroactively adopted Hamas, but in a way that maintains a certain tactical distance between Hamas and the movement. With the publication on August 18, 1988, of the Hamas covenant, it was asserted that "the Islamic Resistance Movement is one of the wings of the Muslim Brothers in Palestine." This formulation achieved a variety of objectives representing the new compromise within the Islamic movement.

First of all, by asserting that there was a relationship between Hamas and the Muslim Brothers, the traditional leaders were responding to internal and external questions regarding the role of the movement in the *intifada*. A new face was thus drawn before public opinion in the Occupied Territories and abroad. Clearly, in order to maintain their influence, the traditional leaders had to transform their negative image among Palestinians. And the covenant went so far as to take responsibility retroactively for starting the *intifada*.

Second, the declared connection between Hamas and the Muslim Brothers was an attempt by the traditional leaders to unite the two major groups within the movement. This was essential in order to calm down the internal unrest, which might have gone so far as to undermine their status. It was a declaration that the leaders of the movement were not defeatists, but that they were prepared to act after study and consultation. The movement's delay in resisting the occupation was due to the fact that it was preparing itself for confrontation. For after proceeding from the stage of "preaching" and "organizing," it had struck out against the enemy when the time was ripe.

Third, the relationship established between the Brotherhood and Hamas is one of connection rather than fusion, and this gives the movement and the traditional leaders room to maneuver. For this relationship may conceivably be cut or negated should conditions so dictate. It should be noted in this regard that Hamas, a "wing" of the Muslim Brothers, has a covenant, but that the mother organization itself does not. Thus the Muslim Brothers may adopt the covenant as long as it is convenient and drop it should this become advisable, since it is not binding on them. This ensures future flexibility.

Fourth, the traditional leaders, through their adoption of Hamas, aimed at continuing their competition with the PLO. They had never, since their emergence in the mid 1970s, recognized the PLO as the sole legitimate representative of the Palestinians. Their stated reason is that the PLO includes communist, Marxist, and generally atheist elements, and that it does not aim at establishing an Islamic state, the only one acceptable to the Islamic movement. In fact, the *intifada* showed once again the depth and breadth of support for the national movement and its leadership, the PLO, among the Palestinians under occupation. The covenant accordingly updates its critique. While declaring friendship and respect for the PLO, it portrays the Muslim Brotherhood as even more patriotic, unwilling to give up any part of Palestine under any conditions. Later communiqués by Hamas were even more explicit in rejecting the resolutions of the Nineteenth PNC, in particular the acceptance of the partition of Palestine and of UN Resolutions 242 and 338, as well as the idea of an international peace conference.

The compromise embodied in the Hamas covenant was generally beneficial to the Muslim Brothers. Elements previously leery of their passivity have now joined the movement, which has spread to various cities, villages, and refugee camps. And it appears that this has resulted in the crystallization of a central leadership for the movement in the Occupied Territories which, it will be remembered, did not exist before the *intifada*. As shown above, unity between new and traditional leaders has been strengthened. And now there is greater coordination between Gaza Strip and West Bank leaderships.

In general, it may be said that the Muslim Brothers have during the *intifada*, after initial setbacks, gone a long way toward achieving political legitimacy. But this was not done at the expense of the mass support of the PLO. While the Muslim Brothers widened their mass base, so too did the national forces. The outcome of the transformations to date in the balance of power among the various forces, taking into account the weakening of the pro-Jordanians and the strengthening of both the national and Islamic groups, continues greatly to favor the PLO, represented by its leadership and program as endorsed by the Nineteenth PNC, which still enjoys the support of the majority of the Palestinians in the Occupied Territories.

CONCLUSION

This chapter has attempted to establish a typology of the structures of the political elites in the Occupied Territories prior to the *intifada,* followed by an account of transformations that took place during its first year, including shifts within the component parts in relation to each other and to the society at large.

It has been seen that, while shifts have taken place, they are marginal in relation to the overall picture. The three main observations are that (1) the national forces, and particularly their organizational leaderships, maintain their predominance over all other Palestinian elites; (2) the relationship between the PLO on the inside and the PLO outside is stronger than ever; and (3) any attempt to foster an alternative leadership is therefore doomed to failure.

NOTES

1. Rabin fostered this view early in the *intifada.* See *al-Quds,* January 21, 1988, and January 6, 1988. Early in 1989 his approach had crystallized in his plan, which called for a solution to the conflict through direct negotiations with ''representatives from the territories.''

2. An example of such an analysis was given by Emile Sahliyeh, a North Texas State

University political scientist, in a lecture given at the Twenty-second Meeting of the Middle East Studies Association in November 1988.

3. From its third communiqué on, UNLU started to include "PLO" in its signature to clear up any doubts as to its close relation with the Palestinian leadership abroad.

4. A somewhat similar typology has been advanced by Ziad Abu-Amr in an article in which he explores the types of Palestinian personalities in the Occupied Territories. Ziad Abu-Amr, "Notes on Palestinian Political Leadership: The Personalities of the Occupied Territories," *Middle East Report*, no. 154 (September-October 1988), pp. 23–25.

5. The influence in the Occupied Territories of the movements based on the outside and forming the National Salvation Front is very limited.

6. Prisons are seen as having great influence in the political socialization of Palestinians. See Abd as-Sattar Qasim et al., *Introduction to the Prison Experience in Israeli Detention Centers* (Beirut: Dar al-Umma, 1986) (in Arabic).

7. The Communist party has its central leadership "inside."

8. On the activities of the mayors and the National Guidance Committee, refer to Ibrahim Dakkak, "Back to Square One: A Study in the Re-emergence of the Palestinian Identity in the West Bank, 1967–1980," in Alexander Schoelch, ed., *Palestinians over the Green Line: Studies on the Relations Between Palestinians on Both Sides of the 1949 Armistice Line Since 1967* (London: Ithaca Press, 1983), pp. 64–101; Emile Sahliyeh, *In Search of Leadership: West Bank Politics Since 1967* (Washington, D.C.: Brookings Institution, 1988), Chap. 4.

9. The concept is Emile Sahliyeh's. Cf. his article, "The West Bank Pragmatic Elite: The Uncertain Future," *Journal of Palestine Studies* 27, no. 4 (Summer 1986): 36–37.

10. Relations between PLO leaders outside and traditional figures inside are complex. See Ziad Abu-Amr and Ali Jarbawi, "The Struggle for West bank Leadership," *Middle East International*, no. 304 (July 1987): 16–18.

11. For a record of Palestinian-Israeli meetings inside and names of Palestinian participants, see Mahdi Abd-al-Hadi, *Notes on Palestinian-Israeli Discussions Inside the Occupied Territories* (Jerusalem: Palestinian Academic Association for International Affairs, 1987).

12. The Islamic Liberation party plays a minor role in the context of this study, so it will not be treated here.

13. Muhammad Shadid, "The Muslim Brotherhood Movement in the West Bank and Gaza," *Third World Quarterly* 10 (April 1988): 660.

14. This section is largely based on personal interviews with various people at different levels of the society.

15. The UNLU as a body does not have direct contact with the leadership abroad. Contact and coordination take place through factional channels of communication.

16. Likely changes will vary from faction to faction, depending on the size of the organization and how badly it is damaged by the occupation authorities.

17. The leaderships in the Gaza Strip and northern West Bank (Jenin, Tulkarem, Qalqilia, and to a lesser extent Nablus) are cases in point.

18. A clear example of this phenomenon occurred when Hanna Siniora returned from abroad, calling for the boycott of Israeli cigarettes.

19. A news conference was held by some public figures at the National Palace Hotel in East Jerusalem on January 14, 1988. After reading a prepared statement, including fourteen demands, they were reluctant to answer questions, either because they lacked

the necessary details or because they were fearful of exposing themselves to prosecution. At any rate, that press conference showed the public figures in the role of communicators rather than participants.

20. The public figures were committed to the position of the UNLU and the PLO and supported boycotting Secretary of State Shultz during his visits to Jerusalem. Shultz was not able to meet with them during any of his three visits in 1988, and was forced to talk to Palestinians in the Occupied Territories through Israeli television. There might be at least a partial correlation between Shultz's snub by the Palestinian public figures and his refusal to grant Yasser Arafat a visa to visit the United States in order to address the UN. The ploy at any rate backfired, because the UN General Assembly moved to Geneva to hear Arafat's speech.

21. Cf. Sari Nusseibeh, "Call for Discussions on the Stages of the Intifada and Its Perspectives," *al-Yom as-Sabe'* (Paris), August 1, 1988 (in Arabic).

22. The inclusion of about 150 names of prospective Palestinian parliament members from the Occupied Territories in the outline independence document caused some worry and discussion among Palestinians, many of whom felt that, from different points of view, it was not representative of the population of the Occupied Territories, and that it included a number of traditional figures whose role was considered to have ended with the *intifada*, while it did not include certain people of greater merit.

23. Lili Galili, "The Period of the Intellectuals," *Ha'aretz*, December 9, 1988 (translated in *al-Quds*, December 11, 1988).

24. Ali Jarbawi, "Severing the Ties Between Tactical Means and Strategic Ends," *al-Bayader as-Siasi* (Jerusalem), August 20, 1988, p. 313 (in Arabic).

25. Cf. UNLU Communiqués No. 2, 4, 5, 8, 9, 10, 11 (the last two of which insisted that West Bank members of the Jordanian parliament should resign), and 17.

V

CONCLUSION

19

The Future in Light of the Past

Jamal R. Nassar and Roger Heacock

THE INTENSITY OF PALESTINIAN HISTORY

The contemporary history of Palestine amply disproves mechanistic and purely *chronological* explanations of the march of time, and illustrates the utility of Bergsonian and Proustian visions of successive expanding and contracting historical phases. The fate of the Palestinian people from 1948 to 1967 was subjectively experienced by them as a barren millennial trek characterized by dispossession, dispersion, alienation, and despair. With the formation of a Palestinian organization twenty years later, a period of rapid consolidation ensued, and the pace of events began to pick up, framed by the PLO in exile and its allies and followers under occupation in their daily struggle against the panoply of measures brought to bear (see Chapters 2 through 5 and Chapter 13). On December 9, 1987, in and from the Israeli-occupied lands history's breath blew with the force of a gale, and it moved forward with the speed and intensity of sheer human energy harnessed to the task of national and social liberation (see Chapters 6 and 7). The intensity of this history presently in the making has few models in modern times (see Chapter 1). One of them is the five-year period in revolutionary France from July 1789 to July 1794, which brought down a 1,000-year-old regime, created the premises for modern Europe, and launched the major ideologies of our age. Interestingly enough, that revolution occurred just 200 years ago, and there are many heady parallels between the two processes with, despite its far more microcosmic nature, an even greater compression and acceleration of events in the present case. The people of France deposed their king and overthrew their ancient monarchy within three years of the storming of the Bastille. King Hussein of Jordan, more intelligent and determined by far than the weak Louis XIV, abdicated as king of the Palestinians on July 29, 1988, only seven and a half months after the outbreak of the *intifada*. This acceleration of events, this compression of time, opens up numerous opportunities, but carries with it countless dangers, since the increased number of decisions to be made means increased possibilities for miscalculation. Indeed, the various protagonists seem conscious of that aspect, although they are for the most part carried along by the swirl of events.

THE TRANSFORMATION OF THE INTERNATIONAL BALANCE

The Palestine question has always been an international issue, dating back to its formulation by imperial/colonial Great Britain in 1917 in the form of the Balfour declaration, through the League of Nations mandate, the UN partition resolution, and numerous UN Security Council and General Assembly resolutions down to the present. The call for an international conference is therefore fully in keeping with the historic treatment of the problem. What is new in the period after December 1987 is the configuration regarding the question. The international community in all of its components has become conscious of the urgency of a solution to the problem. The majority that clamors for the realization of Palestinian rights and a just settlement to the Palestine problem is no longer restricted to progressive, socialist, and nonaligned regimes (see Chapters 15 and 16). It has expanded to include the peoples of the Third World, Western Europe, and North America. Arrayed against them are the governments of the United States and Israel, and a limited but influential portion of the elites, opinion makers, and decision makers in the West. This is a powerful grouping, but a trend has set in and there is every reason to believe that in the medium-term it will prevail in favor of a just solution. This is rendered even more probable by the emerging tri-polarization of Israeli political life (see Chapter 17). If the new center in Israel around Yitzhak Shamir and Yitzhak Rabin fails to implement its Camp David–style program, the new right may then be given its chance. It consists of the Likud right represented by Ariel Sharon and parties to its right. Things will then become much harder for the Palestinians under occupation, since this group advocates harsher measures against the *intifada*. We know from the previous record of Sharon as a military man and defense minister what that means: mass killings, destruction of entire quarters in villages and refugee camps, and implementation of as much of the "transfer" program as the international community is prepared to tolerate. But this program is doomed to failure, because it means war in the Middle East at a time when the Arab states likely to be involved have the means to do significant damage to Israel; and because the example of the Shah of Iran faced with a popular insurrection indicates that the massacre of demonstrating, unarmed civilians only adds oil to the flames. It is likely, therefore, that either because the Israeli leadership will have reached that conclusion without going through the practical stages of its implementation, or after having experimented with hard-line solutions (and this would claim a tragic toll in human suffering at least for the Palestinians, and more likely for all the peoples of the region), it will turn to the third major pole represented by the peace forces. These go from the left of the Labor party to the far left of the political spectrum (and it would seem that the liberal opportunists around Shimon Peres are prepared to join them if there is a clear sign they can come to power). This camp has now come to include all Zionist and non-Zionist elements committed to a genuine program of peace through reconciliation, and enjoys the support of its main potential interlocutor, the PLO. This is a historic turning point, fraught with hope and danger. For the first time, a major sector of the Israeli political elites has come forward with a plan resembling that offered by the other side. Thus, there is hope, because the scenario can be sketched whereby the plan could be politically implemented; and danger, because those irreducibly opposed to it also represent a significant power bloc and might prefer suicidal moves to the consequences of relinqishing power to the peace bloc.

This is, however, where the new international configuration is capable of and likely to play a restraining role. For the forces arrayed against the annexationist right in Israel include the popular conscience—the peoples—of most of the world, including significant sectors in the USSR, Eastern Europe, and the West, which have the moral and material means of imposing limits.

THE NEW SOCIAL BALANCE IN THE OCCUPIED TERRITORIES

The *intifada* has achieved a form of social revolution best defined, in both its depth and its limits, as a revolution of wills. The generational equation has been upset: the young are now in command, the elders are in positions of support; social gaps were for a time closed (see Chapter 10). There was, however, in the first stages of the *intifada*, no transformation in underlying social relations, much less in relations of production. This was to be seen in the continued operation of traditional patterns where women and family life were concerned (see Chapter 8) and in resumed social and class conflict after a few months within various units of production (see Chapter 9). The national struggle, in other words, is giving rise to some of the prerequisites of revolutionary social transformation. At the same time (see Chapter 12) a revolution has taken place. It is a revolution of wills: it has been unanimously determined by the Palestinian people that the *intifada* will continue until its basic objectives (the clear perspective of self-determination) have been realized. And it is at the same time a political revolution, involving the relationship between the masses (that is to say, the people), the political cadres (organizational activists), and the national leadership. All three of these elements have been strengthened their contribution to the uprising (see Chapter 18). But the question remains: What is the emerging relationship between these three components? Depending on whom one asks, one gets a different answer. Some see the leadership as the element responsible for the continuation of the struggle, given the great fatigue evident among the masses. Others tend to emphasize the indispensable role of the intermediate cadre, who keep the popular committees in operation, and who keep the ship afloat through thick and thin. What is certain is that there is competition for influence among various elements, and notably among various levels of political leadership. But the key to the uprising, both its outbreak and its unremittent continuation, is in fact the masses. They rose up without waiting for orders, and they continue to act, as small or large crowds, as producers and consumers, in the same determined way. They too are in a sense competing for influence. They are imposing limits on their leaders in the areas of factional and religious strife. They have demanded and obtained unity in the field. They have marginalized and foiled every attempt to split the ranks of the *intifada*. And they (since nobody else could conceivably do it for them) have decided never to surrender to the counterpressures of the occupiers.

THE ECONOMIC TRANSFORMATION OF THE OCCUPIED TERRITORIES

While not constituting a revolution as theoretically defined by the social sciences, the mutation of various economic indicators in the Occupied Territories in the course of only the first eighteen months of the *intifada* has been dramatic, with indications that the trend will continue and ultimately constitute the essential material basis for national independence from Israel. Several preliminary studies, based on surveys in various areas of the West Bank (areas as different as Jericho in the Jordan Valley and Jerusalem-area villages), indicate that per capita consumption over a twelve-to-fifteen-month period decreased by 40 to 53 percent. Various factors account for that decline, including financial restrictions placed on the people by the occupation, direct measures in the form of taxes, crop destruction, banning of exports and production, reduced work over the Green Line, and voluntary retrenchment. The Israeli defense minister, Yitzhak Rabin, has often made it clear that his government considers economic pressures of that sort as one of the most effective anti-*intifada* measures, presumably because the amount of suffering inflicted is likely to dampen mass enthusiasm for the revolt. In fact, from the Israeli point of view, the decline in per capita consumption has been counterproductive in that it has, along with restrictions on governmental budgets for health and agriculture, and the government closure of schools, including schools under its control, promoted the independence and separation of the Occupied Territories from Israel, and the people's self-reliance.

In this regard, data concerning local production versus imports from Israel are telling. According to Palestinians responsible for implementing the *intifada*'s program of achieving independence in the agricultural field, the following evolution took place from December 1987 to April 1989: cattle production has risen from 14,000 to 27,000 head; the reliance on locally produced eggs has risen from 60 percent to 75 percent; the import of Israeli milk has dropped from 65 percent of total consumption to 20 percent. Animal feed, of which 95 percent was imported, is 60 percent locally produced; and, most importantly, the area of the West Bank under Palestinian cultivation as gone from 1 million to 1.3 million dunums (the situation in land-poor and heavily populated Gaza is different, but the political and economic processes in the two areas are organically linked). To reinforce the dramatic implications of these figures, it appears that 70 percent of the increased agricultural production has been the result of home economy programs by small producers. In industry, the rise in local versus imported Israeli goods has also been impressive, but with less far-reaching implications, because of the limitations imposed on Palestinian industrial production. Soft drinks, cigarettes, and toilet paper are not in themselves revolutionary local achievements. Clearly, industrial development will have to await independence.

Reduced consumption combined with increased self-reliance, as well as clear indications that these trends can be projected into the future: in phantom outline, Palestinian independence is being shaped by producers and consumers alike.

THE QUESTION OF DEMOCRACY

Unlike various other societies involved in revolutionary turmoil, the Palestinians have not put off the question of democracy until some putative future date. It is under consideration in their political organization, the PLO, which gave an example of liberal democratic principles at the Nineteenth PNC when the passage of resolutions was accepted even by those in the minority which had voted against them. However, the question of the type of democracy being sought is still undecided. There is unanimity, outside and inside, *against* the Israeli and U.S. refusal to permit the Palestinians to exercise their right to self-determination on their national soil. But what *positive* form is the decision-making process going to assume after independence? This unanswered question is what the Islamic political forces consider to be their chance for the future (see Chapter 11). But it is clear to those who know the society, in all of its regions, that their hopes are vain. Palestine is not Iran, and the idea of theocracy is rejected by the masses. It has no chance of success. The question then is, What does the future hold in store? It is difficult to imagine that those same masses that surged out of the refugee camps, the villages, and the poor sections of the cities to challenge the occupation will permit a new Palestinian elite, enthroned by the traditional society and the political leadership, to fill the vacuum by itself. Neither the people as a whole, nor in their organized form, the popular committees, whose role continues to be priceless, will ever resign themselves to such a situation. They want a share in the political process and its benefits, and are poised to move to get it. The leadership, both inside and outside, understands this and appears prepared to work on finding the appropriate formula. This is not and will not be an easy task, but rather a great challenge. The competition between the base, the cadre, and the leadership levels, mentioned above, dynamically blends in with this emerging search for the appropriate formula for Palestinian democracy.

OF HISTORICAL OPTIMISM

The *intifada* has shown to those who were inclined to theoretical "realism" and pessimism, translated into practical defeatism, just how wrong they were. By revealing once again the enormous power of the masses when they are armed with courage and determination, it has reinforced the views of those who proclaim historical optimism, those, that is to say, who look to the future as being, if only men and women so will it, better than the past. This message has indeed not been lost on other peoples of the world, from Armenia to Burma to Algeria. Peoples long dormant, struck by the vividness of the image and message of a people unarmed, faced by a hyper-militarized authority and willing and able to confront it, took note and took action, although sometimes with insufficient reflection on relevant local conditions. "Realistic" or "pessimistic" assessments previously dominated historical and political analyses of the Palestinian problem. This is no longer and can never again be the case, no matter what the outcome of the process now under way. This empirically justified historical optimism must be strongly tempered with the objective analysis of conditions on the ground if it is not to lead to disappointment at best, and serious errors at worst. An objective appraisal of the future indicates that it is likely to be a difficult one, as has in so many instances been the case for those peoples and regions having to deal with the painful task of decolonization in the period after World War II. A price has been and will continue to be paid for the shortsightedness and follies of those who peremptorily reshaped the map of the world upon the breakup of European hegemony.

Here again, however, optimism is permitted, based on the impossible history of the *intifada* itself, and based on the length and depth of the Palestinian struggle, with its reflections in ongoing political and moral consciousness. In this way too, the present case is so different from that French model 200 years ago, where a revolutionary movement came from nowhere to seize the reigns of history overnight, without the benefit of decades of reflection and action that occurred here. This drawback of the French Revolution is perhaps found in other revolutionary contexts, including those of other Third World societies, and lends hope that some of the suffering that accompanies liberation and decolonization will be spared the Palestinian people and all those in Israel and the Middle East next to whom they will continue to live.

In this respect, the sufferings endured by the peoples embroiled in the Palestine problem should help in avoiding the worst traps the future will set, for these accumulated sufferings may have paved the way for greater wisdom. All of the peoples of the Mediterranean basin have over the past century and a half realized the goal of national self-determination, with the exception of the Lebanese (fettered from the day of their independence from France by institutionalized sectarianism) and Palestinian peoples. All of the others obtained the chance of independence from the 1820s to the 1950s. The turn of the Palestinians has now come, and the lessons of modern and contemporary history, coupled with the surprise of the *intifada*, show that they must achieve their goal. It is a matter of historical necessity, but also of the mutual interests of all of the states and peoples of the world. The children who have scattered stones all over the roads and alleys of Palestine will some day rebuild the thousand-year-old walls they demolished, in peace and concert with their neighbors.

Appendix
CHRONOLOGY OF THE UPRISING

Facts Information Committee

DECEMBER 1987

Totals: 29 martyrs, 288 demonstrations, 36 curfew days

The uprising was "spontaneous" inasmuch as it had not been planned to begin on a particular day. The initial task was to consolidate the organization of demonstrations, so that protest could continue in spite of 2,000 arrests during the month. On December 18, nine days after the start, the first uprising communiqué was released in the Gaza Strip, signed by "the National Forces in the Gaza Strip." A further three communiqués were subsequently released in Gaza, outlining the main strategic objectives and tactics of the uprising. They were widely distributed in the West Bank as well as Gaza and were influential in establishing the idea of the uprising in the minds of the people. They called for popular organization and adopted the slogan of self-determination and an independent Palestinian state as the movement's demand. One of the first Gaza communiqués predicted that "this movement will end by isolating Israel and will force Israel's friends to condemn it."

Commercial strikes and general strikes (including a boycott of work in Israel) were also initiated in this month in the West Bank. Commercial strikes had been a frequent form of protest in the past; however, the sustaining of a complete general strike had previously been unusual.

During the month massive demonstrations spread across the whole of the West Bank and Gaza, meeting the previously established Israeli response: live ammunition, tear gas, and mass arrests.

The demonstrations received widespread media coverage, and Israel was criticized by the international community for its use of live ammunition. The Israeli Defense Forces were accused of not being properly prepared for riot control.

JANUARY 1988

Totals: 28 martyrs, 563 demonstrations, 112 curfew days.

The first communiqué of the Unified National Leadership of the Uprising (UNLU) was distributed during this month. The first few communiqués were less influential than subsequent ones as they were not actually agreed upon locally by the four major factions of the PLO. The first few communiqués were produced by individual factions or through the collaboration of one or two, and it was only by Communiqué No. 10 that the first genuinely "unified" communiqué was produced (i.e., supported by all four groups). This initial lack of unity was reflected in the timing of the release of the first few communiqués, which were as follows: (1) January 8; (2) January 10; (3) January 18; (4) January 21. The first few communiqués delineated strike days and encouraged the rebellion; in contrast with later communiqués, they contained relatively little political discussion. At times more than one communiqué with the same number was released by different factions, and the Israeli secret police soon began printing their own versions as well.

The importance of forming popular committees began to be emphasized during this month, initially for guarding, food distribution, and the organization of emergency health care. At first they were composed of active youths at the heart of the uprising. Although many of these youths were politically affiliated, the popular committees were organized along geographical rather than factional lines. Their ranks were quickly swollen as people from all walks of life—not just the young—joined the movement. The committees were from the outset democratic in nature and open to the participation of all. Many of the important tactics of the uprising were initiated by these committees and were later adopted by the regional and then the national leadership.

The Voice of Jerusalem radio station (Lebanon/Syria) initially gave a boost to morale by providing music and regular updates on the uprising. Later the station began to broadcast political polemics, which were less popular. Finally the station was successfully jammed by Israel.

During January the number and scale of demonstrations escalated. Israel introduced the "beatings" policy, which led to thousands of brutal beatings with wooden batons, many vividly televised. A policy of enforcing extended twenty-four-hour curfews was also announced, often lasting for several weeks. Food convoys into UNRWA camps under curfew were denied entry by the IDF.

FEBRUARY 1988

Totals: 48 martyrs, 703 demonstrations, 264 curfew days.

The Nablus popular committees announced that shops would open for only three hours per day, and this tactic was subsequently endorsed by the UNLU. The army tried to prevent this by breaking open shops and beating and arresting shopkeepers.

The UNLU announced that the forthcoming visit by Shultz should be boycotted, as he should only negotiate with the PLO. When Shultz visited at the end of the month, he gave a press conference alone in East Jerusalem, as all Palestinians had refused to meet him.

Resignation of appointed councilors and repentance of collaborators began during this month.

The Israelis closed all schools and universities in the West Bank (including East

Jerusalem) until further notice, reduced the amount of money permitted to be brought across the bridge, and began to increase their tax collection efforts.

Israeli violence, including the live burial of young men in Salem, continued to receive international publicity.

The number and scale of demonstrations continued to escalate during the month, as did the number of martyrs.

MARCH 1988

Totals: 57 martyrs, 549 demonstrations, 206 curfew days

In March the demonstrations continued, while the functions of popular committees began to diversify into, for example, agriculture and education. Mass resignations from the police, tax, and car licensing departments were seen as important gains for the uprising, while the failure of the EEC to ratify trade protocols with Israel in protest against Israeli repression was a boost to morale, and cost Israel substantial revenue.

Israel added several new sanctions to the now long list of measures being used against the Palestinians: a night curfew was declared in the whole Gaza Strip until further notice; the entry of Gaza residents into the West Bank or West Bankers into Gaza was banned; international phone lines were cut off from the Occupied Territories; bans on the export of crops from active villages were initiated; the Shabibch youth movement was declared an illegal organization to speed up mass arrests; the right of judicial appeal for administrative detainees was withdrawn; and procedures for ordering administrative detention (without trial) were eased.

The climax of the month came on Land Day on March 30, when the Occupied Territories were declared military areas for three days. In spite of a huge military presence, massive demonstrations continued.

APRIL 1988

Totals: 61 martyrs, 416 demonstrations, 299 curfew days

This month saw the expansion of agricultural activities, with almost every available piece of land being sown to maximize local production. The existing forms of protest—commercial and general strikes and demonstrations—continued, while the army began to enter villages that had been "liberated" zones for some months, with liberal use of live ammunition. The highest number of martyrs, sixty-one, was recorded this month. Shultz visited the area again in April and was again boycotted by the Palestinians.

Israel maintained its previous range of oppressive measures, adding new restrictions on the media by banning the distribution of press releases without permission. The introduction of new IDs in Gaza provided a way of forcing residents to pay outstanding taxes and bills.

The Beita incident, in which settlers clashed with villagers, received much publicity. A settler teenager was killed by a stray bullet fired by another settler; however, the IDF still demolished fourteen houses in the village and issued six deportation orders for Beita residents.

The assassination of Abu Jihad in Tunis sparked off massive demonstrations, and the Occupied Territories were declared a closed military zone for three days.

MAY 1988

Totals: 25 martyrs, 359 demonstrations, 166 curfew days

In May, perhaps in response to the growth of popular education committees, the civil administration announced that it would begin to reopen schools, which had been closed since February. Within a month, however, most of the schools had been closed again.

The conflict between shopkeepers and the army continued during this month. Orders were issued by the army that shops could open only in the afternoon, rather than in the morning as proposed by the UNLU.

The campaign in Gaza to force residents to accept the new ID cards was stepped up. Press censorship increased, as newspapers were forbidden to publish the contents of the UNLU communiqués, and four East Jerusalem editors were placed under administrative detention without trial.

JUNE 1988

Totals: 17 martyrs, 474 demonstrations, 276 curfew days

This month the Arab Summit called for by the Unified Leadership was held. The summit gave verbal support to the uprising and the PLO. That it was convened at all was considered an achievement for the uprising.

By June the army had given up trying to stop the shopkeepers' strikes, and shops were able to open for three hours a day without interference.

During this month there was a heat wave and a spate of fires in Israel that were blamed on the Palestinians. Over the same period soldiers and settlers set fire to large areas of agricultural land in the West Bank, although this received little attention.

Israel issued a new regulation for children under sixteen years of age who were arrested: their parents had to pay 3,000 U.S. dollars for their release, which would be forfeited if they were arrested again. The practice of impounding the cars of those who had not paid their taxes was stepped up.

JULY 1988

Totals: 26 martyrs, 547 demonstrations, 219 curfew days

The beginning of July saw the release and discussion of the Abu Sharif document, which called for negotiations toward a two-state solution to the Palestinian issue in clearer terms than had previously been stated by the PLO. The development received a warm welcome from the majority in the Occupied Territories and was supported by the main East Jerusalem newspapers and by a wide range of local personalities.

In July the IDF once again closed all the schools in the West Bank, this time until the new academic year on October 1.

New regulations were also declared, requiring that all Palestinians who were wounded must pay 150 U.S. dollars before receiving treatment, and any referrals required civil administration approval.

The climax of the month came when King Hussein of Jordan announced his "cutting of the legal and administrative ties with the West Bank" and his "willingness to step aside for the PLO." This move was widely welcomed in the Occupied Territories and signaled the end of the "autonomy" plans of the U.S. and Israeli administrations. King

Hussein's withdrawal was widely seen as an achievement of the uprising. The UNLU has repeatedly expressed direct criticism of the Jordanian role in the Occupied Territories.

AUGUST 1988

Totals: 39 martyrs, 379 demonstrations, 246 curfew days

August saw Israel attempt to respond to the "gap" left by Jordan's disengagement, with declarations that the PLO would not be allowed to take the place of Jordan. Popular committees were declared illegal, and a range of Palestinian institutions was closed down, including the Union of Charitable Societies and the Professional Associations Complex. Mass arrests continued, with the accusation of membership on a popular committee now being enough to warrant six months in the Negev prison camp. Attention was focused on the Negev camp when guards shot and killed two prisoners.

In reality the idea of "filling the gap" left by Jordan was something of a misnomer: the PLO already had the support of the mass of the people, and the popular committees already represented a legitimate alternative to the civil administration.

Meanwhile, active debates were held over the idea of a declaration of Palestinian independence, a government-in-exile, and the adoption of a new political program at the forthcoming PNC.

SEPTEMBER 1988

Totals: 21 martyrs, 326 demonstrations, 228 curfew days

The introduction of a new sharp plastic bullet into the arsenal of the IDF drew strong international condemnation during the month. Rabin defended the policy by stating that his intention was to increase the number of injuries.

Within the national movement discussions were continuing in preparation for the forthcoming PNC.

The Israelis, apparently in order to be seen to be doing something in the run up to the elections, began (yet another) well-publicized policy of mass arrests during the extended curfews.

OCTOBER 1988

Totals: 26 martyrs, 314 demonstrations, 222 curfew days

October was the month before the Israeli and U.S. elections, and the Palestine National Council. With media attention focusing on the Israeli election, the Israeli Labor party sought to project the image of the party of peace, despite the fact that Hussein had publicly distanced himself from the Peres "peace plan." Toward the end of the month Hussein publicly declared his support for Peres, but did not retract his disengagement from the West Bank.

The Palestinians were more concerned with their own National Council, and the UNLU indicated its support for a new political program in a series of communiqués. For example, Communique No. 27 stated, "We are confident that our national council will pursue an agenda and adopt steps capable of translating the slogans of the uprising into further international support for our inalienable rights." Communiqué No. 28 stated, "We are confident that [the PNC] resolutions will be a breakthrough [in] the diplomatic and political arenas.''

This month saw a new Israeli tactic: villages were warned that if there were demonstrations they would be prevented from harvesting or selling their oil, and curfews preventing harvest were imposed in several areas. Tight restrictions were also placed on the export of olive oil, causing a drop in price.

NOVEMBER 1988

Totals: 13 martyrs, 361 demonstrations, 296 curfew days

The Algiers Palestine National Council dominated the month, with the adoption of a new political program and the declaration of the independent state of Palestine. Both were welcomed with celebrations in the West Bank and Gaza, and were considered to be a new step forward for the uprising.

The new political program was followed by a surge of international support for the PLO, particularly after Shultz refused a visa for PLO Chairman Arafat to address the UN General Assembly in New York.

These events sustained high morale in the West Bank and Gaza and were considered as indications that the uprising was reaping its political harvest. At the end of the month sixty countries had recognized the new state.

DECEMBER 1988

Totals: 31 martyrs, 385 demonstrations, 219 curfew days

December saw continuing momentum in the international political arena in the lead up to Arafat's speech to the UN on December 13. As the anniversary of the uprising approached, the predictions of the Gaza communiqué from last December now seemed prophetic: ''This movement will end by isolating Israel, and will force Israel's friends to condemn it.''

Following Arafat's speech to the UN, in which he reiterated the principles of the new Palestinian peace plan, the United States announced its intention to open a diplomatic dialogue with the PLO. This event sent shock waves through the Israeli political establishment, which found itself in a diplomatic corner with no credible peace plan of its own.

DECEMBER 9, 1987-DECEMBER 9, 1988

Totals: 396 martyrs, 5,385 demonstrations, 2,643 curfew days

JANUARY 1989

Totals: 29 martyrs, 390 demonstrations, 207 curfew days

January saw the deepening of political debate within Israel as a whole concerning an appropriate political response to the U.S. dialogue with the PLO. Defense Minister Rabin first promoted the idea of some kind of municipal elections in the Occupied Territories, but within the context of an autonomy arrangement of some kind. The Palestinians rejected the plan and reiterated their demand for an independent state. By the end of the month new political tendencies were emerging within Israel in support of dialogue with the PLO and in support of a Palestinian state, including elements within the Israeli Labor party.

FEBRUARY 1989

Totals: 19 martyrs, 319 demonstrations, 153 curfew days

In February, debate within Israel continued concerning a new political program for the country. Leading Labor party figures began publicly to call for negotiations with the PLO. Shamir, however, rejected such calls.

MARCH 1989

Totals: 30 martyrs, 408 demonstrations, 326 curfew days

March saw efforts by the Israeli government to persuade the United States to break off diplomatic relations with the PLO after DFLP commandos were killed apparently trying to infiltrate the Israeli-occupied Lebanese "security zone." The United States elected to continue its discussions with the PLO. Two events in early March were of importance on the Israeli political front. First, on March 4 Peace Now was prevented by the IDF from holding a series of peaceful demonstrations with Palestinians in the Occupied Territories. The event received much publicity and stimulated debate. Members of the Israeli peace movement claimed that the IDF ban showed that there was no real freedom in the West Bank and Gaza, except for settlers. Peace Now claimed that its membership had grown dramatically over the past few months.

The second event was the release of the report of the Jaffee Center for Strategic Studies, an institute that normally reflects mainstream Labor party thinking. The report suggested that an independent Palestinian state should be considered as a possible outcome of a Middle East peace settlement. This reflected an important change in thinking within the Israeli Labor party.

Toward the end of March there was a political controversy in Israel after Amnon Shahak, head of Israeli Military Intelligence, informed the Knesset Foreign Affairs Committee that there is no alternative leadership to the PLO; that Jordan will not take a leading diplomatic role in the Palestinian issue; that the two-state solution represents a real policy change for the PLO and is not just a maneuver; and that the uprising can only be stopped by a major diplomatic achievement for the Palestinians.

Over the past three months the uprising had sustained its intensity despite the imposition of new and brutal measures by the authorities. The regular general strikes continued, and the general mood was optimistic that, by continuing the uprising, the Palestinians would finally win their goal of an independent state. The state of flux on the Israeli side was seen as a hopeful sign.

Selected Bibliography

Abed, George T. *The Palestinian Economy: Studies in Development Under Prolonged Occupation*. London: Routledge Champan & Hall, 1989.

Abu-Amr, Ziad. "The Palestinian Uprising in the West Bank and Gaza Strip." *Arab Studies Quarterly* 10, no. 4 (Fall 1988).

Amnesty International. *Report 1988*. London: Amnesty International Publications, 1988.

"The Arab-Israeli Conflict—Are These the Solutions?" *Judaism: A Quarterly Journal* 37 (Fall 1988). Special issue.

Aronson, Geoffrey. *Israel, Palestinians and the Intifada: Creating Facts on the West Bank*. London: Routledge Champan & Hall, 1989.

Ashrawi, Hanan Mikhail. *Contemporary Palestinian Literature Under Occupation*. Bir Zeit: Bir Zeit University Publications, 1988.

Bassiouni, M. Cherif, and Louise Cainkar, eds. *The Palestinian Intifada—December 9, 1987-December 8, 1988: A Record of Israeli Repression*. Chicago: Data Base Project on Palestinian Human Rights, 1989.

Baxendale, Sidney J. "Taxation of Income in Israel and the West Bank: A Comprehensive Study." *Journal of Palestine Studies* xviii, no. 3 (Spring 1989).

Beinin, Joel. "Israel at Forty: The Political Economy/Political Culture of Constant Conflict." *Arab Studies Quarterly* 10, no. 4 (Fall 1988).

Benvenisti, Meron. *The West Bank and Gaza Atlas*. Jerusalem: Jerusalem Post Books, 1988.

Boyle, Francis A. "Create the State of Palestine!" *American-Arab Affairs* 25 (Summer 1988).

Cohen, Erik. "A Pilgrimage to Beita." *Jerusalem Quarterly* 49 (Winter 1989).

Farsoun, Samih K. "The Roots of the Intifadah." *The Return* 1, no. 2 (September 1988).

al-Haq: Law in the Service of Man. *Punishing a Nation: Human Rights Violations During the Palestianian Uprising, December 1987-December 1988*. Ramallah: al-Haq, 1988.

Hertzberg, Arthur. "The Illusion of Jewish Unity." *New York Review of Books*, June 16, 1988.

Hiltermann, Joost. "Before the Uprising: The Organization and Mobilization of Palestinian Workers and Women in the Israeli-Occupied West Bank and Gaza Strip." Ph.D. dissertation, University of California at Santa Cruz, June 1988.

Jerusalem Media and Communications Center. *The Siege of Agriculture: Examples of Israeli Sanctions Against Agriculture in the Occupied Territories During the Palestinian Uprising*. Jerusalem: Jerusalem Media and Communication Center, 1988.

Khalidi, Rashid I. "The Uprising and the Palestine Question." *World Policy Journal* 5, no. 3 (Summer 1988).

Krogh, Peter F., and Mary C. McDavid, eds. *Palestinians Under Occupation: Prospects for the Future*. Washington, D.C.: Center for Contemporary Arab Studies, 1989.

Kuttab, Jonathan. "The Children's Revolt." *Journal of Palestine Studies* 17, no. 4 (Summer 1988).

Lesch, Ann M. "Uprising for Palestine: Editorial Commentary." *Journal of South Asian and Middle Eastern Studies* 11, no. 4 (Summer 1988).

Maksoud, Clovis. "The Implications of the Palestinian Uprising—Where from Here?" *American-Arab Affairs*, Fall 1988.

Middle East Report. Special issue, May-June 1988.

Mitchison, Amanda. "Palestine: How Does Your Garden Grow." *New Statesman and Society*, June 21, 1988.

Musallam, S. "Europe and Peace in the Middle East." *Journal of Palestine Studies* vol. 17, no. 2 (Winter 1988).

Nassar, Jamal R. "The Message of the Intifada." *Middle East International*, February 17, 1989.

National Lawyers Guild. *International Human Rights Law and Israel's Efforts to Suppress the Palestinian Uprising*. Washington, D.C.: National Lawyers Guild, 1989.

Palestine Human Rights Information Center. *Human Rights Violations Under Israeli Rule During the Uprising, December 9, 1987-October 9, 1988*. Jerusalem: Data Base Project on Palestinian Human Rights, 1988.

Physicians for Human Rights. *The Casualties of Conflict: Medical Care and Human Rights in the West Bank and Gaza Strip*. Report of a Fact-Finding Mission. Somerville, Mass.: Physicians for Human Rights, 1988.

Pressburg, Gail. "The Uprising: Causes and Consequences." *Journal of Palestine Studies* 17, no. 3 (Spring 1988).

Roy, Sara. "The Gaza Strip: Critical Effects of the Occupation." *Arab Studies Quarterly* 10, no. 1 (Winter 1988).

Sabella, Bernard. "Why the Intifada?" *The Return* 1, no. 5 (December 1988).

Sahliyeh, Emile. *In Search of Leadership: West Bank Politics Since 1967*. Washington, D.C.: Brookings Institution, 1988.

Segal, Jerome M. *Creating the Palestinian State*. Chicago: Independent Publishers Group, 1989.

———. "A Foreign Policy for the State of Palestine." *Journal of Palestine Studies* 18, no. 2 (winter 1989).

————. "The Meaning of the PNC in Algiers." *Tikkun* 4, no. 1 (January-February 1989).

Shadid, Mohammad. "The Muslim Brotherhood Movement in the West Bank and Gaza." *Third World Quarterly* 10, no. 2 (April 1988).

Shehadeh, Raja. "Occupier's Law and the Uprising." *Journal of Palestine Studies* 17, no. 3 (Spring 1988).

Stanley, Bruce. "Raising the Flag over Jerusalem: The Search for a Palestinian Government." *American-Arab Affairs*, Fall 1988.

Steinberg, Gerald. "The 1988 Israeli Elections: The Deadlock Continues." *Midstream*, January 1988.

Tamari, Salim. "What the Uprising Means." *Middle East Report*, no. 152 (May-June 1988).

Umar, Yosuf, and Rex Brynen. "The Revolution Called Intifada." *International Perspectives*, September-October 1988.

Union of Palestinian Medical Relief Committees. *The Uprising: Consequences for Health*. Jerusalem: Union of Palestinian Medical Relief Committees, August 1988.

United States. Department of State. *Country Reports on Human Rights Practices for 1988*. Washington, D.C.: U.S. Government Printing Office, 1989.

Wahdan, Amal. "Living the Intifada Day by Day." *Race and Class* 30, no. 3 (January-March 1989).

Index

About the Contributors

IBRAHIM ABU-LUGHOD is Professor of Political Science at Northwestern University and a member of the Palestine National Council. His many publications include *The Transformation of Palestine* (1987), *Palestinian Rights: Affirmation and Denial* (1982), and *Profile of the Palestinian People* (1987). He is currently working on the issue of state formation in Palestine.

MUSTAFA BARGHOUTHI, a physician employed by Maqassed Islamic Hospital, Jerusalem, is a founder of the Union of Palestinian Medical Relief Committees, and active in promoting primary health care in the Occupied Territories.

HUSAIN JAMEEL BARGOUTI teaches in Bir Zeit University's Cultural Studies Department. His background is in comparative literature, and his current interests lie in rural anthropology and political economy.

HELGA BAUMGARTEN is a political scientist from the Free University of Berlin, specializing in the Palestinian diaspora and Palestinian political movements.

AZMI BISHARA teaches philosophy and cultural studies at Bir Zeit University and currently concentrates on political philosophy.

JEAN-PAUL CHAGNOLLAUD teaches political science at the University of Nancy, France. He has published extensively on the Arab-Israeli conflict and European relations with the Middle East.

FACTS INFORMATION COMMITTEE is a Jerusalem-based group that has, since the second month of the uprising, been issuing regular biweekly updates on events surrounding the *intifada* in the form of the journal *Facts*.

SAMIH K. FARSOUN is Professor and Chair, Department of Sociology, The American University, Washington, D.C.

RITA GIACAMAN teaches at Bir Zeit University's Community Health Department, for which she conducts health research throughout the Occupied Territories.

JOOST R. HILTERMANN is a sociologist and research coordinator with al-Haq/Law in the Service of Man, one of whose areas of specialization is the Palestinian working class.

ISLAH JAD, a political scientist at Bir Zeit's Cultural Studies Department, specializes in Middle Eastern political systems and questions relating to Arab women.

ALI JARBAWI teaches political science at Bir Zeit University. His field is comparative politics, and he has written on the Palestinian movement and modernization in the Arab world.

JEAN M. LANDIS is a doctoral candidate, Department of Sociology, The American University, Washington, D.C.

JEAN-FRANÇOIS LEGRAIN, a researcher at the Centre d'Etudes et de Documentation Economique Juridique et Sociale (CEDEJ), Cairo, Egypt, writes on Islamic political movements.

FOUAD MOUGHRABI is Professor of Political Science at the University of Tennessee, Chattanooga. He is coauthor of *Public Opinion and the Palestine Question* (1987).

SAMIR ABDALLAH SALEH is chairperson of the Economics Department at An-Najah National University, Nablus. He specializes in the economy of the West Bank and Gaza.

GHADA TALHAMI is Associate Professor of Politics at Lake Forest College, Lake Forest, Illinois, specializing in African and Middle Eastern politics. A native of Jerusalem, she received her B.A. (cum laude) from Western College for Women, M.A. from the University of Wisconsin-Milwaukee, and Ph.D. from the University of Illinois-Chicago.

SALIM TAMARI is an urban sociologist teaching at Bir Zeit University. His research has centered on the Palestinian class structure.

LISA TARAKI teaches sociology at Bir Zeit University and is a specialist in political sociology, on which her research and writings have centered.

ADIL YAHYA teaches history at Bir Zeit University and has conducted research on West Bank Palestinian refugees.

About the Editors

JAMAL R. NASSAR is Associate Professor of Political Science at Illinois State University. During the 1987–88 academic year, Professor Nassar was a Senior Fulbright Scholar at Bir Zeit University on the West Bank. He has published many articles in professional journals and chapters in books. Currently, he is on the editorial staff of *Arab Studies Quarterly*

ROGER HEACOCK is Assistant Professor of History at Bir Zeit University. He has taught and published in the field of Modern European and International History. His research interests have centered on the question of relations between the West and the Third World. He has lived in the occupied West Bank since 1983.

DATE DUE